AF213373

Reforming Age Discrimination Law

OXFORD LABOUR LAW

Series Editors: Professor Alan Bogg (University of Bristol Law School), Professor Anne Davies (University of Oxford, Faculty of Law), Professor Keith Ewing (School of Law, King's College London), and Mark Freedland (University of Oxford, Faculty of Law).

The *Oxford Labour Law* series (formerly known as the *Oxford Monographs on Labour Law* series) has come to represent a significant contribution to the literature of British, European, and international labour law. The series recognizes the arrival not only of a renewed interest in labour law generally, but also the need for fresh approaches to the study of labour law following a period of momentous change in the UK and Europe. The series is concerned with all aspects of collective labour law and individual employment law, including the growing role of human rights and discrimination in employment. It is concerned also with the influence of politics and economics in shaping labour law, as well as the importance of legal theory and international labour standards. Recent titles address developments in multiple jurisdictions.

ALSO AVAILABLE IN THE SERIES

Putting Human Rights to Work
Labour Law, The ECHR, and The Employment Relation
Philippa Collins

Strike Ballots, Democracy, and Law
Breen Creighton, Catrina Denvir,
Richard Johnstone, Shae McCrystal,
Alice Orchiston

Living Wage
Regulatory Solutions to Informal and
Precarious Work in Global Supply Chains
Shelley Marshall

A Purposive Approachto Labour Law
Guy Davidov

Reforming Age Discrimination Law

Beyond Individual Enforcement

ALYSIA BLACKHAM
University of Melbourne

OXFORD
UNIVERSITY PRESS

OXFORD
UNIVERSITY PRESS

Great Clarendon Street, Oxford, OX2 6DP,
United Kingdom

Oxford University Press is a department of the University of Oxford.
It furthers the University's objective of excellence in research, scholarship,
and education by publishing worldwide. Oxford is a registered trade mark of
Oxford University Press in the UK and in certain other countries

© Alysia Blackham 2022

The moral rights of the author have been asserted

First Edition published in 2022

Impression: 1

All rights reserved. No part of this publication may be reproduced, stored in
a retrieval system, or transmitted, in any form or by any means, without the
prior permission in writing of Oxford University Press, or as expressly permitted
by law, by licence or under terms agreed with the appropriate reprographics
rights organization. Enquiries concerning reproduction outside the scope of the
above should be sent to the Rights Department, Oxford University Press, at the
address above

You must not circulate this work in any other form
and you must impose this same condition on any acquirer

Public sector information reproduced under Open Government Licence v3.0
(http://www.nationalarchives.gov.uk/doc/open-government-licence/open-government-licence.htm)

Published in the United States of America by Oxford University Press
198 Madison Avenue, New York, NY 10016, United States of America

British Library Cataloguing in Publication Data

Data available

Library of Congress Control Number: 2022937838

ISBN 978–0–19–885928–4

DOI: 10.1093/oso/9780198859284.001.0001

Printed and bound by
CPI Group (UK) Ltd, Croydon, CR0 4YY

Links to third party websites are provided by Oxford in good faith and
for information only. Oxford disclaims any responsibility for the materials
contained in any third party website referenced in this work.

For Kiara—may your world become one where ageing is a joyful opportunity.
And for Bernard—who makes everything possible.

Acknowledgements

This book draws on work conducted as part of a multi-year empirical project funded by the Australian Research Council Discovery Early Career Researcher scheme: DE170100228, 'Addressing Age Discrimination in Employment'. This funding was complemented by an International Grant from the Swedish Research Council for Health, Working Life and Welfare to extend this research to Sweden. I am exceedingly grateful for this ongoing support, which gave me the time and funding to undertake such an ambitious and wide-ranging project. The views expressed herein are my own and are not necessarily those of the Australian government or Australian Research Council.

It has been an incredible privilege to be able to dedicate myself to this topic for such an extended period. My thanks to the Centre for Employment and Labour Relations Law and Melbourne Law School (MLS), University of Melbourne, which have been the best academic 'homes' I could have wished for in undertaking a project of this nature. MLS has supported me through every step of this process, and I am grateful for the mentoring, academic, and practical support I have received—from so many members of the School—to make this project a success. In particular, my deepest thanks to the MLS Academic Research Service, which has provided incredible research assistance throughout this project.

I gratefully acknowledge all my colleagues who have discussed this work with me over the years, in the UK, Sweden, and Australia, and who have contributed to the development of the ideas in this book.

Most importantly, I am exceedingly grateful to the research participants who contributed their time and insights to this project. I hope this work does their complex and nuanced reflections justice, and can contribute to our joint work to build a more age-inclusive future.

Endorsements

Combining scrupulous comparative doctrinal research with meticulous empirical case studies of enforcement, *Reforming Age Discrimination Law* exposes what is going wrong with how the law tackles age discrimination in employment in Australia, Canada, and the United Kingdom. Drawing on a sophisticated account of the regulatory theory and a nuanced understanding of age discrimination, Alysia Blackham proposes innovative and realistic regulatory strategies that deftly and expertly navigate the enduring tensions endemic to age discrimination law. This impressive socio-legal study should be read by anyone interested in realizing equality at work and cultivating age-inclusive employment practices.

Professor Judy Fudge,
FRSC, LIUNA Enrico Henry Mancinelli Professor of Global Labour Issues,
School of Labour Studies, McMaster University

Through meticulous research, Alysia Blackham has produced a groundbreaking commentary on the current landscape of age discrimination. While based on original analysis, her talent for bringing together existing debates across law, sociology, business, and gerontology produces wonderful new theoretical insights and reveals the potential for a more nuanced approach to age inequalities in the labour market. This book is a must-read for academics, students, and practitioners working in the area of ageism at work, one of the most significant challenges in contemporary societies today.

Professor Kathleen Riach,
Adam Smith Business School, University of Glasgow

Alysia Blackham has produced a state-of-the-art study of age discrimination, surely *the* topic of the twenty-first century. It focuses on work that, unsurprisingly, is the central concern of those who lodge formal complaints. The study comprehensively considers the law in the UK, Australia, and Canada with particular regard to the nature of complaints, dispute resolution, modes of enforcement, and positive duties. I recommend this book as the 'go-to' resource on age discrimination law.

Emerita Professor Margaret Thornton,
The Australian National University

This is a remarkably good book, written with clarity, precision, and real expertise. It makes a compelling case for why we need to combat the 'enduring prevalence' of age discrimination in our society and draws upon a range of theoretical and empirical perspectives to map out effective strategies for achieving this aim. Dr Blackham's work really stands out from the field—and will be of interest to anyone engaged with equality law and policy.

Professor Colm O'Cinneide,
UCL Faculty of Laws

This book makes an outstanding contribution to the legal scholarship on age discrimination in the labour market and offers a riveting account of broader, salient issues pertaining to the ineffectiveness of existing enforcement mechanisms, the structural barriers to workplace equality and diversity, and the role of law in transforming societal norms and organizational culture. Academics, policy-makers, lawyers, unions, and workers' rights organizations will find its rich comparative analysis and compelling methodological approach particularly useful in deepening their understanding of one of the most challenging issues of our times—the ageing population.

Associate Professor Pnina Alon-Shenker,
Ted Rogers School of Management and Lincoln Alexander School of Law

In *Reforming Age Discrimination Law: Beyond Individual Enforcement*, Alysia Blackham examines the challenges of addressing workplace age discrimination through individual enforcement and explores options for a preventative approach. Through a refreshingly clear and accessible writing style, Blackham offers a helpful comparative analysis of the legal frameworks in the Australia, UK, and Canada. In particular, reflections on how the law can better respond to intersectionality and how collective enforcement could be enhanced offer valuable insights on what might be needed to reform equality laws everywhere.

Heather Corkhill,
Senior Policy Officer, Queensland Human Rights Commission

Preface

Demographic ageing is a fundamental societal shift facing all nations.[1] As one of the 'most important challenges' confronting Organisation for Economic Co-operation and Development (OECD) countries,[2] without effective government action, population ageing could jeopardize the sustainability of economic, social security, and labour market systems. Giving older workers the opportunity and incentive to participate in paid employment has personal, organizational, and societal benefits, and is a priority for governments. Simultaneously, high youth unemployment is a historical feature of the labour market, and the poor quality of work undertaken by young people is of growing concern to governments and policy makers.

Age is therefore a critical issue for labour market policy. Despite the introduction of age discrimination laws in many jurisdictions, ageism remains prevalent in most labour markets.[3] In 2014 over a quarter (27 per cent) of surveyed Australians aged 50 years and over reported experiencing age discrimination in employment in the previous two years;[4] a 2007 survey of 1,000 Australian employees found that 53 per cent of workers aged 18–24 had personally witnessed youth age discrimination.[5] The stubborn endurance of age discrimination in employment implies that age discrimination laws are largely ineffective at addressing workplace ageism. We need to question whether there are better ways to respond to the challenges experienced by older and younger workers.

There is a need for a critical and nuanced roadmap for the future development of age discrimination law in common law countries. Drawing on normative theoretical and empirical legal scholarship, this book provides a grounded critique of existing age discrimination laws and their enforcement, and posits concrete suggestions for legal change and reform. Leading the way for critical dialogue about the success and failures of existing age discrimination laws, the aim is to provide a concrete, empirically grounded path for legal change and renewal.

These aims are pursued through both a theoretical and empirical lens, focusing on age discrimination in employment. Drawing in particular on theories

1 Department of Economic and Social Affairs, Population Division, 'World Population Ageing 2019: Highlights' (United Nations 2019) ST/ESA/SER.A/430.

2 OECD, *Live Longer, Work Longer* (2006) 9.

3 World Health Organization, 'Global Report on Ageism' (2021) 26–27, 37.

4 AHRC, 'National Prevalence Survey of Age Discrimination in the Workplace: The Prevalence, Nature and Impact of Workplace Age Discrimination amongst the Australian Population Aged 50 Years and Older' (2015).

5 Workplace Info, 'Younger Workers Facing Age Discrimination: Study Shows' (11 October 2007) <http://workplaceinfo.com.au/hr-management/eeo/news/younger-workers-facing-age-discriminat ion-study-shows#.Vq7XrEbwnSg> accessed 1 February 2016.

of reflexive law and democratic experimentalism, and comparative perspectives from the UK, Australia, and Canada, this book critically considers how age discrimination law does (and should) affect or influence the lives of older and younger workers, the demographic composition of the workforce, and our capacity to protect vulnerable members of society. Grounded in the enduring tensions and ambivalences endemic to age discrimination law that make age discrimination law unique, this theoretical work raises issues that are distinct from those in other areas of discrimination.

The empirical components of this research are presented as mixed method case studies of enforcement in two jurisdictions: the UK and Australia. The case studies critically examine the key challenges and limitations of existing legal frameworks and the individual enforcement model for addressing age discrimination in employment. Featuring rigorous doctrinal analysis, qualitative and quantitative content analysis of judicial decisions and conciliation records, qualitative expert interviews with those involved in the enforcement of age discrimination law, surveys of legal practitioners, and analysis of statistical data from courts and statutory agencies, these mixed research methods are integrated to provide an innovative and nuanced critique of the practical operation of age discrimination law in each jurisdiction, at each step of the enforcement process.

Drawing upon these empirical findings allows for the proposition and testing of a normative framework for the future development of age discrimination law, with a particular focus on enforcement. This normative evaluation considers the potential to move beyond individual enforcement models for age discrimination law, to focus on preventative measures that might reduce ageism in employment. Through a canvassing of options including positive duties on employers and other bodies, agency enforcement, and collective approaches, a critical evaluation of both their potential to address the limits of existing laws, and the practical measures necessary to ensure that such strategies succeed is provided.

While much of this empirical research was undertaken prior to the Covid-19 pandemic, the effects of the pandemic echo through this project. Covid-19 has not just created new forms of inequality; it has exacerbated and amplified workplace inequalities that had previously been patched up and glossed over. Over the course of 2020, mass job losses, unemployment, and under-employment became the norm across the world, particularly affecting young people and older people, and especially young women.[6] Even as our lives are fundamentally disrupted by a global pandemic, though, our collective stereotypes of age have remained remarkably resilient. At the same time, Covid-19 has reminded us that an ageing world is

[6] Sharon Goulds, Isobel Fergus, and Esther Winslow, 'Halting Lives: The Impact of COVID-19 on Girls and Young Women' (Report, Plan International 2020) <https://apo.org.au/node/308469> accessed 14 January 2021; Brendan Churchill, 'COVID-19 and the Immediate Impact on Young People and Employment in Australia: A Gendered Analysis' (2021) 28 Gender, Work & Organization 783.

not something we can or should take for granted. The findings of this study have therefore become even more pertinent as we attempt to rebuild our economy and society post-pandemic—and, ideally, to rebuild better, in a way that supports people of all ages.

This work is particularly relevant for labour and discrimination lawyers, socio-legal and empirical legal scholars, and those interested in law in context and access to justice, and will resonate with those in the UK, Australia, and Canada, and other common law jurisdictions. This is a call to action for those involved with the enforcement of age discrimination law, particularly policy-makers, statutory agencies, government, law reform bodies, unions and non-governmental organizations. Moreover, it should capture the imagination of those interested in the practical impact of discrimination law and legal regulation, legal method, and the use of empirical research methods to advance legal scholarship.

Alysia Blackham
14 October 2021

General Editors' Preface

The aim of our monograph series is to publish exceptional scholarship that addresses the most difficult regulatory issues in the fields of labour and social law. In Professor Blackham's new monograph, *Reforming Age Discrimination Law: Beyond Individual Enforcement*, those scholarly virtues are fully realized. Age discrimination represents one of the most pressing and intractable challenges in regulating for decent work. Younger and older workers continue to face legal and social barriers that impede their opportunities to participate in meaningful and rewarding work that respects their dignity. It is a problem that transcends national boundaries. These intergenerational inequities have been intensified by the Covid-19 pandemic, reflected in health and employment outcomes with tragic proportions.

Given this context, Professor Blackham's innovative monograph could not be more timely. She offers a bold and imaginative analysis that integrates doctrinal, comparative, and empirical methodologies to examine the enforcement difficulties that have subverted the realization of substantive age equality at every turn. These rich insights are then used to develop a framework for reconfiguring structures and institutions of enforcement based upon an overarching commitment to solidarity. As the title of the monograph indicates, this takes us far beyond the 'individual enforcement' paradigm to consider a holistic blend of individual and collective strategies. This obviously has far wider resonances as labour lawyers across the world grapple with the general crisis of effectiveness of labour standards.

Political attacks on the enforcement of social law represent the latest pernicious iteration in the genre of market deregulation. Professor Blackham's work will provide an enduring and rigorous academic contribution to the debates around redesign of these mechanisms in age discrimination law and beyond. The editors are delighted to welcome it to the series. We feel sure that it will set the terms of the debate for many years to come.

ALB, ACLD, KDE, MRF
13 January 2022

Contents

Table of Cases

UNITED KINGDOM

AUSTRALIA

Commonwealth

Australian Capital Territory

New South Wales

Queensland

Victoria

Western Australia

CANADA

EUROPE

Table of Legislation

AUSTRALIA

Commonwealth

Australian Capital Territory

New South Wales

Northern Territory

Queensland

South Australia

Tasmania

Victoria

Western Australia

CANADA

EUROPEAN UNION

INTERNATIONAL INSTRUMENTS

List of Abbreviations

2006 Regulations	Employment Equality (Age) Regulations 2006 (UK) SI 2006/1031
A	Agree
ABS	Australian Bureau of Statistics
Acas	Advisory, Conciliation and Arbitration Service
ACAT	Australian Capital Territory Civil and Administrative Tribunal
ACT	Australian Capital Territory
ACTHRC	Australian Capital Territory Human Rights Commission
ADA	Age Discrimination Act 2004 (Cth)
ADEA	US Age Discrimination in Employment Act of 1967
ADNSW	Anti-Discrimination New South Wales
ADR	Alternative dispute resolution
AHRC	Australian Human Rights Commission
ATSI	Aboriginal and Torres Strait Islander
BEIS	Department for Business, Energy & Industrial Strategy
BFOR	Bona fide occupational requirement
BME	Black and minority ethnic
Burden of Proof Directive	Council Directive 97/80/EC of 15 December 1997 on the burden of proof in cases of discrimination based on sex
CAB	Citizens Advice
Charter	Canadian Charter of Rights and Freedoms
CHRC	Canadian Human Rights Commission
CHRT	Canadian Human Rights Tribunal
CJEU	Court of Justice of the European Union
CLC	Community legal centre
COTA	Council on The Ageing
D	Disagree
DWP	Department for Work and Pensions
EASS	Equality Advisory and Support Service
EAT	Employment Appeal Tribunal
ECA	Early conciliation notification
ECHR	Convention for the Protection of Human Rights and Fundamental Freedoms (European Convention on Human Rights, as amended)
ECNI	Equality Commission for Northern Ireland
EHRC	Equality and Human Rights Commission
EIA	Equality impact assessment
EO Act	Equal Opportunity Act 2010 (Vic)
EOT	Equal Opportunity Tasmania

EqA	Equality Act 2010
EqA 2006	Equality Act 2006
ET	Employment Tribunal
EU	European Union
FCA	Federal Court of Australia
FCCA	Federal Circuit Court of Australia
FOI	Freedom of Information
Framework Directive	Council Directive 2000/78/EC of 27 November 2000 establishing a general framework for equal treatment in employment and occupation
FTE	Full time equivalent
FWA	Fair Work Act 2009 (Cth)
FWC	Fair Work Commission
FWO	Fair Work Ombudsman
GB	Great Britain
GSS	General Social Survey
HILDA	Household, Income and Labour Dynamics in Australia
HMRC	Her Majesty's Revenue and Customs
IT	Information technology
JR	Judicial review
LFC	Legal Funding Committee
LRA	Labour Relations Agency
NAD	Neither agree nor disagree
NCAT	New South Wales Civil and Administrative Tribunal
NDAs	Non-disclosure agreements
NGO	Non-governmental organization
NI	Northern Ireland
NI Act	Northern Ireland Act 1998
NI Regulations	Employment Equality (Age) Regulations (Northern Ireland) 2006 (NI)
NIHRC	Northern Ireland Human Rights Commission
NSW	New South Wales
NT	Northern Territory
NTADC	Northern Territory Anti-Discrimination Commission
NTCAT	Northern Territory Civil and Administrative Tribunal
OECD	Organisation for Economic Co-operation and Development
OHS	Occupational health and safety
ONS	Office for National Statistics
OPE inquiry	House of Commons Women and Equalities Committee inquiry on Older People and Employment
PCP	Provision, criterion or practice
PSED	Public Sector Equality Duty
QCAT	Queensland Civil and Administrative Tribunal
QHRC	Queensland Human Rights Commission
QIRC	Queensland Industrial Relations Commission

SA	South Australia
SACAT	South Australia Civil and Administrative Tribunal
SAEOC	South Australia Equal Opportunity Commission
SAEOT	South Australia Equal Opportunity Tribunal
SAET	South Australian Employment Tribunal
SD	Strongly disagree
SETA	Survey of Employment Tribunal Applications
StA	Strongly agree
SwA	Somewhat agree
SwD	Somewhat disagree
TADT	Tasmania Anti-Discrimination Tribunal
TUC	Trades Union Congress
UK	United Kingdom
UN	United Nations
UNISON	R (on the application of UNISON) v Lord Chancellor [2017] UKSC 51
USA	United States of America
VCAT	Victorian Civil and Administrative Tribunal
VEOHRC	Victorian Equal Opportunity and Human Rights Commission
Victorian Charter	Charter of Human Rights and Responsibilities Act 2006 (Vic)
WA	Western Australia
WAEOC	Western Australia Equal Opportunity Commission
WASAT	Western Australia State Administrative Tribunal
WEC	House of Commons Women and Equalities Committee
WERS4	Workplace Employee Relations Survey 4 (1998)
WERS5	Fifth Workplace Employment Relations Survey (2004)
WERS6	Sixth UK Workplace Employment Relations Study (2011)
WGEA	Workplace Gender Equality Agency
WHS	Workplace health and safety

List of Figures

List of Tables

1
The Enduring Challenge of Age Discrimination

I. Introduction

Age discrimination remains an enduring and prevalent phenomenon at work.[1] Despite the introduction of laws making age discrimination unlawful—some of which have been in place for over fifty years—there appears to have been little shift in workplace age norms. The overarching question for this study, then, is why have age discrimination laws been so ineffective at addressing age discrimination in practice? Is this attributable to the limitations of existing legal frameworks? Does it reflect the ambivalent nature of age discrimination and age discrimination law specifically? Or does it reflect broader challenges with equality law and the individual rights model on which it is based? If the latter, how can we move beyond this model of individual rights and individual enforcement, to reinvigorate age discrimination law?

In this comparative, mixed methods study, I draw on six years of empirical legal research, spanning the United Kingdom (UK), Canada, and Australia, to attempt to answer these questions. Using this expansive empirical data, I reflect on the normative role and purpose of age discrimination law—for both older and younger workers—and propose a fourfold programme of reform to address the existing limitations of age discrimination law and its enforcement. This monograph maps the substantial barriers to individual enforcement of age discrimination law, from the initial experience of discrimination itself, all the way to the process of hearing and judgment. These barriers are so significant, and so difficult to surmount, that it is fundamentally unreasonable to depend on individuals to address age inequality at work, even with improvements to the existing legal framework. I therefore put forward three areas in which we can move beyond individual enforcement of age discrimination law, focusing on positive duties, collective action, and statutory agencies.

In this chapter, I provide an introduction to, and overview of, the monograph. The chapter frames the later discussion, drawing on data from the UK, Canada, and Australia relating to demographic ageing, workforce participation rates, and

[1] World Health Organization, 'Global Report on Ageism' (2021) 26–27, 37.

Reforming Age Discrimination Law. Alysia Blackham, Oxford University Press. © Alysia Blackham 2022.
DOI: 10.1093/oso/9780198859284.003.0001

work experiences of older and younger workers, and the prevalence and nature of age discrimination in employment. The chapter also puts forward the theoretical framework and method of the monograph.

II. The Challenge and Opportunity of Demographic Change

Demographic ageing is one of the great success stories of our time. The triumphs of medical technology and public health measures mean people are on average living longer, healthier lives. Those aged 65 and over are steadily increasing as a proportion of the population: in 2018, this group represented 15.6 per cent of the population in Australia, 17.2 per cent in Canada, and 18.3 per cent in Great Britain (GB) (Figure 1.1).[2] At the same time, women have gained more control over their reproduction, leading to greater female workforce participation and declining birth rates. These long-term trends are changing the demographic composition and workforce structure of Organisation for Economic Co-operation and Development (OECD) countries. They offer both incredible opportunities—for longer, better, healthier lives—and exquisite challenges for established work and pension systems.[3]

Longer and healthier lives may also mean people can benefit from longer work careers. Age discrimination laws are potentially an important tool to open up job opportunities for people of all ages. Of course, not everyone wants to continue to work into old age; retirement is a relief for those who have worked in physically intensive roles or jobs that are unrewarding. Age discrimination laws could therefore be seen as part of a neo-liberal ploy to keep older workers employed well beyond the traditional age of retirement.[4] While governments rationalize these laws on the basis of individual 'choice', this choice is firmly bounded by changes to pension laws, which effectively compel individuals (especially those in low paid work) to keep working.[5] There is a tension, then, between what individuals may desire (for some, retirement and a decent pension), and what governments seek to incentivize (individual 'responsibility', longer work careers, and increased tax and pension contributions).[6]

[2] OECD, 'Elderly Population (Indicator)' (2021) <doi:10.1787/8d805ea1-en> accessed 3 November 2020.

[3] See, eg, Alysia Blackham, 'Pensions and the Modern Workforce' in Sinéad Agnew, Paul S Davies, and Charles Mitchell (eds), *Pensions: Law, Policy and Practice* (Hart Publishing 2020).

[4] See, eg, John Macnicol, *Neoliberalising Old Age* (CUP 2015).

[5] Alysia Blackham, 'Addressing the Ageing Workforce: A Critical Examination of Legal Policy Objectives and Values' (2017) 37 Ageing & Society 1362, 1383–84.

[6] ibid 1383.

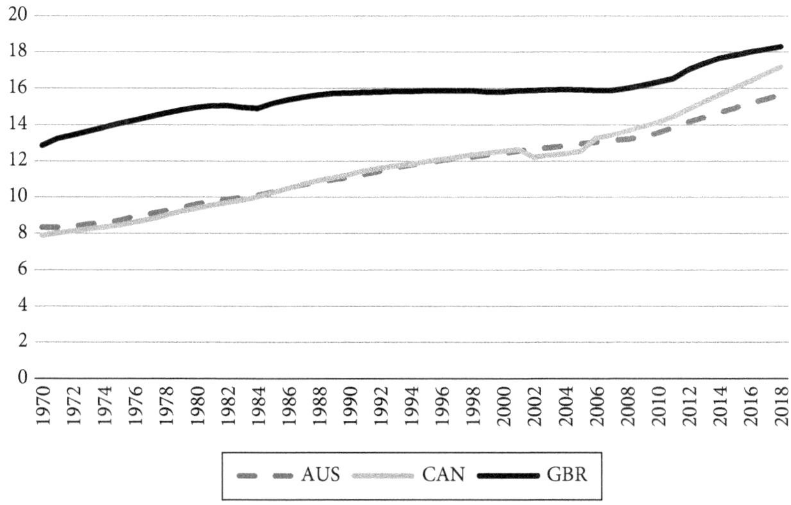

Figure 1.1 Population aged 65+, per cent of total population, 1970–2018

Despite young people and children declining as a proportion of the population in OECD countries,[7] the quality of youth employment remains an enduring and systemic difficulty. Young people are disproportionately affected by precarious and low paid work, workplace accidents, unemployment,[8] and unpaid internships.[9] While this may be partly attributable to broader shifts in the nature of work, away from routine jobs and towards service roles, the historical prevalence and persistence of these trends mean they should be seen as systemic issues, which are unlikely to be rectified with an economic upturn.[10] Indeed, these trends have been substantially exacerbated and intensified by the Covid-19 pandemic, which has led to substantial increases in youth unemployment and under-employment, particularly for young women.[11] Thus, at least to some extent, the enduring difficulties faced by young workers may be attributed to less favourable treatment on the basis of age.

[7] OECD, 'Young Population (Indicator)' (2020) <doi: 10.1787/3d774f19-en> accessed 3 November 2020.

[8] Alysia Blackham, 'Young Workers and Age Discrimination: Tensions and Conflicts' (2019) 48 Industrial Law Journal 1.

[9] Alysia Blackham, 'Working at the Edges of Legal Protection: Equality Law and Youth Work Experience from a Comparative Perspective' in Andrew Stewart and others (eds), *Internships, Employability and the Search for Decent Work Experience* (Edward Elgar 2021).

[10] Blackham, 'Young Workers' (n 8).

[11] Brendan Churchill, 'COVID-19 and the Immediate Impact on Young People and Employment in Australia: A Gendered Analysis' (2021) 28 Gender, Work & Organization 783.

III. Scope and Theoretical Framework

There is a need, then, to consider the way age discrimination continues to manifest at work, and how it can best be addressed, for both older and younger workers. That is the object of this monograph. In the sections that follow, I consider the scope and methods of this work, before considering the ways age discrimination is manifesting at work.

In this study, I have chosen to focus on work for three reasons.[12] First, decent or meaningful work has key emotional, health, financial, and inclusion benefits for those who are able to participate in it.[13] Thus, securing good work for people of all ages achieves a range of other individual, social, and economic benefits.[14] Second, most age discrimination complaints relate to work, and age discrimination is commonly reported at work (Chapter 4). Focusing on the workplace therefore offers a larger (yet still relatively manageable) data set for considering questions of enforcement. Third, and more practically, my focus on work reflects my background as a labour law practitioner and educator.

In considering questions of enforcement and legal efficacy, I use a theoretical framework grounded in reflexive law and regulatory theory. While there are a number of models or theories of this form of regulation—variously called experimentalism, reflexive law, responsive law, regulatory theory, or second-generation regulation—they are united by some key features.

First, these theories de-emphasize command and control regulation, where government *commands* organizations to meet certain standards, and *controls* behaviour with the threat of negative sanctions.[15] This 'first-generation' regulation tends to be grounded in fixed rules prohibiting discrimination, financial penalties for a failure to comply with rules, and a focus on individual enforcement.[16] Negative duties prohibiting discrimination[17] and fixed rules struggle to address structural discrimination,[18] being either too narrow to cover all discriminatory behaviours, or so broad that they create legal uncertainty.[19] Legal uncertainty can

[12] On other areas of public life, see Alysia Blackham, 'Age Discrimination beyond Employment' (2019) 52 Kobe University Law Review 1.

[13] See, eg, Michael F Steger and Bryan J Dik, 'Work as Meaning: Individual and Organizational Benefits of Engaging in Meaningful Work' in Nicola Garcea, Susan Harrington, and P Alex Linley (eds), *Oxford Handbook of Positive Psychology and Work* (OUP 2009); David L Blustein and others, 'Decent Work: A Psychological Perspective' (2016) 7 Frontiers in Psychology 407.

[14] AHRC, 'Willing to Work: National Inquiry into Employment Discrimination Against Older Australians and Australians with Disability' (2016) 12–13, 44–48.

[15] Darren Sinclair, 'Self-Regulation versus Command and Control? Beyond False Dichotomies' (1997) 19 Law & Policy 529, 534.

[16] ibid.

[17] Bob Hepple, 'Enforcing Equality Law: Two Steps Forward and Two Steps Backwards for Reflexive Regulation' (2011) 40 Industrial Law Journal 315, 318.

[18] Susan Sturm, 'Second Generation Employment Discrimination: A Structural Approach' (2001) 101 Columbia Law Review 458, 460.

[19] ibid 461.

lead to organizational 'gestures of compliance' with discrimination law, which are ultimately ineffective at actually addressing discrimination.[20] Command and control regulation is therefore unlikely to lead to reliable organizational change.[21]

Second, then, moving beyond command and control approaches, these theories seek to effect change through second-order effects, via self-regulation and self-scrutiny. For example, reflexive law—grounded in systems theory—posits that legal regulation cannot directly change organizational behaviour: law and organizations occupy discrete sub-systems, which cannot directly interact or communicate.[22] Any communication between systems is mediated by the system's own logic and internal processes for self-reproduction.[23] Law can therefore only 'irritate' other sub-systems;[24] the results of legal change—especially that via command and control regulation—are unpredictable and variable, and legal regulation can have perverse effects.[25] Instead, recognizing these limits, reflexive law seeks to harness and work with organizations' own internal processes of self-regulation, and to use regulatory 'irritations' to effect workplace change.[26]

By contrast, in an experimentalist architecture, change is achieved through 'directly deliberative polyarchy':[27] local actors (such as organizations) are encouraged 'to engage in investigation, information sharing and deliberation' to solve problems,[28] and difficult decisions regarding how to address discrimination are devolved to the local level, accommodating organizational differences.[29] Experimentalism is closely linked to organizational benchmarking[30] and focuses on creating networks of firms that engage in peer review and scrutiny.[31]

Both reflexive law and experimentalism therefore reduce the burden on regulators to monitor organizational compliance: internal processes offer their own form of replication and scrutiny of organizational behaviour, by encouraging

[20] ibid.

[21] Neil Gunningham, 'Introduction' in Neil Gunningham and Peter N Grabosky (eds), *Smart Regulation: Designing Environmental Policy* (Clarendon Press 1998) 12.

[22] Niklas Luhmann, *Law as a Social System* (Fatima Kastner and others trs, OUP 2004).

[23] Gunther Teubner, *Law as an Autopoietic System* (Zenon Bankowski ed, Anne Bankowska and Ruth Adler trs, Blackwell 1993) 62.

[24] Gunther Teubner, 'Autopoiesis in Law and Society: A Rejoinder to Blankenburg' (1984) 18 Law & Society Review 291, 298.

[25] ibid 299–300.

[26] Ralf Rogowski and Ton Wilthagen, 'Reflexive Labour Law: An Introduction' in Ralf Rogowski and Ton Wilthagen (eds), *Reflexive Labour Law: Studies in Industrial Relations and Employment Regulation* (Kluwer Law and Taxation Publishers 1994) 7.

[27] Charles F Sabel and Jonathan Zeitlin, 'Learning from Difference: The New Architecture of Experimentalist Governance in the EU' in Charles F Sabel and Jonathan Zeitlin (eds), *Experimentalist Governance in the European Union: Towards a New Architecture* (OUP 2012) 3.

[28] Charles F Sabel and William H Simon, 'Minimalism and Experimentalism in the Administrative State' (2011–12) 100 Georgetown Law Journal 53, 81.

[29] ibid 56.

[30] See Michael C Dorf and Charles F Sabel, 'A Constitution of Democratic Experimentalism' (1998) 98 Columbia Law Review 267.

[31] Joshua Cohen and Charles Sabel, 'Directly-Deliberative Polyarchy' (1997) 3 European Law Journal 313, 327.

organizations to self-diagnose and self-correct discriminatory processes.[32] These theories therefore offer innovative alternatives to command and control regulation, via a focus on organizational problem-solving, learning, reform, and innovation.[33]

Third, though, these theories see effective 'second generation' regulation as demanding certain institutional structures and preconditions. They all see the state as having a role to play in regulation, focus on organizational self-regulation or problem-solving, and involve stakeholders in the problem-solving process.[34] For example, Hepple argues that the successful deployment of reflexive law requires three 'interlocking mechanisms': internal scrutiny by and of the organization; the involvement of interest groups through participation and consultation; and an external agency to assist, build capacity, and address instances where self-regulation fails.[35]

Similarly, experimentalist organizational deliberation occurs within a specific architecture, highlighting the role of both central institutions (such as government agencies, legislatures, and/or courts), and local institutions (such as employers) in achieving change. In this experimentalist regulatory model, framework goals and measurement criteria are set and revised through joint action between central and lower units;[36] lower-level units report on their performance against agreed goals; and central units monitor performance, pool information, and promote 'aggregate learning' between different local units via a process of 'deliberative engagement'.[37] Experimentalism combines decentralized control as to how goals are to be achieved with centralized coordination of monitoring and evaluation,[38] as part of an iterative cycle.

Thus, while the burden on regulators is reduced, they still perform essential functions. Enforcement must be able to escalate in the case of non-compliance, to support and reinforce self-regulation.[39] In accordance with the 'enforcement pyramid', regulatory intervention moves progressively from 'restorative dialogue', information and persuasion; to internal organizational scrutiny (such as via positive duties); to individual complaints; to agency inquiry and investigation; to compliance notices; to agreements; to sanctions, and (in some systems) criminal penalties.[40] The final step is incapacitation, recognizing that repeated non-compliance

[32] Sabel and Simon (n 28) 88.
[33] See, eg, Christine Parker, *The Open Corporation: Effective Self-Regulation and Democracy* (CUP 2002).
[34] Belinda Smith, 'Not the Baby and the Bathwater: Regulatory Reform for Equality Laws to Address Work-Family Conflict' (2006) 28 Sydney Law Review 689, 710.
[35] Hepple (n 17) 321.
[36] Sabel and Zeitlin (n 27) 3. See also Sabel and Simon (n 28) 79.
[37] Sabel and Simon (n 28) 55.
[38] ibid 79.
[39] Ian Ayres and John Braithwaite, *Responsive Regulation: Transcending the Deregulation Debate* (OUP 1992).
[40] Hepple (n 17).

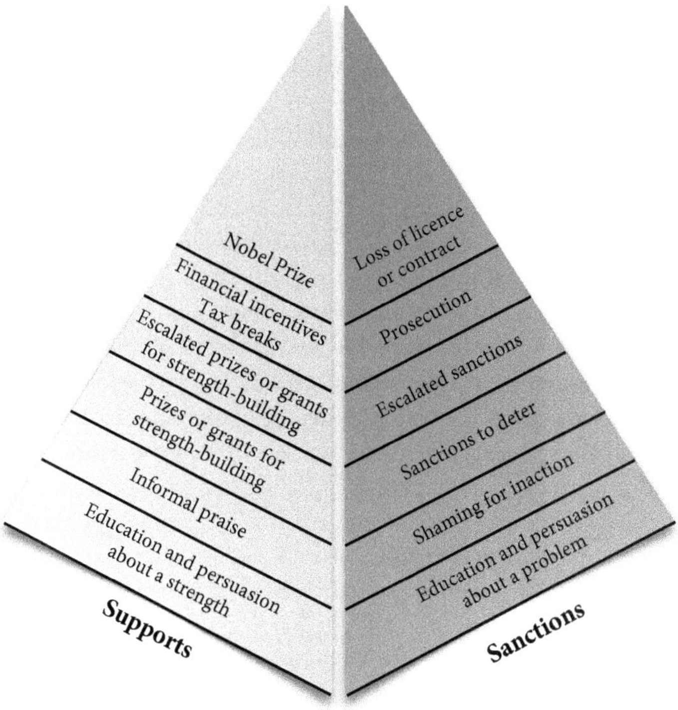

Figure 1.2 Pyramid of supports and sanctions

is often due to a lack of capacity to comply.[41] The enforcement pyramid is complemented by a support pyramid, which focuses on capacity-building (Figure 1.2[42]). For Braithwaite, 'Strengths expand to absorb weaknesses';[43] the emphasis of regulatory activity should therefore be on capacity building, rather than enforcement:[44]

> The first idea, therefore, is to move up a pyramid of supports that allows strengths to expand to solve more and more problems of concern to the regulator; when that fails to solve specific problems sufficiently, the regulator ... starts to move up a pyramid of sanctions.[45]

[41] John Braithwaite, 'The Essence of Responsive Regulation' (2011) 44 University of British Columbia Law Review 475, 485.
[42] Based on ibid 482; Hepple (n 17); Dominique Allen, 'Barking and Biting: The Equal Opportunity Commission as an Enforcement Agency' (2016) 44 Federal Law Review 311.
[43] Braithwaite, 'The Essence of Responsive Regulation' (n 41) 480.
[44] ibid.
[45] ibid 481.

The enforcement pyramid—while compelling in its design and simplicity—focuses on state regulatory action, at the expense of depicting the other 'interlocking mechanisms' of internal scrutiny and involvement of interest groups.[46] It does not show how the actions of different regulatory actors can combine or interact to effect regulatory action.[47] Grabosky therefore proposes a three-dimensional pyramid (a triangular prism), with facets depicting state regulation (the 'enforcement pyramid'); self-regulation (encompassing industry associations); and the role of third parties or interest groups.[48] Regulatory actions, then, exist within the pyramid, being located according to their sponsor(s) and degree of coerciveness.[49] Alternatively or additionally, state regulators could use network partners to escalate or extend the reach of enforcement activity ('networked escalation').[50]

It is not always easy to 'fit' equality law into a reflexive or responsive framework, though many scholars have attempted to do so.[51] As Braithwaite argues, the point is to view responsive regulation 'not as rocket science but as a natural social process',[52] with a focus on unlearning adversarialism and threat-making in favour of a more respectful, natural form of engagement.[53] Thus, it is inconsequential that equality law does not map precisely onto the enforcement pyramid; the point, more generally, is that sanctions should escalate to become more coercive with non-compliance.

In existing legislative models of equality law, the bulk of enforcement action is undertaken by individual claimants pursuing legal rights (Chapter 3). In Braithwaite's model, 'passive responsibility' (holding actors responsible for past wrongs) is only resorted to when 'active responsibility' is not possible (ie, making actors take responsibility to make things right in the future).[54] This compares markedly to the individual enforcement model in equality law. Thus, second generation regulation is perhaps better seen as an aspirational model for existing legal frameworks.[55]

However, if we sought to somehow integrate this focus on individual enforcement as part of a model of second-generation regulation, individual claimants could be depicted as third parties, occupying a pyramid face with other third

[46] PN Grabosky, 'Discussion Paper: Inside the Pyramid: Towards a Conceptual Framework for the Analysis of Regulatory Systems' (1997) 25 International Journal of the Sociology of Law 195, 197.
[47] ibid.
[48] ibid 198.
[49] ibid 200.
[50] Braithwaite, 'The Essence of Responsive Regulation' (n 41) 508, 510.
[51] Hepple (n 17); Smith (n 34); Allen, 'Barking and Biting' (n 42). For detailed consideration, see Alysia Blackham, 'Re-Systematising Labour Law: Beyond Traditional Systems Theory and Reflexive Law?' in Alysia Blackham, Miriam Kullmann, and Ania Zbyszewska (eds), *Theorising Labour Law in a Changing World: Towards Inclusive Labour Law* (Hart Publishing 2019).
[52] Braithwaite, 'The Essence of Responsive Regulation' (n 41) 519.
[53] ibid.
[54] ibid 510.
[55] Hepple (n 17).

parties and interest groups.[56] Alternatively, individual legal action could form a fourth face of the pyramid, representing the pyramid of disputes (Chapter 3).[57]

Overall, then, consolidating these ideas, we are essentially considering a pentagonal pyramid of enforcement, with five sides respectively depicting state sanctions (the 'enforcement pyramid'); state supports; self-regulation; third parties or interest groups; and individual disputes. The simplicity of the enforcement pyramid is long gone.

Reflexive law, and systems theory on which it is based, have been the subject of a number of substantial critiques in the context of equality law.[58] I have questioned elsewhere whether this reflects the imperfect implementation of reflexive law; or more fundamental issues with reflexive law and systems theory themselves.[59] A fundamental challenge with reflexive law is that it is relatively ineffective at addressing disparities of power, including in consultation and engagement processes.[60] Manfredi and others argue:

> reflexive regulation does not address deep structural inequalities and the inequality of power relations operating within organisations. Instead, as with other forms of second-generation regulation, the implementation of social tasks that should be the concern of the state, such as the development of institutional equality, is externalised to become an internal organisational interest, albeit within the public sector.[61]

Thus, reflexive law may fail to address or even 'reinforce the neo-liberal turn in economic policies which may be at the root of inequality'.[62] Any model of second-generation regulation must therefore be constantly attuned to the way in which power is replicated, reinforced, or hidden through regulatory techniques. While recognizing these limitations, in this research I use a theoretical framework grounded in reflexive law and regulatory theory, as a lens for critiquing the enforcement and legal efficacy of age discrimination laws.

[56] Grabosky (n 46) 198.

[57] See, eg, Laura Beth Nielsen and Robert L Nelson, 'Scaling the Pyramid: A Sociolegal Model of Employment Discrimination Litigation' in Laura Beth Nielsen and Robert L Nelson (eds), *Handbook of Employment Discrimination Research: Rights and Realities* (Springer 2005).

[58] See Blackham, 'Re-Systematising Labour Law' (n 51).

[59] ibid.

[60] See, eg, Hepple (n 17) 323.

[61] Simonetta Manfredi, Lucy Vickers, and Kate Clayton-Hathway, 'The Public Sector Equality Duty: Enforcing Equality Rights Through Second-Generation Regulation' (2018) 47 Industrial Law Journal 365, 376.

[62] ibid 377.

IV. Method

This study employed an empirical mixed methods research design, synthesizing qualitative, quantitative, doctrinal, and comparative research methods. Comparative legal doctrinal research, spanning the UK, Canada, and Australia, is complemented by empirical case studies of enforcement in the UK and Australia.

Mixed methods research meaningfully combines or integrates—*mixes*—qualitative and quantitative research methods to understand a research problem.[63] The aim of this mixing is to make use of the different strengths and advantages of qualitative and quantitative research methods,[64] thereby increasing research validity[65] and enriching understanding of a topic.[66] I have written more about mixed methods—and my rationale for using this design—in my previous work.[67] More particularly, this study draws on comparative legal doctrinal research, content analysis, quantitative data analysis, qualitative expert interviews, and a survey of advocates.[68]

Legal doctrinal research involves the hermeneutic study of legal texts.[69] It is a 'two-part process', involving both identification[70] and interpretation of texts.[71] Legal doctrinal method is essentially a search for coherence across legal texts, combining 'specific interpretations of legal principles, rules and concepts in a (newly) systematised whole'.[72] As van Hoecke argues, however, 'coherence' is not innate or intrinsic to legal texts[73]—hermeneutic analysis must be complemented with empirical analysis and normative decision-making to find legal 'meaning'.[74] Thus, legal doctrinal research and empirical research are not so far removed.

This study draws on ***comparative*** legal doctrinal research, spanning the UK, Canada, and Australia. Given the UK, Canada, and Australia share a common legal tradition, and have framed their equality laws on an individual rights model, there

[63] Vicki L Plano Clark and others, 'Mixing Quantitative and Qualitative Approaches: An Introduction to Emergent Mixed Methods Research' in Sharlene Nagy Hesse-Biber and Patricia Leavy (eds), *Handbook of Emergent Methods* (Guilford Press 2008) 364.

[64] Michael Quinn Patton, *Qualitative Evaluation and Research Methods* (2nd edn, SAGE 1990) 13.

[65] Jerome Kirk and Marc L Miller, *Reliability and Validity in Qualitative Research* (SAGE 1986) 30.

[66] Jennifer C Greene, Valerie J Caracelli, and Wendy F Graham, 'Toward a Conceptual Framework for Mixed-Method Evaluation Designs' (1989) 11 Educational Evaluation and Policy Analysis 255, 258.

[67] Alysia Blackham, *Extending Working Life for Older Workers: Age Discrimination Law, Policy and Practice* (Hart Publishing 2016) ch 2.

[68] Research materials used in this study are available on the project website: <http://www.ageworks.info>.

[69] Mark van Hoecke, 'Legal Doctrine: Which Method(s) for What Kind of Discipline?' in Mark van Hoecke (ed), *Methodologies of Legal Research: What Kind of Method for What Kind of Discipline?* (Hart Publishing 2011) 17.

[70] Texts might include normative cases, legislation, and treaties and authoritative non-binding cases and scholarly writings: ibid 11.

[71] Terry Hutchinson and Nigel Duncan, 'Defining and Describing What We Do: Doctrinal Legal Research' (2012) 17 Deakin Law Review 83, 110.

[72] van Hoecke (n 69) 17.

[73] ibid 3, 6.

[74] ibid 10.

is significant scope for mutual learning between the jurisdictions. Explanatory comparative legal analysis, then, seeks to identify similarities and differences between jurisdictions, and account for these variances.[75] My interest in these jurisdictions reflects what Örücü describes as a 'problem-solving' or sociological approach to comparative law, examining how different legal systems have responded to similar problems in contrasting ways: here, age discrimination at work.[76] The fact that these jurisdictions are facing a similar problem warrants the comparison;[77] differences in national context increase the potential for mutual learning.[78]

In additional to doctrinal analysis, this study uses ***qualitative and quantitative content analysis*** to analyse age discrimination cases in the UK and Australia.[79] Unlike doctrinal analysis, which aims to harmonize or systematize texts, content analysis focuses on themes in texts.[80] This approach is apt where there are many decisions of a similar precedential weight (ie many first instance decisions, as in discrimination law) and where we are concerned with the *pattern* across cases, rather than a nuanced and deep understanding of one case.[81] What matters for content analysis is the collective—not individual—insights from cases.[82]

In Australia, my universe of documents for analysis included all judgments relating to age discrimination, including those under discrimination legislation and industrial relations legislation (including unfair dismissal law where age was alleged to be a factor in the dismissal) handed down in all Australian jurisdictions, from the commencement of age discrimination legislation in Australia until 31 December 2017. The refined sample included 108 decisions.[83]

In the UK, I analysed all Employment Tribunal (ET) decisions relating to age discrimination published on the GOV.UK ET decisions website, from the first decisions being uploaded to the website (February 2017) until 17 April 2019,[84] and

[75] Maurice Adams, 'Doing What Doesn't Come Naturally: On the Distinctiveness of Comparative Law' in Mark van Hoecke (ed), *Methodologies of Legal Research: What Kind of Method for What Kind of Discipline?* (Hart Publishing 2011) 237.

[76] Esin Örücü, 'Developing Comparative Law' in Esin Örücü and David Nelken (eds), *Comparative Law: A Handbook* (Hart Publishing 2007) 52.

[77] ibid.

[78] Dagmar Schiek, 'Enforcing (EU) Non-Discrimination Law: Mutual Learning between British and Italian Labour Law?' (2012) 28 International Journal of Comparative Labour Law and Industrial Relations 489, 508.

[79] Lisa Webley, 'Qualitative Approaches to Empirical Legal Research' in Peter Cane and Herbert M Kritzer (eds), *The Oxford Handbook of Empirical Legal Research* (OUP 2010) 941.

[80] See van Hoecke (n 69) 11–17.

[81] Mark A Hall and Ronald F Wright, 'Systematic Content Analysis of Judicial Opinions' (2008) 96 California Law Review 63, 66.

[82] ibid 76.

[83] This method and sample selection is discussed in detail elsewhere: Alysia Blackham, 'Why Do Employment Age Discrimination Cases Fail? An Analysis of Australian Case Law' (2020) 42 Sydney Law Review 1.

[84] GOV.UK, 'Employment Tribunal Decisions' <https://www.gov.uk/employment-tribunal-decisions> accessed 27 February 2017. Some decisions handed down earlier than February 2017 had been uploaded to the website, dating back to 14 July 2016. These decisions were included for the purposes of this analysis, adding four decisions to the sample which were decided prior to February 2017. I have written in detail elsewhere about how this sample was refined and analysed: Alysia Blackham, 'Enforcing Rights

decisions uploaded to the Northern Ireland (NI) tribunal website over the same period.[85] Data were updated for the case numbers within the sample to reflect all case developments up to 11 January 2020. Cases were compared and linked to those heard in the Employment Appeal Tribunal (EAT) and Court of Appeal, to include subsequent case developments. The UK sample included 1,208 age discrimination cases and 1,563 published decisions, covering 7,829 pages.

Cases with multiple decisions (eg, a preliminary hearing and/or on appeal) were only considered once, aggregating the issues for consideration. Decisions were coded manually using themes derived from the literature and the documents themselves,[86] and analysed using qualitative and quantitative methods.[87]

Quantitative data analysis was used at various points in this study to analyse the prevalence and outcomes of age discrimination claims. These analyses used both publicly available data from statutory agencies (such as that included in annual reports), and additional data sourced through freedom of information (FOI) requests and by liaising with the agencies themselves. Data were collected and updated to the point of writing (June 2020).

Gathering and collating this data was one of the more onerous aspects of this project. Equality agencies do not publicly report on many aspects of their operations, due to onerous secrecy obligations imposed by their founding statutes, budget cuts, and the extensive use of non-disclosure agreements (NDAs) in conciliated equality disputes.[88] Within these limits, statutory equality agencies retain substantial discretion in determining what and how they report on data. In many cases, data on age discrimination claims were not collected centrally[89] or were collected by a different body,[90] numbers of complaints were too small to provide detail beyond that in the annual report,[91] there were inconsistencies in how individual consents to participate in research were noted centrally,[92] data were promised but

in Employment Tribunals: Insights from Age Discrimination Claims in a New "Dataset"' (2021) 41(3) Legal Studies 390.

[85] Northern Ireland Office of Industrial Tribunals and Fair Employment Tribunals, 'Decisions Search' (28 September 2006) <https://employmenttribunalsni.co.uk/OITFET_IWS/DecisionSearch.aspx> accessed 27 April 2021.

[86] Gery W Ryan and H Russell Bernard, 'Data Management and Analysis Methods' in Norman K Denzin and Yvonna S Lincoln (eds), *Collecting and Interpreting Qualitative Materials* (2nd edn, SAGE 2003) 275–76.

[87] Further details of these methods and results are on file with the author and available on request.

[88] Dominique Allen and Alysia Blackham, 'Under Wraps: Secrecy, Confidentiality and the Enforcement of Equality Law in Australia and the UK' (2019) 43 Melbourne University Law Review 384. See also Women and Equalities Committee, *The Use of Non-Disclosure Agreements in Discrimination Cases* (2017–19 HC 1720).

[89] Federal Court of Australia (FCA), Federal Circuit Court of Australia (FCCA), Fair Work Commission (FWC), Victorian Civil and Administrative Tribunal (VCAT).

[90] UK Equality and Human Rights Commission (EHRC) and Equality Advisory and Support Service (EASS).

[91] Northern Territory (NT).

[92] New South Wales (NSW).

not provided[93] or concerns were expressed about how data were recorded and its consistency.[94]

After over four years of negotiation, I managed to obtain long-term, detailed complaint and conciliation data for only three jurisdictions: Queensland, Western Australia (WA), and South Australia (SA). To comply with statutory secrecy obligations, the equality agencies de-identified all conciliation records, so no personally identifiable information was provided. I obtained additional, less expansive data from Acas (the Advisory, Conciliation and Arbitration Service), the Equality Advisory and Support Service (EASS), the Australian Human Rights Commission (AHRC), Tasmania, and the Fair Work Ombudsman (FWO).

The data I obtained are often incomplete, contain errors, and jurisdiction-specific in the way they are reported. Key variables are often missing from the data, making it difficult to analyse questions of intersectionality, particularly due to ethnicity and indigeneity. Rather than applying complex statistical models, I have used descriptive statistics to analyse data as and where relevant.

One of the key findings of this project, then, is the extent to which data on individual discrimination complaints are incomplete, dispersed, potentially inaccurate, and difficult to obtain, across both the UK and Australia. This makes it difficult to evaluate the practical operation of enforcement mechanisms. Increasing transparency, including through better data collection and communication, is a key reform for advancing age equality in practice.[95]

To complement this limited quantitative data, ***semi-structured qualitative expert interviews*** were conducted across the Australian states and territories, and the UK nations. A first series of ten pilot interviews was conducted with twelve respondents in New South Wales (NSW) and Victoria in July 2015, to develop the themes and scope of this project. A second series of interviews was conducted across all Australian states and territories and the UK nations between March 2018 and September 2020.[96]

'Experts' were defined as those who were actively involved in the enforcement of age discrimination law, as it related to work.[97] Experts were sampled purposively[98] by approaching agencies and individuals who had key roles in the enforcement

[93] Victoria (Vic).

[94] South Australia (SA), UK Advisory, Conciliation and Arbitration Service (Acas).

[95] Alysia Blackham, 'Positive Equality Duties: The Future of Equality and Transparency?' (2021) 37(2) Law in Context 98.

[96] Five organizations were interviewed in both the pilot interviews and the subsequent interviews; however, in the intervening period, all respondent officeholders in these organizations had turned over, meaning the interviews were with different individuals at each time point. Both the pilot and subsequent interviews were therefore included in the data analysis.

[97] Michael Meuser and Ulrike Nagel, 'The Expert Interview and Changes in Knowledge Production' in Alexander Bogner, Beate Littig, and Wolfgang Menz (eds), *Interviewing Experts* (Palgrave Macmillan 2009) 24.

[98] Robert Stake, 'Qualitative Case Studies' in Yvonna Lincoln and Norman Denzin (eds), *Strategies of Qualitative Inquiry* (3rd edn, SAGE 2008) 130.

of age discrimination law, as identified from the legal framework, government reports, and searches of internet databases. Respondents included representatives from equality bodies, legal practice, age lobby groups, government, unions, and academia. Over time, theoretical sampling was used to identify further respondents who were likely to extend or further develop emerging concepts and theory,[99] and snowball sampling[100] was used to expand the pool of respondents.[101]

Some community legal centres and practitioners declined to be interviewed, on the basis that they were not actively involved in age discrimination matters. I was also unable to secure an interview with the Labour Relations Agency (LRA) in NI. ET judges were not interviewed in GB, as judicial participation in research projects will only be approved if judicial participation is deemed 'necessary'.[102] Given the publicly available data on these issues, ET judges' perspectives are arguably not 'necessary' to corroborate the findings of this study.

In total, sixty-eight expert interviews were conducted with 101 respondents, as depicted in Table 1.1 and Table 1.2. Interviews were mostly conducted in person, though phone and Zoom interviews were conducted if in person meetings could not be arranged (including during the Covid-19 pandemic). Where necessary or expedient, group interviews were conducted, such as when interviewing equality agencies or community legal centres with multiple people involved in age discrimination matters. As Table 1.1 demonstrates, some jurisdictions were over-represented in the sample (such as England and Victoria): this, in part, reflected where agencies and practitioners were active in age discrimination law (and, conversely, where there was minimal activity, and/or respondents did not agree to be interviewed, such as in Queensland and SA).

Interviews were conducted with non-directive questions and a broad topic guide, and typically lasted for an hour. Respondents were asked their views on the effectiveness of the enforcement of age discrimination legislation, barriers and limitations to the enforcement of age discrimination law (for both older and younger workers), and suggestions for law reform and change. Interviews were recorded and transcribed; content analysis was then used to categorize key patterns in the data.[103] Transcripts were inductively coded, using themes derived from the literature and the transcripts themselves,[104] with the assistance of NVivo

[99] Kathleen M Eisenhardt, 'Building Theories from Case Study Research' in A Michael Huberman and Matthew Miles (eds), *The Qualitative Researcher's Companion* (SAGE 2002) 13; Juliet M Corbin and Anselm L Strauss, *Basics of Qualitative Research: Techniques and Procedures for Developing Grounded Theory* (3rd edn, SAGE 2008) 117.

[100] That is, where experts identify other potential respondents.

[101] Tim May, *Social Research: Issues, Methods and Process* (Open University Press 1993) 100; Webley (n 79) 934.

[102] Courts and Tribunals Judiciary, 'Judicial Participation in Research Projects' (15 August 2019) <https://www.judiciary.uk/publications/judicial-participation-in-research-projects/> accessed 16 June 2020.

[103] Patton (n 64) 381.

[104] Ryan and Bernard (n 86) 275–76.

Table 1.1 Interviews and respondents by jurisdiction

Jurisdiction	Number of interviews	Number of respondents
England	10	11
NI	5	6
Wales	4	9
Scotland	6	9
Tasmania	4	10
WA	4	5
NT	4	7
ACT	6	7
NSW	6	7
Victoria	11	17
Queensland	1	2
Federal	5	7
SA	1	4
Total	**68**	**101**

Table 1.2 Number of interviews by respondent type

Respondent type	Number of interviews	Number of respondents
Agency	27	46
Practitioner	19	26
Academic	1	1
Government	3	4
Union	3	3
NGO	15	21

qualitative data analysis software. Data were anonymized and each interview allocated an identifier in accordance with a classification scheme.[105] Respondents were invited to review and check how their responses were being reported, and to

[105] Stephen McNair, Matthew Flynn, and Nina Dutton, 'Employer Responses to an Ageing Workforce: A Qualitative Study' (2007) Research Report 455, 161–62. Interviewees have been classified according to their jurisdiction: A for Australia, UK for the UK, then allocated a number.

amend information to ensure fairness, accuracy, or relevance;[106] one substantive change was made through this process.

To complement this qualitative data, I conducted a ***survey of advocates*** to gather a broader range of perspectives on how age discrimination law is operating in practice. The survey sought qualitative and quantitative data about practitioners' and advocates' experiences in the enforcement of age discrimination law, their opinions regarding any barriers to enforcement, and possible legal reforms. It was conducted using Qualtrics survey software. Respondents were not required to answer every question on the survey.

The survey was distributed in June 2020 to legal practitioners and industrial advocates operating in the UK and Australia. Individual practitioners working in the area of age discrimination law were identified from the analysis of ET decisions and Australian case law. Where practitioners had a publicly accessible email address (153 UK practitioners, 67 Australian practitioners), a link to the survey was sent directly to them.[107] In many cases (seventy-eight UK practitioners, six Australian practitioners), public emails were generic email addresses, or emails for barristers' clerks. In this case, clerks, law firms, or chambers were contacted and asked to pass the survey link on. A survey link was also sent to 295 law societies, bar associations and community legal centres, unions, and industrial advocates in Australia and the UK for distribution. A public call for respondents was also made on Twitter.

In total, seventy-six survey responses were received between June and September 2020. Of those who identified their jurisdiction (forty-one respondents), twenty-seven respondents were based in Australia (seven in Victoria, twelve in NSW, two in SA, and six in Queensland), and fourteen in the UK; of respondents who identified their gender (thirty-seven), seventeen identified as female and twenty as male. The majority (thirty-three of forty-one responses) regularly represented claimants or workers; eight represented employers or respondents. Of those who identified their professional role (thirty-seven), most were barristers (twenty-seven), though respondents also included union officials (two), other legal practitioners (seven), and a tribunal member.

This study synthesizes multiple, overlapping, and mutually enriching sources of data. While recognizing the limits of each of these methods—which are all partial, incomplete, and limited in different ways—this study aims to make use of the different strengths and advantages of qualitative and quantitative research methods, to enrich our understanding of how age discrimination law is operating in practice.

Using these mixed methods, we can turn to consider the ways in which age discrimination continues to affect both older and younger workers, and why we might

[106] See Helen Simons, *Case Study Research in Practice* (SAGE 2009) 102–03.

[107] This meant many barristers were contacted directly, as barristers were more likely than solicitors to list their email publicly.

question the success of existing age discrimination laws at effecting change. The enduring prevalence of age discrimination at work presents a strong case for critique and reform of the legal framework; indeed, the very nature of age discrimination may make existing models of enforcement problematic.

V. The Enduring Prevalence of Age Discrimination

There is a general perception that age discrimination in employment remains common. Butler defines age discrimination or ageism as 'prejudice by one age group toward other age groups'.[108] However, ageism and ageist sentiment can also be internalized, so that individuals make assumptions about their *own* age group. Age discrimination is often grounded in age norms, or widely shared judgements of the standard or typical ages of individuals holding a role or status.[109] Age norms are still firmly entrenched in society, as age continues to be a category deployed to help make sense of the world.[110] Where individuals breach these age norms, they may experience less favourable or unfair treatment. The endurance of age norms means that age discrimination is often taken less seriously than other forms of discrimination; indeed, age is often treated less favourably than other protected grounds in discrimination law itself, with broader exceptions and wider defences to the statutory prohibition of discrimination.[111]

Australian survey evidence indicates that age discrimination is widespread in Australian workplaces. In a 2014 prevalence survey of age discrimination in the workforce, based on telephone interviews with 2,109 Australians aged 50 years and over, the AHRC found that 27 per cent of respondents reported experiencing age discrimination in employment in the previous two years.[112] Further, 32 per cent of respondents were aware of other people experiencing discrimination because of their age in the workplace in the last two years.[113] Age discrimination was more

[108] Robert N Butler, 'Age-Ism: Another Form of Bigotry' (1969) 9 Gerontologist 243, 243.

[109] BS Lawrence, 'Organizational Age Norms: Why is it so Hard to Know One When You See One?' (1996) 36 Gerontologist 209, 209.

[110] John Macnicol, 'Dilemmas of Age Discrimination' (Paper presented at the Third International Conference on Policy Transferability, Aix-en-Provence, France, September 2002) 16, quoted in Colin Duncan, 'The Dangers and Limitations of Equality Agendas as Means for Tackling Old-Age Prejudice' (2008) 28 Ageing & Society 1133, 1146.

[111] Blackham, *Extending Working Life* (n 67); Alysia Blackham, 'A Compromised Balance? A Comparative Examination of Exceptions to Age Discrimination Law in Australia and the UK' (2018) 41 Melbourne University Law Review 1085; Alysia Blackham, 'Defining "Discrimination" in UK and Australian Age Discrimination Law' (2018) 43 Monash University Law Review 760.

[112] AHRC, 'National Prevalence Survey of Age Discrimination in the Workplace: The Prevalence, Nature and Impact of Workplace Age Discrimination amongst the Australian Population Aged 50 Years and Older' (2015) 18. Respondents were asked: 'during 2013 and 2014, have you at any time during those two years, been treated less favourably than other people in a similar situation because of your age or because of assumptions made about older people?': ibid 79.

[113] ibid 23.

commonly experienced by those aged 55–59 (31 per cent of respondents) and 60–64 (32 per cent) than by those aged 65 and older (20 per cent);[114] and more likely to be experienced by those seeking paid work (58 per cent) than by those who worked for a wage or salary (28 per cent) or who were self-employed (26 per cent).[115] Of those who experienced discrimination, two thirds (65 per cent) were explicitly told that their age was the reason for the treatment they experienced.[116] Eighty per cent of respondents who experienced discrimination reported a negative impact as a result;[117] for many, this negative impact related to a loss of self-esteem, decline in mental health, or increase in stress (60 per cent); others reported a negative impact on family, career, or finances (54 per cent).[118] The AHRC has therefore found that age discrimination is a pervasive, systemic, damaging, and often accepted part of Australian workplace culture.

In our analysis of the 2014 General Social Survey (GSS) conducted by the Australian Bureau of Statistics (ABS),[119] Temple and I found that, of all respondents reporting discrimination, age was the second most common ground reported (at 21.3 per cent), after country of birth (a composite variable which included race, ethnicity, language, and skin colour) (34.4 per cent).[120] In relation to age discrimination specifically, those aged 60 and over were most likely to report discrimination on the basis of age (at 38.4 per cent), though age discrimination was also common among those aged 18 to 34 (21.1 per cent) and 35 to 59 (16.9 per cent) (Table 1.3). Age discrimination was slightly more likely to be reported by women, those born in Australia, those with a disability, heterosexuals, and non-parents.

For those reporting age discrimination, the most common context reported was at work (63.8 per cent), though the majority (57 per cent) of those reporting age discrimination report experiencing it in multiple contexts. The GSS offers high quality evidence of the enduring prevalence of age discrimination in Australian workplaces.

Similar results have been found in the UK. In Britain, for example, a 2017–18 national survey of prejudice canvassing 2,853 adults (using NatCen Panel surveys and an additional survey to capture minority groups) found that age discrimination was the most common form of prejudice British adults reported experiencing, affecting 26 per cent of respondents (though this was not confined to the workplace).[121] Those under 35 were more likely to report experiencing age prejudice (39 per cent of respondents) than those aged 35–54 (22 per cent) or over 55

[114] ibid 18.
[115] ibid 19.
[116] ibid 35.
[117] ibid 45.
[118] ibid 46.
[119] Alysia Blackham and Jeromey Temple, 'Intersectional Discrimination in Australia: An Empirical Critique of the Legal Framework' (2020) 43 University of New South Wales Law Journal 773.
[120] Though note the large number of 'other', at 48.6 per cent.
[121] Dominic Abrams, Hannah Swift, and Diane Houston, 'Developing a National Barometer of Prejudice and Discrimination in Britain' (2018) Research Report 119, 22, 24.

Table 1.3 Age discrimination reported by demographic characteristics (per cent)

		Age Discrimination Reported (%)
Age	18–34	21.1
	35–59	16.9
	60+	38.4
Sex	Male	19.7
	Female	22.7
Country of Birth	Australia	24.7
	MESB	22.2
	NESB	11.7
Disability	No	19.9
	Yes	23.7
Heterosexual	No	20.4
	Yes	21.5
Parent	No	22.6
	Yes	19.7
All		21.3

Table notes:
MESB = Mainly English-Speaking Background countries
NESB = Non-English Speaking Background countries
Source: 2014 GSS

(20 per cent).[122] Nearly half of all respondents (46 per cent) who had experienced prejudice had done so in employment or at work.[123] At the same time, though, across all respondents, over half (54 per cent) thought that the issue of age discrimination was not at all or only slightly serious.[124]

Of course, self-reported discrimination does not necessarily reflect the actual prevalence of discrimination in society:[125] the difficulty of perceiving discrimination can mean that individuals under-report discrimination.[126] Further,

122 ibid 25.
123 ibid 27.
124 ibid 28.
125 Ralph Fevre, Heidi Grainger, and Rioch Brewer, 'Discrimination and Unfair Treatment in the Workplace' (2011) 49 British Journal of Industrial Relations s207.
126 ibid s212.

individuals often assume that workplace practices prevent discrimination, and guarantee equal opportunities, reducing their tendency to report discrimination:[127] Fevre and others describe this as a 'belief in the benign effects of instrumental rationality in the workplace'.[128] This may mean that large-scale surveys significantly under-state the prevalence of discrimination in society. Overall, though, while it is difficult to assess the prevalence of age discrimination, it appears that a sizeable proportion of workers experience age discrimination in employment, flagging the importance of effective mechanisms to address and remedy discrimination.

Supplementing this statistical data, the expert interviews conducted in this study reveal telling insights about how age discrimination is manifesting in the workplace. Age discrimination is seen as the biggest issue facing older workers at work;[129] indeed, experiencing age discrimination is a close to universal experience for those who are older: 'we go to the senior's expo and everybody who walks past us has got the basis for a complaint about something.'[130] Age discrimination is subtle and rarely overt,[131] occurring across the life-cycle of employment, from recruitment to termination.

Age discrimination was seen as common in recruitment,[132] affecting both older and younger workers. In some cases, age discrimination was imported into recruitment processes through ostensibly age-neutral criteria, like 'experience'. While these criteria can be legitimate, they can also be a cloak for age discrimination: 'Experience is really just a synonym for time'.[133] Issues could be encountered in recruitment if applicants did not fit the stereotype of those who perform that particular job (eg, dental hygienists tend to be young, attractive women).[134] This flags the particular challenges faced by older women in recruitment, as they experience the double jeopardy of age and gender discrimination (Chapters 2 and 4).

To some extent, difficulties in recruitment could reflect a skills mismatch between what employers require and what non-prime age workers are able to offer. For older workers, particular issues can arise where people have worked in manual industries throughout their career, but no longer have the physical capacity to maintain a manual role,[135] or such industries have shut down.[136] These workers are expected to be technologically literate to obtain a new role[137] or to 'retool':[138] 'you are sort of left out or an expectation about teaching yourself all these skills and you

127 ibid s222.
128 ibid s227–28.
129 UK81.
130 A105.
131 A10; A100; A101; A102; A103; A113; A150; A153; UK78; UK84. cf UK80; UK81.
132 A5; A10; A98; A102; A113; A156; UK80; UK162.
133 A159.
134 A106.
135 A109.
136 A110.
137 UK84; UK152.
138 A110.

can't.'[139] Upskilling is seen as an individual responsibility;[140] lower-skilled workers are rarely seen by employers as 'people to develop, they're just seen as a resource'.[141] For younger workers, employers may not recognize or value the skills that they bring to a particular role.[142]

Within work, age discrimination manifests as a lack of voice[143] and invisibility, for both older and younger workers.[144] Age-based stereotypes are pervasive within the workplace,[145] seeing younger workers as lazy,[146] and regarding older workers as having poor information technology (IT) skills, an inability or unwillingness to learn,[147] 'just going through the motions',[148] or making assumptions that skills or capacity will decline with age.[149]

These stereotypes can be conscious or unconscious;[150] regardless, they have a substantial impact on older and younger workers' experiences at work. Age-based stereotypes mean employers often invest less in older workers,[151] meaning older workers have more limited access to training and skills development than their younger peers.[152] In some cases, older workers might be penalized for making mistakes at work, in situations that could have been readily resolved or avoided through better training and support.[153] A lack of training may push older workers to retire or resign, especially if they feel their skills are not keeping up with organizational change, or if technology is changed abruptly.[154]

Employers also sometimes fail to encourage older workers to make use of policies that might assist them, such as those around flexible working.[155] Indeed, an older worker may not be employed due to a fear of needing to provide flexible working conditions in the future.[156] Equally, an illness or injury that might be tolerated in a younger worker may not be accepted in an older worker: 'It's a whole package of thought around their value to a company'.[157] This reflects the

[139] UK84.
[140] UK152.
[141] A110.
[142] A156; A159.
[143] A156.
[144] A156; UK90.
[145] A3.
[146] A156.
[147] A113; UK78; UK92.
[148] A111.
[149] A99; A103. See also Richard A Posthuma and Michael A Campion, 'Age Stereotypes in the Workplace: Common Stereotypes, Moderators, and Future Research Directions' (2009) 35 Journal of Management 158; Hannah J Swift and others, 'The Risks of Ageism Model: How Ageism and Negative Attitudes toward Age Can Be a Barrier to Active Aging' (2017) 11 Social Issues and Policy Review 195.
[150] A113.
[151] UK88.
[152] UK86; UK88.
[153] A106.
[154] UK152.
[155] UK88.
[156] A104.
[157] A101.

substantial discretion that employers have around how these policies operate in practice.[158]

In some cases, employers avoid having difficult conversations with older workers, or undertaking succession planning, for fear of being seen as 'ageist'.[159] This can lead to age discrimination against younger workers, who are expected to over-perform and are subjected to performance management processes;[160] this can 'create intergenerational stress within teams'.[161] By not having these conversations, employers also miss an opportunity to identify where issues around performance can be supported and rectified, through both training and flexible work arrangements for those with caring responsibilities.[162]

The performance management of older workers can also raise age-based issues.[163] In some cases, there is a sense that these processes have been driven by age, or manifest some age bias, even if there are also legitimate performance concerns:[164] '[w]ith any discrimination claim, what you find is that there's always mixed elements.'[165] Poor disciplinary processes can be perceived as having an element of age bias, though there is often limited evidence to back this up.[166] That said, often poor processes can be attributable to a breakdown in communication[167] and, in some cases, a failure to accommodate a disability.[168]

Both older and younger workers experience excessive paternalism at work. For younger workers, this could manifest as unhelpful 'mentoring'.[169] For older workers, this manifested—in the particular context of Covid-19—in being more likely to be furloughed or stood down from work.[170] While employers might see this as helping their workers, it is not necessarily in their best interests, as it limits pay and promotional opportunities.[171]

Less benevolently, youth wages can lead to discrimination as workers grow older and become eligible for higher pay rates. As one practitioner noted: 'I had quite a few complaints where ... people were saying, "Look, you know, I've suddenly turned this age, and suddenly my shifts have disappeared." '[172] Older workers may

[158] UK88. See similarly Vanessa Beck and Glynne Williams, 'The (Performance) Management of Retirement and the Limits of Individual Choice' (2015) 29 Work, Employment & Society 267.
[159] UK88; UK89.
[160] UK88.
[161] ibid.
[162] ibid.
[163] A109.
[164] A111; UK117.
[165] A111.
[166] A108.
[167] UK117.
[168] ibid.
[169] A156.
[170] UK117.
[171] ibid.
[172] A102. See also A160.

also experience pejorative terms and age-based name-calling, including terms like 'cranky old bitch', 'old fart', 'geriatric', or 'dinosaur'.[173]

In relation to termination, older workers could be pushed to leave work,[174] especially when a new manager was appointed,[175] ostensibly on the basis of seeking 'fresh blood',[176] 'fresh ideas',[177] or 'renewal'.[178] Workers often experienced pressure to retire,[179] which could be exerted subtlety or indirectly: '[i]t's just a sense of being pushed out, a sense of being less valued.... a general sense that you are not welcome here anymore.'[180] Older workers—especially older women[181]—might also be targeted in redundancy exercises.[182] Some older workers were subject to non-genuine redundancy situations,[183] where roles and responsibilities were moved around, to be undertaken by a different employee.[184] This might be done to make way for a new, more affordable, and often younger staff member.[185] In other cases, older workers are sidelined in workplace restructures due to their age,[186] including by being pushed aside, having managerial responsibilities removed, or not being considered for other roles.[187] Older workers experienced subtle coercion to accept voluntary redundancy packages.[188] This is perhaps partly due to older workers' average higher level of seniority: those in more senior positions are more likely to be targeted by voluntary redundancy processes,[189] being more expensive to employ.[190] Indeed, redundancies are only likely to be attractive to older workers with long periods of service.[191] Conversely, in some organizations, those who have failed to achieve a certain level of seniority by a particular age may be seen as ineffective or less effective than their peers, and targeted for redundancy: 'there must be something wrong with you for not having ascended the ladder in that way.'[192] Even if a redundancy is not discriminatory, it can lead to a fear of not regaining work, particularly for older women.[193]

173 A151.
174 ibid.
175 A100; UK117.
176 A108; A151.
177 A154.
178 ibid.
179 A99; A105; A106.
180 A115.
181 A100.
182 A98; A100; A113.
183 A109.
184 ibid.
185 A111.
186 A101.
187 A103; A151.
188 A104.
189 ibid.
190 A111.
191 A154.
192 A104.
193 A108; UK152.

Overall, this discussion reveals some of the striking similarities and parallels between the experiences of age discrimination of different (non-prime) age groups, uniting the experiences of older and younger workers.[194] Age discrimination remains an enduring problem for both older and younger workers across the life-cycle of employment.

VI. The Nature of Age Discrimination: Compounding the Difficulties of Enforcement

The nature of age discrimination, and the way it affects the practical enforcement of age discrimination law, is a recurring theme taken up in the chapters that follow. At this stage, however, it is important to make three thematic points.

First, the difficulties faced by many older workers in recruitment and at the end of the employment relationship can be partly attributable to the enduring age-norms around retirement,[195] and the idealized view of older age as a period of leisure and recreation. Unfortunately for many workers—especially older women, those with caring responsibilities, and those with limited pensions—this ideal does not reflect their reality.[196] Thus, while societal views of ageing do not match the reality of many older people, they continue to have an enduring influence on how workplaces are structured.

Second, in some instances, taken in isolation, age discrimination could be seen as trivial or 'trifling':[197]

> I call them 'cup of tea' cases because people put in a claim and they say, 'My boss never made me a cup of tea' and you look at that and you think, 'Really? Is this your problem?' But actually, if you think about it and somebody comes into work and says, 'Hi. Good morning. Do you want a cup of tea? Hi Susan. I'll get you a coffee' and they go through the whole office and they look straight past you and do that day after day after day . . . actually that's very distressing.[198]

It can be difficult to articulate, then, why age discrimination is harmful when it appears so trivial when documented.[199] Claimants are aware of this, and it can affect their confidence:

194 Blackham, 'Young Workers' (n 8) 31.
195 See, eg, Martin Kohli, 'The Institutionalization of the Life Course: Looking Back to Look Ahead' (2007) 4 Research in Human Development 253.
196 A103.
197 A150.
198 UK78.
199 A150.

> the question I get asked in training by women more than any other is, am I being over-sensitive, do you think I'm exaggerating this? … when they do voice their concerns, they're shut down, and given the snowflake treatment. And so they're really afraid that they are over-sensitive because that's what they're told all the time.[200]

Claimants may not even recognize behaviour as being discriminatory or use that label to describe their experiences. This is, in part, because age discrimination is not well understood[201] and is normalized and tolerated in society:[202]

> they're just not predisposed to think in those terms, especially if it's the kind of indirect discrimination of being ignored, of being invisible, of being not listened to. … I guess it's the frog in the pot thing that it happens gradually over time and they just have come to expect that that's how it is for older women and haven't framed it in those terms of, is this discrimination and is it something I can do something about?[203]

Thus, the degree to which age discrimination is seen as trivial or insignificant is also bound up with enduring age norms, and the degree to which age discrimination is seen as more socially acceptable than other types of discrimination.[204] Age is an important personal characteristic,[205] which is used extensively as a social stratifier: 'we like being able to discriminate on these grounds.'[206] This is given legislative form through the many exceptions to the prohibition of age discrimination.[207] The fact that age discrimination is subtle and socially accepted makes it even more difficult to challenge through legal proceedings.[208]

Third, it can be difficult to disaggregate age discrimination from other systemic trends. Age-based vulnerability can be driven by systemic factors, such as the changing nature of work and the workplace,[209] offshoring of manufacturing, outsourcing (including of recruitment),[210] workplace automation,[211] and the

[200] A99. This is arguably a form of gaslighting: see Paige L Sweet, 'The Sociology of Gaslighting' (2019) 84 American Sociological Review 851; Kate Abramson, 'Turning up the Lights on Gaslighting' (2014) 28 Philosophical Perspectives 1.
[201] A151; UK152.
[202] A150.
[203] A99.
[204] UK80.
[205] UK82.
[206] ibid.
[207] Blackham, 'A Compromised Balance?' (n 111).
[208] A159; UK80.
[209] A6.
[210] A10.
[211] A102.

growth in insecure and temporary work,[212] which affect different age groups differently.

For example, the most junior workers tend to experience very poor treatment at work, sometimes due to hazing and bullying, sexual harassment, or just poor working conditions and long working hours.[213] Younger workers are also over-exposed to exploitation, wage theft, internships, and unpaid work experience.[214] This is a particular problem in hierarchical workplaces[215] and in the context of apprenticeships, where (often young) workers are dependent on a particular employer for training.[216] Younger workers may also be more vulnerable because they tend to occupy industries characterized by insecure work, low unionization, and poor working conditions, such as retail and hospitality.[217]

Similarly, it is difficult to disaggregate potential age discrimination from a lack of experience, or a lack of the *right* experience.[218] In competitive employment markets, experience—or a lack thereof—becomes a key distinguishing factor in recruitment. To be employed, people need the perfect level and type of experience.[219] Young people may have insufficient experience, and older workers too much. However, employers cannot (and should not) be prevented from seeking recruits with a reasonable level of experience or expertise.

Equally, too, a lack of experience—combined with relative youth—could make young people more vulnerable to exploitation at work, in part because their expectations of the workforce are lower.[220] Some younger workers are still coming to understand what is acceptable behaviour at work.[221] As one practitioner noted: 'the employer assumes, this young person doesn't know their rights . . . it's their first job, so they should just be lucky to have that job and they can get away with treating them terribly.'[222] Some employers might have a strategic preference for younger workers, who are less experienced and less likely to assert their employment rights.[223] Thus, age interacts with and compounds other forms of vulnerability, and can act as a signifier to unscrupulous employers that a worker is especially vulnerable to exploitation.

[212] A6; A102. Though we need to recognize the diversity of different age groups: for example, some older workers quite like flexible, casual roles and zero-hours contracts if they have a good pension and do not need to work to sustain themselves financially: A104; UK166.
[213] A3; A6; A115; A160; A164.
[214] A6; A105; A112; A159; A160; A169. Blackham, 'Working at the Edges of Legal Protection: Equality Law and Youth Work Experience from a Comparative Perspective' (n 9).
[215] A164.
[216] A107; A115; A160.
[217] A160; A169.
[218] A163.
[219] ibid.
[220] A164.
[221] A3.
[222] A108.
[223] A110.

Age therefore becomes 'a different category of vulnerability'[224] and overlaps with other forms of vulnerability.[225] This does not fit easily within the statutory framework as 'age discrimination', but there is an element of discrimination in how these workers are treated: the poorest treatment is reserved for the weakest of the cohort, typically those who are young and the least experienced at work.[226] That said, these cases would rarely be pursued as an age discrimination claim, even if age is a factor.[227]

It may not be practically possible—or necessary—to distinguish between these interlinked factors:[228] issues can have more than one cause, and can be addressed through more than one solution. That said, structural issues can be intensified by age-based law and policy, such as the use of youth wages, which de-value younger workers.[229] Further, these structural trends directly challenge the way age discrimination law is implemented and enforced;[230] with minimal job security, individuals will not risk their job to make a discrimination complaint[231] (Chapter 4). Discrimination law, with its strict division between direct and indirect discrimination, may therefore be inappropriate for capturing the complex ways discrimination manifests in society, and its effects on individuals.[232] How legislation is framed can limit our perception and understanding of discrimination and its effects.[233] Evaluating the degree to which the legislative framework is appropriate for conceiving of, and addressing, age discrimination at work is the key aim of the chapters that follow.

VII. Chapter Overview

Age discrimination therefore remains widespread, despite legal reform to make age discrimination at work unlawful. The House of Commons Women and Equalities Committee inquiry on Older People and Employment (WEC OPE inquiry) concluded that: 'Ageism remains a significant problem within British society and is affecting the ability of people to continue working into later life, despite long-standing laws against age discrimination.'[234]

The question, then, is why does age discrimination endure? In her oral evidence to the inquiry, barrister Dee Masters summed up the issues thus:

224 A169.
225 A112.
226 A115; A159; A164.
227 A108.
228 A164.
229 A159; A160.
230 A154.
231 A159.
232 A111.
233 ibid.
234 Women and Equalities Committee, *Older People and Employment* (2017–19, HC 359) 13.

> In theory, we have a very robust legal system. We have the Equality Act, which prohibits all forms of age discrimination. The real issue, it seems to me, is one of enforcement.... as a practitioner I very rarely see discrimination claims, and not just on age but in respect of any of the protected characteristics. It is very unusual for people to put their heads above the parapet and bring an age discrimination complaint and hold organisations to account. One of the reasons for this is that discrimination is very rarely overt; it is unusual for an organisation to explicitly say, 'We're not giving you this job because, frankly, we think you're past it.' Discrimination is often motivated by unconscious stereotypes or prejudices.[235]

This book exposes what is going wrong with the enforcement of age discrimination law, across Australia, the UK, and Canada. It considers how the limitations of the legal framework are impacting on individual, collective, and agency enforcement, and how the system might be improved to better address age discrimination at work. Drawing on six years of empirical research conducted in Australia and the UK, it maps the barriers to claiming across the life-cycle of a dispute, and considers how legal barriers might inhibit our ability to achieve an age-diverse workplace. The book offers a critical and nuanced roadmap for the future development of age discrimination law in common law countries. It draws on normative theoretical and empirical legal scholarship to offer a grounded critique of existing age discrimination laws and their enforcement and posits concrete suggestions for legal change and reform. It aims to promote critical dialogue about the success and failures of existing age discrimination laws, and to provide a concrete, empirically grounded path for legal change and renewal. It pursues these goals through three key areas of scholarship.

First, in Part 1, drawing on comparative perspectives from the UK, Australia, and Canada, it develops a normative case for preventing age discrimination in employment (Chapter 2). It critically considers how age discrimination law does (and should) affect or influence the lives of older and younger workers, the demographic composition of the workforce, and our capacity to protect vulnerable members of society. The comparative approach adopted offers a critical means of evaluating and illuminating the different practices in common law countries, and builds on the successes of different nations to construct a more developed normative model for the future development of age discrimination law. The common challenges faced by these common law countries—demographic ageing, poor youth employment, and persistent age discrimination—make this comparative analysis particularly relevant.

[235] House of Commons, 'Oral Evidence: Older People and Employment' (2018) HC 359 Q43 <http://data.parliament.uk/writtenevidence/committeeevidence.svc/evidencedocument/women-and-equalities-committee/older-people-and-employment/oral/76656.html> accessed 17 March 2022.

This theoretical work is grounded in the enduring tensions and ambivalences endemic to age discrimination law.[236] It is these tensions that make age discrimination law unique, and these issues distinct from those arising in other areas of discrimination. Age discrimination is seen as 'different' to, and less harmful than, other forms of discrimination. Unlike many prohibited grounds of discrimination, there is no single group who may benefit from its protection: in the countries under study, age discrimination legislation protects all people and all ages. While age discrimination is undesirable, it is often seen as less undesirable than other forms of discrimination and, indeed, potentially beneficial and efficient in some circumstances, including where ageing is assumed to be associated with declining physical and mental capacity. Age discrimination legislation is therefore caught in a fundamental conflict between its intrinsic and instrumental aims. Unlike other forms of discrimination, age discrimination is less likely to be viewed as a human rights issue: instrumental goals generally take priority. Further, entrenched social and cultural views on age make age discrimination a difficult problem to tackle using legal incentives and sanctions. While research on other forms of discrimination informs this theoretical discussion, it is necessary to consider age discrimination separately, as an issue with its own unique complexities and conceptual controversies.

Part 1 goes on to consider the issue of enforcement of age discrimination law from a theoretical perspective, offering a normative and theoretical critique of the individual enforcement model and its alternatives (Chapter 3). This discussion draws on doctrinal analysis of the law in the UK, Canada, and Australia, to frame the empirical results reported in subsequent chapters.

Second, in Part 2, building on this theoretical work, and focusing on two empirical mixed method case studies of the enforcement of age discrimination law in the UK and Australia, the book critically examines the key practical challenges and limitations of relying on the individual enforcement model for addressing age discrimination in employment. These case studies feature rigorous doctrinal analysis, content analysis of judicial decisions, qualitative expert interviews, surveys of legal practitioners, and analysis of statistical data from courts, tribunals, and statutory agencies. These mixed research methods are integrated to offer an innovative and nuanced critique of the practical enforcement of age discrimination law in each jurisdiction, across the stages of claiming (Chapter 4), negotiation and alternative dispute resolution (ADR) (Chapter 5), and hearing and judgment (Chapter 6). These case studies identify a number of critical limitations for pursuing age discrimination claims in each jurisdiction, including: limited claiming by particular groups, especially younger workers and older women; extensive reliance on confidential ADR to resolve claims; difficulties in proving discrimination; and potential

[236] See, eg, Blackham, 'Young Workers' (n 8).

gaps in relation to intersectional or dual discrimination. Overall, the cost of complaining well exceeds any perceived benefit.

Third, then, in Part 3, drawing on these empirical findings, and comparative experiences from the UK, Australia, and Canada, the book proposes and tests a normative framework for the future development of age discrimination law, with a particular focus on enforcement. This normative evaluation considers the potential to move beyond individual enforcement models for age discrimination law, to instead focus on preventative measures that might reduce ageism in employment. It canvasses options such as positive duties on employers and other bodies (Chapter 7), agency enforcement (Chapter 8), and collective approaches (Chapter 9), critically evaluating both their potential to address the limits of existing laws, and practical measures that are essential to ensure that such strategies are successful in practice. To be effective, all of these strategies require a renewed focus on and prioritization of age equality.

The book concludes in Chapter 10 with reflections on the key tensions of age discrimination law, both in relation to the prohibition of age discrimination generally, and the practical enforcement of law.

VIII. Conclusion

In the context of rapid demographic change, this work offers new and innovative insights into the operation of age discrimination laws in common law countries. This research represents the first focused, in-depth study of the legal effectiveness of age discrimination laws from a theoretical and empirical legal perspective, and is the first substantial work to integrate rigorous and detailed comparative doctrinal analysis on age discrimination law with comprehensive empirical data. It offers a normative model for the development of age discrimination law in common law countries, and a new conceptual framework for thinking about age discrimination and equality law.

The focus of this book is, by necessity, limited. It only considers age discrimination at work and how it is addressed. It does not consider broader questions of how we should better reshape the workforce and support services to support older workers,[237] age discrimination beyond the workplace (though discrimination experienced in other areas of public life can strongly influence our behaviour and experience at work),[238] or how we can prompt broader cultural change—including in workplaces—to better value age diversity[239] and improve workplace management

[237] See Women and Equalities Committee, *Older People and Employment* (n 234); AHRC, 'Willing to Work' (n 14).

[238] Blackham and Temple (n 119).

[239] Blackham, *Extending Working Life* (n 67).

and communication,[240] including through flexible work.[241] It does not consider the broader range of policy instruments used to address demographic ageing and improve youth employment.[242] This book, and the evidence within it, offers just one piece of a complex puzzle.

However, while the scope of this work is limited, its findings are relevant not just to age discrimination, but to equality and workplace law more generally: many of these issues are relevant to all protected grounds.[243] The findings and recommendations herein therefore use age as a lens to help us rethink our approach to discrimination law and workplace rights. It is therefore part of a broader and ongoing conversation about we can secure fairness, dignity, and wellbeing at work and promote access to justice.

[240] A98; A99; A151; UK88; UK92; UK117; Alysia Blackham, 'Interrogating the "Dignity" Argument for Mandatory Retirement: An Undignified Development?' (2019) 48 Industrial Law Journal 377.

[241] A99; A151; Alysia Blackham, 'Rethinking Working Time to Support Older Workers' (2015) 31 International Journal of Comparative Labour Law and Industrial Relations 119.

[242] Miriam Hartlapp, 'Deconstructing EU Old Age Policy: Assessing the Potential of Soft OMCs and Hard EU Law' (2012) 16 European integration online papers 1; Blackham, 'Addressing the Ageing Workforce' (n 5); Alysia Blackham, 'Values Driving Ageing Law and Policy in Europe' in Mia Rönnmar and Jenny Julén Votinius (eds), *Festskrift Till Ann Numhauser-Henning* (Juristförlaget i Lund 2017).

[243] A112; A115.

PART I

THE NORMATIVE FOUNDATION OF AGE DISCRIMINATION LAW AND ITS ENFORCEMENT

2

Towards a Theory of Age Discrimination Law

The Normative Basis for Preventing Age Discrimination

I. Introduction

In Chapter 1, I mapped the enduring prevalence of age discrimination at work, using both quantitative and qualitative data. This chapter builds on this to provide a theoretical and normative account and critique of age discrimination law. Drawing on discrimination law theory and theories of intersectionality and vulnerability as they relate to age, I consider the normative basis and rationale for addressing age discrimination in employment. This theoretical and normative discussion is grounded in examples from three common law jurisdictions: the United Kingdom (UK), Canada, and Australia.

Age discrimination has been prohibited in employment in Canada since the 1980s,[1] in the Australian states and territories progressively since the 1990s, at the federal level in Australia since 2004,[2] and in the UK since 2006.[3] While age discrimination legislation is arguably now an established feature of the anti-discrimination law landscape, there is no coherent empirically informed account of why age discrimination should be prohibited at a theoretical and practical level.[4] This may explain why scholars continue to question whether age discrimination is morally wrong or harmful.[5]

This has serious consequences for the development and coherence of age discrimination law as a whole. Indeed, as Fredman argues, one of the key challenges for age discrimination law is to distinguish between acceptable and unacceptable age discrimination:[6] this will have implications for the scope, exceptions, and

[1] Morley Gunderson, 'Age Discrimination in Employment in Canada' (2003) 21 Contemporary Economic Policy 318, 320.

[2] Age Discrimination Act 2004 (Cth) (hereafter ADA).

[3] Employment Equality (Age) Regulations 2006, SI 2006/1031 (hereafter 2006 Regulations), and later consolidated into the Equality Act 2010 (hereafter EqA).

[4] Though see the account for why age is not a less serious form of discrimination in Stuart Goosey, 'Is Age Discrimination a Less Serious Form of Discrimination?' (2019) 39 Legal Studies 533. See also the discussion in Lucy Vickers, *Comparative Discrimination Law: Age as a Protected Ground* (Brill 2018).

[5] See Pnina Alon-Shenker, 'Capabilities and Age Discrimination' in Brian Langille (ed), *The Capability Approach to Labour Law* (OUP 2019) 278–79.

[6] Sandra Fredman, *Discrimination Law* (2nd edn, OUP 2011) 101.

Reforming Age Discrimination Law. Alysia Blackham, Oxford University Press. © Alysia Blackham 2022.
DOI: 10.1093/oso/9780198859284.003.0002

judicial development of age discrimination law. Without a coherent account of what age discrimination law is attempting to achieve, it is difficult to model age discrimination law in a way that addresses social harm effectively. Thus, interrogating the rationale and purpose of age discrimination law is essential to inform its future development.

In this chapter, then, I consider the fundamental normative questions underlying statutory age discrimination law. First, I ask how age discrimination law can be justified; to answer this question, I interrogate dignity-based, redistributive, and liberty-based arguments in favour of equality law, and consider how they apply to age discrimination. Second, I ask what age discrimination law adds, over and above other prohibitions of discrimination. To answer this, I consider whether intersectionality or other theories of discrimination might accommodate age-based disadvantage, making age discrimination law unnecessary. Third, I ask what role age discrimination law might play in a modern society, and consider its enduring role in regulating behaviour. Fourth, I draw out the fundamental tensions that endure in age discrimination law, and consider how they might impact the framing of age discrimination legislation and its enforcement. By considering these fundamental theoretical questions, I seek to explore why age discrimination remains 'the "Cinderella" of the protected characteristics',[7] and how the tensions and theoretical framing of age discrimination law might flow through to the legislative framework and the way age discrimination law is enforced.

II. Theories of Discrimination Law

To start, then, I consider theories of discrimination and equality law, and how they might be used to justify a prohibition of age discrimination, particularly in the workplace. To do that, it is first necessary to clarify what is meant by 'discrimination' and 'equality', before considering the social harm that discrimination or equality law might seek to prevent. 'Non-discrimination' and 'equality' may logically be seen as different concepts: for McColgan, discrimination law imposes an obligation to desist from discriminatory conduct, whereas equality law involves positive obligations.[8]

The debate over the meaning and purpose of discrimination law is normative,[9] and has generated strong disagreement about the fundamental principles

[7] UK79.

[8] Aileen McColgan, *Discrimination, Equality and the Law* (Hart Publishing 2014) 14. However, in much of the literature on the rationales of discrimination and equality law, little distinction is made between the two terms. Thus, the discussion that follows uses the terms interchangeably, while noting the difficulty of this position.

[9] Tarunabh Khaitan, *A Theory of Discrimination Law* (OUP 2015) 6.

underlying discrimination law.[10] Identifying what is meant by 'discrimination' or 'equality' will necessarily direct attention to certain types of harm (or away from certain types of harm). Thus, how 'discrimination' is described and defined is inherently political and contentious, and will reflect broader social and political theories, including about the desirable limits of state intervention.

Various attempts have been made to synthesize the voluminous literature on the theory or rationale of discrimination and equality law. For example, Hellmann makes a distinction between (non-comparative) liberty and (comparative) equality-based accounts of discrimination.[11] This distinction is critiqued by Moreau, who argues there is not as much distinction between the two schools as Hellmann depicts.[12] This chapter does not seek to provide a comprehensive account of all theories of discrimination and equality law. Instead, I draw out some key themes and rationales that emerge in the literature, and attempt to identify synergies between various scholars' views.

While the discussion that follows divides theories of discrimination into different themes or categories, there is much overlap between these ideas. Theorizing 'equality' arguably requires a pluralist approach, evading any singular definition.[13] This is, perhaps, because our understanding of discrimination has evolved as the nature of discrimination has evolved: as Sturm argues,

> the 'wrong' of second generation discrimination cannot be reduced to a single, universal, or simple theory of discrimination.... Instead, the applicable normative theories are plural, subtle, and, not surprisingly, more complex.[14]

Within this pluralistic understanding of (in)equality, six potential theories of or justifications for discrimination law emerge from the literature, focusing on stereotypes, power and disadvantage, autonomy and liberty, (re)distribution, social inclusion, and efficiency.

First, then, one rationale for discrimination law is that it is designed to *address stereotypes and group-based assumptions*, to advance individual dignity and recognition. For Macnicol, for example, discrimination is the application of assumed group characteristics to an individual, regardless of their actual personal characteristics.[15] In employment, this results in decisions based on particular protected

[10] Colm O'Cinneide, 'Fumbling Towards Coherence: The Slow Evolution of Equality and Anti-Discrimination Law in Britain' (2006) 57 Northern Ireland Legal Quarterly 57, 64.

[11] Deborah Hellman, 'Equality and Unconstitutional Discrimination' in Deborah Hellman and Sophia Moreau (eds), *Philosophical Foundations of Discrimination Law* (OUP 2013).

[12] Sophia Moreau, 'In Defense of a Liberty-Based Account of Discrimination' in Deborah Hellman and Sophia Moreau (eds), *Philosophical Foundations of Discrimination Law* (OUP 2013).

[13] Sophia Reibetanz Moreau, *Faces of Inequality: A Theory of Wrongful Discrimination* (OUP 2020) 11.

[14] Susan Sturm, 'Second Generation Employment Discrimination: A Structural Approach' (2001) 101 Columbia Law Review 458, 473.

[15] John Macnicol, *Neoliberalising Old Age* (CUP 2015) 183.

grounds, rather than a person's actual productivity.[16] Group generalizations can be a useful cognitive tool:[17] mental shortcuts are often expedient, and allow us to quickly make sense of a complex world. The issue, of course, is that stereotypes can be wrong, outdated, or not apply to all members of a group. The challenge is to find a balance between the efficiency of mental shortcuts and a prohibition of discrimination. The question, then, is why (or, more accurately, when or where) we would seek to prevent discrimination, and avoid the use of group generalizations: should society be trying to be blind to different individual characteristics,[18] and, if so, in what context(s)?

Second is a view of discrimination that focuses on *power and disadvantage*. Roseberry describes discrimination as the use of power by persons who can claim membership in a dominant identity group to bring about, maintain, and enforce a social and economic hierarchy in which targeted groups are excluded from social and economic opportunities and from which the dominant group obtains benefits.[19] Thus, for Roseberry, discrimination is about power and exclusion, which coalesces around dominant and subordinate identity groups. Khaitan similarly sees discrimination as the wrongful and unjustified exacerbation of relative group disadvantage.[20]

A third approach to discrimination law focuses on *individual autonomy or liberty*: autonomy can be progressed by treating individuals on the basis of individual merit rather than group-based characteristics.[21] Thus, discrimination law is grounded in the pursuit of liberal goals such as autonomy and individualism; this manifests in a conception of equality of fairness as consistency.[22] Similarly, Moreau sees discrimination law as being directed to protecting individual 'deliberative freedoms', that is, 'freedoms to have our decisions about how to live insulated from the effects of normatively extraneous features of us, such as our skin color or gender'.[23] Discrimination law therefore protects people from personal wrongs (as in tort law), as discriminatory acts interfere with an individual right to deliberative freedoms.[24] For Schiek, this 'individuation' aspect of equality law requires that people be allowed to 'move outside the box created by expectations based on ascribed otherness'.[25] Sen also focuses on individual freedom in his conception

[16] ibid.
[17] ibid.
[18] McColgan (n 8) 2.
[19] Lynn Roseberry, 'Multiple Discrimination' in Malcolm Sargeant (ed), *Age Discrimination and Diversity: Multiple Discrimination from an Age Perspective* (CUP 2011) 33.
[20] Khaitan (n 9) 18. Gardner also sees discrimination as being concerned with relative positions: John Gardner, 'Discrimination as Injustice' (1996) 16 Oxford Journal of Legal Studies 353, 355.
[21] Sandra Fredman, 'Equality: A New Generation?' (2001) 30 Industrial Law Journal 145, 154.
[22] ibid.
[23] Sophia Moreau, 'What is Discrimination?' (2010) 38 Philosophy & Public Affairs 143, 147. See also Moreau, *Faces of Inequality* (n 13) ch 3.
[24] Moreau, 'What is Discrimination?' (n 23) 147.
[25] Dagmar Schiek, 'Intersectionality and the Notion of Disability in EU Discrimination Law' (2016) 53 Common Market Law Review 35, 51.

of equality, though moves beyond a focus on 'equality of opportunities' (which tends to be more restrictive, with a focus on barriers)[26] to argue for a freedom to achieve.[27] Thus, Sen argues for 'real' equality of opportunities, through an equality of capabilities approach.[28] This, then, is a substantive view of individual liberty and autonomy, which may require positive action to achieve full individual freedom.[29]

Fourth, discrimination law can be focused on *(re)distribution*. For Gardner, discrimination is a form of injustice; justice is concerned with reasons for or against altering a person's position relative to other people.[30] Discrimination is therefore concerned with distributive justice, or changing a person's relative position other than by returning to the status quo.[31] Similarly, Khaitan sees the role of discrimination law as reducing or eliminating pervasive, abiding and substantial relative disadvantage between groups, to advance access to negative freedoms, valuable opportunities, and self-respect, which are necessary for a good life.[32] Khaitan's conception therefore sees a focus on distribution and relative disadvantage as being necessary for the pursuit of individual autonomy, reflecting the potential overlap between these ideas and theories.

A fifth approach to discrimination law focuses on *social inclusion and participation*, and remedying social exclusion. Fredman has described the central aim of equality as facilitating equal participation of all in society, based on equal concern and respect for the dignity of each individual.[33] In a similar vein, Schiek sees anti-discrimination law as being designed to address 'exclusion in the market place based on a specific kind of de-recognition' which is not 'linked to any rationality'.[34] De-recognition is linked to elements of people's identities (and therefore has dignity or stereotyping implications) and can have redistributive effects.[35] Thus, Schiek's theory again emphasizes the overlap between these schools of thought. Fundamentally, though, for Schiek the 'wrong' of discrimination law is social disadvantage from labour market discrimination, which is triggered by 'ascribed otherness'.[36]

Collins sees equality law as being justified on the basis of social inclusion,[37] which is an 'aim or principle of justice ... concern[ed] about outcomes or

[26] Amartya Sen, *Inequality Reexamined* (15th impr, OUP 2010) 7.
[27] ibid 3.
[28] ibid 7.
[29] Alon-Shenker, 'Capabilities and Age Discrimination' (n 5) 274.
[30] Gardner (n 20) 353.
[31] ibid 357–58.
[32] Khaitan (n 9) 18, 91.
[33] Sandra Fredman, 'The Age of Equality' in Sandra Fredman and Sarah Spencer (eds), *Age as an Equality Issue: Legal and Policy Perspectives* (Hart Publishing 2003) 46.
[34] Dagmar Schiek, 'Revisiting Intersectionality for EU Anti-Discrimination Law in an Economic Crisis: A Critical Legal Studies Perspective' [2016] Sociologia del Diritto 23, 35.
[35] ibid.
[36] ibid 40.
[37] Hugh Collins, 'Discrimination, Equality and Social Inclusion' (2003) 66 Modern Law Review 16.

distributive patterns'.[38] Social inclusion aims to 'establish conditions and opportunities that induce all citizens to participate in society and to come to value its institutions and potentials', thereby promoting social cohesion and solidarity.[39] Social inclusion is not concerned with *relative* disadvantage; instead, Collins argues the focus should be on *absolute disadvantage* of particular groups.[40] The aim of social inclusion is to achieve a 'minimum level of welfare for every citizen', not equality of welfare.[41] Discrimination laws are therefore designed to intervene to respond to 'structural or systematic disadvantage for protected groups',[42] which occurs where (1) there are patterns of disadvantage, or groups that are 'disproportionately and persistently in worse positions' and socially excluded;[43] and (2) there are 'certain permanent arrangements, practices, institutions, and social structures that produce this outcome.'[44]

Further, Collins sees equality law as being about the 'achievement of outcomes, not just life-chances'.[45] For Collins, this conception of equality overcomes tension between the equal treatment principle and substantive conceptions of equality.[46] At the same time, Collins's conception of equality is more paternalistic and coercive than other theorists' ideas:[47] individuals can be compelled to undertake actions that promote social inclusion, rather than just being offered the opportunity to take such actions. O'Cinneide has criticized Collins's argument on the basis that social inclusion does not adequately capture the transformative potential of discrimination law,[48] instead focusing on (potentially coercive) integration of disadvantaged groups into social processes.

Sixth, discrimination law may be justified on the basis of *efficiency* and practical considerations. While group generalizations might be 'economical' for individual decision-making, they are inefficient on a societal scale. For Macnicol, then, discrimination law can be justified on the basis of economic efficiency, as it encourages people to discriminate on the rational basis of 'productivity'[49] which, in turn, should maximize workforce productivity.[50]

Even if discrimination law is justified on the basis of economic efficiency, there may still be a need to recognize difference and individuals' particular circumstances

[38] ibid 22.
[39] ibid 24.
[40] ibid 22.
[41] ibid.
[42] ibid 26.
[43] ibid 27.
[44] ibid 26.
[45] ibid 23. Similarly, Moreau emphasizes access to 'basic' goods: Moreau, *Faces of Inequality* (n 13) ch 4.
[46] Collins (n 37) 17–18.
[47] ibid 24–25.
[48] O'Cinneide, 'Fumbling Towards Coherence' (n 10) 62–63.
[49] Macnicol (n 15) 183.
[50] ibid 184.

(eg the vulnerability of old age).[51] A focus on social neutrality—enforced through a productivity lens —can blur or conceal society's insistence that individuals conform to dominant social values.[52] For Fredman, conformity is enforced through the process of comparison, which creates an ideal of equality grounded in eliminating difference.[53] Understandably, this creates conformist pressures,[54] as individuals are expected to meet the 'norm'. There is therefore a more compelling question of when the recognition of difference will be good, or bad.[55] Similarly, Macnicol argues that there is a need to recognize individual difference in any assessment of productivity: treating people equally does not necessarily mean treating them the same.[56] Thus, Schiek argues that discrimination law should focus on respecting and accommodating difference.[57]

This brief summary of the literature has identified at least six potential theories of, or justifications for, discrimination law, focusing on stereotypes, power and disadvantage, autonomy and liberty, (re)distribution, social inclusion, and efficiency.

Given the enduring differences (and noticeable overlaps) between these theoretical viewpoints, it is unsurprising that the idea of 'equality' has been operationalized in varying ways in statute: there is limited agreement as to what 'equality' entails at either the UK or the European Union (EU) level.[58] 'Equality' therefore cannot be seen as a unitary concept with one clear meaning, and what it entails in practice (like in theory) will never be straightforward.[59] Hepple identifies seven meanings of 'equality' evident in the Equality Act 2006 and government equality reviews:

- Respect for equal worth, dignity, and identity as fundamental human rights;
- Eliminating status discrimination and disadvantage;
- Consistent treatment/formal equality;
- Substantive equality of opportunity;
- Equality of capabilities;
- Equalities of outcomes; and
- Fairness.[60]

Alternatively, equality could be defined as encompassing:

[51] ibid 185.
[52] Fredman, 'Equality' (n 21) 154.
[53] ibid 160.
[54] ibid.
[55] McColgan (n 8) 3.
[56] Macnicol (n 15) 185.
[57] Schiek, 'Intersectionality and the Notion of Disability' (n 25) 51.
[58] Colm O'Cinneide, 'The Uncertain Foundations of Contemporary Anti-Discrimination Law' (2011) 11 International Journal of Discrimination and the Law 7, 10–11.
[59] See Fredman, 'The Age of Equality' (n 33) 37–46.
[60] BA Hepple, *Equality: The Legal Framework* (2nd edn, Hart Publishing 2014) 18–31.

- Consistency (that is, like individuals being treated alike);
- Individual merit (that is, treating individuals according to merit, free from stereotypical assumptions);
- Treating individuals differently according to their needs;
- Achieving a fair distribution of social resources;
- Equality of opportunities;
- Treating individuals with equal dignity and concern; and/or
- Full participation and inclusion in social institutions.[61]

Reconciling these forms of equality, and the substantive underpinnings of equality law, Fredman argues for a 'multi-dimensional concept' of substantive equality, pursuing redistributive, recognition (promoting respect and dignity), transformative (accommodating difference and achieving structural change), and participative (social inclusion and political voice) dimensions.[62] Thus, Fredman's approach integrates the various purposes and meanings of 'equality' to create a composite approach. Applying this to Canadian age discrimination law, Alon-Shenker argues for a 'Dignified Lives Approach' to age discrimination law, grounded in equal concern and respect, which requires compliance with five principles: individual assessment, equal influence, sufficiency, social inclusion, and autonomy.[63]

Rejecting the relevance of Fredman's account for Australian law,[64] and drawing on Gardner's work and Brest's analysis of United States of America (USA) discrimination law,[65] Hewitt argues that discrimination law (as opposed to equality law) in Australia can be justified by two rationales: multiplicity of harm and redistributive justice. 'Harm' in Hewitt's conception can relate to the denial of opportunities to obtain a benefit; infliction of psychological injury; pervasive injury (or compounded forms of discrimination); and unfairness.[66] It is the simultaneous existence of multiple harms that justifies governmental intervention in the field of discrimination law:[67] this, then, integrates both material harms and intrinsic harms. However, Hewitt sees this approach as merely a way of illuminating the rationale of discrimination law, rather than something that should be used as a concrete limit of legal intervention.[68]

[61] See Fredman, 'The Age of Equality' (n 33) 37–46. See also Fredman, *Discrimination Law* (n 6) 8–19.

[62] Fredman, *Discrimination Law* (n 6) 25–33.

[63] Pnina Alon-Shenker, '"Age is Different": Revisiting the Contemporary Understanding of Age Discrimination in the Employment Setting' (2013) 17 Canadian Labour & Employment Law Journal 31, 34, 44.

[64] Anne Hewitt, 'Can a Theoretical Consideration of Australia's Anti-Discrimination Laws Inform Law Reform?' (2013) 41 Federal Law Review 35, 43.

[65] Paul Brest, 'Foreword: In Defense of the Antidiscrimination Principle' (1976–77) 90 Harvard Law Review 1.

[66] Hewitt (n 64) 44–47.

[67] ibid 48.

[68] ibid 62–63.

III. Relating Theories of Discrimination Law to Age

A. The Normative Question of 'Grounds'

The scope of discrimination law—and the grounds it protects—is a contested normative question.[69] Indeed, even the framing of discrimination law around protected characteristics or 'grounds' is contested. Khaitan argues that groups are a condition to enliven the norms of discrimination law,[70] and grounds are used to class people into groups.[71] Khaitan's analysis of discrimination case law posits two criteria to add grounds to discrimination law:[72] first, there must be groups, at least one of which suffers material disadvantage;[73] and, second, these groups must be grounded in some immutable or fundamental choice, which is normatively irrelevant to the groups' treatment.[74]

Similarly, Moreau sees the choice of grounds in discrimination law as reflecting decisions about traits individuals should not need to factor into their life decision-making: grounds are normatively extraneous traits.[75] Unlike Khaitan, Moreau does not see grounds as needing to be immutable or fundamental, chosen or unchosen: rather, 'whatever the nature of the trait, the burdens that result from it are not ones that we believe its possessors should have to factor into their deliberations in these particular social contexts'.[76] The choice of grounds, then, is a normative decision, which depends on 'whether people have a right to make decisions in a manner that is free from the sorts of institutional and attitudinal pressures that are encountered by those with that trait'.[77] The sort of reasoning used to resolve this normative dilemma could vary from ground to ground:

> it seems unlikely that there could be a single principled explanation of what makes each ground of discrimination worthy of the status of a ground. All that we can say is that each ground reflects a judgment that people have a right to make decisions in these social contexts in a manner that is insulated from the burdens imposed by these traits, or by other people's assumptions about them.[78]

For Moreau, then, the inclusion of age as a protected characteristic reflects a normative decision that age should be irrelevant in individual life decision-making.

69 McColgan (n 8) 2.
70 Khaitan (n 9) 29.
71 ibid 30.
72 ibid 50.
73 ibid 31.
74 ibid 56.
75 Moreau, 'What is Discrimination?' (n 23) 156.
76 ibid.
77 ibid.
78 ibid 157.

The justification for including age as a ground does not need to conform to the reasoning used for other protected characteristics: its rationale could be uniquely its own.

This style of group-based analysis is questioned by Fredman, who argues that 'groups' are not fixed:[79] a 'group' is made by a social process of interaction and subjective affirmation of affinity.[80] Like any social interactive process, groups can change, merge, and evolve over time. Further, groups often intersect.[81] Creating any demarcation between groups requires the fraught drawing of bright lines. This process of line-drawing assumes that groups are mutually exclusive; serves to highlight the differences between groups, while blurring differences within groups; and defines groups as though they are unchanging and fixed, which they are not.[82] These sorts of bright line distinctions are confounded by intersectionality (see below).[83]

Going further, Fineman argues for a 'post-identity' approach to equality law, which does not focus on discrimination against 'defined groups', but instead looks to vulnerability and patterns of power, privilege, and favour in society.[84] For Fineman, 'defined groups' or grounds are both too broad—in that they include successful individuals who fall within disadvantaged identity groups—and too narrow—as they exclude consideration of poverty, denial of dignity, and deprivation.[85] They also risk pitting groups against each other, and deflect attention from the institutional arrangements that perpetuate disadvantage.[86] A focus on 'vulnerability' as 'a universal, inevitable, enduring aspect of the human condition'[87] instead recognizes that abilities change over a lifetime, and that dependency is a common trait of humans at the start and end of their lives.[88] For Fineman, vulnerability is therefore a more useful touchstone than grounds, groups, or identity-based measures. However, if discrimination endures 'along identity lines' (as it is likely to do), there will still be a need to remedy and address identity (and ground-based) discrimination.[89]

79 Fredman, 'Equality' (n 21) 159.
80 ibid.
81 ibid.
82 ibid, 158.
83 ibid 159.
84 Martha Albertson Fineman, 'The Vulnerable Subject: Anchoring Equality in the Human Condition' (2008) 20 Yale Journal of Law & Feminism 1, 1.
85 ibid 4.
86 ibid 20.
87 ibid 8.
88 ibid 12.
89 ibid 17.

B. Age as a Protected Ground

If continuing to rely on groups or grounds to anchor discrimination law, it becomes a normative question as to which grounds should be protected, or who should be the beneficiary or subject of discrimination law.[90] Drawing on the theoretical discussion above, extending discrimination law to the ground of age could be justified on the basis that law is necessary to: protect dignity or prevent stereotypes on the basis of age; for redistribution or to protect against age-based disadvantage or power differentials; to protect autonomy or liberty, or prevent the use of age as an extraneous factor in decision-making; to promote social inclusion of people of different ages; and/or to promote economic and organizational efficiency.

As Moreau has recognized, these arguments could be adapted or modified in relation to age, or may be extended to reflect the unique features of age as a protected characteristic.[91] Thus, the rationale for including age as a protected characteristic is not confined to general justifications for discrimination law.[92] Indeed, age does not operate like other protected characteristics: age is not an unchanging or acquired attribute,[93] instead being both universal and temporal.[94] Age can be both positive and negative at different life stages.[95] Further, the impact of age depends on class, socio-economic status,[96] and other protected characteristics. Age's 'special nature' may mean that protection from age discrimination should not necessarily be identical to other grounds like sex;[97] equally, though, treating age differently might undermine intersectional protection given the close relationship between age and other grounds.[98]

Rationalizing or justifying age as a protected ground is therefore complicated by the nature of 'age' itself. Further, while we most commonly perceive age as *chronological* age, age could be interpreted in other ways. Chronological age is 'an "empty" variable ... it is whatever age presumably indexes that is thought to be important';[99] despite this, chronological age is often a poor proxy or indicator for other forms or indicators of age and ageing.[100] Other measures—such as

[90] McColgan (n 8) 2.
[91] Moreau, 'What is Discrimination?' (n 23) 157.
[92] ibid.
[93] Malcolm Sargeant, 'Mandatory Retirement Age and Age Discrimination' (2004) 26 Employee Relations 151, 154.
[94] Nick Adnett and Stephen Hardy, 'The Peculiar Case of Age Discrimination: Americanising the European Social Model?' (2007) 23 European Journal of Law & Economics 29, 38.
[95] McColgan (n 8) 68.
[96] ibid.
[97] ibid 67.
[98] Malcolm Sargeant, 'For Diversity, Against Discrimination: The Contradictory Approach to Age Discrimination in Employment' (2005) 21 International Journal of Comparative Labour Law and Industrial Relations 629, 643–44.
[99] Richard A Settersten and Karl Ulrich Mayer, 'The Measurement of Age, Age Structuring, and the Life Course' (1997) 23 Annual Review of Sociology 233, 239–40.
[100] ibid 240.

biological or physiological, psychological, or social age[101]—may be better indicators of individual ability and capacity to work,[102] and better recognize the diversity of different age cohorts.[103] Much legal regulation, however, focuses on chronological age,[104] though this is often implicit rather than explicit. The Australian Age Discrimination Act 2004 (Cth) s 5 (ADA), and UK Equality Act 2010 s 5 (EqA), for example, simply define age as including membership of an age group. Under the ADA, discrimination can be due to the age of the claimant, a characteristic that appertains generally to persons of that age, or a characteristic that is generally imputed to persons of that age (ss 14, 16). This all likely hinges on chronological age.

Like our notion of 'age' itself, age discrimination law is inherently limited by a general lack of clarity regarding its aims and objectives.[105] Age discrimination law in the context of employment is justified in the literature by two (potentially conflicting) aims or objectives. First, the laws may secure *instrumental* economic ends, by increasing the efficiency of organizations and labour markets, avoiding irrational and economically inefficient prejudice,[106] and thereby helping to relieve pressure on pension systems or the labour market from demographic ageing (that is, an efficiency argument).[107] Second, age discrimination laws may achieve *intrinsic* ends, having value in and of themselves in acknowledging the dignity and inherent worth of older workers.[108] For Manfredi and Vickers, these dual aims represent 'a fundamental tension at the heart of the call for age equality'.[109]

In Australia, the objects of the ADA focus particularly on dignity and age-based stereotypes, including aims such as: 'to promote recognition and acceptance within the community of the principle that people of all ages have the same fundamental rights';[110] to ensure that people of all ages have the 'same rights to equality before the law';[111] and 'to respond to demographic change by ... changing negative stereotypes about older people'.[112] The ADA touches only briefly on redistribution or disadvantage, and only in relation to the provision of age-based benefits and assistance.[113] However, the ADA also makes reference to the need 'to respond to

[101] ibid 239–40.
[102] Helen Meenan, 'Reflecting on Age Discrimination in the European Union: The Search for Clarity and Food for Thought' (2009) 10 ERA Forum 107, 110.
[103] ibid 111.
[104] ibid 110.
[105] Simonetta Manfredi and Lucy Vickers, 'Pensioning off the Mandatory Retirement Age: Implications for the Higher Education Sector' (2013) 33 Legal Studies 289, 310.
[106] Simonetta Manfredi and Lucy Vickers, 'Retirement and Age Discrimination: Managing Retirement in Higher Education' (2009) 38 Industrial Law Journal 343, 344–45.
[107] See also Dagmar Schiek, 'Age Discrimination before the ECJ: Conceptual and Theoretical Issues' (2011) 48 Common Market Law Review 777, 779.
[108] Manfredi and Vickers, 'Retirement and Age Discrimination' (n 106) 344.
[109] Manfredi and Vickers, 'Pensioning off the Mandatory Retirement Age' (n 105) 311.
[110] ADA (n 2) s 3(d).
[111] ibid s 3(b).
[112] ibid s 3(e)(ii).
[113] ibid s 3(c).

demographic change by ... removing barriers to older people participating in society, particularly in the workforce'.[114] This flags the importance of economic efficiency and social inclusion arguments, particularly as they relate to the need to extend working lives to respond to demographic pressures.

The UK Employment Equality (Age) Regulations 2006, SI 2006/1031 (2006 Regulations) were also justified on the basis of both instrumental and intrinsic aims, though with a stronger focus on efficiency. The Regulatory Impact Assessment for the Regulations anticipated that they would 'increase the participation of older and younger workers in the economy, while at the same time helping employers draw on a wider pool of workers.'[115] Thus, the Regulations were geared to achieving greater economic and organizational efficiency, which would otherwise be prevented by age discrimination:

> Discrimination results in poorer quality matches in labour markets, which leads to lower national output.... The risk that exists currently is that [older and younger workers] are not participating fully in the workforce and so human resources are wasted.[116]

Thus, the 2006 Regulations were grounded in economic and efficiency considerations, with less focus on intrinsic aims. Macnicol therefore argues that anti-ageism is a legitimating principle behind the labour market activation of older people, and an argument that helps to undermine social rights, such as through the raising of the state pension age:[117] anti-discrimination 'rights' are balanced by the 'responsibility' to get a job.[118] Instead of being focused on dignity, then, age discrimination legislation serves to individualize the life course and individualize the risks of ageing. Similarly, in my study of UK policy documents, I found that the values and objectives driving ageing law and policy all had an individualistic focus, with individual 'choice' emphasized throughout.[119]

Going beyond the rationales presented in government documents and legislative materials, it is worth scrutinizing further arguments in favour of government intervention to address age discrimination. Some scholars have argued that age discrimination law is unnecessary, 'inefficient', and even harmful, and that the market should be allowed to resolve any issues of discrimination through the operation

[114] ibid s 3(e)(i).
[115] Regulatory Impact Assessment for the Employment Equality (Age) Regulations 2006, SI 2006/1031, [3].
[116] ibid [5].
[117] Macnicol (n 15) 171.
[118] ibid 173.
[119] Alysia Blackham, 'Addressing the Ageing Workforce: A Critical Examination of Legal Policy Objectives and Values' (2017) 37 Ageing & Society 1362, 1383. See also Alysia Blackham, 'Values Driving Ageing Law and Policy in Europe' in Mia Rönnmar and Jenny Julén Votinius (eds), *Festskrift Till Ann Numhauser-Henning* (Juristförlaget i Lund 2017).

of competitive pressures.[120] However, the sections that follow illustrate that there are at least two compelling areas in which the market is unable to resolve issues of age discrimination without regulatory intervention: in relation to dignity and age-based stereotypes; and in relation to redistribution and disadvantage. These arguments, which draw on the interconnected theoretical ideas above, provide a strong rationale and justification for laws prohibiting discrimination on the basis of age.

C. Dignity and Stereotypes

For Bamforth, Malik, and O'Cinneide, eliminating irrational stereotyping and prejudice on the basis of age is a key rationale for age discrimination law.[121] 'Age stereotyping' is generally defined as associating certain characteristics (or not associating certain characteristics) with people of particular ages.[122] Ageism, age-based stereotypes, and a preference for 'prime age' workers may significantly limit opportunities for older and younger workers in the labour market.[123] Stereotypes can create both socio-cultural[124] and economic disadvantage for people of different ages. Legal intervention could therefore be required to secure the autonomy and liberty of people of all ages, including by preventing the use of age as an extraneous factor in decision-making. As Alon-Shenker argues,

> age-based distinctions are not merely wrong when they are based on stereotypes and prejudice; they are primarily wrong because they fail to treat older workers as real agents who are capable of making their own choices, and because they undermine their sets of capabilities.[125]

Thus, there is clear interplay between rationales based on dignity, autonomy, disadvantage, and stereotyping. Studies have identified a consistent and persistent prevalence of negative attitudes towards older workers.[126] Stereotypes associated with older workers can be positive or negative: in practice, though, stereotypes are often negative, inaccurate, or distorted.[127] Drawing on a meta-analysis of 117 studies on

[120] Richard Posner, *Aging and Old Age* (University of Chicago Press 1995) 319; Richard Allen Epstein, *Equal Opportunity or More Opportunity? The Good Thing about Discrimination* (Civitas 2002) 19–20.

[121] Nicholas Bamforth, Maleiha Malik, and Colm O'Cinneide, *Discrimination Law: Theory and Context: Text and Materials* (1st edn, Sweet & Maxwell 2008) 1104–06.

[122] Malcolm Sargeant, 'Ageism and Age Discrimination' in Malcolm Sargeant (ed), *Age Discrimination and Diversity: Multiple Discrimination from an Age Perspective* (CUP 2011) 1.

[123] See Age UK, 'Grey Matters: A Survey of Ageism across Europe: EU Briefing and Policy Recommendations' (2011) 11–12.

[124] Khaitan (n 9) 53.

[125] Alon-Shenker, 'Capabilities and Age Discrimination' (n 5) 284.

[126] Kelly Harris and others, 'Ageism and the Older Worker: A Scoping Review' (2018) 58 Gerontologist e1.

[127] Richard A Posthuma and Michael A Campion, 'Age Stereotypes in the Workplace: Common Stereotypes, Moderators, and Future Research Directions' (2009) 35 Journal of Management 158, 160.

age stereotypes in the workplace, Posthuma and Campion identify stereotypes that older workers: have lower ability, are less motivated, and less productive; are harder to train, less adaptable, less flexible, and more resistant to change; have a lower ability to learn, and therefore less development potential; have shorter job tenure; are more costly; and are more stable, dependable, honest, trustworthy, loyal, committed to the job, and less likely to miss work.[128] Ng and Feldman similarly identify six key negative stereotypes about older workers: that they are poorer performers, less motivated, less willing to participate in training and career development, more resistant and less willing to change, less trusting, less healthy, and more vulnerable to work–family imbalance.[129] Drawing on a meta-analysis of 418 empirical studies, Ng and Feldman found that only one of these stereotypes was consistent with empirical evidence (ie, that older workers were less willing to participate in training and career development activities).[130] Despite the lack of evidence supporting age stereotypes, these ideas have an enduring impact. Studies have repeatedly found negative intentions towards older workers, especially in recruitment,[131] and age discriminatory behaviour.[132] Numerous studies have traced the impact of age stereotypes on the outcomes of employment-related decisions, resulting in (for example) lower ratings for older workers in interviews and performance appraisals.[133]

Stereotypes do not just affect older workers: they also affect the young. Stereotypes associated with younger workers include that they are frivolous, lazy, and apathetic; or, conversely, are a threat or danger to society. Giroux identifies a public perception of young people in the USA as 'variously lazy, stupid, self-indulgent, volatile, dangerous and manipulative'.[134] This is not a new phenomenon: USA youth have been perceived to be immature and 'specifically irresponsible' since the 1940s.[135] Stereotypes and portrayals of young people that demonize and vilify have led to a 'diminishing public concern about their care, dignity and future'.[136] As one interview respondent noted, 'I have been amazed in training by the hostility of middle aged and older people towards millennials.... it's so visceral and it's so like extreme'.[137]

[128] ibid 161–63.
[129] Thomas WH Ng and Daniel C Feldman, 'Evaluating Six Common Stereotypes about Older Workers with Meta-Analytical Data' (2012) 65 Personnel Psychology 821.
[130] ibid.
[131] Harris and others (n 126) e8.
[132] ibid e9.
[133] Posthuma and Campion (n 127) 163–64.
[134] Henry A Giroux, *Youth in a Suspect Society: Democracy or Disposability?* (Palgrave Macmillan 2010) 14.
[135] Talcott Parsons, 'Age and Sex in the Social Structure of the United States' (1942) 7 American Sociological Review 604, 606.
[136] Giroux (n 134) 14.
[137] A99.

These negative stereotypes mean both older and younger workers may struggle to obtain employment and might be subject to discriminatory action on the basis of age. Oswick and Rosenthal argue that jobs are often 'age-typed', with some jobs being seen as 'older jobs' and others as 'younger jobs'.[138] Older workers will be preferred where a job requires stability, loyalty, and maturity—on the stereotypical assumption that older workers will be a 'good fit' with the job requirements—and younger workers are preferred where a job is physically demanding or requires high energy or intensity.[139] Age discrimination, then, occurs due to a 'lack of fit' between stereotypical assumptions about certain ages and job requirements.[140]

This implies that age *is* influencing—and restricting—individuals' abilities to plan their own life path. If age is normatively irrelevant (as, indeed, it appears to be empirically irrelevant in most cases), there appears to be a strong basis for age discrimination laws to address prevailing stereotypes around age, to protect the dignity and autonomy of both older and younger workers. However, Bamforth, Malik, and O'Cinneide note that, while age stereotyping is a problem, it does not 'take the same virulent forms' as for other grounds of discrimination.[141] That said, stereotypes do not need to be virulent or based on bigotry or hatred[142] to be destructive. Thus, as Bamforth, Malik, and O'Cinneide conclude, even if age discrimination is perceived to be 'milder' or less violent than other forms of discrimination, it still warrants legal intervention.[143]

D. Redistribution and Disadvantage

It is difficult to generally classify people as 'advantaged' or 'disadvantaged' on the basis of age.[144] While both older and younger workers face issues in the labour market,[145] and many elderly people (especially women) suffer financial disadvantage,[146] some older households are very wealthy, and pensioners tend to receive a lot of state support in the form of subsidies and pensions.[147] Further, unlike other protected characteristics, age is 'dynamic' and 'transient', as individuals move in and out of advantaged and disadvantaged age groups over time.[148] Age discrimination

[138] <Cliff Oswick and Patrice Rosenthal, 'Towards a Relevant Theory of Age Discrimination in Employment' in Mike Noon and Emmanuel Ogbonna (eds), *Equality, Diversity and Disadvantage in Employment* (Palgrave Macmillan 2001) 168.
[139] ibid.
[140] ibid.
[141] Bamforth, Malik, and O'Cinneide (n 121) 1111.
[142] ibid.
[143] ibid 1112.
[144] McColgan (n 8) 67.
[145] ibid.
[146] ibid.
[147] ibid.
[148] Oswick and Rosenthal (n 138) 165.

may also be perpetuated by older workers against other older workers (and by younger workers against other younger workers), meaning the identity of 'advantaged' discriminators is blurred: 'the purveyors of ageism are also in other circumstances its recipients.'[149] Overall, it is difficult to identify a clear distinction between advantaged and disadvantaged groups on the basis of age.[150] McColgan therefore argues that: 'Neither the young nor the elderly, much less those in other age categories, are oppressed by reason of their age.'[151]

It is important, then, to recognize the diversity of age cohorts, particularly when it comes to disadvantage. As one respondent noted,

> it is socioeconomic because ... the very wealthy, powerful people in our society ... who are ... generally men and I think kind of older at some stage, we see [older people] associated with that. So I think we associate all older people with that ... relatively small group of powerful and wealthy individuals. When in reality, actually, [that] power and financial advantage kind of reflects the socioeconomic make up of our society.[152]

It is a mistake, then, to assume that all older people or all younger people fall within a privileged class. We therefore need to adopt a more nuanced, intersectional view of how disadvantage might be related to age.

Without this nuance, using age discrimination law to redress disadvantage or facilitate redistribution might be seen as exacerbating intergenerational tensions between older and younger workers. 'Intergenerational solidarity' is often seen as requiring older workers to 'make way' for the young, allocating positions 'fairly' between the generations.[153] This is driven by the 'fair innings' argument, which asserts that employment policy should take into account all the benefits older workers have received over their lifetime.[154] The tension, then, is seen as between older workers' rights to not be discriminated against, and younger people's interests in having access to employment opportunities.[155]

In practice, though, the disadvantages faced by older and younger workers may have more in common than these arguments imply. In considering social inclusion on the basis of age, Collins argues that high levels of unemployment among older workers mean that age becomes a 'serious disadvantage' in the labour market from

[149] ibid.
[150] ibid 166.
[151] McColgan (n 8) 67.
[152] UK80.
[153] See Elaine Dewhurst, 'Intergenerational Balance, Mandatory Retirement and Age Discrimination in Europe: How Can the ECJ Better Support National Courts in Finding a Balance between the Generations?' (2013) 50 Common Market Law Review 1333.
[154] Fredman, 'The Age of Equality' (n 33) 47.
[155] Lucy Vickers and Simonetta Manfredi, 'Age Equality and Retirement: Squaring the Circle' (2013) 42 Industrial Law Journal 61, 68.

around the age of 55.[156] Thus, Collins argues that age discrimination law should regulate discrimination in hiring practices that serves to exclude or disadvantage those over the age of 55.[157] Collins also flags that a 'similar finding of disadvantage' might require the protection of workers under the age of 22.[158] Rather than having interests that are in tension, older and younger workers may be subjected to parallel forms of disadvantage in the workplace.

On statistical measures, young workers certainly appear to be disadvantaged in the labour market, being more exposed to unemployment;[159] work precarity[160] and insecurity;[161] low wages;[162] under-employment;[163] under-utilization;[164] unpaid internships;[165] and unpaid work experience[166] than both prime-age and older workers. These measures hold across jurisdictions, indicating that younger workers are especially disadvantaged in the labour market.[167] Equally, older workers experience significant difficulties in recruitment, and are overexposed to some dimensions of precarious work.[168] Addressing disadvantage is therefore a key rationale for legal intervention.

IV. Tensions in Age Discrimination Law

While there may be strong theoretical and practical arguments for ensuring protection from age discrimination at work, the way age discrimination law has been developed and implemented is beset by enduring tensions. These tensions are revealed in the way the law is framed, implemented, and perceived at an individual

156 Collins (n 37) 27.

157 ibid.

158 ibid.

159 Foundation for Young Australians, 'How Young People Are Faring: The National Report on the Learning and Earning of Young Australians' (2012) 11, 44–45.

160 Robert MacDonald, 'Precarious Work: Risk, Choice and Poverty Traps' in Andy Furlong (ed), *Handbook of Youth and Young Adulthood: New Perspectives and Agendas* (Routledge 2009) 168–69.

161 Matthew Pennycook, Giselle Cory, and Vidhya Alakeson, 'A Matter of Time: The Rise of Zero-Hours Contracts' (Resolution Foundation 2013) 10.

162 Eurostat Structure of Earnings Survey 2010; Australian Characteristics of Employment Survey 2016.

163 That is, employed persons who want, and are available for, more hours of work than they currently have: see Australian Bureau of Statistics 6202.0 Labour Force, Australia (2017).

164 That is, the sum of the number of persons unemployed and the number of persons in under-employment, expressed as a proportion of the labour force: Australian Bureau of Statistics 6202.0 Labour Force, Australia (2017).

165 See Kayte Lawton and Dom Potter, 'Why Interns Need a Fair Wage' (2010) <https://www.ippr.org/files/images/media/files/publication/2011/05/Why%20interns%20need%20a%20fair%20wage_1788.pdf> accessed 9 February 2022.

166 Damian Oliver and others, 'Unpaid Work Experience in Australia: Prevalence, Nature and Impact' (2016) 5 <https://docs.employment.gov.au/node/37506> accessed 19 July 2017.

167 Alysia Blackham, 'Young Workers and Age Discrimination: Tensions and Conflicts' (2019) 48 Industrial Law Journal 1.

168 Alysia Blackham, 'Reforming Default Retirement Ages: Regulating Out Precariousness for Older Workers?' (2016) 7 European Labour Law Journal 4.

and societal level; thus, while these tensions are flagged in this part, they shape the chapters that follow, and will be returned to throughout this work.

A. Economic and Human Rights Goals

First, as flagged above, there is an abiding tension in age discrimination law between its economic or instrumental goals (in promoting efficiency, avoiding irrational or inefficient prejudice, integrating workers of all ages into the economy, and avoiding economically harmful age stereotypes)[169] and its human rights or dignity goals (in recognizing the inherent and equal worth and dignity of people of all ages).[170] This tension could be framed as being between the individual right not to be discriminated against and collective labour market needs,[171] or between human rights and economic justifications.[172] For Hendrixx, this represents the 'double bind' of age discrimination law.[173]

While a human rights approach would emphasize the broadest possible protection from age discrimination, an economic focus is more likely to make concessions to the ways in which age facilitates and enables economic and workplace decision-making. This raises a further tension, then, between productivity and efficiency, and securing individual dignity or equal treatment. While age equality law may boost productivity and efficiency, by avoiding irrational stereotyping and employing the most capable workers,[174] fears of age-related performance decline may beset older workers,[175] and younger workers may be perceived as lacking sufficient experience to work productively. These productivity concerns for older workers are a driving force behind mandatory retirement ages;[176] for younger workers, they have led to youth pay rates, benefits tied to length of experience or service, and less favourable treatment in lay-offs and redundancy.[177] While age discrimination law should obviously not force employers to engage unqualified

[169] Manfredi and Vickers (n 106) 344–45.

[170] Sargeant, 'For Diversity, Against Discrimination: The Contradictory Approach to Age Discrimination in Employment' (n 98).

[171] Malcolm Sargeant, 'The Default Retirement Age: Legitimate Aims and Disproportionate Means' (2010) 39 Industrial Law Journal 244, 247.

[172] Malcolm Sargeant, 'Distinguishing between Justifiable Treatment and Prohibited Discrimination in Respect of Age' (2013) 4 Journal of Business Law 398, 399.

[173] Frank Hendrickx, 'Age and European Employment Discrimination Law' in Frank Hendrickx (ed), *Active Ageing and Labour Law: Contributions in Honour of Professor Roger Blanpain* (Intersentia 2012) 5.

[174] See, eg, Fredman, 'The Age of Equality' (n 33) 48.

[175] Sargeant, 'The Default Retirement Age: Legitimate Aims and Disproportionate Means' (n 171) 250.

[176] *Seldon v Clarkson Wright & Jakes (A partnership)* [2012] UKSC 16, [2012] WLR(D) 124, [57]–[58].

[177] Declan O'Dempsey and Anna Beale, 'Age and Employment' (2011) 93 <http://ec.europa.eu/justice/discrimination/files/age_and_employment_en.pdf> accessed 2 April 2015.

staff,[178] these measures tend to conflate age and productive capacity.[179] With a growth in unskilled work, age and length of service are being increasingly disaggregated from productivity.[180]

Similarly, while a human rights justification would seek to reduce or end discrimination, an economic rationale might instead aim to increase participation in the workforce. This reveals a further tension between achieving an age diverse workforce, via the integration of workers of all ages into the economy,[181] and individual dignity. Not all jobs are 'good' or advance individual dignity;[182] as a result, not all social inclusion will advance individual dignity. Reducing workers' terms and conditions, ostensibly to promote employment and economic 'integration', can deeply undermine individual dignity and equal treatment. For older workers, this has occurred through the use of fixed-term contracts;[183] for younger workers, the use of lower youth wages.[184] Both measures seek to reduce the cost or 'risk' of employing non-prime age workers, thereby increasing employer 'demand' for their labour and promoting work integration.[185] While these measures might increase participation, they may not be dignity enhancing.

Overall, then, an economic approach is less likely to disrupt the existing age stratification of society, the economy, and the workplace; or may lead to coercive or paternalistic measures to advance age inclusion. It is unclear how any tension between economic and human rights goals should be resolved, particularly where they become inconsistent or contradictory.[186] While Fredman acknowledges the conflict between the instrumental and intrinsic aims of age discrimination law,[187] she argues that the law is primarily derived from an economic impetus, not some 'sudden appreciation of the need for fairness'.[188] Thus,

[178] Preamble to Council Directive 2000/78/EC of 27 November 2000 establishing a general framework for equal treatment in employment and occupation [2000] OJ L303/16, [17] (hereafter Framework Directive).

[179] *Seldon v Clarkson Wright & Jakes (A partnership)* (n 176) [57].

[180] Rosemary Lucas and Shobana Nair Keegan, 'Young Workers and the National Minimum Wage' (2007) 26 Equal Opportunities International 573.

[181] Regulatory Impact Assessment for the Employment Equality (Age) Regulations 2006, SI 2006/1031, [3].

[182] Sharon C Bolton, 'Dignity in and at Work: Why It Matters' in Sharon C Bolton (ed), *Dimensions of Dignity at Work* (Elsevier 2007) 8.

[183] *Mangold v Helm* [2006] 1 CMLR 43.

[184] David Plowman, 'Wage Differentials and Youth Unemployment' (1994) 5 Economic and Labour Relations Review 21; John Mangan and John Johnston, 'Minimum Wages, Training Wages and Youth Employment' (1999) 26 International Journal of Social Economics 415. See further National Minimum Wage Act 1998 (UK); National Minimum Wage Regulations 1999 (UK) SI 1999/584.

[185] This has not been effective in practice, especially for youth wages: Shobana Nair Sehkaran and Rosemary Lucas, *The National Minimum Wage and Young Workers: A Comparison between Urban and Rural Areas* (Centre for Hospitality Employment Research 2001); Grant Belchamber, 'Minimum Award Wages for Young Workers Must Be Reformed' (1999) 32 Australian Economic Review 390.

[186] Manfredi and Vickers (n 105) 310.

[187] Fredman, *Discrimination Law* (n 6) 106.

[188] ibid 103–04.

it is more likely that economic objectives will be prioritized in the event of conflict.[189]

In practice, too, this conflict has seemingly been resolved in favour of economic rationales[190] through the introduction of wide justifications and exceptions to age discrimination laws.[191] The legal framework seeks to simultaneously address age discrimination in employment, and to give governments and employers ways to sidestep age discrimination legislation; for Meenan, this is 'something of a paradox lying at the heart' of age discrimination law.[192] Thus, Dickens argues that fairness and human rights arguments are only pursued to the extent they are commensurate with efficiency or economic ends,[193] including through the broad use of exceptions in equality statutes.[194]

B. Tensions between the Individual and Collective

Second, there are numerous tensions between the individual and the collective within age discrimination law. For Meenan, this is a tension between age *groups* and *individuals*;[195] but there are also tensions between individual interests—such as remaining in work—and collective interests, as manifested in intergenerational solidarity and pension systems.[196] A further associated tension exists between collectively negotiated outcomes—which reflect the interests and preferences of the *average* bargaining unit member—and actual individual interests.[197] For Meenan, age discrimination 'can only be fully understood if it is looked at through the eyes of the individual'[198] due to the variability of ageing.[199] Conversely, for Numhauser-Henning, 'the overall concern should be intergenerational solidarity and sustainable societies' rather than individual interests.[200] Thus, the way we resolve or regard

[189] D Schiek, 'Age Discrimination before the ECJ: Conceptual and Theoretical Issues' (2011) 48 Common Market Law Review 777, 778–79.

[190] Matthew Flynn, 'The United Kingdom Government's "Business Case" Approach to the Regulation of Retirement' (2010) 30 Ageing & Society 421, 423.

[191] Malcolm Sargeant, 'Age Discrimination' in Malcolm Sargeant (ed), *The Law on Age Discrimination in the EU* (Kluwer Law International 2008) 3, 5.

[192] Helen Meenan, 'Age Equality after the Employment Directive' (2003) 10 Maastricht Journal of European and Comparative Law 9, 10.

[193] Linda Dickens, 'The Road is Long: Thirty Years of Equality Legislation in Britain' (2007) 45 British Journal of Industrial Relations 463, 468–71.

[194] ibid 470–71.

[195] Meenan, 'Age Equality after the Employment Directive' (n 192) 17.

[196] Ann Numhauser-Henning, 'The EU Ban on Age-Discrimination and Older Workers: Potentials and Pitfalls' (2013) 29 International Journal of Comparative Labour Law and Industrial Relations 391, 413.

[197] Kenneth WM Thornicroft, 'The Uncertain State of Mandatory Retirement in Canada' (2016) 67 Labor Law Journal 397, 405.

[198] Meenan, 'Age Equality after the Employment Directive' (n 192) 17.

[199] See further Helen Meenan, 'Age: The Individual and the Law: Part 1' (2002) 10 Irish Law Times 154, 154.

[200] Numhauser-Henning, 'The EU Ban on Age-Discrimination and Older Workers' (n 196) 402.

tensions between the individual and the collective is likely to be contextually and nationally driven.[201]

For Numhauser-Henning, tensions between individual and societal interests are navigated—in the EU and UK—by the ability to justify direct age discrimination:

> Whereas the ban on direct age discrimination fulfils the 'classical' purpose of being a basis for individual claims of non-discrimination—to uphold individual dignity—the opening for justification makes room for collective interests at a more societal level, in terms of age as a traditional stratifier but also (competing) active ageing strategies of a more instrumental nature.[202]

Thus, for Numhauser-Henning, age discriminatory measures like mandatory retirement can promote societal interests, such as upholding the standard employment contract, promoting employment protection, and resisting flexibilization.[203] Similarly, in Canada, mandatory retirement was part of the social contract,[204] derived largely from collective bargaining—not statute—until its legislative abolition;[205] this was upheld by the Supreme Court of Canada as constitutional, in part given the importance of collective bargaining.[206]

While prompted by legitimate societal interests, national or collectively negotiated solutions tend to focus on the 'normal' or normative worker. As Fudge and Zbyszewska argue, the model underlying many of these collective arrangements is no longer consistent with economic and social reality, as fewer people follow a fixed life course or fit the norm of the full-time employed worker.[207] Indeed, specific groups of workers—such as women, those with caring responsibilities, those with disabilities, and migrant workers—have never been the 'norm'.[208] Collective or intergenerational compromises tend to exclude and disadvantage those who do not fit the normative model of work.[209] 'Standard'

[201] Ann Numhauser-Henning, 'The Elder Law Individual versus Societal Dichotomy: A European Perspective' in Ann Numhauser-Henning (ed), *Elder Law: Evolving European Perspectives* (Edward Elgar Publishing 2017).

[202] Ann Numhauser-Henning, 'Ageism, Age Discrimination and Employment Law in the EU' in Israel Doron and Nena Georgantzi (eds), *Ageing, Ageism and the Law: European Perspectives on the Rights of Older Persons* (Edward Elgar 2018) 105.

[203] ibid 107. Somek argues that discrimination law and flexibilization go hand-in-hand: Alexander Somek, *Engineering Equality* (OUP 2011) 2–3.

[204] Thornicroft (n 197) 397.

[205] Robert E Charney and Matthew Horner, 'Defending Age Distinctions in Employee Benefits after the Elimination of Mandatory Retirement' (2013) 17 Canadian Labour and Employment Law Journal 255, 258.

[206] *McKinney v University of Guelph* [1990] 3 SCR 229; 76 DLR (4th) 545. See ibid 258–62.

[207] Judy Fudge and Ania Zbyszewska, 'An Intersectional Approach to Age Discrimination in the European Union: Bridging Dignity and Distribution?' in Ann Numhauser-Henning and Mia Rönnmar (eds), *Age Discrimination and Labour Law: Comparative and Conceptual Perspectives in the EU and Beyond* (Kluwer Law International 2015) 146.

[208] ibid.

[209] ibid.

employment relationships—and rules designed to protect them—do not assist all workers;[210] rather,

> many ageing workers have not historically followed the normative employment pattern inherent in the standard employment contract and life course on which the prevalent notion of inter-generational solidarity is based; therefore, policy rules that seek to uphold that solidarity tend to disadvantage these workers in ways that are not only unfair but also inherently systematic.[211]

Views of the 'collective' therefore need to be scrutinized to identify those better equated with the status quo. Indeed, many age-related policies, which are predicated on the standard employment relationship, may serve to increase disadvantage related to other protected characteristics.[212]

A capabilities approach to age discrimination law offers one way in which we might navigate these tensions between individual and collective interests. Capabilities are for *each person*; while individual and social goals may be pursued, they cannot undermine an adequate threshold of capabilities of each individual, and benefits in some areas cannot be offset against detriments in others.[213] That said, socially oriented policies (such as mandatory retirement) might still be acceptable if they are supported by evidence and provide for alternative ways of securing relevant functionings (such as access to social spheres).[214]

C. Intergenerational Tensions

Third, as foreshadowed above, there is a potential tension between the interests of older workers and the interests of younger workers. Despite both older and younger workers experiencing age discrimination and age-based disadvantage,[215] age discrimination law may have come to embody a conflict between generations. In the EU and UK, arguments relating to 'intergenerational fairness' can be used to justify direct age discrimination.[216] This risks pitching different generations as being in conflict or competition for jobs and employment opportunities.[217]

210 ibid 151.
211 Numhauser-Henning, 'Ageism' (n 202) 111.
212 Fudge and Zbyszewska (n 207) 151.
213 Alon-Shenker, 'Capabilities and Age Discrimination' (n 5) 285.
214 ibid.
215 Hilary Metcalf and Pamela Meadows, 'Second Survey of Employers' Policies, Practices and Preferences Relating to Age, 2010' (2010) DWP Research Report 682, 33–34 <http://research.dwp.gov.uk/asd/asd5/rports2009-2010/rrep682.pdf> accessed 16 November 2011.
216 Dewhurst (n 153).
217 Vickers and Manfredi (n 155) 67–69.

For example, where positions are finite, discrimination against older workers (such as through mandatory retirement ages) is seen as facilitating young people's participation in the workforce, by 'freeing up' positions occupied by older workers for the next generation. This has been described (in rather unsavoury terms) as 'bed blocking' or making way for 'young blood'.[218] Mandatory retirement may not achieve intergenerational balance at a macro level:[219] intergenerational arguments only hold in very specific firms, with limited entry pathways and finite positions.[220] At a macro-economic level, jobs create more jobs.

As barrister Dee Masters therefore noted in her evidence to the House of Commons Women and Equalities Committee inquiry on Older People and Employment, intergenerational fairness can be a difficult thing to navigate in the context of age discrimination law:

> the notion of intergenerational fairness is a very broad umbrella and encapsulates all sorts of different tensions between different age groups. Some of those tensions are legitimate, and so it is justified to treat people differently, and others are derived from stereotypical views, which we need to be cautious about.[221]

Focusing on 'generations' and 'intergenerational fairness' tends to obscure the diversity *within* age cohorts. While 'a constant narrative in the media',[222] intergenerational tensions have limited basis in reality, being grounded in generalizations.[223] In these narratives, older people tend to be associated with those who are wealthy and powerful, who are generally men.[224] This does not provide an accurate picture of the diversity of older people.[225] Those who are the most privileged also have 'voice',[226] meaning they are likely to be the most visible in public life. Those who are less privileged 'are just trying to get on with their day-to-day lives.'[227]

Despite their limited empirical basis, assumptions about the tensions between different generations strongly influence how older people are perceived and treated,[228] and can be used to minimize the concerns of older people, and

[218] Performance and Innovation Unit, 'Winning the Generation Game: Improving Opportunities for People Aged 50–65 in Work and Community Activity' (2000) 3, 6.

[219] Dewhurst (n 153) 1350–59.

[220] PB Doeringer and MJ Piore, *Internal Labor Markets and Manpower Analysis* (Heath Lexington Books 1971) xi, 2, 3, 43.

[221] House of Commons, 'Oral Evidence: Older People and Employment' (2018) HC 359 Q67 <http://data.parliament.uk/writtenevidence/committeeevidence.svc/evidencedocument/women-and-equalities-committee/older-people-and-employment/oral/76656.html> accessed 9 February 2022.

[222] UK84. See also A112.

[223] UK167.

[224] UK80; UK84.

[225] UK80.

[226] UK81.

[227] ibid.

[228] UK80; UK84.

reduce public provision for the most vulnerable.[229] A nuanced understanding of age discrimination and age discrimination law must therefore acknowledge that age cohorts have more differences than similarities, and seek to move beyond age stereotypes. Further, it is important to recognize the similarities and common experiences across generations: the challenges faced by older and younger workers can be similar, meaning non-prime age workers have more similarities than differences in the treatment they experience.[230]

At a theoretical level, intergenerational equity and solidarity can be thought about in a number of different ways; 'intergenerational solidarity' itself is an evolving and contested idea. While ideas of solidarity prevalent since the 1970s required older workers to retire,[231] evolving views of solidarity require older workers to continue to contribute to society, including through work.[232] There is a need, then, to continue to review and reconceive our view of the 'intergenerational contract' to accommodate changing social mores.[233]

At its core, though, intergenerational solidarity embodies a form of social cohesion,[234] bonding,[235] or contract[236] between and across generations. It recognizes a social responsibility[237] or collective obligation[238] to other age groups, grounded in reciprocity[239] and intergenerational transfers.[240] Even in these conceptions, though, the interests of different age groups are not necessarily seen as being mutually *enhancing*, but something to be negotiated and balanced. Thus, the idea of 'intergenerational solidarity' itself continues to embody an ambivalence towards age and ageing.[241]

229 Select Committee on Intergenerational Fairness and Provision, 'Tackling Intergenerational Unfairness' (UK Parliament 2019) Report of Session 2017–19 HL Paper 329.

230 A154; Blackham, 'Young Workers' (n 167).

231 Anne-Marie Guillemard and Martin Rein, 'Comparative Patterns of Retirement: Recent Trends in Developed Societies' (1993) 19 Annual Review of Sociology 469, 474.

232 HM Government, 'Opportunity Age: Meeting the Challenges of Ageing in the 21st Century' (2005) 2.

233 Donna M Butts, 'Key Issues Uniting Generations' in María Amparo Cruz-Saco and Sergei Zelenev (eds), *Intergenerational Solidarity: Strengthening Economic and Social Ties* (Palgrave Macmillan 2010) 94.

234 Vern L Bengtson and Petrice S Oyama, 'Intergenerational Solidarity and Conflict' in María Amparo Cruz-Saco and Sergei Zelenev (eds), *Intergenerational Solidarity: Strengthening Economic and Social Ties* (Palgrave Macmillan 2010) 35.

235 María Amparo Cruz-Saco, 'Intergenerational Solidarity' in María Amparo Cruz-Saco and Sergei Zelenev (eds), *Intergenerational Solidarity: Strengthening Economic and Social Ties* (Palgrave Macmillan 2010) 9.

236 Bengtson and Oyama (n 234) 38.

237 Eurofound, 'Foundation Findings: Intergenerational Solidarity' (2012) 3.

238 Alain Supiot, *Homo Juridicus: On the Anthropological Function of the Law* (Verso 2007) 208.

239 Misa Izuhara, 'Introduction' in Misa Izuhara (ed), *Ageing and Intergenerational Relations: Family Reciprocity from a Global Perspective* (Policy Press 2010) 5.

240 Bengtson and Oyama (n 234) 36; Ariela Lowenstein, 'Determinants of the Complex Interchange among Generations: Collaboration and Conflict' in María Amparo Cruz-Saco and Sergei Zelenev (eds), *Intergenerational Solidarity: Strengthening Economic and Social Ties* (Palgrave Macmillan 2010) 58.

241 See Blackham, 'Addressing the Ageing Workforce' (n 119) 1378–79.

This is captured by Alon-Shenker and Lurie's threefold typology for how intergenerational tensions might be approached in the workplace:

(1) a conflict approach, where the interests of older and younger workers are seen as inherently conflictual and zero-sum game;
(2) an 'important but separate' approach, where interests neither conflict nor align; and
(3) a solidarity approach, which values interaction, solidarity, and enrichment across generations, and sees the interests of different age groups as being mutually enhancing.[242]

While age discrimination law often adopts a 'conflict approach', a 'solidarity approach' may be less influenced by age stereotypes. A solidarity approach better reflects both macro-economic conditions and the lived experiences of different age groups. Often, though, a mix of different approaches will be adopted, reflecting an 'intergenerational ambivalence'.[243] If not appropriately acknowledged, intergenerational ambivalence in law can lead to legal vagueness and contradictory legal norms.[244]

To address this ambivalence, it helps to take a broader view: instead of focusing on the tensions between older and younger generations (ie synchronic relations), we can think about the relationship between current generations and the generations of the future[245] (ie diachronic relations).[246] In this view, current generations have a point of similarity, as they are all in existence *now*, and can all make a difference now.[247] Focusing on these points of commonality, rather than difference, can bridge perceived tensions between generations.

Further, conflict approaches tend to assume that resources are so finite that the needs of all generations cannot be met simultaneously. As government policy responses to Covid-19 have shown, resources are not as finite as governments might represent:

> I think we all can be winners. It's just that where society slices the cake or cuts the pie. There's enough to go around.... how we order our society is a choice. There is

[242] Pnina Alon-Shenker and Lilach Lurie, 'Do Trade Unions Promote Age Diversity and Intergenerational Solidarity in the Workplace? A View from Canada and Israel' (2019) 70 Labor Law Journal 103, 106.

[243] ibid.

[244] Jenny Julén Votinius and Mia Rönnmar, 'Intergenerational Aspects of Elder Law: Conflict, Solidarity: Or Ambivalence' in Ann Numhauser-Henning (ed), *Elder Law: Evolving European Perspectives* (Edward Elgar Publishing 2017) 137, 144–48.

[245] UK85.

[246] Votinius and Rönnmar (n 244) 148.

[247] UK85.

> enough resource to go around. But I think for some people … it's to their benefit to play off different generations. It's not helpful. But it's a tricky one to challenge.[248]

The question, then, is how we can best challenge this narrative of intergenerational conflict. Overcoming ageism and intergenerational tensions is largely about 'recognising the rights and legitimacy of older people as human beings, as individuals'.[249] This could be supported by the development of international rights of older persons.[250] It is important, too, to see cohorts as groups of diverse individuals, and respond to their particular needs.[251]

D. Public and Private Spheres

Fourth, there is a tension between the public and the private spheres in age equality law.[252] Consistent with liberal democratic theory, 'inequities in the private sector are treated as though they were naturally beyond the purview of the state'.[253] While the public sphere is 'one of order', the private sphere allows for the 'untrammelled pursuit of personal desires'.[254] As a result of this limited focus, the private sector has tended to lag in its pursuit of equality.[255] This is especially problematic given the private sector's importance as an employer and its growing role in the delivery of essential services.[256]

In a practical sense, this public/private divide manifests in the exclusion of the domestic sphere from the scope of age equality legislation in a number of Australian jurisdictions.[257] In the UK, positive duties are limited to public entities and those performing public functions (Chapter 7). The direct application of positive duties to private entities and employers is far more contentious, though indirect effects may be achieved through procurement.

[248] UK86.

[249] UK80.

[250] See, eg, Israel Doron and Itai Apter, 'The Debate Around the Need for an International Convention on the Rights of Older Persons' (2010) 50 Gerontologist 586.

[251] UK88.

[252] Margaret Thornton, *The Liberal Promise: Anti-Discrimination Legislation in Australia* (OUP 1990) 103.

[253] ibid 102.

[254] ibid 103.

[255] Dickens, 'The Road is Long' (n 193) 474.

[256] ibid.

[257] Alysia Blackham, 'A Compromised Balance? A Comparative Examination of Exceptions to Age Discrimination Law in Australia and the UK' (2018) 41 Melbourne University Law Review 1085, 1094–96.

The public/private divide also manifests in the use of private, confidential conciliation to resolve the vast majority of claims (Chapter 5):[258] discrimination is seen as a private wrong, best settled behind closed doors.[259] As Thornton argues,

> While anti-discrimination legislation purports to express public disapprobation of discriminatory acts committed in the public arena, it is nevertheless nervous about public scrutiny of those acts, the wrongfulness of which is contentious. Therefore, violations are treated not as public transgressions in the way that crimes are treated, but as private pecadilloes [sic] … [to] be dealt with primarily in a confidential and non-threatening privatised environment.[260]

There is a related tension, then, between privacy and transparency in the field of age equality. As in equality law generally, many age discrimination complaints are resolved in private, and subject to confidential conciliation and non-disclosure agreements (NDAs).[261] This has led to equality law being shrouded in secrecy, both in relation to its processes and outcomes.[262] Indeed, many statutory equality agencies are subject to onerous secrecy obligations, which limit their ability to make information about age discrimination claims public.[263] This can be a substantial barrier to transparency and public understanding of age discrimination law.

There is also limited data collected about older people, including their experiences of age discrimination:[264] 'there is ageism within data collection'.[265] While this may, in part, reflect our devaluing of age equality, it may also be easier to avoid measuring a problematic area: 'there's just a reluctance. There's so many problems out there that the best way to ward off criticism is by not measuring it.'[266] This lack of data raises difficult questions about how we can effectively evaluate and measure age discrimination, especially where government data collection is not thorough or consistent:[267] 'we don't have enough data to really show what's happening.'[268] This also makes it nearly impossible for equality agencies and governments to target their activities: 'unless you can see where a problem is, it's difficult to take

[258] Alysia Blackham and Dominique Allen, 'Resolving Discrimination Claims Outside the Courts: Alternative Dispute Resolution in Australia and the United Kingdom' (2019) 31 Australian Journal of Labour Law 253.

[259] Dominique Allen and Alysia Blackham, 'Under Wraps: Secrecy, Confidentiality and the Enforcement of Equality Law in Australia and the UK' (2019) 43 Melbourne University Law Review 384, 395.

[260] Thornton, *The Liberal Promise* (n 252) 144.

[261] See, eg, Women and Equalities Committee, *The Use of Non-Disclosure Agreements in Discrimination Cases* (2017–19 HC 1720).

[262] Allen and Blackham (n 259).

[263] ibid.

[264] UK152.

[265] UK80.

[266] ibid.

[267] ibid; UK81.

[268] UK80.

that enforcement action.'[269] The need for greater public transparency and data collection is a recurring theme in the chapters that follow.

E. Views of Equality

Fifth, there is a potential tension between a view of equality as 'sameness' or equal treatment; and a view of equality as recognizing difference. This is reflected in organizations' hesitancy to adopt positive action measures that seek to promote and accommodate the different needs of different people, and in legislative provisions that firmly restrict the ability to take such positive action measures.[270] Further, legislation tends to adopt a symmetrical approach to addressing inequality, where both historically advantaged and disadvantaged groups are protected equally (the exception, of course, being in relation to disability discrimination law, which is asymmetric).[271] In reality, however, any potential tension between these views of equality can be surmounted by adopting a more nuanced view of what equality entails, as discussed in Part II above.

F. Agency and Protection

Sixth, there is a potential tension between what might paternalistically be seen as in people's 'best interests' and what they might actually choose—that is, what is consistent with individual agency and choice.[272] This plays out in statutes that introduce protective measures for older and younger workers, including those relating to workplace health and safety, working time, and involvement in particular industries or 'risky' work.[273] It is also evident in laws and regulations relating to mandatory retirement: in the UK, for example, I have traced how changes to mandatory retirement were driven by a desire to enhance individual 'choice'. This choice, though, was firmly bounded by government policy, so that many individuals were left with little real agency as to when and how they retired.[274]

These tensions between protection and agency are largely determined at the policy level, rather than at the point of an individual complaint of age

[269] UK81.

[270] Dickens, 'The Road is Long' (n 193) 473–74.

[271] ibid.

[272] In relation to children, see Jonathan Herring, 'Children's Rights for Grown-Ups' in Sandra Fredman and Sarah Spencer (eds), *Age as an Equality Issue: Legal and Policy Perspectives* (Hart Publishing 2003) 153–54.

[273] See, eg, Council Directive 94/33/EC of 22 June 1994 on the Protection of Young People at Work [1994] OJ L216/12; Working Time (Amendment) Regulations 2002, SI 2002/3128; Management of Health and Safety at Work Regulations 1999, SI 1999/3242, reg 19; Education and Skills Act 2008, ss 1–2.

[274] Blackham, 'Addressing the Ageing Workforce' (n 119) 1383.

discrimination.[275] These policy decisions have often operated to expand exceptions to age discrimination law, and are not always driven by evidence.[276] This may substantially limit the scope for discrimination law to offer individuals protection.[277]

V. The Challenge of Intersectionality

Discrimination on the grounds of age is often linked to other types of discrimination:[278] there is intersectionality between age and other grounds such as gender[279] (including pregnancy or potential pregnancy,[280] and menopause[281]), ethnicity[282] (including English proficiency[283]) and indigeneity,[284] mental health[285] and disability,[286] sexuality[287] and caring responsibilities.[288] 'Discrimination blends together' as age interacts with other protected grounds.[289] This is particularly acute for Australian Aboriginal and Torres Strait Islanders, where 'appalling' morbidity rates mean 'older age' is categorically different than for other groups.[290]

In Australia, women, those with a disability and the Australian-born are more likely to report age discrimination.[291] For older women, both age and gender influence their experiences: 'Neither age nor gender can be removed from the analysis without losing an essential aspect of the discriminatory practice.'[292] McGann and others argue that the ageism experienced by older women job-seekers is qualitatively different to that encountered by older men, with women encountering issues of 'lookism' which do not affect male job-seekers.[293] Women who experience age

[275] A8.
[276] ibid.
[277] Alysia Blackham, 'A Compromised Balance?' (n 257).
[278] Sargeant, 'Ageism and Age Discrimination' (n 122) 13.
[279] A99; A100; A102; A103; A104; A107; A112; A115; A150; A154; A155; A156; A163; A164; A169; UK80; UK165; UK84; UK90; UK152.
[280] A102; A108; A157.
[281] UK90; UK152.
[282] A99; A100; A102; A153; A154; A156; A164; UK80.
[283] A100.
[284] A113; A99.
[285] A156; UK152.
[286] A1; A9; A99; A100; A101; A104; A108; A109; A112; A113; A151; A153; A155; A164; UK94.
[287] A99.
[288] A163; UK84; UK88; UK90; UK152; Sian Moore, '"No Matter What I Did I Would Still End up in the Same Position" Age as a Factor Defining Older Women's Experience of Labour Market Participation' (2009) 23 Work, Employment & Society 655.
[289] A164.
[290] A99; Zoë Hyde and others, 'Prevalence and Incidence of Frailty in Aboriginal Australians, and Associations with Mortality and Disability' (2016) 87 Maturitas 89.
[291] Alysia Blackham and Jeromey Temple, 'Intersectional Discrimination in Australia: An Empirical Critique of the Legal Framework' (2020) 43 UNSW Law Journal 773.
[292] Roseberry (n 19) 37.
[293] Michael McGann and others, 'Gendered Ageism in Australia: Changing Perceptions of Age Discrimination among Older Men and Women' (2016) 35 Economic Papers: A Journal of Applied Economics and Policy 375, 386.

discrimination tend to see it as 'bound up' with discrimination on other grounds—especially gender and race—making it hard to identify instances of age discrimination specifically.[294]

The nature of age discrimination can change as it interacts with other grounds,[295] and age (and older age specifically) can intensify the impacts of work segregation (including by occupation and sector) and non-linear work careers.[296] 'Age touches everything',[297] and 'turns the temperature up' for other forms of vulnerability.[298] Age exacerbates other forms of disadvantage (eg on the grounds of gender or ethnicity),[299] and can make people vulnerable to particular types of wrong.[300] As the House of Commons Women and Equalities Committee (WEC) concluded, age is an 'amplifier' of other forms of inequality.[301]

Age discrimination therefore cannot be seen or interpreted in a vacuum: disadvantage is complex, overlapping and intertwined across multiple grounds, including age. In developing a justification for the prohibition of age discrimination, it is therefore necessary to embrace and accommodate the diversity of different age cohorts,[302] and to move beyond a focus on one protected characteristic; disadvantage and discrimination form a complex web.[303]

Intersectionality challenges equality law to 'embrace the complexities of compoundedness'[304] and understand people's identities in a holistic way.[305] Existing models of discrimination law encourage thinking 'along a single categorical axis',[306] focusing inquiry on privileged members of a group, and ignoring other forms of disadvantage.[307] *Intersectional* discrimination recognizes that disadvantage is compounded across different grounds: the sum of disadvantage is greater than its individual parts.[308] This intersection creates disadvantage which is unique and distinct to that from any one ground alone.[309] Meaningfully addressing

[294] Moore (n 288) 660.
[295] Australian Human Rights Commission (AHRC), 'Willing to Work: National Inquiry into Employment Discrimination Against Older Australians and Australians with Disability' (2016) 71–74.
[296] Moore (n 288) 659.
[297] UK90.
[298] A99.
[299] McColgan (n 8) 68.
[300] ibid 69.
[301] Women and Equalities Committee, *Older People and Employment* (2017–19, HC 359) 14.
[302] UK92; Sargeant, 'Ageism and Age Discrimination' (n 122) 7.
[303] A5.
[304] Kimberle Crenshaw, 'Demarginalizing the Intersection of Race and Sex: A Black Feminist Critique of Antidiscrimination Doctrine, Feminist Theory and Antiracist Politics' [1989] University of Chicago Legal Forum 139, 166.
[305] Shreya Atrey, *Intersectional Discrimination* (1st edn, OUP 2019) 2.
[306] Crenshaw (n 304) 140.
[307] ibid.
[308] Beth Gaze and Belinda Smith, *Equality and Discrimination Law in Australia: An Introduction* (CUP 2017) 84; Sarah Hannett, 'Equality at the Intersections: The Legislative and Judicial Failure to Tackle Multiple Discrimination' (2003) 23 Oxford Journal of Legal Studies 65, 68.
[309] Mary Eaton, 'Patently Confused: Complex Inequality and Canada v. Mossop' (1993–94) 1 Review of Constitutional Studies 203, 229. cf the idea of 'multiple' discrimination, where disadvantage is

intersectionality requires a fundamental rethink of existing structures[310] and discrimination law.[311]

Recognizing the importance of intersectionality, Schiek has argued for the consolidation of equality law around the nodes of gender/sex, ethnicity/'race' and disability/impairment.[312] For Schiek, this 'recategorization' 'counteracts the arbitrariness of limitless proliferation of discrimination grounds'.[313] However, Schiek's recategorization fails to recognize the complexity of age discrimination: for Schiek, age discrimination is contained within 'discrimination on grounds of being too slow in moving' as part of the disability node[314] or, perhaps, just contained within the disability node.[315] This ignores the prevalence of youth age discrimination, and the multiple ways in which age discrimination may manifest, many of which are unrelated to disability (Chapter 1). This consolidated approach is unable to accommodate the diversity of older and younger workers' experiences.

Sen adopts a different response to the challenge of applying equality law to a diverse population.[316] For Sen, the fundamental question of equality law is which *aspect* should be chosen in assessing equality: equality of *what*?[317] There are multiple spaces of equality,[318] and multiple variables by which equality can be judged.[319] This is a question for all of equality law: age is not unique in this sense, and each person can be categorized in multiple ways based on multiple protected characteristics. This is one of the dilemmas of discrimination law framed on the basis of grounds or protected characteristics:[320] on the basis of some grounds, people will be advantaged by discrimination; on the basis of others, they will be disadvantaged.[321] People may simultaneously suffer and profit from discrimination.[322] So, for example, an older white man may be advantaged on the basis of his gender and race, but disadvantaged on the basis of his age. In practice, too, it may be that older, white men are the primary beneficiaries of statutory protection against age discrimination and the most likely to enforce their claims in court;[323]

additive: Gaze and Smith (n 308) 84; Hannett (n 308) 68. Atrey describes these ideas as lying on a continuum, with single-axis discrimination at one end, and intersectionality at the other: Atrey (n 305) 78.

310 Crenshaw (n 304) 140.
311 Atrey (n 305) 2–3.
312 Schiek, 'Revisiting Intersectionality' (n 34) 23.
313 ibid 32.
314 ibid.
315 Schiek, 'Intersectionality and the Notion of Disability' (n 25) 52.
316 Sen (n 26) 1.
317 ibid 14.
318 ibid.
319 ibid 1.
320 Schiek, 'Intersectionality and the Notion of Disability' (n 25) 49.
321 ibid.
322 ibid 50.
323 Alysia Blackham, 'Why Do Employment Age Discrimination Cases Fail? An Analysis of Australian Case Law' (2020) 42 Sydney Law Review 1.

this may arguably serve to cut across or undermine other areas of discrimination law.[324]

That said, there is nothing *intrinsic* in age discrimination law that cuts across other areas:[325] trends in enforcement can be divorced from the underlying logic or rationale of age discrimination law. Thus, as is the case for other grounds, recognition of intersectionality and group diversity does not necessarily mean that age discrimination should be omitted from statutory regulation: age adds an extra dimension to the discrimination that people already suffer,[326] and age cannot be divorced from intersectional experiences. Thus, it is arguable that age discrimination needs specific legal protection,[327] and cannot be subsumed within protection on the basis of other grounds.

Fineman has critiqued ideas of intersectionality on the basis that multiple identities (or grounds) do not 'intersect to produce compounded inequalities'.[328] Instead, Fineman suggests that 'systems of power and privilege ... interact to produce webs of advantages and disadvantages',[329] emphasizing the importance of institutional structures in creating and compounding inequalities. Indeed, disadvantage can be related to systems of power and privilege traditionally beyond the scope of equality law, such as visa status,[330] dependency on a particular employer,[331] limited knowledge of employment rights,[332] socio-economic status,[333] undertaking manual or physically demanding work,[334] broken work histories,[335] and work quality.[336] Discrimination tends to affect the most vulnerable,[337] and vulnerability can arise in a range of ways, including due to social isolation[338] and power disparities.[339]

Similarly, Solanke has critiqued intersectionality for its reliance on 'grounds', which are grounded in the 'logic of immutability':[340] that is, that grounds are

[324] Bamforth, Malik, and O'Cinneide (n 121) 1111.
[325] ibid 1112.
[326] Sargeant, 'Ageism and Age Discrimination' (n 122) 7.
[327] McColgan (n 8) 69.
[328] Fineman (n 84) 16.
[329] ibid.
[330] A107; A108; A115; A157.
[331] A107.
[332] A108; A110; A157.
[333] A103; A104; A108; A159; UK80; UK86; UK92.
[334] A100; A108; A115; UK86.
[335] A104; UK152.
[336] A99; UK86.
[337] UK90.
[338] A99.
[339] A102; A107; A109.
[340] Iyiola Solanke, 'Stigma: A Limiting Principle Allowing Multiple-Consciousness in Anti-Discrimination Law?' in Dagmar Schiek and Victoria Chege (eds), *European Union Non-Discrimination Law: Comparative Perspectives on Multidimensional Equality Law* (Routledge-Cavendish 2009) 115. This is echoed in Khaitan's argument that groups or grounds must be grounded in some immutable or fundamental choice, which is normatively irrelevant to the groups' treatment: Khaitan (n 9) 56. cf Moreau, who does not see grounds as needing to be immutable or fundamental: Moreau, 'What is Discrimination?' (n 23) 156.

permanent and involuntary,[341] and cannot recognize the complexity of modern discrimination.[342] Instead, Solanke argues for the use of 'stigma' as a limiting principle for discrimination law, which draws on a 'spectrum of characteristics'.[343] This recognizes that various forms of stigma can interact, without drawing firm boundaries between different groups or grounds.[344]

Age is a key site of both stigma and power disparities. While recognizing the importance of intersectionality and the complexity of disadvantage, this is not a basis for ignoring inequality on the basis of age: age remains an essential lens for interrogating discrimination and inequality, and cannot be abandoned or excluded from the legal framework. Instead, intersectionality can be used as a lens to reveal disparities of power and distribution, and to 'bridge' the competing interests and tensions in age discrimination law.[345] Recognizing these nuances should not be complicated: 'it's just the world. It's just who we are.'[346]

VI. Conclusion

This chapter has illustrated the difficulty of developing any clear or unified rationale for discrimination and equality law: while six overlapping themes emerge from the theoretical literature, there is no clear consensus as to how discrimination law might best be justified. Instead, discrimination and equality law are better seen through a pluralist frame, pursuing multiple yet often complementary objectives. Similarly, age discrimination law could be justified on the basis of a number of rationales. Ultimately, the decision as to which justification(s) to adopt reflects a normative stance on the purposes of discrimination law, and the limits of government action. Further, retaining age as a protected characteristic reflects a normative stance as to the importance (or, more accurately, irrelevance) of age in individual and organizational decision-making.

Going beyond the standard dual justifications of age discrimination law of intrinsic and instrumental aims, this chapter has mapped the relevance of upholding dignity and addressing stereotypes, and redistribution to address disadvantage on the basis of age, as justifications for age discrimination law. Further, it has mounted a case for retaining statutory age discrimination law, even while recognizing the challenges of intersectionality and diversity within age groups. Thus, it provides

[341] Solanke (n 340) 117.
[342] ibid 130.
[343] ibid 115.
[344] ibid 121.
[345] Fudge and Zbyszewska (n 207) 149.
[346] A102.

a strong basis for maintaining age as a protected characteristic, while recognizing the enduring tensions embedded within age discrimination law. In the chapters that follow, I turn my gaze to the way in which age discrimination has been regulated in different national settings, to consider the extent to which law and legal regulation are addressing age discrimination at work.

3
Models for Enforcing Age Discrimination Law

I. Introduction

Chapters 1 and 2 have illustrated the ways in which age discrimination endures at work, and offered a theoretical account and justification for the prohibition of age discrimination. In this chapter, then, I consider how this prohibition of age discrimination has been effected in practice across different national jurisdictions, drawing on doctrinal analysis of the law in the United Kingdom (UK), Canada, and Australia.

In these jurisdictions, national models of age discrimination law primarily rely on individual enforcement models for the prevention and redress of age discrimination at work; individual enforcement is the primary mechanism by which rights to be protected from discrimination are enforced. As a result, the weight of enforcement has fallen on individuals.[1]

In this chapter, I provide a theoretical framing and critique of the individual enforcement model adopted by domestic models of age discrimination law. Drawing on legal and interdisciplinary literature, and the empirical results of this study, I illustrate the ways in which reliance on individual enforcement is fundamentally flawed for addressing age discrimination at work. I flag three alternatives to relying on individual enforcement, including agency enforcement, positive duties, and collective action. Mapping age discrimination laws in the UK, Australia, and Canada, I consider the way in which individual enforcement is deployed, and the extent to which alternative enforcement mechanisms are adopted.

II. The Theory and Rationale of Individual Enforcement

Individual enforcement models rely on individuals commencing legal action to pursue their rights to be protected from discrimination.[2] Dickens describes this as

[1] Linda Dickens, 'The Road is Long: Thirty Years of Equality Legislation in Britain' (2007) 45 British Journal of Industrial Relations 463, 475.

[2] Women and Equalities Committee, *Enforcing the Equality Act: The Law and the Role of the Equality and Human Rights Commission* (2017–19 HC 1470) 7.

Reforming Age Discrimination Law. Alysia Blackham, Oxford University Press. © Alysia Blackham 2022.
DOI: 10.1093/oso/9780198859284.003.0003

a '"victim complains", self-service approach'.[3] A focus on individual enforcement is not always by design: rather, Dickens argues that the UK enforcement model is 'the result of historical accident, political convenience and ad hoc responses to particular needs, rather than one informed by a logic of enforcement designed to make employment rights effective'.[4]

For labour law rights more generally, the shift to individual enforcement reflects historical trends away from collective regulation.[5] In employment law, there has been a post-war shift from a voluntarist system—characterized by limited legal regulation and employment regulation through collective bargaining—to a focus on individual legal rights.[6] While the number and scope of individual legal rights has expanded, there has been no accompanying focus on how these rights are enforced.[7]

Not coincidentally, the era in which employment law shifted its focus to individual rights was the same period in which equality law was developed and refined.[8] In Great Britain (GB), for example, individual complaints have been key to the legislative framework since its earliest days. Britain's first equality statute, the Race Relations Act 1965, which prohibited racial discrimination in certain public settings, was enforced by individual complaints to a statutory agency—the Race Relations Board.[9] The Race Relations Act 1968—which extended protection to housing and employment—provided for conciliation of employment complaints via existing mechanisms already available in industry, in priority to those on offer by the Race Relations Board.[10] Further enforcement could then only be pursued by the Race Relations Board;[11] this was used infrequently.[12] With the passing of the Sex Discrimination Act 1975, individuals were given the right to claim compensation for unlawful discrimination directly. Thus, while equality law in GB progressed towards individual enforcement in the courts, even the earliest statutes

[3] Linda Dickens, 'Introduction: Making Employment Rights Effective: Issues of Enforcement and Compliance' in Linda Dickens (ed), *Making Employment Rights Effective: Issues of Enforcement and Compliance* (Hart Publishing 2012) 2.

[4] ibid 3.

[5] Judy Fudge, 'Labour as a "Fictive Commodity": Radically Reconceptualizing Labour Law' in Guy Davidov and Brian Langille (eds), *The Idea of Labour Law* (OUP 2011) 124.

[6] Dickens, 'Introduction' (n 3) 1; Gillian S Morris, 'The Development of Statutory Enforcement Rights in Britain and Enforcement Mechanisms' in Linda Dickens (ed), *Making Employment Rights Effective: Issues of Enforcement and Compliance* (Hart Publishing 2012).

[7] Dickens, 'Introduction' (n 3) 1.

[8] Indeed, the development of an individual right to unfair dismissal was, in part, justified on the basis of the UK government's commitment to introduce discrimination legislation on the basis of race: see Lord Donovan (Chair), *Royal Commission on Trade Unions and Employers' Associations* (Cmnd 3623, 1968) 146 [543].

[9] Race Relations Act 1965, s 2. Injunctions could also be sought by the Attorney-General in civil proceedings: s 3.

[10] Race Relations Act 1968, s 16. See also UK Parliamentary debate, HC Deb 23 April 1968, vol 763, col 57 (James Callaghan).

[11] Race Relations Act 1968, s 19; UK Parliamentary debate, HC 23 April 1968, vol 763, col 56 (James Callaghan).

[12] BA Hepple, *Equality: The Legal Framework* (2nd edn, Hart Publishing 2014) 12.

made provision for individual complaints to a statutory agency. These legislative developments were informed by the experience of the United States of America (USA).[13] The individual enforcement model adopted in the UK is also reflected in European Union (EU) law; though whether EU law echoes that of the UK or vice versa is a matter of debate.[14]

Even if the UK has adopted an individual enforcement model somewhat unthinkingly, and Australia has thereafter followed the UK,[15] there are a number of potential rationales for relying on individual enforcement to secure equality rights. First, at a theoretical level, individual enforcement is consistent with a model of individual equality. An individual justice model—or 'individualistic vision'[16]—of equality focuses on protecting individuals from unfair treatment on the basis of a protected ground—here, age.[17] In this model, the remedial aims of equality law are to compensate individuals for the detriment caused by discrimination.[18] If equality law is focused on protecting and compensating individuals, it makes sense for individuals to take responsibility for enforcement. This is consistent with a view of human rights as protecting individuals from interference by the state; rights vest in individuals, and remedies are available for individuals who can establish in court that their rights have been breached.[19] This leads to a view of equality as a negative duty: a 'duty of restraint' to stop the state or individuals discriminating against other individuals.[20] Again, this is enforced by individuals in court, requires proof of breach, and focuses on individualized and retrospective remedies.[21]

Second, at a practical level, if an individual experiences discrimination or inequality at work, they are potentially in a strong position to recognize that discrimination has occurred and have a clear personal interest in seeing that discrimination remedied. Individuals are more likely to be able to identify discrete instances of discrimination than, say, equality agencies, which are tasked with the oversight of significant numbers of employers: agencies cannot be in every location or monitor every workplace at once. Further, collective groups (such as unions) may not have a particular interest in securing the enforcement of equality rights, especially where doing so would challenge the established status quo (if the status quo is advantageous to their members). Individuals, therefore, are potentially in the best position to *identify* discriminatory behaviour and have the strongest *motive or drive*

13 Dickens, 'The Road is Long' (n 1) 466.

14 ibid 467.

15 Margaret Thornton, *The Liberal Promise: Anti-Discrimination Legislation in Australia* (OUP 1990) 1.

16 S Fredman, 'Equality: A New Generation?' (2001) 30 Industrial Law Journal 145, 156.

17 Mark Bell and Lisa Waddington, 'Reflecting on Inequalities in European Equality Law' (2003) 28 European Law Review 349, 351.

18 Fredman, 'Equality' (n 16) 156.

19 Sandra Fredman, 'Changing the Norm: Positive Duties in Equal Treatment Legislation' (2005) 12 Maastricht Journal of European and Comparative Law 369, 370.

20 ibid.

21 ibid.

to address such behaviour. An individual rights model is therefore key to the effective enforcement of equality rights; there is an obvious rationale for allowing and empowering individuals to enforce rights to be protected from discrimination.

III. Limits of Individual Enforcement

Despite the notional strengths of individual enforcement, concerns have been expressed for many years about its theoretical and practical limits.[22] The House of Commons Women and Equalities Committee (WEC) has concluded that individual enforcement of equality law 'is not fit for purpose' and should be 'only rarely needed'.[23] More specifically, individual enforcement of equality law is not fit for purpose at both a theoretical and practical level.

A. Theory: A Limited View of Equality

At a theoretical level, individual enforcement is only effective if we perceive discrimination to be an individual wrong, requiring individual solutions.[24] Discrimination is arguably better perceived in other, non-individualized ways; this critique demands a shift in focus, from the individual justice model, to thinking about (in)equality via a (1) group-oriented approach, (2) a focus on organizational change, and/or (3) recognition of inequality as a societal harm.

First, the individual justice model underlying individual enforcement struggles to accommodate structural or institutional discrimination, which is not directed to one specific person, but instead disadvantages a group.[25] A focus on individuals runs directly counter to the way age discrimination actually manifests at work, which is often group-based, systemic, and structural.[26] It fails to recognize the inherently collective nature of inequality, where disadvantage is due to actual or perceived membership of, or association with, a particular group.[27] Relying on individual enforcement means that structural or systemic discrimination—where no one individual may have been sufficiently impacted to prompt a claim—goes unaddressed.[28] Focusing on individuals ignores or minimizes problems that are

[22] See, eg, Beth Gaze, 'The Sex Discrimination Act after Twenty Years: Achievements, Disappointments, Disillusionment and Alternatives' (2004) 27 University of New South Wales Law Journal 914, 919.

[23] Women and Equalities Committee, *Enforcing the Equality Act* (n 2) 3.

[24] UK81.

[25] Bell and Waddington (n 17) 352.

[26] A160.

[27] Bell and Waddington (n 17) 353.

[28] Belinda Smith, 'It's about Time: For a New Regulatory Approach to Equality' (2008) 36 Federal Law Review 117, 134.

repeated,[29] systemic, self-perpetuating, and embedded in workplace cultures, at a workplace, sectoral, and national level: individual rights models do not necessarily effect systemic solutions.[30]

A group-oriented approach, which focuses less on individual merit and fault and more on addressing discriminatory barriers, may be more appropriate for addressing structural or 'second generation' discrimination.[31]

Second, an individual—rather than organizational—focus[32] seeks to adapt individuals to fit existing structures, rather than focusing on how structures can be adapted to accommodate everyone.[33] This is a more limited approach to equality than one which is focused on organizational change and transformation. Over-reliance on individual complaints therefore risks undermining the broader public message conveyed by equality law to organizations and employers: as Fredman argues,

> Anti-discrimination legislation which relies wholly on individual claims to tribunals might well signal to employers, State agents, and other major actors that the function of the law extends no further. As long as they can avoid tribunal claims, and pay out compensation where necessary, the problem of discrimination has been dealt with.[34]

Relying primarily on individual enforcement in the courts has resulted in intervention that is 'random and *ad-hoc*', potentially meaning many workplaces are untouched by equality litigation and enforcement.[35] This may serve to legitimize the status quo, as practices that are not challenged successfully come to be regarded as 'normal' or 'acceptable'.[36] Rather than supporting the aims of equality law, then, an excessive focus on individual enforcement might dampen the potential of equality law.[37] Anti-discrimination law has therefore had limited impact as a 'lever for change',[38] including due to its limited focus on individual compensation and settlements.[39]

Third, and relatedly, focusing on individuals and individual enforcement minimizes any regard for inequality as a *societal* wrong and form of harm. Equality law

[29] UK81.
[30] A160; Smith 'It's about Time: For a New Regulatory Approach to Equality' (n 28) 134.
[31] Fredman, 'Equality' (n 16) 156.
[32] Dickens, 'The Road is Long' (n 1) 472.
[33] ibid.
[34] Sandra Fredman, *Discrimination Law* (2nd edn, OUP 2011) 279–80.
[35] Fredman, 'Changing the Norm' (n 19) 372.
[36] Colm O'Cinneide, 'Positive Duties and Gender Equality' (2005) 8 International Journal of Discrimination and the Law 91, 93–94.
[37] See, eg, Lizzie Barmes, *Bullying and Behavioural Conflict at Work: The Duality of Individual Rights* (OUP 2016) 242.
[38] O'Cinneide (n 36) 93–94.
[39] Women and Equalities Committee, *Enforcing the Equality Act* (n 2) 8.

has evolved from a tort-based model to where 'it's supposed to be about larger-scale social change';[40] this is not reflected, though, in its enforcement mechanisms. For Thornton, addressing inequality through an individual, complaint-driven model reflects a choice not to 'exert the punitive force of the law'.[41] Unlike other public harms, discrimination is seen as something which is individual and private, to be resolved via the use of confidential conciliation rather than public proceedings.[42] Individualized enforcement is therefore also privatized enforcement,[43] which minimizes any public interest in addressing inequality. As Thorton argues, individuals do not have a right to equality as such; rather, they have a right to complain about discrimination.[44] The emphasis on conciliation in equality law both reflects the individualized nature of discrimination law, and makes the process and outcomes of equality law more atomized:

> The atomism inherent within the confidential conciliation process underscores the notion that acts of discrimination are of an isolated and individualistic nature and that individualistic solutions alone are appropriate.[45]

Rather than being an unthinking development, then, Thornton perceives the focus on individual enforcement in Australia as undermining the importance and transformative potential of equality law: through individual enforcement and private conciliation, discrimination law has become an empty 'liberal promise', confined to individual redress rather than societal change.[46]

B. Practice: False Assumptions and Barriers to Enforcement

In addition to challenging the theoretical view of (in)equality underlying the individual enforcement model, we also need to re-examine the assumptions underlying individual enforcement itself. Reliance on individual enforcement presupposes that those who experience discrimination fit the archetype of the rational, utility maximizing individual, who is able to (1) perceive discrimination and (2) who will logically wish to see discrimination addressed and remedied, including through financial compensation. As Fredman notes: 'The individualisation of rights assumes that the subject is an autonomous and discrete individual, whose self-realisation

[40] UK81.
[41] Thornton, *The Liberal Promise* (n 15) 37.
[42] Margaret Thornton, 'Equivocations of Conciliation: The Resolution of Discrimination Complaints in Australia' (1989) 52 Modern Law Review 733, 735.
[43] Trevor Colling, 'No Claim, No Pain? The Privatization of Dispute Resolution in Britain' (2004) 25 Economic and Industrial Democracy 555.
[44] Thornton, *The Liberal Promise* (n 15) 38.
[45] Thornton, 'Equivocations of Conciliation' (n 42) 741.
[46] Thornton, *The Liberal Promise* (n 15) 38, 151.

consists in protecting his or her freedom of choice and action.'[47] This model is likely gendered, classist, and racist:

> our system is predicated on a certain kind of Western subject who has agency and that is a very white male, middle class construction of the subject, which has traditionally made it difficult for non-white, for women, for people in minorities, for people in other cultures.... the Act says that somebody who has experienced the discrimination must complain and complaining is not a normal form of behaviour. It requires a certain kind of agency that many people do not have.... it requires a certain kind of culture to even accept help, let alone seek it.[48]

Understandably, then, the assumptions underlying the individual enforcement model do not hold in the practical context of equality law; the reality for many individuals is messy, driven by emotion, and contextually contingent.

At a basic level, individual enforcement depends on individuals having an awareness of their rights—and how to enforce them—and having capacity and willingness to enforce those rights in practice.[49] Rights awareness is not evenly distributed;[50] the most vulnerable workers may be particularly disadvantaged in this context, lacking both rights awareness and the capacity to pursue their entitlements.[51] As Smith concisely summarizes:

> Anti-discrimination legislation is designed to protect disempowered groups—those who traditionally experience marginalisation and exclusion. Expecting members of such groups to have the time, security and resources to pursue legal action in order to gain compensation and possibly bring about wider change represents a fundamental regulatory weakness.[52]

Individuals who experience discrimination tend to experience multiple, overlapping forms of disadvantage;[53] those who are most disadvantaged are most likely to experience discrimination, but also the least equipped to file a complaint.[54] Thus, 'reliance on individual complainants is problematic because it places the greatest burden on those with the fewest resources to file formal complaints'.[55]

47 Fredman, 'Changing the Norm' (n 19) 371.
48 A99.
49 Dickens, 'Introduction' (n 3) 3; Smith, 'It's about Time: For a New Regulatory Approach to Equality' (n 28) 118.
50 Dickens, 'The Road is Long' (n 1) 479.
51 Dickens, 'Introduction' (n 3) 3.
52 Smith, 'It's about Time: For a New Regulatory Approach to Equality' (n 28) 132.
53 Alysia Blackham and Jeromey Temple, 'Intersectional Discrimination in Australia: An Empirical Critique of the Legal Framework' (2020) 43 University of New South Wales Law Journal 773.
54 Sara Wakefield and Christopher Uggen, 'The Declining Significance of Race in Federal Civil Rights Law: The Social Structure of Employment Discrimination Claims' (2004) 74 Sociological Inquiry 128, 150.
55 ibid.

Those who experience discrimination may be especially vulnerable[56] and lack the confidence to bring a complaint;[57] indeed, experiencing discrimination can lead to a decline in individual confidence,[58] further undermining individual enforcement:

> I think often the people we see are so vulnerable and so damaged by their experiences that ... even with good support in family and friends and [representation], do not feel like they can elect to continue and would rather ... let it be.[59]

Some advocates and agencies therefore saw their role as supporting individuals to build the necessary confidence to bring a claim;[60] other respondents felt only the strongest claimants would be able to navigate a claim.[61]

C. Naming, Blaming, and Claiming

The potential barriers to bringing a discrimination claim can be more clearly articulated using the lens of 'naming, blaming, and claiming' as a theoretical framework to describe the emergence and transformation of disputes.[62] Even prior to encountering the legal system, for individual enforcement to be effective, potential claimants must first undergo a process of 'naming, blaming, and claiming'.[63]

First, *naming* requires individuals to transform an unperceived injurious experience into a perceived injurious experience[64]—that is, they must perceive that an injury has occurred. However, modern manifestations of discrimination—across all protected grounds—are increasingly more subtle and less overt.[65] Age discrimination is generally subtle and insidious;[66] conversely, individuals are more likely to both identify discrimination and take action when the discrimination they experience is overt.[67] Thus, the nature of modern discrimination may make naming problematic.

56 A100.
57 A102.
58 A98; A99; A100; A101. See Laura Smart Richman and Mark R Leary, 'Reactions to Discrimination, Stigmatization, Ostracism, and Other Forms of Interpersonal Rejection: A Multimotive Model' (2009) 116 Psychological Review 365, 368.
59 A100.
60 A98; A101; A102.
61 A103.
62 William LF Felstiner, Richard L Abel, and Austin Sarat, 'The Emergence and Transformation of Disputes: Naming, Blaming, Claiming ...' (1980) 15 Law & Society Review 631, 632.
63 ibid.
64 ibid 633.
65 Susan Sturm, 'Second Generation Employment Discrimination: A Structural Approach' (2001) 101 Columbia Law Review 458, 459–60.
66 A158; UK117; UK78; UK80.
67 Alex Lindsey and others, 'When Do Women Respond against Discrimination? Exploring Factors of Subtlety, Form, and Focus' (2015) 45 Journal of Applied Social Psychology 649, 657.

This is compounded by *attributional ambiguity* theories. Behaviour and events—and subtle discrimination[68]—can be ambiguous. It is often difficult to identify—or 'attribute'—why behaviour has occurred.[69] Attributional ambiguity makes it difficult to both (1) realize that you have been subjected to discrimination, and (2) prove that discrimination has occurred; this is especially the case for 'everyday' discrimination.[70] To identify discrimination, claimants may need to interpret events in aggregate, and infer discrimination from that collection of events. How people decipher events—and whether they subsequently infer discrimination—depends on both individual and contextual factors, including prior experiences of discrimination.[71] People may tend to err on the side of deciding that something is not discriminatory, especially if they have low self-esteem or self-worth,[72] instead attributing behaviour to their own personal limits or failings. It may also be 'easier to endure' behaviour that is interpreted as not being discriminatory.[73] Further, personal-group discrimination discrepancy (PGDD) means that people may be less likely to perceive their own treatment as discrimination, than that experienced by others; individuals deny or minimize their own experiences of discrimination.[74] This may be due to a need to protect their own self-esteem or identity (and not be labelled as a victim), difficulties in attributing ambiguous individual events, or due to cognitive bias in discounting individual experiences.[75] Attributional ambiguity may therefore lead to the under-reporting of discrimination where surveys ask people to self-report discrimination,[76] and makes the process of naming far from straightforward.

While a failure to identify discrimination is common across all protected grounds, this is particularly acute in relation to age discrimination due to the strength of internalized age stereotypes.[77] Internalized age norms and ageist sentiments reduce our ability to perceive age discrimination as an injurious experience.[78]

[68] Kristen P Jones and others, 'Subtle Discrimination in the Workplace: A Vicious Cycle' (2017) 10 Industrial and Organizational Psychology 51, 53.

[69] Jennifer Crocker and others, 'Social Stigma: The Affective Consequences of Attributional Ambiguity' (1991) 60 Journal of Personality and Social Psychology 218.

[70] Elizabeth A Deitch and others, 'Subtle yet Significant: The Existence and Impact of Everyday Racial Discrimination in the Workplace' (2003) 56 Human Relations 1299, 1302–03.

[71] Lisa Feldman Barrett and Janet K Swim, 'Appraisals of Prejudice and Discrimination' in Janet K Swim and Charles Stangor (eds), *Prejudice: The Target's Perspective* (Academic Press 1998) 19–20.

[72] Jennifer Crocker, Brenda Major, and Claude Steele, 'Social Stigma' in Daniel T Gilbert, Susan T Fiske, and Gardner Lindzey (eds), *The Handbook of Social Psychology*, vol 2 (McGraw-Hill 1998) 520–21.

[73] Joe R Feagin, 'The Continuing Significance of Race: Antiblack Discrimination in Public Places' (1991) 56 American Sociological Review 101, 103.

[74] See, eg, Bernard E Whitley Jr and Mary E Kite, *The Psychology of Prejudice and Discrimination* (Thomson Wadsworth 2006) 466–70.

[75] Lindsey and others (n 67) 650.

[76] Deitch and others (n 70) 1303.

[77] UK81; Kelly Harris and others, 'Ageism and the Older Worker: A Scoping Review' (2018) 58 Gerontologist e1, e7.

[78] Alysia Blackham, 'Normative Visions of Age: Progress and Change in Australian Labour Law' in John Howe, Anna Chapman, and Ingrid Landau (eds), *The Evolving Project of Labour Law: Foundations, Development and Future Research Directions* (The Federation Press 2017).

Unlike other forms of discrimination, 'age differentiation within society [can be] entirely legitimate, accepted and acceptable'.[79] Internalized age norms may mean that people expect[80] and accept poor treatment on the basis of age.[81] This particularly affects groups at the intersection of different protected grounds.[82] Internalized age norms mean individuals do not identify behaviour as age discrimination,[83] or do not see it as a legal wrong.[84] Ageism is ingrained[85] as something that is normal and acceptable,[86] rather than something to be treated seriously:[87] 'everyone knows the other types of discrimination are plainly wrong. . . . [But people] just expect a bit of age discrimination.'[88] Rather than address any dissonance between age norms of old age and their own personal experience of ageing, older people may deny that they are old at all, a form of adaptive coping.[89] Denying that you are old means that it is effectively impossible to experience (old) age discrimination.[90]

A cultural acceptance and expectation of age discrimination may also mean age-based treatment—even where it is recognized as such—is not seen as a form of harm: indeed, in the Australian Human Rights Commission's (AHRC) *National Prevalence Survey*, when asked why they did not take action in relation to age discriminatory behaviour, 27 per cent of respondents said that they were not offended or affected by the action in question.[91] Overall, then, a failure to identify age discrimination, or to see it as a form of harm, may fundamentally undermine the process of 'naming', and, as a result, the individual enforcement model more generally.

Second, for a perceived injurious experience to translate to a grievance, the individual must attribute the injury to the fault of another;[92] that is, they must feel wronged and believe that something might be done.[93] This is the process of *blaming*. It may be difficult to identify who is to blame for discriminatory treatment, especially in recruitment, where systems are often opaque. Asymmetries of information may therefore inhibit the process of blaming (Chapter 4). Third, individuals must voice their grievance to the person or entity believed to be responsible, and

[79] UK81.
[80] A115.
[81] A98; A110; A112; A115; A118; UK93; UK84; UK86.
[82] UK80; UK84; UK90.
[83] A5; A98; UK84; UK93; A110; UK78; UK117.
[84] A8; UK78.
[85] UK84.
[86] A8; A112; A115; UK80; UK84; UK86.
[87] UK86.
[88] A115.
[89] UK86; Pnina Ron, 'Elderly People's Attitudes and Perceptions of Aging and Old Age: The Role of Cognitive Dissonance?' (2007) 22 International Journal of Geriatric Psychiatry 656, 660.
[90] UK86; UK80.
[91] AHRC, 'National Prevalence Survey of Age Discrimination in the Workplace: The Prevalence, Nature and Impact of Workplace Age Discrimination amongst the Australian Population Aged 50 Years and Older' (2015) 70.
[92] Felstiner, Abel, and Sarat (n 62) 635.
[93] ibid.

seek a remedy: the process of *claiming*.[94] A claim becomes a dispute when it is rejected in whole or part.[95]

The process of naming, blaming, and claiming is subjective, unstable, reactive, complicated, and incomplete.[96] Only a small fraction of perceived injurious experiences translate into disputes,[97] and most attrition from this process occurs in the early stages.[98] A failure to transition to a dispute may be related to both an individual's social position as well as their individual characteristics.[99] Going further, though, it can also be attributed to structural factors embedded in the legal process, which deter or inhibit claiming.

D. Responding to Disputes

Even once a dispute exists, individuals face a range of choices about how to respond to the situation. For Regan, this involves a (potentially unconscious) weighing of costs and benefits of various courses of action.[100] Individuals may choose to 'lump it' or put up with the situation, avoid it (including through exit), use self-help, talk with family or friends, consult a third party (such as a mediator, lawyer, or statutory agency), or consult with a manager or colleagues.[101] Regan sees this process as involving a range of 'filters', with disputes being filtered out at various levels, and not necessarily involving any linear process from one action to another.[102] A claim may be filtered by individuals themselves if they decide it is not worth proceeding; or by a dispute-processing mechanism.[103] As a result, few disputes will progress to the legal arena; even seeking third party help to resolve a dispute is rare.[104]

In the AHRC's *National Prevalence Survey*, there was significant 'filtering' by those who had experienced age discrimination. Forty-three per cent of respondents who reported experiencing age discrimination at work in the last two years (n = 309) did not take any action;[105] of those who took action, only 5 per cent raised the matter with an external organization, 14 per cent raised the matter with their organization, and 15 per cent raised the matter with family, friends, or colleagues.[106] The most common form of action was to think about leaving the job in

94 ibid 635–36.
95 ibid 636.
96 ibid 637.
97 ibid 636.
98 ibid.
99 ibid.
100 Francis Regan, 'Dilemmas of Dispute Resolution Policy' (1997) 8 Australian Dispute Resolution Journal 5, 7.
101 ibid.
102 ibid.
103 ibid.
104 ibid 8. This corresponds with the pyramid of disputes: see below.
105 AHRC, 'National Prevalence Survey' (n 91) 67.
106 ibid 68.

question (17 per cent of respondents);[107] a further 8 per cent considered changing career or profession, and 6 per cent actually left their job.[108] Thus, for 31 per cent of respondents, taking 'action' involved contemplating or actually exiting the situation. Similarly, exit was a major form of resolution: while the majority of survey respondents (58 per cent) who experienced discrimination felt that the issue had not been resolved,[109] for those who achieved a full or partial resolution, 17 per cent quit their job, and 12 per cent found another job.[110] Only 5 per cent discussed the issue with their employer or other parties, and 3 per cent received an apology.[111]

Behavioural science and psychology literature offer further insights into how people variously respond when they experience discrimination, and how this might inhibit individual enforcement. For Smart Richman and Leary, experiencing discrimination—like experiencing other negative interpersonal events—has the 'potential to lower people's perceived relational value', that is, 'the degree to which they believe that others value having relationships with them'.[112] This challenges our fundamental need for acceptance and belonging,[113] and leads to hurt feelings[114] and lowered self-esteem.[115]

These feelings are universal, but people's *behaviour* in reaction to these feelings can vary; people simultaneously experience different motives that can lead to competing behaviour.[116] These motives are threefold: first, a desire to regain *social connection* and acceptance; second, an antisocial or angry urge to *defend oneself* or hurt the discriminator ('make them pay'); third, a wish to *avoid* future hurt or rejection, including by withdrawing from social contact.[117] Which motive dominates depends on how people construe the discrimination; this is impacted by the perceived fairness (or otherwise) of the treatment, subjective expectations of relationship repair, pervasiveness or chronicity of the rejection, value of the relationship, perceived costs of the rejection, and the possibility of alternative relationships.[118] For example, if the treatment is perceived as being unfair, this is more likely to lead to an antisocial, aggressive response. If a relationship is highly valued, is seen as salvageable, and the costs of exit are high, people are more likely to pursue prosocial actions. If rejection is pervasive or chronic, or an alternative relationship is available, then a person is more likely to withdraw.[119]

107 ibid.
108 ibid.
109 ibid 71.
110 ibid 72.
111 ibid.
112 Smart Richman and Leary (n 58) 366.
113 ibid.
114 That is, 'a distinct negative emotion that is associated with feeling devalued, unwanted, and rejected': ibid 367.
115 ibid 368.
116 ibid.
117 ibid.
118 ibid.
119 ibid.

An individual enforcement model is only likely to be used by claimants where the second, antisocial motive is dominant; seeking legal redress is a 'confrontational response'.[120] These are likely to be the claimants who are the most angry, willing to engage in antisocial behaviour, and who feel 'wronged'. Thus, an individual enforcement model is only likely to attract and capture a very select type of claimant. By contrast, a quest for social connection may lead to attempts to repair a relationship, which is generally seen as inconsistent with engaging with an adversarial legal model (Chapters 4 and 5).

People seeking to avoid future hurt are particularly unlikely to engage with legal complaint mechanisms. Those who seek to avoid future hurt do not just avoid contact with those who have discriminated against them: they may also withdraw from contact with those 'whose acceptance they doubt'.[121] As Smart Richman and Leary argue,

> withdrawal may be motivated by a desire to avoid additional decrements in belonging and the accompanying emotional pain. This consideration may even lead people to avoid interacting with those who were not involved in the initial rejection episode unless their acceptance is assured. Once they are rejected by one person, people may temporarily lose confidence in their acceptability to others.[122]

Thus, the ripple effects of experiencing discrimination can spread far further than the initial interaction. This 'avoidance effect' means that trying to address social exclusion and inequality through redress for individual experiences and instances of discrimination is fundamentally flawed; such individuals may well withdraw from or avoid both complaints mechanisms and future interactions that risk rejection. For older workers, this might mean avoiding certain recruitment processes[123] and, in some cases, withdrawing from the labour market entirely.[124] Those who have most often experienced discrimination are also those most likely to withdraw.[125] This means legal processes are least likely to assist those most exposed to discrimination.

Of course, Smart Richman and Leary's framework is just that, *a framework*: actual human behaviour in response to discrimination is highly diverse and individual; it is messy, dynamic, and bound up in emotion, and a framework cannot fully capture that complexity.[126] The point, though, is that people will react to their experiences differently, and how individuals react to their experiences may change

[120] Feagin (n 73) 103.
[121] Smart Richman and Leary (n 58) 368.
[122] ibid 376.
[123] A104; A110; A157; UK90; UK152.
[124] A109; A163; UK84; UK152.
[125] Smart Richman and Leary (n 58) 367–68.
[126] ibid 378.

with time.[127] An individual enforcement model engages only one type of human behaviour. Further, imposing strict time limits on individual claims means there is no scope for individuals to change their approach over time, even if their reactions do change with time.[128]

Overall, then, discrimination law is a limited tool for addressing the range of behaviours people demonstrate in response to discrimination. Individual claiming is likely to be a rare response: it requires a perfect confluence of individual, contextual, and structural factors for an individual to name, blame, and claim, and then pursue their complaint. As a result, the individual enforcement model is likely to address only a small minority of instances of discrimination, avoidance, and exclusion. In practice, individual enforcement is likely to be the exception, not the norm.

E. Summary: The Limits of Individual Enforcement

Assuming this perfect confluence of factors, and that an individual actually pursues a complaint, the individual enforcement model then raises a number of other overarching challenges. First, in the context of work, the model is beset by the significant power disparities between employers and employees—a paradigmatic case of inequality of bargaining power.[129] Employers have substantial power derived from their access to information, documents, and witnesses, as well as structural ideologies.[130] These power disparities substantially inhibit the individual enforcement model, particularly in areas such as proof and evidence, and the conduct of negotiation. Further, claimants rarely use legal mechanisms ('one-shotters') whereas respondents tend to be 'repeat players'; for repeat players, the stakes of any one claim are low, they have resources to pursue their long-term interests through favourable precedents, they know the legal system, and have access to expertise.[131] Understandably, then, respondents tend to 'come out ahead' in individual enforcement.[132]

Second, in relation to remedies, many people who experience discrimination do not primarily want financial compensation, and the individual enforcement model is ill-equipped to offer other remedies that might be seen as more meaningful. Individual enforcement is primarily oriented to after-the-fact vindication;[133] it is reactive, and seeks to remedy harm after it has occurred. Financial compensation

[127] ibid 379.
[128] A103.
[129] Thornton, 'Equivocations of Conciliation' (n 42) 743.
[130] ibid.
[131] Marc Galanter, 'Why the "Haves" Come out Ahead: Speculations on the Limits of Legal Change' (1974) 9 Law & Society Review 95, 97–104.
[132] ibid.
[133] Barmes (n 37) 242.

cannot 'fix' the harm occasioned by discrimination; this may deter individual complaints.

Third, an emphasis on individual enforcement puts substantial pressure on community groups and the voluntary sector to support individual claimants, particularly with the decline in unionization in the UK and Australia and reductions in legal aid funding.[134] Thus, a focus on individual enforcement puts the burden of achieving structural change and addressing discrimination on individuals and community groups, rather than government and organizations, who are arguably in a better position to effect meaningful change.

Overall, then, relying on individuals to address discrimination through individualized complaints-based mechanisms is highly unrealistic. The fundamental limits of the individual enforcement model are evident in the discussion above, and repeatedly illustrated by the statistics and findings of the chapters that follow. While there are particular doctrinal limitations with the way age discrimination law has been drafted and framed (Chapter 6), at its heart, discrimination law overlooks cases where claimants are prosocial or choose to withdraw. This is a fundamental limitation of existing individualized legal models.

Unsurprisingly then, there was a strong consensus in the expert interviews that individualized, complaints-based models were ineffective for addressing age discrimination.[135] Even the strongest legislative framework 'falls down before people have even got through the door'.[136] Individual enforcement is limited for achieving systemic change[137] and for addressing subtle discrimination,[138] given its reactive nature.[139] Its effectiveness depends on individual capacity,[140] knowledge of legal rights,[141] and willingness to both challenge an employer[142] and to pursue a claim.[143] Overall, 'in reality the steps that you've got to take to realising these rights under that legislation are too many and too big really . . . to surmount';[144] the onus on the individual is just too much.[145]

These barriers to, and limits of, individual enforcement are developed further in the chapters that follow, across the various life stages of an age discrimination complaint. However, it is important to note that these barriers and limits often impact

[134] Stephanie Tailby and others, 'Under-Funded and Overwhelmed: The Voluntary Sector as Worker Representation in Britain's Individualised Industrial Relations System: Individualised Industrial Relations System in Britain' (2011) 42 Industrial Relations Journal 273.

[135] A3; A5; A10; A71; A153; A160; A164; UK78; UK80; UK81; UK97; A99; A100; A101; A103; A104; A108; A115; UK117; UK162.

[136] A104.

[137] A3; A5; UK78; A100; A101; A160.

[138] UK78.

[139] A164.

[140] A5; UK80; A99.

[141] UK81.

[142] ibid; A104; A153.

[143] A10; A108.

[144] UK80.

[145] A108. See also UK117.

every stage of a claim: it is artificial to distinguish the factors that deter claiming, for example, from those that deter proceeding to a court hearing. That said, the relative importance and way those factors operate may shift over the life of a claim. Wherever possible, I have attempted to reduce duplication and repetition across the parts of this book, though it is important to acknowledge that things are rarely this clear cut in practice.

More fundamentally, too, there is a normative question as to whether individuals *should* have to bear the burden of addressing systemic discrimination.[146] Discrimination often goes beyond any one person; issues are structural, embedded, and integral in employment practices and interpersonal interactions.[147] Individuals both cannot and should not bear the burden of addressing and challenging this sort of discrimination. Further, individual enforcement is typically reactive, and does not directly aim to prevent harm occurring.[148] It is important, then, to consider both the extent to which individual enforcement is paradigmatic in national models of equality law, and the degree to which alternative models exist and are utilized.

IV. National Models of Enforcement

Australia, the UK, and Canada have grounded their age discrimination laws in an individual rights model, with a primary focus on individual enforcement via complaints for remedying discrimination in employment. However, there is provision—at least in theory—for alternative forms of enforcement, via statutory agencies, collective action, and positive duties.

The national models are described in broad terms below; specific doctrinal provisions are developed in more detail in later chapters. In all jurisdictions, though, individual claims must scale a pyramid of disputes: following the process of naming, blaming, and claiming, disputes must progress through various stages of alternative dispute resolution (ADR) before proceeding to a court or tribunal hearing and judgment (Figure 3.1). The apex of the pyramid—court or tribunal decisions—is reached by only a minute proportion of claims.

A. UK

In the UK, age discrimination is regulated by both human rights law and equality law. EU law on age discrimination, as contained within Council Directive 2000/78/

[146] Thornton, 'Equivocations of Conciliation' (n 42) 760.
[147] Sturm (n 65) 468.
[148] A164.

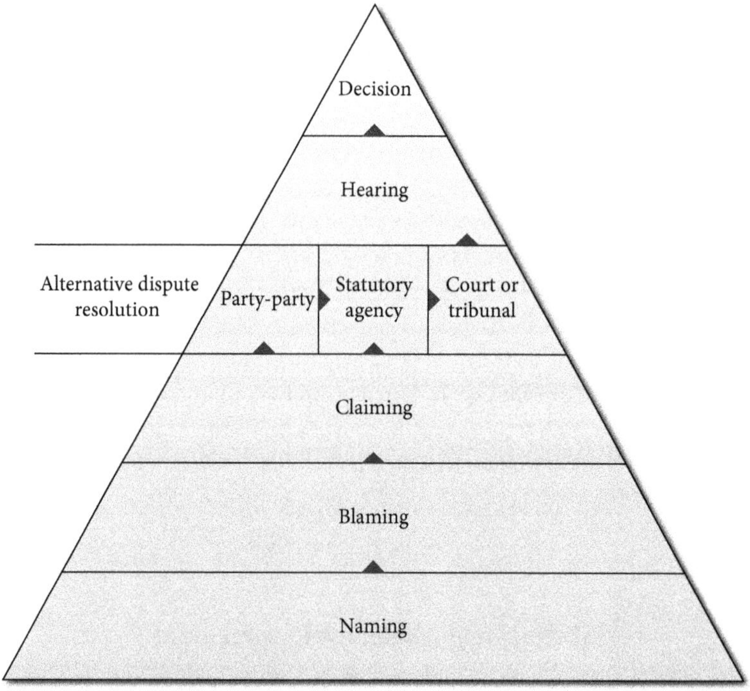

Figure 3.1 Pyramid of disputes

EC of 27 November 2000 establishing a general framework for equal treatment in employment and occupation[149] (and, later, the Charter of Fundamental Rights of the European Union[150]) prompted UK legislative activity in this area (Employment Equality (Age) Regulations 2006, SI 2006/1031) (the 2006 Regulations). In GB, this was later consolidated in the Equality Act 2010 (EqA); in Northern Ireland (NI), equality law has not been consolidated.

This flags, then, the devolved nature of some equality regulation in the UK: while legislative powers have been progressively transferred or devolved to Wales,[151] Scotland,[152] and NI,[153] devolution in the UK is asymmetrical: different countries have different legislative competences.[154] Thus, while equality law is a

[149] [2000] OJ L303/16 (hereafter Framework Directive).

[150] Article 21. Though see Angela Ward, 'The Impact of the EU Charter of Fundamental Rights on Anti-Discrimination Law: More a Whimper than a Bang?' (2018) 20 Cambridge Yearbook of European Legal Studies 32.

[151] Government of Wales Act 1998; Government of Wales Act 2006; Wales Act 2014; Wales Act 2017.

[152] Scotland Act 1998; Scotland Act 2012; Scotland Act 2016.

[153] Northern Ireland Act 1998.

[154] Paul Chaney, 'Equality and Territorial (in-)Justice? Exploring the Impact of Devolution on Social Welfare for Older People in the UK' (2013) 33 Critical Social Policy 114, 116.

transferred matter in NI, it is a reserved matter in Wales[155] and Scotland.[156] Even where equality law is reserved, there is still scope for the nations to have an impact in this area, including, for example, in relation to the specific duties under the Public Sector Equality Duty (PSED) (Chapter 7).[157] The chapters that follow flag relevant differences between the statutory frameworks in GB and NI; for the most part, though, the frameworks are similar, both being grounded in the Framework Directive.[158]

In relation to human rights law, age discrimination is prohibited by the European Convention on Human Rights (at least in relation to Convention rights).[159] It is unclear what impact—if any—Brexit will have on equality law in the UK. Freed from the need to implement EU Directives, it is possible that equality rights will be weakened or undermined.[160] Further, the UK will not be required to implement any future Directives relating to discrimination. Given that UK age discrimination law is directly attributable to the need to implement the Framework Directive, leaving the EU may well operate to stultify age equality law in the UK.

1. Legal framework

In GB, the EqA defines direct age discrimination as being where:

> If, because of age, A treats B less favourably than A treats or would treat others; *unless* A can show A's treatment of B to be a proportionate means of achieving a legitimate aim.[161]

The ability to justify direct age discrimination as a proportionate means of achieving a legitimate aim is unique to age discrimination; it does not apply to any other protected characteristic.

Indirect age discrimination is defined as where:

> A applies to B a provision, criterion or practice ('PCP') which is discriminatory in relation to B's age.

155 Government of Wales Act 2006, sch 7A, N1.

156 Scotland Act 1998, sch 5, L2.

157 Equality Act 2010, s 153(2)–(3) (hereafter EqA).

158 The key difference between the two statutory frameworks relates to the regulation of age discrimination beyond employment: see Alysia Blackham, 'Age Discrimination beyond Employment' (2019) 52 Kobe University Law Review 1.

159 Article 14. See also Human Rights Act 1998. See further the Charter of Fundamental Rights of the European Union, art 21 (which relates to EU institutions and bodies, and Member States when implementing EU law). On how these provisions have been used in practice, see Blackham, 'Age Discrimination beyond Employment' (n 158).

160 Sandra Fredman and others, 'The Impact of Brexit on Equality Law' (2021) <https://ohrh.law.ox.ac.uk/wp-content/uploads/2021/04/The-Impact-of-Brexit-on-Equality-Rights-1.pdf> accessed 18 March 2022.

161 EqA (n 157) s 13(1)–(2).

This occurs if:

(a) A applies, or would apply, the PCP to persons with whom B does not share the characteristic of age,
(b) the PCP puts, or would put, persons with whom B shares the characteristic of age at a particular disadvantage when compared with persons with whom B does not share the characteristic of age,
(c) the PCP puts, or would put, B at that disadvantage, and
(d) A cannot show the PCP to be a proportionate means of achieving a legitimate aim.

Intersectionality is not explicitly recognized in the EqA: s 14, which makes provision for combined discrimination on the basis of two protected characteristics, has never become operative.

In NI, the Employment Equality (Age) Regulations (Northern Ireland) 2006 (NI) (NI Regulations) make similar provision in their prohibition of both direct and indirect age discrimination:

. . . a person ('A') discriminates against another person ('B') if—
(a) on the grounds of B's age, A treats B less favourably than he treats or would treat other persons, or
(b) A applies to B a provision, criterion or practice which he applies or would apply equally to persons not of the same age group as B, but—
  (i) which puts or would put persons of the same age group as B at a particular disadvantage when compared with other persons, and
  (ii) which puts B at that disadvantage,

and A cannot show the treatment or, as the case may be, provision, criterion or practice to be a proportionate means of achieving a legitimate aim.[162]

The EqA prohibits age discrimination in work against employees and applicants, including in relation to recruitment; terms and conditions; access to opportunities for promotion, transfer or training or for receiving any benefit, facility or service; dismissal; any other detriment; victimization;[163] and harassment.[164] Similar provision is made in the NI Regulations, though protection from age discrimination in

[162] Employment Equality (Age) Regulations (Northern Ireland) 2006 (NI), reg 3 (hereafter NI Regulations).
[163] EqA (n 157) s 39.
[164] ibid s 40.

recruitment does not apply to those at the employer's normal retirement age or age 65, or within six months of that age.[165]

Discrimination is also prohibited by the EqA against contract workers,[166] partners,[167] members of limited liability partnerships,[168] barristers[169] and advocates,[170] personal offices[171] and public offices,[172] and members of local authorities;[173] and by those who facilitate access to work, such as qualifications bodies,[174] employment service providers,[175] and trade organizations.[176] Similarly, the NI Regulations prohibit age discrimination in work by those with a statutory power to select employees for others,[177] against contract workers,[178] office holders,[179] barristers and pupils,[180] partners;[181] and by those who facilitate access to work, such as trade organizations,[182] qualifications bodies,[183] training providers,[184] and employment agencies.[185]

There are substantial exceptions to the prohibition of age discrimination in the UK.[186] One of the most contentious is the ability to justify direct age discrimination as a proportionate means of achieving a legitimate aim.[187] There has been much litigation on this point, particularly in relation to mandatory retirement ages.[188] While the EqA used to contain an exception for the national default retirement age of 65, and employers' normal retirement ages,[189] retirement ages now need to be justified as a proportionate means of achieving a legitimate aim. That is not the case in NI, where the prohibition of age discrimination against employees does not 'render unlawful the dismissal of a person to whom this regulation applies

165 NI Regulations (n 162) reg 7(4).
166 EqA (n 157) s 41.
167 ibid s 44.
168 ibid s 45.
169 ibid s 47.
170 ibid s 48.
171 ibid s 49.
172 ibid ss 50–1.
173 ibid s 58.
174 ibid s 53.
175 ibid s 55.
176 ibid s 57.
177 NI Regulations (n 162) reg 8.
178 ibid reg 10.
179 ibid reg 13.
180 ibid reg 17.
181 ibid reg 18.
182 ibid reg 19.
183 ibid reg 20.
184 ibid reg 21.
185 ibid reg 22.
186 Alysia Blackham, 'A Compromised Balance? A Comparative Examination of Exceptions to Age Discrimination Law in Australia and the UK' (2018) 41 Melbourne University Law Review 1085.
187 EqA (n 157) s 13.
188 See, eg, *Seldon v Clarkson Wright and Jakes (A Partnership)* [2012] UKSC 16 (25 April 2012), [2012] WLR(D) 124.
189 This exception was removed by the Employment Equality (Repeal of Retirement Age Provisions) Regulations 2011, SI 2011/1069.

at or over the age of 65 where the reason for the dismissal is retirement'.[190] Given the extensive and detailed literature on the matter of mandatory retirement, I will not explore these issues in detail, though I return to the question of justification in Chapter 6.

2. Enforcement

Enforcement of age discrimination law in the UK primarily relies on individuals bringing claims to enforce their rights. In GB, for claimants who need advice, the Equality Advisory and Support Service (EASS) is an outsourced service (that was previously run by the Equality and Human Rights Commission (EHRC)) providing 'informal advice, guidance and support' and may be able to help individuals locate legal assistance. It does not comment on individual cases or their merits.[191] Individuals may be able to obtain more specific advice from a law centre, legal aid, trade union, or Citizens Advice (CAB).

To bring a claim of age discrimination that relates to work, claimants must generally notify the statutory body Acas (the Advisory, Conciliation and Arbitration Service) before lodging a claim at the Employment Tribunal (ET) (the 'early conciliation' process).[192] Acas offers individual conciliation of claims.[193]

Participating in conciliation is not compulsory, though some claimants confuse compulsory *notification* with compulsory *conciliation*. In the first-year survey of claimants who had notified Acas of their claims, 30 per cent participated in conciliation because they thought it was compulsory.[194] This confusion might have been resolved over time; however, given most claimants are 'one-shotters',[195] it is likely that at least some confusion endures.

If a claim is not resolved at conciliation, a claimant may choose to pursue their claim to the ET (though ETs may also refer a claim back to Acas for conciliation, or a claim may be subject to judicial mediation: Chapter 5). ETs are independent judicial bodies designed to offer a more efficient and less formal venue for resolving disputes than traditional courts;[196] this has not necessarily been realized in

[190] NI Regulations (n 162) reg 32(2).

[191] Equality Advisory and Support Service, 'Contact Us' <https://www.equalityadvisoryservice.com/app/ask> accessed 29 May 2020.

[192] Enterprise and Regulatory Reform Act 2013, s 7; The Employment Tribunals (Early Conciliation: Exemptions and Rules of Procedure) Regulations 2014, SI 254/2014. Notification was not compulsory prior to 2014.

[193] For further on ADR in the UK, see Alysia Blackham and Dominique Allen, 'Resolving Discrimination Claims Outside the Courts: Alternative Dispute Resolution in Australia and the United Kingdom' (2019) 31 Australian Journal of Labour Law 253.

[194] Matthew Downer and others, 'Evaluation of Acas Early Conciliation 2015' (Acas Research Paper 04/15) 5 <https://webarchive.nationalarchives.gov.uk/ukgwa/20210104113851mp_/https://archive.acas.org.uk/media/4335/Evaluation-of-Acas-Early-Conciliation-2015/pdf/Evaluation-of-Acas-Early-Conciliation-2015.pdf> accessed 18 March 2022.

[195] Galanter (n 131) 97–104.

[196] Dickens, 'The Road is Long' (n 1) 478.

practice.[197] Decisions can be appealed to the Employment Appeal Tribunal (EAT), and thereafter to the Court of Appeal and Supreme Court.

Complaints relating to work under the EqA are subject to time limits under s 123(1), which says:

> proceedings … may not be brought after the end of—
> (a) the period of 3 months starting with the date of the act to which the complaint relates, or
> (b) such other period as the employment tribunal thinks just and equitable

though this period is extended to facilitate Acas conciliation.[198] Conduct which extends 'over a period is to be treated as done at the end of the period'.[199] This is a shorter time limit than that for claims in the civil courts (the latter is set at six months).[200]

Consistent with EU law,[201] there is a legislative shifting of the burden of proof in the UK: s 136 of the EqA provides:

> (2) If there are facts from which the court could decide, in the absence of any other explanation, that a person (A) contravened the provision concerned, the court must hold that the contravention occurred.
> (3) But subsection (2) does not apply if A shows that A did not contravene the provision.[202]

Two government reforms have substantially inhibited access to justice for those who experience discrimination at work. First, from 29 July 2013 to 26 July 2017, ETs charged substantial fees to hear claims or appeals.[203] In *R (UNISON) v Lord Chancellor*,[204] the UK Supreme Court found the ET fees regime to be unlawful, given its potential to inhibit access to justice; the Employment Tribunals and Employment Appeal Tribunal Fees Order 2013 was quashed. While fees are no longer charged for ET claims, the long-term impact of the fee regime is likely to be

[197] See, eg, ibid; Susan Corby, 'British Employment Tribunals: From the Side-Lines to Centre Stage' (2015) 56 Labor History 161.
[198] EqA (n 157) s 140B. See similarly NI Regulations (n 162) reg 48(1).
[199] EqA (n 157) s 123(3).
[200] ibid s 118.
[201] Council Directive 97/80/EC of 15 December 1997 on the Burden of Proof in Cases of Discrimination Based on Sex [1998] OJ L14/6 (hereafter Burden of Proof Directive); Council Directive 98/52/EC of 13 July 1998 on the Extension of Directive 97/80/EC on the Burden of Proof in Cases of Discrimination Based on Sex to the United Kingdom of Great Britain and Northern Ireland [1998] OJ L205/66; Framework Directive (n 149) art 10.
[202] See also NI Regulations (n 162) reg 42(2).
[203] HM Courts & Tribunals Service, *Employment Tribunal Fees for Individuals*, T435, November 2013.
[204] [2017] UKSC 51, [2017] 3 WLR 409.

substantial, both for individuals who did not pursue their claim, and given reduced opportunities for the development of case law over that four-year period.

Second, the adverse impact of fees on claiming behaviour has been exacerbated by the general exclusion of employment matters from legal aid funding.[205] While legal aid is available for discrimination claims, it is not generally available for representation in the ET. Though claimants can apply for 'exceptional case funding' for this purpose, from 2013–14 to 2017–18 not one of the ten applications for exceptional case funding was granted.[206] The EHRC has therefore concluded that changes to legal aid mean 'vulnerable people who are unable to represent themselves in complex Employment Tribunal cases are being deprived of access to justice'.[207] While ET fees have been declared unlawful, legal aid reforms endure.

Enforcement of age discrimination law in NI largely mirrors the situation in GB. However, there are five important differences between the jurisdictions. First, fees were never charged in NI tribunals; thus, the long-term impact of the fees regime is unlikely to apply in NI.

Second, the Equality Commission for Northern Ireland (ECNI) has retained its advisory role, and runs a telephone advice line for those who experience discrimination. By contrast, in GB, this function is outsourced to EASS (Chapter 4).

Third, the ECNI actively offers claimants legal support, through applications to its Legal Funding Committee (LFC). While the EHRC may also assist individual claimants, this occurs on a larger scale in NI. In 2018–19, for example, of 317 applications to the LFC, 67 were granted legal assistance (21 per cent of applications).[208] Thus, the ECNI plays an obvious and tangible role in assisting claimants to navigate the legal system. In exchange for this support, ECNI asks claimants to participate in publicity around their claim, and to refuse any confidentiality clauses in settlement deeds (Chapter 5). This has resulted in ECNI developing a substantial database of successfully conciliated outcomes, and a significant public media presence in NI.

Fourth, the early conciliation process—where claimants *must* notify the NI Labour Relations Agency (LRA) before proceeding to tribunal—was only introduced in NI from 27 January 2020.[209] By contrast, in GB, the early conciliation regime has been in place since 2014. In practice, this may redirect a significant number of cases away from the tribunal system.

Fifth, discrimination claims in NI may be pursued in the Fair Employment Tribunal (which considers claims of religious belief and political opinion

205 See Legal Aid, Sentencing and Punishment of Offenders Act 2012, sch 1, pt 1, s 43.

206 Equality and Human Rights Commission, 'Access to Legal Aid for Discrimination Cases' (2019) 10, 38 <https://www.equalityhumanrights.com/sites/default/files/access-to-legal-aid-for-discrimination-cases-our-legal-aid-inquiry.pdf> accessed 29 May 2020.

207 ibid.

208 Equality Commission for Northern Ireland, 'Legal Services Report: Review of Legal Services 2018–19' (2019) 3.

209 The Industrial Tribunals and Fair Employment Tribunal (Early Conciliation: Exemptions and Rules of Procedure) Regulations (Northern Ireland) 2020 (NI).

discrimination) and Industrial Tribunals (which consider discrimination on other grounds). Unlike in GB, NI tribunal decisions relating to age discrimination have historically been published online, with online decisions dating back to 19 December 2007.[210] Given that most of the provisions of the NI Regulations only commenced on 1 October 2006, it is likely that this online collection of decisions represents all first instance decisions made under the NI Regulations to date.

3. Beyond individual enforcement

A move away from individual enforcement could be facilitated by vesting a statutory agency with enforcement powers to secure compliance with equality law. There is some scope for agency enforcement of age discrimination law in GB. The EHRC is empowered to take enforcement action in relation to equality complaints, including investigations, unlawful act notices, compliance notices relating to the PSED, action plans, agreements, applications to restrain, conciliation, and legal proceedings.[211] However, these powers are rarely exercised in practice,[212] particularly in relation to age discrimination: significant budget and staffing cuts have limited the efficacy of the EHRC's operations.[213] Agency enforcement is only effective if supported by adequate personnel and funding: at present, the EHRC has neither. The weight of enforcement has therefore fallen on individual claimants.

Alternatively or additionally, Barmes has emphasized the need to collectivize the enforcement and implementation of individual rights.[214] This could occur via trade unions, community groups and non-governmental organizations (NGOs), or groups of workers themselves. Indeed, a trend towards collectivized enforcement can already be seen among some vulnerable workers who experience workplace problems.[215] The question, though, is how this can be strengthened and improved in relation to age discrimination in particular, including for those who are not members of trade unions.

Age discrimination may also be proactively prevented via the PSED. The use of positive duties in equality law may help to require organizations to develop their own solutions to equality issues,[216] promoting a more proactive approach

[210] *McCoy v James McGregor & Sons Ltd* [2007] NIIT 00237/07IT (19 December 2007).

[211] Equality Act 2006, ss 16, 20–22, 32.

[212] Historically, see Linda Dickens, 'Road Blocks on the Route to Equality: The Failure of Sex Discrimination Legislation in Britain' (1991) 18 Melbourne University Law Review 277, 285–86.

[213] *HRreview*, Budget Cuts May Leave to All White Management at EHRC' (10 September 2012) <http://www.hrreview.co.uk/hr-news/diversity-equality/budget-cuts-may-leave-to-all-white-management-at-ehrc/38788> accessed 6 September 2013; Bob Hepple, 'Enforcing Equality Law: Two Steps Forward and Two Steps Backwards for Reflexive Regulation' (2011) 40 Industrial Law Journal 315.

[214] Barmes (n 37).

[215] Anna Pollert and Andy Charlwood, 'The Unorganised Worker: Problems at Work, Routes to Support and Views on Representation' (2008) Working Paper 11, 42 <https://uwe-repository.worktribe.com/output/1021196/the-unorganised-worker-problems-at-work-routes-to-support-and-views-on-representation-the-unrepresented-worker-survey-2004-working-paper-11-who-experiences-problems-at-work-what-problems-do-they-experience-what-do-they-do-about-them-and-what-happen> accessed 18 March 2022.

[216] Sandra Fredman, 'The Public Sector Equality Duty' (2011) 40 Industrial Law Journal 405, 419.

to the implementation of equality law,[217] and reducing reliance on individuals to reactively enforce their rights after discrimination has occurred.[218] In GB, the PSED requires a public authority or those exercising public functions to:

> … in the exercise of its functions, have due regard to the need to—
> (a) eliminate discrimination, harassment, victimisation and any other conduct that is prohibited by or under [the EqA];
> (b) advance equality of opportunity between persons who share a relevant protected characteristic and persons who do not share it;
> (c) foster good relations between persons who share a relevant protected characteristic and persons who do not share it.[219]

A failure to comply with the PSED can lead to action by the EHRC (including a compliance notice),[220] or proceedings for judicial review. The PSED has been criticized for its use of the 'due regard' standard,[221] which is seen as 'too flimsy'[222] and vague to operate effectively;[223] ongoing reliance on judicial review to enforce the duty, which may cultivate a 'tick box' mentality among public authorities and a focus on 'mere procedural compliance';[224] and its limited application to the private sector. Despite these criticisms, the PSED is seen as having the potential to prompt a shift away from reactive individual enforcement towards a more proactive organizational approach to equality issues. The extent to which the PSED has been successful in practice at addressing age discrimination is considered in Chapter 7.

The GB PSED was based on the statutory duty in NI, which requires a public authority to:

> in carrying out its functions relating to Northern Ireland have due regard to the need to promote equality of opportunity … between persons of different … age[s].[225]

The powers and functions of the ECNI relating to positive duties differ substantially to those of the EHRC; in essence, the ECNI is tasked with a more intensive

[217] O'Cinneide (n 36).
[218] Sandra Fredman and Sarah Spencer, 'Delivering Equality: Towards an Outcome-Focused Positive Duty: Submission to the Cabinet Office Equality Review and to the Discrimination Law Review' (2006) 6–7; Sandra Fredman, 'Breaking the Mold: Equality as a Proactive Duty' (2012) 60 American Journal of Comparative Law 265, 266.
[219] EqA (n 157) s 149(1).
[220] Equality Act 2006, s 32.
[221] Fredman, 'The Public Sector Equality Duty' (n 216).
[222] ibid 419.
[223] ibid 411.
[224] ibid 420; Fredman, 'Breaking the Mold' (n 218) 276.
[225] Northern Ireland Act 1998, s 75(1).

role in relation to positive duties than the EHRC (Chapter 7). At the same time, the responsibility for human rights oversight in NI lies with the Northern Ireland Human Rights Commission (NIHRC); in GB, this also sits with the EHRC. Overall, while there are measures in place in the UK to move beyond individual enforcement, their potential has not yet been realised in practice.

B. Australia

Australia is a federal nation with eight states and territories and a federal Commonwealth government. Federalism divides (rather than devolves) powers;[226] in Australia, the federal government has a limited number of exclusive powers,[227] and a larger number of powers exercised concurrently with the states.[228] Residual powers remain with the states. Where there is inconsistency between federal and state laws, the Commonwealth law prevails, and state law is invalid to the extent of any inconsistency.[229]

Australia as a whole does not have a bill of rights or human rights charter; the *Australian Constitution* makes limited provision for individual rights, and does not consider age discrimination. However, Victoria,[230] the Australian Capital Territory (ACT)[231] and Queensland[232] have adopted human rights instruments, which offer protection from discrimination and establish positive equality duties.

1. Legal framework

Age discrimination at work is regulated by state, territory, and federal equality law; and via industrial regulation (at the federal level, the Fair Work Act 2009 (Cth) (FWA)). It is only possible to pursue a claim in one jurisdiction. The choice of jurisdiction—which is largely up to the claimant—will determine which body receives, conciliates, and hears the claim; the specific legal rules to be applied; and the scope for agency enforcement.

The FWA establishes a federal industrial relations regime. The scope of federal industrial legislation reflects the cobbling together of different statutory powers, with legislative authority from powers relating to trade and commerce,[233] corporations,[234] the Commonwealth public service,[235] the territories,[236] and the referral

226 Vernon Bogdanor, *Devolution in the United Kingdom* (OUP 2001) 3.
227 See, eg, Australian Constitution, s 52.
228 See, eg, Australian Constitution, s 51.
229 Ibid s 109.
230 Charter of Human Rights and Responsibilities Act 2006 (Vic), s 8(3)–(4).
231 Human Rights Act 2004 (ACT), s 8(3).
232 Human Rights Act 2019 (Qld), s 15.
233 Australian Constitution, s 51(i).
234 ibid s 51(xx).
235 ibid s 52(ii).
236 ibid s 122.

of state powers.[237] The FWA only applies to employees of 'national system employers': these are defined as including:

- Constitutional corporations;
- The Commonwealth;
- A Commonwealth authority;
- Those employing a flight crew officer, a maritime employee, or a waterside worker, in connection with constitutional trade or commerce;
- A body corporate incorporated in a territory; and
- A person who carries on an activity in a territory.[238]

The regime also extends to employers in states that have referred their industrial relations powers to the federal government.[239] This has led to some coverage of state and local government employees by the federal system.[240] Thus, the federal system continues to exist side-by-side with state industrial relations regimes in some jurisdictions.

The FWA establishes a general protections regime, which includes protection for employees and prospective employees against 'adverse action'[241] 'because of' age.[242] 'Adverse action' against employees includes dismissal, being injured in employment, prejudicial altering of a position, and discriminating between employees.[243] Against prospective employees, adverse action includes a refusal to employ, or discriminating in the terms and conditions offered.[244] 'Employee' and 'employer' are (rather unhelpfully) defined in s 335 as having 'their ordinary meanings'.

Protections against adverse action do not apply if: action is not unlawful under any anti-discrimination law; it is because of the 'inherent requirements' of the position; or it is in a religious institution, and done in good faith 'to avoid injury to the religious susceptibilities of adherents of that religion or creed.'[245] Complaints under the FWA are handled by the Fair Work Commission (FWC), which conducts voluntary conciliation, formal hearings, and determinative conferences.

The FWA regime is notable in Australia for three reasons. First, there is a reverse onus of proof under s 361 of the FWA. This is the only discrimination law in Australia with a shifting onus of proof (Chapter 6).[246] Second, the FWA regime is

237 ibid s 51(xxxvii).
238 Fair Work Act 2009 (Cth), s 14 (hereafter FWA).
239 ibid ss 30D, 30E.
240 ibid ss 30L, 30G, 30R.
241 ibid s 342.
242 ibid s 351(1).
243 ibid s 342(1).
244 ibid s 342(1).
245 ibid s 351(2).
246 Though, for claims that are referred to the Australian Capital Territory Civil and Administrative Tribunal (ACAT), there is a rebuttable presumption that discrimination has occurred if the claimant can establish that treatment was unfavourable, or a condition or requirement has, or is likely to have, the

supported by the Fair Work Ombudsman (FWO), a statutory authority tasked with ensuring compliance with workplace laws. The FWO's powers are more extensive than those typically held by statutory equality agencies (Chapter 8). Third, though, the FWA has the strictest time limits in the country for claims relating to dismissal, which must be brought within twenty-one days of the dismissal taking effect.[247] The FWC may allow a further period only in 'exceptional circumstances'.[248]

In equality law, laws prohibiting age discrimination at work are in place at the federal, state, and territory level. At the federal level, the Age Discrimination Act 2004 (Cth) (ADA) is again grounded in an array of legislative heads of power,[249] including those relating to corporations,[250] the Commonwealth public service,[251] the territories,[252] banking,[253] insurance,[254] trade and commerce,[255] and the external affairs power.[256] With its reliance on the external affairs power, the ADA has effect in relation to age discrimination to the extent it gives effect to: the Discrimination (Employment and Occupation) Convention, 1958; the International Covenant on Civil and Political Rights; the International Covenant on Economic, Social and Cultural Rights; the Convention on the Rights of the Child; or relates to matters external to Australia or of international concern.[257] This potentially enables the ADA to cover most instances of age discrimination in Australia, though the territorial limits and scope of the ADA have not been tested thoroughly in the courts.

Given the potential overlap between the ADA and state and territory laws, s 12(3) of the ADA provides that it is 'not intended to exclude or limit the operation of a law of a State or Territory that is capable of operating concurrently with this Act'. However, if there is overlap between the federal law and the law of a state or territory, and a person makes a complaint at the state or territory level, then they are not entitled to make a complaint at the federal level in relation to the same allegedly discriminatory act.[258] If behaviour constitutes an offence against both federal and state or territory statutes, then that behaviour can be prosecuted at both levels,[259] though it cannot be punished

effect of disadvantaging them; and presents evidence that would enable the Tribunal to decide, in the absence of any other explanation, that the treatment or disadvantage was because of a protected attribute: Human Rights Commission Act 2005 (ACT), s 53CA(2). This still imposes a significant burden on claimants to establish discrimination.

247 FWA (n 238) s 366(1)(a).
248 ibid s 366(2).
249 Age Discrimination Act 2004 (Cth), ss 9, 10 (hereafter ADA).
250 Australian Constitution, s 51(xx).
251 ibid s 52(ii).
252 ibid s 122.
253 ibid s 51(xiii).
254 ibid s 51(xiv).
255 ibid s 51(i).
256 ibid s 51(xxix).
257 ADA (n 249) s 10(7).
258 ibid s 12(4).
259 ibid s 12(5).

twice.[260] The AHRC may also decide not to inquire into a complaint if it 'has been adequately dealt with', a more appropriate remedy is available, or it 'could be more effectively or conveniently dealt with by another statutory authority'.[261]

Under the ADA, age discrimination is either direct or indirect. Direct age discrimination is where:

(a) the discriminator treats or proposes to treat the aggrieved person less favourably than, in circumstances that are the same or are not materially different, the discriminator treats or would treat a person of a different age; and
(b) the discriminator does so because of:
    (i) the age of the aggrieved person; or
    (ii) a characteristic that appertains generally to persons of the age of the aggrieved person; or
    (iii) a characteristic that is generally imputed to persons of the age of the aggrieved person.[262]

Indirect discrimination occurs where:

(a) the discriminator imposes, or proposes to impose, a condition, requirement or practice; and
(b) the condition, requirement or practice is not reasonable in the circumstances; and
(c) the condition, requirement or practice has, or is likely to have, the effect of disadvantaging persons of the same age as the aggrieved person.[263]

The discriminator or respondent has the burden of proving that the condition, requirement, or practice is reasonable.[264] If an act is done for two or more reasons, and one of those reasons is age, then the act is 'taken to be done because of the age of the person'.[265]

In the context of work, the ADA prohibits discrimination in recruitment; determining terms and conditions of employment; access to promotion, transfer, training, or benefits; dismissal; and in relation to any other detriment.[266] The prohibition of discrimination applies to 'employees' and persons in recruitment. 'Employment' is defined broadly, to include part–time and temporary

[260] ibid s 12(6).
[261] Australian Human Rights Commission Act 1986 (Cth), ss 20(2)(c)(iii)–(vii), 32(3)(c)(iii)–(vii).
[262] ADA (n 249) s 14.
[263] ibid s 15(1).
[264] ibid s 15(2).
[265] ibid s 16. This section previously required that age be the 'dominant' reason: see Disability Discrimination and Other Human Rights Legislation Amendment Act 2009 (Cth) sch 1.
[266] ADA (n 249) s 18(1)–(2).

employment; and work 'under a contract for services' (ie, independent contractors or the self-employed).[267] Other parts of the ADA prohibit discrimination against commission agents,[268] contract workers,[269] and partners (in partnerships of six or more);[270] and by qualifying bodies,[271] employer and employee organizations,[272] and employment agencies.[273]

There are substantial exceptions to the prohibition of discrimination in the ADA as it relates to work, including for domestic duties,[274] the inherent requirements of the position,[275] youth wages, positive discrimination,[276] governing rules of charities,[277] religious bodies,[278] superannuation[279] and insurance,[280] pensions and social security,[281] taxation,[282] government employment programmes,[283] compliance with other laws and court orders,[284] and exemptions granted by the AHRC.[285] These exceptions significantly limit the scope and protection afforded by the ADA; many of these exceptions are replicated at state and territory level.[286]

Each state and territory in Australia has its own statute prohibiting age discrimination at work. These differ from federal laws in key respects. First, states and territories have adopted unified anti-discrimination statutes, with each jurisdiction having one piece of legislation that covers all protected grounds. By contrast, at the federal level, there are five separate discrimination statutes, four of which are based on different protected grounds.

Second, in relation to the definition of discrimination, most jurisdictions have separate definitions of direct and indirect discrimination.[287] Some states have adopted more flexible tests for determining when direct discrimination occurs. For example, rather than requiring a comparator, Victoria, the ACT, and South Australia (SA) define direct discrimination as being treated 'unfavourably',[288]

[267] ibid s 5.
[268] ibid s 19.
[269] ibid s 20.
[270] ibid s 21.
[271] ibid s 22.
[272] ibid s 23.
[273] ibid s 24.
[274] ibid s 18(3).
[275] See, eg, ibid s 18(4).
[276] ibid s 33.
[277] ibid s 34.
[278] ibid s 35.
[279] ibid s 38.
[280] ibid s 37.
[281] ibid s 41.
[282] ibid s 40.
[283] ibid s 41A.
[284] ibid s 39.
[285] ibid s 44.
[286] Blackham, 'A Compromised Balance?' (n 186).
[287] See, eg, Equal Opportunity Act 2010 (Vic), ss 8, 9.
[288] Equal Opportunity Act 2010 (Vic), s 8(1); Discrimination Act 1991 (ACT), s 8(2); Equal Opportunity Act 1984 (SA), s 85A.

rather than *less* favourably. In the Northern Territory (NT), though, no distinction between direct and indirect discrimination is made:[289] discrimination is defined broadly as including 'any distinction, restriction, exclusion or preference made on the basis of an attribute that has the effect of nullifying or impairing equality of opportunity.'[290]

Third, in relation to causation, most jurisdictions require discrimination to occur because of,[291] on the grounds of,[292] or 'on the basis of'[293] age. However, age does not need to be the only, sole, or dominant reason,[294] though in some jurisdictions it must be 'a substantial reason.'[295] In the ACT, too, the statute is explicitly required to be interpreted in a way that is beneficial to those with protected attributes.[296]

Intersectionality is generally not recognized in Australian equality law.[297] The exception is in the ACT, which recognizes additive discrimination in s 8 of the Discrimination Act 1991 (ACT):

> (2) … a person directly discriminates against someone else if the person treats, or proposes to treat, another person unfavourably because the other person has 1 or more protected attributes.
>
> (3) … a person indirectly discriminates against someone else if the person imposes, or proposes to impose, a condition or requirement that has, or is likely to have, the effect of disadvantaging the other person because the other person has 1 or more protected attributes.[298]

Accommodating additive discrimination does not fully reflect the complex 'compoundedness' of intersectionality.[299]

2. Enforcement

While the process of individual enforcement varies from jurisdiction to jurisdiction, there are noticeable similarities. In all jurisdictions bar Victoria, claims under equality law must first be lodged with the relevant statutory equality commission,

289 Anti-Discrimination Act 1992 (NT), s 20.
290 ibid s 20(1).
291 Equal Opportunity Act 2010 (Vic), s 8(1); Equal Opportunity Act 1984 (SA), s 85A; Discrimination Act 1991 (ACT), s 8(2).
292 Anti-Discrimination Act 1977 (NSW), s 49ZYA; Equal Opportunity Act 1984 (WA), s 66V.
293 Anti-Discrimination Act 1998 (Tas), s 14(2); Anti-Discrimination Act 1992 (NT), s 20(1); Anti-Discrimination Act 1991 (Qld), s 10(1).
294 Equal Opportunity Act 2010 (Vic), s 8(2); Anti-Discrimination Act 1992 (NT), s 20(3); Anti-Discrimination Act 1998 (Tas), s 14(2).
295 See, eg, Equal Opportunity Act 2010 (Vic), s 8(2); Anti-Discrimination Act 1991 (Qld), s 10(4).
296 Discrimination Act 1991 (ACT), s 4AA.
297 Blackham and Temple (n 53) 778–81.
298 See Human Rights Commission Act 2005 (ACT), s 42(2).
299 Blackham and Temple (n 53) 780–81.

and parties must undertake compulsory and confidential ADR before proceeding to court or tribunal. Complaints under the ADA, for example, are filed with the AHRC. Similarly, under industrial law, parties must undertake conciliation at the FWC. The vast majority of discrimination complaints are resolved via ADR, and few claims progress further.[300]

Victoria is exceptional, in that claimants may apply directly to the Victorian Civil and Administrative Tribunal (VCAT), whether or not they have brought their dispute to the Victorian Equal Opportunity and Human Rights Commission (VEOHRC),[301] and conciliation at the VEOHRC is voluntary.[302] However, it appears comparatively rare for claimants to bypass the VEOHRC's mechanisms.[303]

If conciliation is unsuccessful, a claimant may file at—or have their complaint referred to—a court or tribunal. It is here that state and territory laws diverge from the federal system. First, in the states and territories, discrimination complaints are typically heard by tribunals at first instance, not formal courts. This allows for a more flexible approach to procedural rules. VCAT, for example, is 'bound by the rules of natural justice', but not by rules of evidence or procedure.[304] VCAT 'may inform itself on any matter as it sees fit' and is required to 'conduct each proceeding with as little formality and technicality, and ... as much speed, as ... a proper consideration of the matters before it permit'.[305] At the federal level, though, if a complaint is terminated by the AHRC, a claimant may make an application to either the Federal Circuit Court of Australia (FCCA) (formerly the Federal Magistrates Court) or the Federal Court of Australia (FCA),[306] and proceedings will be conducted in accordance with fairly onerous procedural rules.[307]

Second, while costs may be awarded in state and territory tribunals, this is far less likely than at the federal level. In federal courts, costs typically follow the event,[308] except in proceedings under the FWA.[309] In its 2016 *Willing to Work* report, the AHRC recommended that parties to discrimination matters in the federal

300 Therese MacDermott, 'Resolving Federal Age Discrimination Complaints: Where Have All the Complainants Gone?' (2013) 24 Australasian Dispute Resolution Journal 102.

301 Equal Opportunity Act 2010 (Vic), s 122.

302 ibid s 112(d).

303 Dominique Allen, 'Addressing Discrimination Through Individual Enforcement: A Case Study of Victoria' (2019) 19.

304 Victorian Civil and Administrative Tribunal Act 1998 (Vic), s 98(1)(a)–(b).

305 ibid s 98(1)(c)–(d).

306 Australian Human Rights Commission Act 1986 (Cth), s 46PO(1).

307 See, eg, Federal Circuit Court of Australia Act 1999 (Cth), ss 43, 81; Federal Circuit Court Rules 2001.

308 Federal Circuit Court of Australia Act 1999 (Cth), s 79; Federal Court of Australia Act 1976 (Cth), s 43.

309 Federal Circuit Court of Australia Act 1999 (Cth), s 79(1); Federal Court of Australia Act 1976 (Cth), s 43(1)(b). In those proceedings, costs may only be awarded if the proceedings were initiated 'vexatiously or without reasonable cause'; the party's unreasonable behaviour caused the other party to incur costs; or the party unreasonably refused to participate in the proceedings: FWA (n 238) s 570(2). Cost orders may also be made against a state or territory (s 569A) or the Commonwealth (s 569) if they intervene in proceedings or institute an appeal.

courts bear their own costs, with the court retaining a discretion to make costs orders in some circumstances.[310] This is consistent with the situation in state and territory jurisdictions.[311] That said, even if tribunals rarely award costs, claimants may be fearful of exposing themselves to cost orders (Chapter 4).

Third, time limits vary across the jurisdictions. In some states and territories, there is no fixed time limit on claiming: rather, the equality agency may choose to decline to conciliate,[312] terminate a complaint,[313] close a complaint,[314] or decline a complaint[315] if the claim is out of time. This time period is twelve months in New South Wales (NSW)[316] and Victoria;[317] two years in the ACT;[318] and six months at the AHRC.[319] Other jurisdictions have more fixed time requirements: in Tasmania, SA, NT, Western Australia (WA), and Queensland, for example, complaints must be filed within twelve months; a complaint may be accepted outside this window in Tasmania if the Commissioner is 'satisfied that it is reasonable to do so';[320] in Queensland if 'satisfied the complainant has shown good cause';[321] if 'appropriate to do so' in NT;[322] in WA on 'good cause being shown';[323] and in SA if there is 'good reason' why the claim was out of time or it is just and equitable to do so.[324]

3. Beyond individual enforcement

Australian statutory equality agencies typically have very limited enforcement powers.[325] By contrast, industrial regulation bodies (such as the FWO) have far more extensive powers.[326] Thus, agency enforcement of anti-discrimination law by the FWO is at least possible,[327] so long as age discrimination becomes an ongoing priority for the FWO (Chapter 8).

[310] AHRC, 'Willing to Work: National Inquiry into Employment Discrimination Against Older Australians and Australians with Disability' (2016) 21, 337–8.

[311] See, eg, Victorian Civil and Administrative Tribunal Act 1998 (Vic), ss 109(1), 109(3).

[312] Equal Opportunity Act 2010 (Vic), s 116(a).

[313] Australian Human Rights Commission Act 1986 (Cth), s 46PH(1)(b).

[314] Human Rights Commission Act 2005 (ACT), s 78(1)(a).

[315] Anti-Discrimination Act 1977 (NSW), s 89B(2)(b).

[316] ibid s 89B(2)(b).

[317] Equal Opportunity Act 2010 (Vic), s 116(a).

[318] Human Rights Commission Act 2005 (ACT), s 78(1)(a).

[319] Australian Human Rights Commission Act 1986 (Cth), s 46PH(1)(b).

[320] Anti-Discrimination Act 1998 (Tas), s 63.

[321] Anti-Discrimination Act 1991 (Qld), s 138.

[322] Anti-Discrimination Act 1992 (NT), s 65.

[323] Equal Opportunity Act 1984 (WA), s 83(4)–(5).

[324] Equal Opportunity Act 1984 (SA), s 93(2)–(2a).

[325] Dominique Allen, 'Barking and Biting: The Equal Opportunity Commission as an Enforcement Agency' (2016) 44 Federal Law Review 311.

[326] Therese MacDermott, 'Affirming Age: Making Federal Anti-Discrimination Regulation Work for Older Australians' (2013) 26 Australian Journal of Labour Law 141, 150–51; Therese MacDermott, 'Challenging Age Discrimination in Australian Workplaces: From Anti-Discrimination Legislation to Industrial Regulation' (2011) 34 University of New South Wales Law Journal 182, 206–07.

[327] MacDermott, 'Affirming Age' (n 326) 150–51; MacDermott, 'Challenging Age Discrimination' (n 326) 206–07. See *Fair Work Ombudsman v Theravanish Investments Pty Ltd* [2014] FCCA 1170.

There is limited collective enforcement of age discrimination law in Australia; age equality is rarely a priority for groups or unions. In the 2016 *Willing to Work* report, the AHRC recommended a review of standing provisions in federal discrimination law, with a view to allowing initiation of matters by representative organizations with leave of the court.[328] Even in the context of low union density, reforms to the legal process may help to facilitate the collective enforcement of equality rights (Chapter 9).

Positive duties are generally uncommon in Australia, though limited positive duties are imposed on employers in Victoria, Tasmania, Queensland, and the ACT, through both equality law and human rights law. The AHRC has recommended that the government consider the benefits of a positive duty to 'promote substantive equality or eliminate discrimination' being added to federal discrimination laws in Australia.[329] MacDermott has argued that such a duty will be of assistance to older workers only if it is 'framed in a robust way that focuses on the steps necessary to achieve equality, applies to both the public and private sectors, and includes details on the specific obligations that underpin the general duty'.[330] Framed in this way, positive duties could change the landscape of discrimination law in Australia, representing a fundamental shift away from individual enforcement (Chapter 7). Overall, then, as in the UK, the weight of enforcement of age discrimination law has fallen on individuals, across all Australian jurisdictions.

C. Canada

Like Australia, Canada is a federal nation. However, unlike Australia, the Canadian Parliament has a broad power to legislate 'for the Peace, Order, and good Government of Canada',[331] except in areas exclusively reserved for the Provinces.[332] Equality rights are protected at federal, provincial, and territorial level.

1. Legal framework

At the federal level, equality rights are framed as human rights.[333] The *Canadian Charter of Rights and Freedoms*,[334] which applies to Canadian governments and legislatures,[335] says in s 15:

[328] AHRC, 'Willing to Work' (n 310) 21, 332–33.
[329] ibid 21, 334.
[330] MacDermott, 'Affirming Age' (n 326) 156.
[331] Constitution Acts, 1867 to 1982, c 91.
[332] ibid c 92.
[333] On the development of these provisions, see Kathleen Mahoney, 'The Constitutional Law of Equality in Canada' (1992) 44 Maine Law Review 229.
[334] Part I of the Constitution Act, 1982, enacted as sch B to the Canada Act 1982, c 11 (UK) (Charter).
[335] ibid s 32(1).

> (1) Every individual is equal before the and under the law and has the right to the equal protection and equal benefit of the law without discrimination and, in particular, without discrimination based on race, national or ethnic origin, colour, religion, sex, age, or mental or physical disability.
>
> (2) Subsection (1) does not preclude any law, program or activity that has as its object the amelioration of conditions of disadvantaged individuals or groups including those that are disadvantaged because or race, national or ethnic origin, colour, religion, sex, age, or mental or physical disability.[336]

This right is 'subject only to such reasonable limits prescribed by law as can be demonstrably justified in a free and democratic society'.[337] Rights in the Charter may be enforced by individuals.[338]

The Canadian Human Rights Act (RSC, 1985, c H-6) prohibits discrimination on the grounds of age.[339] The purpose of the Act is framed broadly: it is

> to give effect ... to the principle that all individuals should have an opportunity equal with other individuals to make for themselves the lives that they are able and wish to have and to have their needs accommodated, consistent with their duties and obligations as members of society, without being hindered in or prevented from doing so by discriminatory practices based on ... age ....[340]

In relation to employment, s 7 says

> It is a discriminatory practice, directly or indirectly,
> (a) to refuse to employ or continue to employ any individual, or
> (b) in the course of employment, to differentiate adversely in relation to an employee,
>
> on a prohibited ground of discrimination.[341]

[336] In *McKinney v University of Guelph* [1990] 3 SCR 229, 76 DLR (4th) 545, this was used to challenge the Ontario Human Rights Code, which in s 10(1) defined 'age' as being between 18 and 65 years, excluding protection for those beyond this age range. The Supreme Court of Canada held that the limit was reasonable under s 1. See further Robert E Charney and Matthew Horner, 'Defending Age Distinctions in Employee Benefits after the Elimination of Mandatory Retirement' (2013) 17 Canadian Labour and Employment Law Journal 255, 258–62.

[337] Charter s 1. This exception has proven fatal to many age-based claims: see Kenneth WM Thornicroft, 'The Uncertain State of Mandatory Retirement in Canada' (2016) 67 Labor Law Journal 397, 398–400.

[338] Charter s 24(1). On the theory and implementation of s 15, see Fay Faraday, Margaret Ann Denike, and M Kate Stephenson (eds), *Making Equality Rights Real: Securing Substantive Equality under the Charter* (Irwin Law 2006).

[339] Canadian Human Rights Act (RSC, 1985, c. H-6), s 3(1).

[340] ibid s 2.

[341] See ibid s 8 in relation to recruitment, s 9 in relation to employee organizations, and s 10 in relation to discriminatory practices.

The Act also prohibits harassment[342] and retaliation for filing a complaint.[343] Exceptions are provided for bona fide occupational requirements (BFOR), minimum and maximum ages under employment laws, discrimination in a manner deemed by guidelines to be reasonable,[344] and special programmes.[345] This may mean mandatory retirement remains legally permitted in many contexts.[346] Similar protection from age discrimination is afforded at the provincial and territorial level in relation to non-federally regulated entities.[347]

Compared to the UK and Australia, the Canadian legal framework is exceptional for five key reasons.[348] First, Canadian discrimination law has a stronger basis in human rights law than that in other jurisdictions, especially given rights in the Charter can be enforced by individuals. This influences how discrimination law is interpreted:[349] Smith argues that the open-textured nature of Canadian discrimination law has led to more purposive and sophisticated judicial interpretation than in Australia.[350] Canadian courts have emphasized the need for substantive equality and change, rejecting an approach grounded in formal equality.[351]

Second, Canadian law makes no distinction between direct and indirect discrimination, instead adopting a unified approach.[352] Further, the law does not strictly require the use of a comparator,[353] though comparisons are sometimes used, especially in age discrimination cases.[354]

Third, as under the EqA and FWA, there is a shifting burden of proof in Canada.[355] Once a claimant can show that a standard is prima facie discriminatory, the burden shifts to the employer to justify the standard as a BFOR.[356]

[342] ibid s 14.
[343] ibid s 14.1.
[344] ibid s 15.
[345] ibid s 16(1).
[346] Thornicroft (n 337).
[347] At the provincial level, taking British Columbia as an example, see the Human Rights Code [RSBC 1996, ch 210]. On the interplay between provincial and federal law, see Charney and Horner (n 336).
[348] See Belinda Smith and Dominique Allen, 'Whose Fault is it?: Asking the Right Question to Address Discrimination' (2012) 37 Alternative Law Journal 31, 34.
[349] Belinda Smith, 'Rethinking the Sex Discrimination Act-Does Canada's Experience Suggest We Should Give Our Judges a Greater Role?' in Margaret Thornton (ed), *Sex Discrimination in Uncertain Times* (ANU E Press 2010) 246.
[350] ibid 255–56.
[351] *Andrews v Law Society of British Columbia* [1989] 1 SCR 143; *Law v Canada* [1999] 1 SCR 497, [25].
[352] *British Columbia (Public Service Employee Relations Commission) v BCGSEU* [1999] 3 SCR 3, [50]–[53].
[353] See Beth Gaze and Belinda Smith, *Equality and Discrimination Law in Australia: An Introduction* (CUP 2017) 281–84. One basis on which the Canadian Supreme Court rejected strict reliance on a comparator was due to the need to accommodate intersectionality: *Withler v Canada* [2011] 1 SCR 396, [58].
[354] Pnina Alon-Shenker, '"Age is Different": Revisiting the Contemporary Understanding of Age Discrimination in the Employment Setting' (2013) 17 Canadian Labour & Employment Law Journal 31, 35. See, eg, *Law v Canada* (n 351) [56]–[58].
[355] *Ontario Human Rights Commission v Simpsons-Sears* [1985] 2 SCR 536, [28].
[356] See, eg, *British Columbia (Public Service Employee Relations Commission) v BCGSEU* (n 352) [54], [70]; *Bhinder v Canadian National Railway Company* [1985] 2 SCR 561, [42].

Fourth, through this shifting burden of proof, reasonable accommodations are required for all protected grounds, not just disability. To establish that treatment is a BFOR under the Canadian Human Rights Act, for example,

> it must be established that accommodation of the needs of an individual or a class of individuals affected would impose undue hardship on the person who would have to accommodate those needs, considering health, safety and cost.[357]

Thus, a requirement to accommodate individual needs is built into the BFOR defence. Alon-Shenker criticizes this as being part of an affirmative *defence* rather than an affirmative *duty*.[358] The duty only arises in response to an individual request for accommodation, and employers are only required to prove accommodation once an employee files and establishes a prima facie case of age discrimination.[359] Thus, the duty is likely to have limited effect in practice; few cases relate to the duty to accommodate older workers, and those that do adopt a narrow interpretation of the duty.[360] There is a need, then, for courts and tribunals to interpret the duty of accommodation more broadly, reflecting a shift from individual accommodation to systemic accommodation;[361] this is consistent with a Dignified Lives Approach to age (Chapter 2).[362]

Fifth, unlike in Australia and the UK, the Canadian Human Rights Act (RSC, 1985, c H-6) contains specific provision for intersectionality (or, at least, additive and compound discrimination): s 3.1 says,

> For greater certainty, a discriminatory practice includes a practice based on one or more prohibited grounds of discrimination or on the effect of a combination of prohibited grounds.

Intersectionality has been recognized by Canadian courts as part of a contextual approach to understanding (in)equality.[363] That said, it is still common for courts to consider individual protected grounds in isolation.[364]

[357] Canadian Human Rights Act (RSC, 1985, c H-6) s 15(2). Alon-Shenker and Davidov argue that this test for bona fide occupational requirements implicitly reflects a proportionality test: Pnina Alon-Shenker and Guy Davidov, 'Applying the Principle of Proportionality in Employment and Labour Law Contexts' (2013) 59 McGill Law Journal 375, 396–99.

[358] Pnina Alon-Shenker, 'Legal Barriers to Age Discrimination in Hiring Complaints' (2016) 39 Dalhousie Law Journal 289, 317.

[359] ibid.

[360] Pnina Alon-Shenker, 'Duty to Accommodate Senior Workers: Its Nature, Scope and Limitations' (2012–13) 38 Queen's Law Journal 165, 194.

[361] Alon-Shenker, 'Legal Barriers to Age Discrimination in Hiring Complaints' (n 358) 323.

[362] Alon-Shenker, 'Duty to Accommodate Senior Workers' (n 360).

[363] See, eg, *Withler v Canada* [2011] 1 SCR 396, [58]; *Turner v Canada (Attorney General)* [2012] FCA 159, [48]–[49]; *Turner v Canada Border Services Agency* [2020] CHRT 1 (CanLII) <https://canlii.ca/t/j81w8> accessed 26 March 2021.

[364] Pnina Alon-Shenker and Therese MacDermott, 'Intersecting Age and Gender in Workplace Discrimination Complaints' (2020) 41 Comparative Labor Law and Policy Journal 521, 531.

Together, Smith and Allen argue that these features of discrimination law in Canada 'combine to transform a negative duty of non-discrimination into a positive obligation to promote equality'.[365] Canadian scholars take a more circumspect approach, especially in the context of age equality. For example, Fudge argues that, despite very different regulatory frameworks, the approach to resolving claims by older workers is virtually the same in the Supreme Court of Canada and the Court of Justice of the European Union.[366] Alon-Shenker argues that the Canadian test for discrimination (based on the Charter case of *R v Kapp*[367]) fails to accommodate the nature of age discrimination, and places too little value on age equality, instead over-emphasizing stereotyping or prejudice and the 'fair innings' argument.[368] Similarly, Bisnar and McIntyre argue for the need to frame Charter claims as intersectional, in order to surmount the idea that age discrimination is 'different' to other grounds of discrimination.[369] Alon-Shenker therefore puts forward a Dignified Lives Approach as an alternative approach to age discrimination matters;[370] this broader approach would encourage a more just approach to cases of age discrimination.

2. Enforcement

The Canadian Human Rights Commission (CHRC) is responsible for the administration of the Canadian Human Rights Act (RSC, 1985, c H-6) and receives complaints under Part III of the Act. A discriminatory act may be the subject of a complaint to the CHRC by an individual or group who have reasonable grounds to believe a person is engaging or has engaged in a discriminatory practice.[371] The person affected does not necessarily need to file the complaint. However, if the person impacted does not consent to the complaint, then the CHRC may refuse to deal with the matter.[372] The CHRC itself may also initiate a complaint where it has reasonable grounds to believe a person has engaged or is engaging in a discriminatory practice.[373] Separate complaints may be dealt with together if they involve substantially the same issues of fact and law.[374]

A complaint may not be dealt with if:

[365] Smith and Allen (n 348) 35.

[366] Judy Fudge, 'Dignity, Disadvantage, and Age: Putting Constitutional and Fundamental Rights to Work for Older Workers' in Ann Numhauser-Henning (ed), *Elder Law: Evolving European Perspectives* (Edward Elgar 2017) 84.

[367] [2008] 2 SCR 483.

[368] Alon-Shenker, '"Age is Different"' (n 354) 35–42.

[369] Danielle Bisnar and Elizabeth McIntyre, 'Lessons for Litigators from ONA v. Chatham-Kent: A Union Perspective' (2013) 17 Canadian Labour & Employment Law Journal 225, 227–28.

[370] Alon-Shenker, '"Age is Different"' (n 354) 44.

[371] Canadian Human Rights Act (RSC, 1985, c. H-6) s 40(1).

[372] ibid s 40(2).

[373] ibid s 40(3).

[374] ibid s 40(4).

- It purely relies on statistical information to argue that a group is under-represented in the workforce;[375]
- There are other grievance or review procedures that are reasonably available;
- The complaint is more appropriately dealt with under a different Act;
- The complaint is beyond the Commission's jurisdiction;
- The complaint is trivial, frivolous, vexatious, or made in bad faith; or
- The acts occurred more than one year prior to the complaint, or such longer period of time considered appropriate by the CHRC.[376]

The CHRC may investigate a complaint, including by entering and searching premises with a warrant and requiring the production of documents.[377] The report of an investigation can lead to an inquiry by the Canadian Human Rights Tribunal (CHRT),[378] or to the appointment of a conciliator to attempt settlement[379] (this can also be done immediately upon the filing of a complaint). Terms of settlement must be approved or rejected by the CHRC.[380]

In conducting an inquiry, proceedings of the CHRT must be 'conducted as informally and expeditiously as the requirements of natural justice and the rules of procedure allow'.[381] The CHRT is to inquire into the complaint; the complainant and respondent—and potentially other interested parties—can present evidence and make representations.[382] In appearing at an inquiry, the CHRC can adopt whatever position it deems to be in the public interest.[383]

If an inquiry finds a complaint is substantiated, an order may be made against the person who committed the discriminatory practice, including that they: cease the discriminatory practice; take measures to redress it or prevent it occurring in the future; make available to the victim any rights, opportunities, or privileges they were denied; and/or compensate the victim for any expenses and/or for pain and suffering (the latter not exceeding $20,000).[384] Additional compensation may be awarded for wilful or reckless discriminatory practices (again not exceeding $20,000).[385] The CHRT cannot require an employer to adopt a special programme to increase the representation of certain groups in the workforce,[386] as opposed to ceasing a discriminatory practice.[387]

375 ibid s 40.1(2).
376 ibid s 41(1).
377 ibid s 43.
378 ibid ss 44(3), 49.
379 ibid s 47.
380 ibid s 48.
381 ibid s 48.9(1).
382 ibid s 50(1).
383 ibid s 51.
384 ibid s 53(2).
385 ibid s 53(3).
386 ibid s 54(2).
387 ibid s 54(3).

The Canadian system of enforcement is notable for two key reasons. First, there is a broader approach to enforcement, as claims may be filed by an individual or group with reasonable grounds to believe a person is engaging or has engaged in a discriminatory practice[388] or the CHRC itself, even if the person impacted does not file a complaint. This places less responsibility on impacted individuals to navigate the process of naming, blaming, and claiming.

Second, the Canadian system integrates a public aspect into private conciliation and individual complaints. This occurs through the CHRC itself initiating complaints, potential investigation of complaints by a public body, the review of settlement terms by the CHRC, and the CHRC's appearance at inquiries. This public aspect is not routinely or explicitly integrated into individual enforcement in Australia or the UK.

How these provisions are operating in practice can be gleaned to some extent from the annual reports of the CHRC. In its 2019 Annual Report, the CHRC reported receiving 36,000 contacts, which led to 1,203 complaints being accepted by the Commission.[389] Nearly half (42 per cent) of the complaints received were from Ontario;[390] and 58 per cent related to employment.[391] Nine per cent of accepted complaints related to age.[392] In 2019, one in three accepted complaints were mediated, and 52 per cent of these reached a settlement.[393] The CHRC represented the public interest in more than 200 cases before the CHRT in 2019.[394] An additional eighty-five cases were referred to the CHRT in 2019, 77 per cent of which related to employment.[395] This represents around 7 per cent of accepted complaints.

In practice, then, the way discrimination law operates in Canada at the federal level appears similar to Australia, with the CHRC receiving and mediating many complaints. The difference, though, is that a higher proportion of complaints proceed to the CHRT. It is up to the CHRC to refer complaints to the CHRT; in Australia, this relies on individuals pursuing their claim to court. Like in Australia, there is limited official data on age discrimination complaints in Canada, and data is not well disaggregated at provincial level.[396] Thus, federal systems of government may well make data collection more complex in this field.

As in Australia and the UK, few cases proceed to hearing in Canada: in Ontario, for example, in 2017–18 only 97 cases were decided 'on the merits' by the Ontario Human Rights Tribunal.[397] Like in other jurisdictions, Canadian claimants

[388] ibid s 40(1).
[389] Canadian Human Rights Commission, 'Stand Together: The Canadian Human Rights Commission's 2019 Annual Report to Parliament' (2020) 51 <https://www.chrc-ccdp.gc.ca/sites/default/files/publication-pdfs/chrc_ar_2019-eng_0.pdf> accessed 18 March 2022.
[390] ibid 52.
[391] ibid 53.
[392] ibid 54.
[393] ibid 58.
[394] ibid 61.
[395] ibid 62.
[396] Alon-Shenker, 'Legal Barriers to Age Discrimination in Hiring Complaints' (n 358) 298–99.
[397] Alon-Shenker and MacDermott (n 364) 534.

encounter issues of proof or evidence, especially where age discrimination is subtle or systemic;[398] many cases settle.[399] Reviewing sixty-nine Ontario Human Rights Tribunal decisions from 2004–15 on age discrimination in hiring, Alon-Shenker argues that few complaints are upheld (only six in this sample), flagging difficulties in the way Canadian discrimination law has responded to hiring complaints.[400] In Ontario, men are more likely to file a complaint of age discrimination than women: examining 313 age discrimination in employment complaints filed over a ten year period, Alon-Shenker and MacDermott found 196 complaints filed by men, 112 filed by women, and five filed by both genders.[401] Intersectional complaints were rare,[402] flagging difficulties with the way the law is enforced in practice. Thus, the apparent strengths of the Canadian legal framework do not necessarily flow through to better outcomes for claimants in practice.

3. Beyond individual enforcement

Recognizing the limits of the individual enforcement model, Alon-Shenker identifies a need for unions to better support job applicants in challenging age discrimination in recruitment; and for simplified mechanisms for bringing class actions or NGO-initiated complaints.[403]

There are few positive obligations or duties on Canadian employers in relation to age. The Employment Equity Act (SC 1995, c 44), which creates positive duties for the employment of women, Aboriginal peoples, persons with disabilities, and members of visible minorities, does not apply to age. Alon-Shenker therefore suggests adopting legislation to promote age equality in the workplace, including by requiring written hiring policies that promote age diversity, introducing reporting duties regarding selection processes, and to broaden the scope of the duty of accommodation.[404] In Canada, like in Australia and the UK, mechanisms beyond individual enforcement have not yet been fully realized in practice.

V. Conclusion

Age discrimination legislation has significant potential to respond to the challenges and opportunities of demographic ageing, and to facilitate decent work for those of all ages. However, while the UK, Canada, and Australia have grounded their age discrimination laws on an individual enforcement model, it appears unrealistic to

398 Alon-Shenker, 'Legal Barriers to Age Discrimination in Hiring Complaints' (n 358) 300–01.
399 Alon-Shenker and MacDermott (n 364) 534.
400 Alon-Shenker, 'Legal Barriers to Age Discrimination in Hiring Complaints' (n 358) 300.
401 Alon-Shenker and MacDermott (n 364) 535.
402 ibid 535–46.
403 Alon-Shenker, 'Legal Barriers to Age Discrimination in Hiring Complaints' (n 358) 323–24.
404 ibid 324.

rely on individual litigation as the primary means of addressing age-based discrimination in employment. Those who experience discrimination are unlikely to have the awareness, capacity, and willingness to enforce these rights in practice. This chapter has therefore identified significant theoretical and practical limitations of the individual enforcement model, including its limited view of equality, and inability to deal with avoidance and withdrawal behaviours. In Part II of this book, I draw on two empirical case studies of the individual enforcement of age discrimination law in the UK and Australia to further illustrate the practical limitations of the individual enforcement model, and the way in which it fails to address the needs of particular claimants.

This chapter has flagged three alternatives to individual enforcement models, including positive duties, agency enforcement, and collective structures. These options are explored in more detail in Part III, in Chapters 7, 8 and 9 respectively. However, it is important to complement alternative models with individual enforcement; abandoning or severely restricting individual claims is counterproductive. Thus, this book puts forward a quadripartite model of reform, encompassing improvements to individual enforcement, as well as reforms to strengthen positive duties, agency enforcement, and collective structures.

PART II

ENFORCING AGE DISCRIMINATION LAW

Empirical Case Studies

Chapter 3 has identified substantial theoretical and practical limitations of the individual enforcement model. At the same time, individual enforcement remains the primary mechanism for preventing and addressing age discrimination at work in the United Kingdom (UK) and Australia. The question, then, is how are these mechanisms working in practice? Are the risks of the individual enforcement model being realized? Or is enforcement generally working, despite the potential risks and limits of the individual enforcement model? Could individual enforcement be improved, to strengthen outcomes for claimants, respondents, and the general public?

It is to these questions that Part II turns. Drawing on empirical case studies of the enforcement of age discrimination law in the UK and Australia, Chapters 4, 5, and 6 examine how these laws are operating in practice. Utilizing mixed methods, including doctrinal analysis, qualitative expert interviews, quantitative analysis of data from equality agencies, courts and tribunals, a survey of advocates, and content analysis of cases, the chapters provide compelling empirical evidence of the barriers inhibiting individual enforcement in practice. Building on a 'naming, blaming, and claiming' lens and the pyramid of disputes (as put forward in Chapter 3), the chapters map the limits of individual enforcement across the stages of claiming (Chapter 4), alternative dispute resolution (Chapter 5), and hearing and judgment (Chapter 6).

As these chapters show, individual enforcement of age discrimination law is not, for the most part, working. Not only are the risks of the individual enforcement model being realized in practice, but it appears that reliance on individual enforcement is substantially disadvantaging particular groups, including older women and younger workers. These chapters therefore put forward a range of specific reforms which could help to strengthen individual enforcement. Overall, though, these empirical case studies provide a compelling case for the need to look beyond individual enforcement: this is taken up in Part III.

4
Claiming

I. Introduction

As Chapter 3 has mapped, individual enforcement fundamentally depends on individuals first navigating the fraught process of 'naming, blaming, and claiming',[1] even prior to encountering the legal system. Naming and blaming may be especially problematic in the context of age discrimination law, as individuals may fail to identify conduct as being discriminatory,[2] including due to internalized age norms;[3] or may be unable to identify who to blame for particular conduct. Assuming, though, that naming and blaming occurs, individual enforcement then requires *claiming*: that is, for individuals to voice their grievance, and seek a remedy.[4] A rejected claim then becomes a dispute.[5] Claims could be raised with respondents directly; or could be directed to third parties for assistance, such as unions, advocates, or statutory agencies.

Using empirical case studies of the enforcement of age discrimination law in the United Kingdom (UK) and Australia, in this chapter I consider the process of *claiming*, and identify potential gaps in enforcement even at this preliminary stage of pursuing individual rights. Drawing on enquiry and claim statistics from statutory agencies and community legal centres (CLCs), qualitative expert interviews and a survey of advocates, I consider why age discrimination claims are so infrequent, given the reported prevalence of age discrimination in employment (mapped in Chapter 1). I argue that the fraught process of transforming injuries into disputes, and the filtering of claims, means individual age discrimination claims occur at far lower rates than might be expected based on the prevalence of discriminatory treatment. This chapter therefore highlights the fundamental limits of relying on individual claims to address age discrimination, even at this preliminary stage of enforcement.

[1] William LF Felstiner, Richard L Abel, and Austin Sarat, 'The Emergence and Transformation of Disputes: Naming, Blaming, Claiming . . .' (1980) 15 Law & Society Review 631, 632.

[2] Ralph Fevre, Heidi Grainger, and Rioch Brewer, 'Discrimination and Unfair Treatment in the Workplace' (2011) 49 British Journal of Industrial Relations s207, s212.

[3] Kelly Harris and others, 'Ageism and the Older Worker: A Scoping Review' (2018) 58 Gerontologist e1, e7.

[4] Felstiner, Abel, and Sarat (n 1) 635–36.

[5] ibid 636.

Reforming Age Discrimination Law. Alysia Blackham, Oxford University Press. © Alysia Blackham 2022.
DOI: 10.1093/oso/9780198859284.003.0004

II. A Lost Area of Claiming?

A. Infrequent Complaints

There is a noticeable absence of age discrimination claims in both Australia[6] and the UK. In Australia, complaints are 'relatively low' compared to complaints on the basis of other protected attributes.[7] In the Australian Human Rights Commission's (AHRC) *Willing to Work* inquiry, under-reporting of age discrimination was the most frequently raised concern relating to the effectiveness of the legal framework.[8] The inquiry concluded that 'many people in the community who experience discrimination on the basis of their age ... do not take any action in response'.[9] Similarly, in Great Britain (GB), Julie Dennis, Head of Diversity and Inclusion at Acas (the Advisory, Conciliation and Arbitration Service), noted in her evidence to the House of Commons Women and Equalities Committee (WEC) that age discrimination notifications 'are really low'.[10]

In this study, there was a strong sense among respondents that age discrimination complaints are relatively infrequent, across both Australia and the UK. Indeed, when asked how effective the enforcement of age discrimination law is in practice, one respondent noted: 'It's not'.[11] This is not because people are not experiencing age discrimination at work; rather, people are not pursuing formal complaints to address the discrimination they experience.[12] CLCs and practitioners rarely receive enquiries about age discrimination;[13] complaints are 'almost unheard of'.[14] The number of age discrimination complaints received by equality agencies is 'relatively low', meaning there is likely more discrimination occurring than what comes to the agencies.[15] There was a general consensus on this point across nearly all respondents, in all jurisdictions.[16]

This is not what had been expected when age discrimination laws were introduced: according to one equality agency in the UK, they had been warned by colleagues in other (non-UK) jurisdictions that they would experience an avalanche of complaints when the laws commenced.[17] That had not

[6] Therese MacDermott, 'Resolving Federal Age Discrimination Complaints: Where Have All the Complainants Gone?' (2013) 24 Australasian Dispute Resolution Journal 102.

[7] AHRC, 'Willing to Work: National Inquiry into Employment Discrimination Against Older Australians and Australians with Disability' (2016) 59, 61.

[8] ibid 320.

[9] ibid 321.

[10] House of Commons, *Oral Evidence: Older People and Employment* HC 2018, 359 Q57 <http://data.parliament.uk/writtenevidence/committeeevidence.svc/evidencedocument/women-and-equalities-committee/older-people-and-employment/oral/76656.html> accessed 21 March 2022.

[11] A101.

[12] UK80; UK78; A3; A4; A5; A101; A103; A105; A108; A112; A113; A158; A169.

[13] A5; A107; A108; A112; UK78.

[14] A169.

[15] A99. See also A3; A4; A101; A102; A105; A110; A113; A150; A151; A155.

[16] cf A153.

[17] UK97.

occurred.[18] That said, one agency noted that they had previously received many age discrimination complaints, but that number had since 'just flat lined'.[19] Another agency noted that they received very few complaints about work particularly:[20] this might be because the costs of mobilizing or complaining in the workplace are potentially so much higher (see Part IV.C).

While a number of UK surveys have examined how people respond to problems at work,[21] their findings tend to be dated, and rarely focus on age discrimination specifically.[22] What these surveys do indicate, though, is that—consistent with the literature discussed in Chapter 3—many people fail to take action when they experience problems at work, though people often seek advice.[23] Very few people engage with formal legal processes:[24] individuals are far more likely to 'lump it', exit, or attempt to resolve a matter internally than to approach external agencies or bring legal proceedings. This is consistent with the findings of the AHRC's *National Prevalence Survey*: of those who had experienced age discrimination in the last two years (n = 309), 43 per cent took no action. The least likely course of action was to discuss or raise the issue with an external organization (5 per cent)—this was less common than leaving the job (6 per cent).[25] Raising or discussing the issue with an external organization also does not necessarily mean filing a complaint—many would have simply made an enquiry or called a phone line. This limited engagement with legal processes therefore represents a systemic limitation of the individual enforcement model, across both jurisdictions.

[18] ibid.

[19] A99.

[20] A105.

[21] For example, the 2008 Fair Treatment at Work survey: Ralph Fevre and others, 'Fair Treatment at Work Report: Findings from the 2008 Survey' (2009) Employment Relations Research Series 103 126–27. See also the 2006–09 English and Welsh Civil and Social Justice Survey: Pascoe Pleasence and others, 'Civil Justice in England and Wales 2009: Report of the 2006–9 English and Welsh Civil and Social Justice Survey' (2010) 49. The 2004 Unrepresented Worker Survey is discussed below: Anna Pollert and Andy Charlwood, 'The Vulnerable Worker in Britain and Problems at Work' (2009) 23 Work, Employment and Society 343, 350.

[22] See the summary in Lizzie Barmes, *Bullying and Behavioural Conflict at Work: The Duality of Individual Rights* (OUP 2016) 28–37.

[23] Anna Pollert and Andy Charlwood, 'The Unorganised Worker: Problems at Work, Routes to Support and Views on Representation' (2008) Working Paper 11 36 <https://uwe-repository.worktribe.com/output/1021196/the-unorganised-wohttprker-problems-at-work-routes-to-support-and-views-on-representation-the-unrepresented-worker-survey-2004-working-paper-11-who-experiences-problems-at-work-what-problems-do-they-experience-what-do-they-do-about-them-and-what-happen> accessed 21 March 2022. See Fevre and others (n 21) 126–27; Pleasence and others (n 21) 49.

[24] In the 2008 Fair Treatment at Work survey, around 3 per cent of respondents made an application to an ET: Fevre and others (n 21) 136. In the 2004 Unrepresented Worker Survey, only 2.4 per cent of respondents began ET proceedings: Pollert and Charlwood, 'The Vulnerable Worker in Britain and Problems at Work' (n 21) 351. These surveys were conducted before the introduction and subsequent abolition of ET fees.

[25] AHRC, 'National Prevalence Survey of Age Discrimination in the Workplace: The Prevalence, Nature and Impact of Workplace Age Discrimination amongst the Australian Population Aged 50 Years and Older' (2015) 68.

At a practical and structural level, it is not surprising that claiming is so infrequent. The *Willing to Work* report identified a myriad of factors that may limit individual enforcement of age discrimination legislation, including: a lack of access to legal assistance; legal complexity; lack of awareness of rights; insufficient financial resources, the potential costs of legal action and fear of adverse costs orders; power disparities between employers and employees, including in relation to financial resources and access to legal advice; the emotional toll of pursuing a complaint; the difficulty of proving discrimination; challenges in meeting the comparator test, particularly in cases of intersectional discrimination; fear of victimization; insufficient remedies, including a lack of reinstatement opportunities and low damages; and that making a complaint will not achieve systemic change.[26] The WEC, following its inquiry into the enforcement of the Equality Act 2010 (EqA), identified similar barriers to individual enforcement of discrimination rights in the UK, including poor rights knowledge, power disparities, legal complexity, gaps in specialist legal support and legal aid, and the cost (financial and emotional) of legal action.[27]

These barriers are recurring themes in the chapters that follow, and affect the stages of claiming (Chapter 4), alternative dispute resolution (ADR) (Chapter 5), and hearing and judgment (Chapter 6). In the face of these substantial barriers, it is perhaps surprising that so many disputes progress as far as they do. That said, these barriers are not unique to age discrimination law; indeed, many affect all protected grounds, and—to some extent—other individual employment rights. The question, then, is why age discrimination law in particular leads to so few complaints.

B. The Particular Limits of Age Discrimination Claiming: Intersectionality and Universality

Age discrimination has a number of specific challenges and limits that might inhibit claiming and reduce claim numbers. While cases might raise age-related issues, age discrimination is rarely the primary or major ground of complaint:[28] age is an 'afterthought', not the 'primary driver'.[29] Claims are more likely to relate primarily to sex,[30] sexual harassment,[31] or disability,[32] flagging the inherently intersectional nature of age-based disadvantage. Even if age is initially raised as an additional or subsidiary ground of complaint, this typically 'falls away pretty

26 AHRC, 'Willing to Work' (n 7) 321–27.

27 Women and Equalities Committee, *Enforcing the Equality Act: The Law and the Role of the Equality and Human Rights Commission* (2017–19 HC 1470) 7–8.

28 A99; A100; A169.

29 A99.

30 A169.

31 A100.

32 A113.

quickly'.[33] Given the way discrimination statutes are framed, there is no benefit to pursuing multiple grounds of claim:[34] pursuing two grounds simply means there is a requirement to prove discrimination on the basis of two attributes.[35] It is easier to simply focus on the obvious and easier ground, which is only rarely age.[36] Thus, while age may amplify other forms of inequality and discrimination, limited statutory provision for intersectionality may limit the extent to which this is reflected and accommodated in legal claiming.

At the same time, the universality of age may affect claim numbers. Every claimant has an age, meaning every claimant can potentially list age as a ground of discrimination. Some claimants tick every box (including age) when they file a complaint, particularly if they are unrepresented.[37] This is understandable, given the complexity of identifying and attributing discrimination:

> the form's complicated. The law's complicated. Like, it could be my accommodation status, but it might be because I'm female or it might be because I'm a white female person of X age.... what I feel is I've been treated badly or unfairly or unreasonably and how am I supposed to narrow down what the thinking was on the other side of the table? ... fundamentally what they're saying is I think my right to equality has been breached.[38]

Claimants may perceive that the more boxes that are ticked, the stronger their claim becomes:[39] the opposite, of course, is often true. In some jurisdictions, this is described as an 'ambit complaint', and the complaint is disregarded from data reporting; in small jurisdictions, ambit complaints can substantially skew agency data.[40] In one jurisdiction, when ambit complaints are excluded from the data, most age discrimination complaints also disappear.[41] In other jurisdictions, the phrase 'ambit complaint' is no longer used.[42] Instead, equality agencies work with claimants to refine and further develop the complaint, together ascertaining which grounds are relevant;[43] claims are carefully screened to make sure they actually relate to a particular ground.[44] Thus, agency complaints data is likely to be influenced by how complaints are managed and recorded; this is not always consistent across jurisdictions.

33 A169.
34 ibid.
35 ibid.
36 ibid. See also A9; A158; UK166.
37 A112; A153.
38 A105.
39 A99.
40 ibid; A102.
41 A99.
42 A101.
43 A105.
44 A101.

C. The Nature of Complaints Made

Where age discrimination claims are made, they are not always strong claims. Claims are not always submitted on a form or in a standard format: in one jurisdiction, '[p]eople just email in complaints, now. You'll get, you know, six lines, or a page and a half of outrage at something.'[45] In two jurisdictions, age discrimination complaints were noted as often being vexatious,[46] brought by 'frequent flyers' experiencing mental health issues[47] or who were particularly aggrieved.[48] Complainants in this area can be 'bloody-minded' and emotional,[49] though statutory equality agencies work hard to ensure these claims are given proper consideration.[50]

Weak complaints may reflect a public misunderstanding of the nature and technicalities of discrimination law. Some claimants misunderstand the legal distinction between unfairness and discrimination, and seek to use discrimination law to address unfairness.[51] Just because conduct is unfair, it does not mean that it is unlawful:[52] 'even though conceptually that's the idea, there's not necessarily that direct parallel between fair and equality.'[53] This represents a disjunction between the *legal* view and the *public* or colloquial view of discrimination law.[54] Many of the queries received by agencies relate to behaviour that is not 'nice', but is not technically discrimination.[55] This can lead to frustration or anger on the part of claimants, as it appears the law is doing little to support them.[56]

There is also a lack of understanding—among both claimants and practitioners—about how discrimination law works, and its 'nuances'.[57] This may mean people with a potentially arguable case plead badly, or do not give enough information to ground their claim.[58] These errors can be corrected fairly easily with 'reframing' and the right legal advice.[59] However, a lack of familiarity with discrimination law can deter practitioners from pursuing it as an avenue of redress;[60] this is compounded by a lack of case law.[61] There is also confusion between the requirements of discrimination law and the way in which employers might cater to the needs

45 A155.
46 A99.
47 ibid; A151.
48 A151.
49 A155.
50 A99.
51 A118.
52 A151.
53 A155.
54 A5; A112; UK167.
55 UK167.
56 A5; A151.
57 A105.
58 UK162.
59 ibid.
60 A105; A107.
61 A107.

of different age groups;[62] distinctions between formal and substantive equality are not well understood. Thus, limited public and practitioner understanding of age equality law might inhibit the claiming process.

III. Claim Statistics: Interrogating the Narrative

To more critically explore this issue, it is necessary to examine statistics on enquiries and formal complaints of age discrimination made to statutory bodies in the UK and Australia. Statutory agencies filter the vast majority of formal discrimination claims. Examining this data can therefore help to answer two key questions: first, are age discrimination claims so infrequent as experts believe? Second, what gaps, if any, exist in enforcement, even at this preliminary stage of pursuing individual rights? However, gathering data on age discrimination complaints is not straightforward: agency data are rarely consistent, reliable and accessible,[63] reflecting variations in the quality of centralized record management, and in the level of detail and format that is recorded.[64] This makes it difficult to make comparisons across jurisdictions, or even within jurisdictions over time.[65] The haphazard and piecemeal data that are available from equality agencies have serious implications for the transparency of age discrimination law, and limit the degree to which we can reliably answer these questions.

A. Enquiries and Complaints

Within the data obtained, statistics can be broken down into two categories (1) enquiries received (typically via a phone line, website, or email), which may or may not lead to a complaint; and (2) formal complaints received.

Some issues may be resolved at the enquiry stage by, for example, assisting a person to raise an issue directly with an employer. For enquiries that are not resolved, equality agencies encounter substantial difficulties in translating *enquiries* to *complaints*:[66] 'the vast majority of people are going to self-select themselves out . . . Especially people who have only invested a phone call in it.'[67] Young people in particular do not translate enquiries to complaints.[68] In some cases, individuals

[62] UK81.
[63] A9; A10; A113.
[64] A9; A10; A113.
[65] In WA, for example, where data were obtained for age discrimination complaints received from 2014–19, the data collected changed in nearly every year of reporting, to increase the sorts of data collected, but also to change the way data were categorized. This made comparisons over time difficult.
[66] A10; A101; A102; A110; UK97.
[67] UK97.
[68] House of Commons (n 10) Q52.

will make an enquiry, become aware of their rights, and still choose not to proceed further,[69] perhaps reflecting the high costs of claiming (discussed in Part IV.C). Even asking complainants to write down a complaint could prove to be a barrier to progressing further.[70] Taking complaints over the phone may help to address this; if a complainant later decided to withdraw the complaint, the record could at least be used to consolidate the agency's data collection.[71] However, this would be resource-intensive for the agency, so is not often done in practice.[72]

Enquiries are more likely to be withdrawn or abandoned if individuals are referred between agencies: 'when you start to move matters around you lose people.'[73] This is particularly relevant in Australia where individuals have a choice of jurisdiction and claims could be raised at state or federal level or under industrial law. This is addressed, to some extent, in small jurisdictions, where relevant agencies all operate from within the same building, and can refer complaints between themselves.[74] This might, however, flag potential problems with referring claimants between the Equality Advisory and Support Service (EASS) and Acas in GB.

While there are clear difficulties in translating enquiries to complaints, it is challenging to numerically quantify the problem: not all complaints will originate as enquiries, some enquiries may be resolved without a complaint, and not all enquiries have the basis for a complaint, so claims cannot be easily traced from one stage to the other. Regardless, as the statistics below illustrate, there tend to be far more enquiries than complaints, across all jurisdictions, and some groups appear more likely to enquire than to complain. Even at this preliminary stage, then, gaps are emerging in the claiming process.

1. Australia

Australian agencies report highly variable data relating to age discrimination complaints and enquiries (Table 4.1).[75]

Despite this variable reporting, key trends emerge. First, where enquiry data is reported, enquiries well exceed complaints received, across all jurisdictions. This

69 A108.
70 A101.
71 ibid.
72 ibid.
73 A105.
74 ibid.
75 In Tasmania, age discrimination complaints are reported separately to 'prohibited conduct', that is, unlawful conduct other than discrimination, such as offensive conduct, sexual harassment, incitement, and victimization. In 2018–19, for example, there were twenty-two prohibited conduct complaints relating to age, and twenty-five age discrimination complaints, but only twenty-eight complaints overall. Thus, there is a lot of overlap between these categories, which cannot be accurately assessed by the publicly released data: the total numbers cited here were obtained directly from the Tasmanian equality body. Table 4.1 therefore reports just the age discrimination complaints presented in annual reports, recognizing that this might under-represent total numbers if including prohibited conduct complaints.

Table 4.1 Complaints (C) and Enquiries (E) relating to Age Discrimination (AD) and Age Discrimination in Employment (ADE), Australia, 2010–19

	NSW			Victoria			WA			SA			FWO	FWC	AHRC		Queensland		NT		Tasmania		ACT	Total	
	E	C		E	C		E	C		E	C		E	C	C		C		C		C		C	C	
	ADE	AD	ADE	AD	AD	ADE	AD	AD	ADE	AD	AD	ADE	ADE	ADE (dismissal)	AD	ADE	AD	ADE	AD	ADE	AD	ADE	AD	AD	ADE
2010–11	190	86	44	329	160	108		35	21		30	21			175	195[1]	*	*	37	27	20	*	7	550	416
2011–12	148	55	30	384	199	109		52	30		44	27			196	134	24	14	48	46	15	*	6	575	390
2012–13	212	61	35	426	141	84		51	26		17	10		1	157	103	33	16	34	21	21	26	3	518	321
2013–14	175	83	47	461	140	77		37	*	97	18	9		29	184	128	30	18	35	23	22	7	6	555	309
2014–15	110	79	52	500	145	90		53	*	86	26	18		104	149	103	29	23	37	16	17	9	4	539	311
2015–16	80	77	29	402	123	83		26	*	59	14	10	62 (r)	85	161	105	24	17	45	21	23	10	2	481	275
2016–17	100	75	38	411	131	82	73	34	*	36	10	5	48 (r)	85	154	100	34	23	55	*	39	23	4	536	271
2017–18	95	63	30	318	94	64	90	38	*	28	13	11	83 (c)	112	172	105	27	21	45	*	23	12	8	483	243
2018–19	70	68	29	331	100	49	74	33	*	38	4	3		90	137	83	48	29	*	*	25	10	7	422	193

Source: Annual Reports, bodies themselves, and author's own calculations

Table notes:
* = not reported

r = received

c = completed

[1] One complaint can have multiple different areas, which is why ADE exceeds AD in this reporting period; in total, age discrimination complaints had 297 areas in 2010–11; ADE complaints represented 66 per cent of all areas.

may mean that enquiries do not always progress to become complaints, flagging the need to support the transition from enquiry to complaint.

Second, while there is limited demographic data on those who make enquiries, in South Australia (SA), women, those with caring responsibilities, and those over 60 appear more likely to enquire than to complain. In 2010–14, for example, SA recorded 256 enquiries relating to age discrimination in employment, and sixty-seven complaints. Women represented 51.95 per cent of enquirers (133 of 256 enquiries; nine enquiries where gender was unknown or not specified), but only 40.29 per cent (twenty-seven of sixty-seven) of complainants. Workers over the age of 50 were more likely to both enquire and complain (Table 4.2). Those aged 60–69 represented 50.54 per cent of enquirers where age was specified, but only 24.59 per cent of complainants. This may reflect a reluctance to pursue rights; or it might be that older workers are more likely to use telephone lines as a first point of information (rather than, say, the agency's website). Indeed, a number of enquiries did not relate to a specific event; rather, they were requests for information (Table 4.3).

SA data also identify where enquiries and complaints related to other protected characteristics as well as age (Table 4.4). Disability was the most common additional protected characteristic for both enquiries and complaints, and sex was the second most frequent additional ground. Race was slightly more common as an additional ground in complaints than in enquiries. Only four enquiries were received from those who identified as Aboriginal and Torres Strait Islander (ATSI) (all women); three of these enquiries involved race. Not one complainant was identified as being Aboriginal or a Torres Strait Islander. For complainants who listed

Table 4.2 Age of complainant, complaints and enquiries, SA, 2010–14

Age range	Enquiries	% of Enquiries	Complaints	% of complaints
10–19	1	1.08	3	4.92
20–29	10	10.75	8	13.11
30–39	5	5.38	11	18.03
40–49	6	6.45	7	11.48
50–59	18	19.35	16	26.23
60–69	47	50.54	15	24.59
70–79	5	5.38	1	1.64
80+	1	1.08	0	0
Total specified	93	100.00	61	100

Source: SA Attorney-General's Department, Discrimination Complaints and Enquiries (2015) <https://data.sa.gov.au/data/dataset/aff12383-bb28-4a97-9c75-fbbcf9eeec7e> and author's own calculations

Table 4.3 Reason for enquiry or complaint, SA, 2010–14

	Enquiries	% total	Complaints	% total
Treatment during recruitment	106	41.41	20	29.85
Treatment at work	119	46.48	19	28.36
Refused (entry, service, housing, etc.)	7	2.73	4	5.97
Manner of provision	7	2.73	30	44.78
Dismissed	21	8.20	1	1.49
No event	21	8.20	0	0.00

Source: SA Attorney-General's Department, Discrimination Complaints and Enquiries (2015) <https://data.sa.gov.au/data/dataset/aff12383-bb28-4a97-9c75-fbbcf9eeec7e> and author's own calculations

Table 4.4 Additional protected characteristics, enquiries and complaints, SA, 2010–14

	Enquiries	Complaints
Sex	25	13
Disability	29	17
Industrial	8	0
Caring	14	2
Bullying	15	0
Race	12	14
Victimization	7	4
Pregnancy	2	1
Unfair dismissal	1	0
Marital status	2	1
Sexuality	1	0
Sexual harassment	1	1
Religion	1	0
Appearance	1	0
Whistleblower	0	5
Association	1	1

Source: SA Attorney-General's Department, Discrimination Complaints and Enquiries (2015) <https://data.sa.gov.au/data/dataset/aff12383-bb28-4a97-9c75-fbbcf9eeec7e> and author's own calculations

race as a ground (fourteen), nine were born in Australia, one in Chile, and one in Poland. In three cases birthplace was not identified.

The highest disparities between enquiries and complaints were in relation to industrial matters (eight to zero) and bullying (fifteen to zero). It is possible that these enquiries were directed to the federal industrial jurisdiction. However, only nine matters were referred elsewhere as being beyond the SA Equal Opportunity Commission's (SAEOC) jurisdiction, including one bullying matter and the unfair dismissal matter. Thus, these matters have not necessarily been dealt with elsewhere. Even less explicable is the disparity for those with caring responsibilities (fourteen enquiries and two complaints); it is likely that many of these enquirers are simply not pursuing their rights further.

In the more recent SA data, 128 enquiries were received from 2014 to 2020 relating to age discrimination at work: sixty-two from men, and forty-three from women (twenty-three unknown). The age of the enquirer was discernible in only thirty-four cases, meaning it is difficult to generalize across the data. The subject of the enquiry was evident in just over half of matters (seventy-one cases); of these, forty-two related to recruitment, and seven related to harassment or bullying. Twenty-three enquiries were referred to a legal advice clinic; this appeared common practice from the start of 2019. Sixteen enquiries were on behalf of someone else, often a parent, spouse, child, or co-worker. In this data, each enquiry or complaint was assigned a case number for internal reference; no complaints and enquiries were assigned the same case number, though this does not necessarily mean that enquiries did not proceed to become complaints (ie, they might have been assigned a different case number).

2. UK

In GB, enquiries have been outsourced from the Equality and Human Rights Commission's (EHRC) helpline to EASS since 2012.[76] There is limited public information about how EASS is run; data sourced from EASS directly provides a limited picture of the enquiries received. In the first quarter of 2019, age discrimination represented 4.8 per cent of enquiries received by EASS; over half (54 per cent) of all enquiries related to work. The total number of enquiries was not specified. Throughout 2018, however, EASS received 44,500 total contacts, and 31,693 'cases' overall. Age enquiries remained uncommon.

In Northern Ireland (NI), the Equality Commission for Northern Ireland (ECNI) has retained its advice function, and enquiry data is reported in ECNI Legal Services Reports. Table 4.5 shows age and total enquiries received and dealt

[76] GOV.UK, 'New Equality Advisory and Support Service is Launched' (15 November 2012) <https://www.gov.uk/government/news/new-equality-advisory-and-support-service-is-launched> accessed 25 May 2020. This is discussed further in Chapter 8.

Table 4.5 Enquiries, ECNI, 2011–12 to 2019–20

Year	Age Enquiries	Total Enquiries	Age as % of total
2011–12	320	3,200	10
2012–13	297	3,300	9
2013–14	300	3,330	9.01
2014–15	265	3,313	8
2015–16	dns	3,412	dns
2016–17	287	3,454	8.31
2017–18	251	3,680	6.82
2018–19	332	4,144	8.01
2019–20	dns	3,922	7.5

Table notes:
dns = did not specify
Source: ECNI Annual Reports

with by the ECNI each year. Age represents a higher proportion of all enquiries in NI than in GB.

Acas runs a helpline accessible to both employers and employees. The helpline received 2,903 calls relating to age discrimination in 2018–19; from 2014 to 2019, calls relating to age discrimination consistently represented 0.4–0.5 per cent of all calls received. Acas receives more calls from women employees than men employees relating to age discrimination (Table 4.6). The overrepresentation of women among enquirers is consistent with the SA data. However, Acas statistics relate to the gender of the *caller*, not necessarily the person who experienced age discrimination; a call could be made by a partner, friend, or parent of the person concerned. Further, Acas helpline staff discern the gender of the caller from their voice, rather than asking specifically; this data may reflect 'misgendering' of callers.

Acas statistics likely represent a fairly complete picture of formal age discrimination complaints relating to work in GB, at least since the commencement of Early Conciliation in 2014.[77] As Table 4.7 shows, age discrimination notifications are fairly stable as a proportion of all notifications received by Acas, at between 1.71 and 2.06 per cent of all notifications. Men are slightly more likely to make an age

[77] The Employment Tribunals (Early Conciliation: Exemptions and Rules of Procedure) Regulations 2014, SI 2014/254. However, according to Acas, jurisdiction is typically only recorded against early conciliation notifications where the matter is progressing to conciliation—jurisdictions are not selected when submitting the notification. This may mean that early conciliation notifications that do not progress to conciliation have not been counted in Acas statistics.

Table 4.6 Calls to the Acas helpline relating to age discrimination by gender, 2014–15 to 2018–19

	Female	Male
2014–15	61%	39%
2015–16	58%	42%
2016–17	61%	39%
2017–18	60%	40%
2018–19	62%	38%

Source: Acas

Table 4.7 Age discrimination notifications received by Acas, 2014–15 to 2018–19

	Early conciliation notifications	Employer notifications	Age as % of all notifications
2014–15	1,415	15	1.71
2015–16	1,856	44	2.06
2016–17	1,821	35	2.01
2017–18	2,000	54	1.88
2018–19	2,303	84	1.80

Source: Acas

discrimination notification than women;[78] this is the opposite of the gender make up of enquirers to the Acas helpline, where women are the majority of callers in age discrimination matters.

In NI, the Labour Relations Agency (LRA) has historically received and dealt with few age complaints each year (Table 4.8). These numbers are likely to substantially increase with early conciliation. Indeed, in 2019–20, 1,406 cases received by the LRA fell within the age discrimination jurisdiction;[79] this is fifteen times greater than the number of age complaints received in 2018–19.

[78] House of Commons (n 10) Q57.
[79] Labour Relations Agency, 'Conciliation Statistics 2019–2020' <https://www.lra.org.uk/resources/conciliation-statistics-2019-2020> accessed 23 March 2021.

Table 4.8 Age complaints, LRA, 2005–06 to 2018–19

	Received	Dealt with	Conciliation - settled	Withdrawn	Referred to tribunal
2005–06	0	0	0	0	0
2006–07	24	0	0	0	0
2007–08	65	36	17	17	2
2008–09	76	65	21	37	7
2009–10	137	103	34	57	12
2010–11	95	117	38	62	17
2011–12	189	109	51	40	18
2012–13	199	158	48	95	15
2013–14	80	106	33	54	19
2014–15	114	182	48	117	17
2015–16	104	120	43	66	9
2016–17	226	86	36	44	6
2017–18	128	75	37	30	8
2018–19	93	106	50	43	13

Source: LRA Annual Reports

B. Claimant Demographics

Factors that may affect claiming behaviour—and can be measured with available data—relate to age, sex or gender, job security, and the area of claim (and, perhaps, its potential impact or monetary worth).[80] Equality agencies felt the law was being used by people from a certain demographic group: 'that's what we see—you know, the older white male cohort benefitting from the case law.'[81] However, who benefits from *case law* may well be different to who is *complaining*. The question, then, is: which individuals are making complaints of age discrimination? This can be investigated using the detailed complaint data obtained from Queensland, Western Australia (WA), Tasmania, and SA, supplemented by demographic information

[80] Other factors, which are harder to evaluate with the data available, relate to the legal and economic climate, power disparities, organizational characteristics, and other individual factors such as employability, caring responsibilities, support structures, mental and physical health, financial position, and protected characteristics beyond gender and age.

[81] UK79. See also UK97.

available in selected agencies' annual reports. These data are not collected by Acas, so the discussion below focuses on Australian jurisdictions. It is possible, though, that these trends also apply in the UK.

1. Age

How age discrimination is experienced changes with age;[82] claiming behaviour may therefore also change with age. Older workers may be more affected by age discrimination,[83] or more sensitized to age discrimination,[84] and therefore more likely to make a formal complaint. Claiming behaviour is also likely to be shaped by practical considerations: older workers are more likely to have resources (financial and otherwise) that assist them to bring a complaint, reducing the relative costs of claiming. Further, in cases relating to dismissal or redundancy in particular, older workers may anticipate experiencing age discrimination in recruitment for a new job. In this context, hesitancy to bring a claim is likely outweighed by the potential value of a complaint, and the difficulty of just 'moving on'. Older workers may also be more likely to identify or recognize age discrimination at work, meaning they are more likely to 'name' their experience as discrimination. That said, experiences of age discrimination are shaped by social norms: those over 'pension age' may be less likely to engage in paid employment, limiting their exposure to discrimination at work.[85] Complaints relating to work may therefore be less likely among older age demographics (ie, those over the age of 65).

In the expert interviews, there was a clear sense that older workers were more likely to bring an age discrimination claim than younger workers.[86] Rather than reflecting the over-representation of older workers, though, this likely reflects the *under-representation* of younger workers. Equality agencies receive few claims from young workers, whether or not the complaint relates to age discrimination.[87] The process of making a complaint may be intimidating for young people;[88] even relatively informal processes can be alienating and intimidating.[89] While young workers have a comparatively low tolerance of discriminatory behaviour,[90] they

[82] Colin Duncan and Wendy Loretto, 'Never the Right Age? Gender and Age-Based Discrimination in Employment' (2004) 11 Gender, Work & Organization 95, 105–06.

[83] Tanja Rabl and María del Carmen Triana, 'How German Employees of Different Ages Conserve Resources: Perceived Age Discrimination and Affective Organizational Commitment' (2013) 24 International Journal of Human Resource Management 3599, 3607.

[84] Joe R Feagin, 'The Continuing Significance of Race: Antiblack Discrimination in Public Places' (1991) 56 American Sociological Review 101, 114–15.

[85] Though experiences of age discrimination still remain high in other settings, especially health and government: see Alysia Blackham and Jeromey Temple, 'Intersectional Discrimination in Australia: An Empirical Critique of the Legal Framework' (2020) 43 University of New South Wales Law Journal 773; Table 2; Table 3.

[86] A99; A101; A102; A105; A150; A153; A155; UK97; UK79.

[87] A99; A101; A150; A153; A155; UK79; UK97.

[88] A99.

[89] A160; A99.

[90] A99; A156.

are unlikely to bring a formal complaint.[91] Young workers are more likely to engage with an equality agency to seek assistance for someone else (ie, make a third-party complaint).[92] While young people are very reluctant to make a report to a statutory agency,[93] their parents might file a complaint on their behalf.[94] This reluctance to become involved in formal processes makes it difficult for youth-focused advocacy groups to advance or address issues relating to age.[95] In some jurisdictions, too, there is a sense that younger people do not have very high rights awareness, or a good understanding of age discrimination law.[96]

The findings from the expert interviews are reinforced by claim statistics. At the AHRC, across all age discrimination complaints received from 2011–19, the 55–64 age group brought 29.52 per cent of complaints; 50.27 per cent of complaints were raised by those aged 55 to 74. Young people were far less likely to bring a complaint of age discrimination: those aged 18 to 24 brought only 7 per cent of complaints across this period.

In Queensland, from 2009–19, the largest number of age discrimination complaints about work were brought by those aged 55 to 64, at 31.8 per cent of complaints; young people aged 15–24 brought only 9.3 per cent of complaints.

In WA, age groups used for categorizing data changed from 2014–19. Again, though, complaints increased substantially into middle and older age, with those aged 55 and over bringing 28.13 per cent of complaints, and a further 28.13 per cent of complaints falling within the 40–64 age group.

In SA, over half (57.14 per cent) of complaints received between 1 July 2014 and 30 June 2020 relating to age discrimination at work were filed by those aged 50 to 69. Those aged 50 to 59 brought nearly 34.92 per cent of complaints.

Overall, then, it is clear that age discrimination law is being used, and complaints are being made, far more frequently by older workers than younger workers, especially those aged in their 50s. This trend holds across jurisdictions.

2. Gender

Gender and age is a 'particularly toxic combination'[97] of protected characteristics as women experience the 'double jeopardy' of ageism and sexism.[98] It is not just older women who experience the intersection of age and gender; these issues affect women of nearly all ages.[99] Essentially, women are *never* the right age, continuing to experience gendered ageism across the life course, even among younger cohorts.

[91] A99; A100.
[92] A99.
[93] A7; A159.
[94] A7.
[95] A159.
[96] A102.
[97] UK165.
[98] Duncan and Loretto (n 82) 110.
[99] A154.

While both men and women are affected by age discrimination at work,[100] older women may be less likely to challenge workplace discrimination, having experienced discriminatory treatment throughout their working lives.[101] Women may be more likely to internalize discrimination or just accept it:[102] 'it's just something else to deal with.'[103] Older women in particular have been culturally conditioned to accept discrimination.[104] Women in older cohorts are more likely to be a 'secondary bread winner',[105] and generally have lower workforce participation rates.[106] They therefore possibly also have a weaker attachment to work, due to intermittent work patterns in the past, and concurrent caring responsibilities (for parents, spouses, children, or grandchildren) in the present:[107] 'They've always had a more fluid identity so they would just go and explore another part of their identity [if they experienced discrimination].'[108] Thus, detaching from the workforce can be a rational choice for many women.[109]

Detachment from the labour market has a number of implications for claiming: first, potential compensation will be lower, reflecting women's (on average) lower pay, part-time status, and lower level of seniority at work; and, second, the costs of exit from work will be lower, as women are less likely to feel that work is essential to their identity or personal sense of self. This may mean that men are more likely to bring an age discrimination claim than women.[110] In practice, older women rarely bring complaints of age discrimination, despite being particularly exposed to discrimination.[111] Older women may not be fully aware of their rights, may lack confidence in pursuing legal claims, and may not see their treatment as ageism.[112]

For older white men, though, age discrimination could be their first experience of discrimination: 'they suddenly really understand what discrimination means.'[113] While equality agencies receive many claims from older men, 'they're probably also more likely to be vexatious.'[114] Thus, these are not necessarily *strong* complaints, just common.[115] Some male age discrimination complainants were

[100] AHRC, 'National Prevalence Survey' (n 25) 18–19.
[101] Diane Grant, 'Older Women, Work and the Impact of Discrimination' in Malcolm Sargeant (ed), *Age Discrimination and Diversity: Multiple Discrimination from an Age Perspective* (CUP 2011) 43, 62.
[102] UK84; A101.
[103] UK90.
[104] A99. See Grant (n 101).
[105] A103.
[106] A105.
[107] Grant (n 101) 58–59.
[108] A150.
[109] Grant (n 101) 59.
[110] House of Commons (n 10) Q57.
[111] A99; A100; A101; UK84.
[112] A98.
[113] UK90.
[114] A99.
[115] A112.

especially aggrieved by their experiences, pursuing a claim beyond the point where it was beneficial or helpful.[116]

In the Australian state jurisdictions, though, women and men appear to have similar claiming patterns at agency level, with women slightly overrepresented in some jurisdictions. In Victoria, from 2010–16, women represented 50.84 per cent of age discrimination claimants on average each year. However, this was lower than women's representation across all grounds of complaint (57.85 per cent of claimants). In Queensland, where gender was identifiable from the complaint summary (317 of 387 complaints), women (52 per cent of identifiable complaints) appeared slightly more likely to bring a complaint than men. This is consistent with WA data, where women brought 55 per cent of complaints across the five-year period. In Tasmania, in 2017–18, sixteen age complaints were made by men and thirteen by women; in 2018–19, eighteen age complaints were made by women (with one complaint having two women co-complainants) and eleven by men. In SA, complaints received between 1 July 2014 to 30 June 2020 relating to age discrimination at work were evenly distributed across men (thirty-two) and women (thirty-one).

By contrast, at the federal AHRC, from 2016–19, men brought 57.39 per cent of all age discrimination complaints. Thus, the gender profile of complainants is *reversed* compared with state jurisdictions. This implies that the 'high stakes' federal jurisdiction—with more formal court processes, and where costs can be awarded—is more likely to attract complaints from men than women; conversely, the 'low stakes' state jurisdictions—where proceedings are informal, and costs are generally not available—see the opposite trend.[117]

3. Job security

Another factor that may influence claiming behaviour is job (in)security. Fear of retribution for making a claim is particularly acute for those in precarious or insecure work.[118] Employers' control of working time can facilitate retribution or victimization, and this is likely to increase the perceived costs of claiming. Job insecurity also adds another dimension to the discussion of age, gender, and claiming. Age is fundamentally related to employment security: younger workers and women are far more likely to be in casual positions.[119] Thus, job insecurity may be one reason why younger workers are less likely to lodge an age discrimination

[116] A151.

[117] In the UK, Acas does not collect data relating to the characteristics of individuals who participate in dispute resolution. If data is recorded, it is in the case notes of each dispute, is not searchable, and is typically purged from the system in accordance with Acas's data handling procedures. Thus, it is not possible to map the gender of claimants.

[118] A154; A159; UK84. See Catherine Barnard, Amy Ludlow, and Sarah Fraser Butlin, 'Beyond Employment Tribunals: Enforcement of Employment Rights by EU-8 Migrant Workers' (2018) 47 Industrial Law Journal 226, 241–43.

[119] ABS, *6333.0 Characteristics of Employment, Australia* (August 2019).

complaint. These characteristics—of age, gender, and job insecurity—therefore cannot be disentangled.

The impact of job security on claiming is illustrated by CLC and agency data. Between September 2018 and September 2019, an Australian women's industrial advocacy centre received 67.2 per cent of long contacts (across all matters) from those in permanent full-time positions, and another 10.6 per cent of contacts from those in permanent part-time positions. Only 22.2 per cent of contacts were from those in fixed-term, casual, self-employed, or insecure roles. By contrast, the Australian Bureau of Statistics (ABS) estimates that those without paid leave entitlements (a proxy for casual employment) represented 24.35 per cent of employees in Australia in 2019, and 20 per cent of all employed persons; a further 17.29 per cent of all employed persons were classed as independent contractors or other business operators.[120] Those occupying insecure jobs were therefore significantly less likely to approach the advocacy centre than those in permanent positions.

In Queensland, a substantial proportion of complaints were received from those in permanent full- or part-time work (47.8 per cent). Those in casual, temporary, or contract roles cumulatively raised only 17.6 per cent of complaints, substantially lower than their representation in the workforce. In WA, those in secure jobs (permanent, full time, or part time) represented eighteen complaints, or 30 per cent of complaints where employment status was known. Those who were unemployed represented 32 per cent of complainants, reflecting the volume of complaints relating to recruitment processes. Casual staff raised 25.4 per cent of complaints where employment status was known; this is on par with rates of casual work in the general workforce.

4. Intersectionality

While the legal framework arguably accommodates intersectionality poorly, it is possible for individuals to bring claims based on multiple grounds; for example, for both age discrimination and disability discrimination. Few intersectional claims progress to a full court hearing and judgment.[121] Complaints to equality bodies therefore potentially reveal far more than court decisions about the prevalence and importance of intersectionality to understanding age discrimination.

In Queensland, the most common additional grounds discernible in complaint descriptions were disability (flagged in forty-nine of 387 complaints) and sex (forty complaints). In WA, fifty-one complaints did not flag any additional grounds. Victimization was the most common additional ground raised (seventeen complaints), followed by sex (fourteen), and impairment (twelve). In SA, twenty-nine

[120] ibid.
[121] Blackham and Temple (n 85).

of sixty-three complaints (46 per cent) involved multiple grounds. The most common additional grounds were sex (eleven complaints), race (ten) and disability (ten).

These data indicate that multiple grounds of claim are common at complaint stage: 47 per cent of complaints in WA and 46 per cent in SA included something additional to age. It is likely, then, that an intersectional lens is key to understanding experiences of age discrimination.

5. Area of claim

Finally, some substantive issues may be more likely to be the subject of an age discrimination complaint than others. For example, people may be more likely to complain about forced retirement or redundancy—where it is no longer possible to salvage or repair the employment relationship, there is no fear of retribution, and the likely compensation or benefit for a complaint is higher—than issues such as access to training or promotion. Complaints about recruitment may also be unlikely due to attributional ambiguity and difficulties of proof; equally, though, there is minimal risk of retribution and no employment relationship to salvage in these cases. This might encourage claiming.

In Queensland, based on the complaint summary, the largest proportion of complaints (ninety-four or 24 per cent) related to recruitment or advertising of positions. A significant number (eighty-seven or 22 per cent) related to harassment or age-based treatment, though this may reflect how the complaints were coded: where age-based treatment or name-calling was alleged, this was coded as 'harassment', even if it was unlikely to meet the statutory definition of harassment. This category therefore includes a number of examples of what might be called 'casual' or 'everyday' ageism.

In WA, a substantial number of complaints (thirty-six or 37.5 per cent) related to applying for a job. Dismissal was the next most common area of complaint (nine or 9 per cent). Seven complaints related to working time, including the allocation of casual shifts. In Tasmania, over a two-year period, the agency received five complaints relating to sexual harassment of younger workers, two relating to age-based comments at work, four relating to being 'pushed out' of work, and three complaints relating to recruitment. Complaints relating to recruitment are therefore far more common than might be predicted: recruitment—not dismissal—is the most common substantive issue in complaints.

IV. Where Have All the Complaints Gone?

Overall, age discrimination complaints are rare. These complaint statistics are difficult to comprehend in abstract terms, particularly given population differences. However, if compared with the population of older workers in each jurisdiction (given older workers bring the vast majority of claims), the statistics arguably become more informative.

According to the ABS, in November 2019 (pre-Covid-19) there were 3,264,622 older workers aged between 50 and 64 participating in the labour force.[122] The AHRC estimates around 27 per cent of older workers report experiencing age discrimination in employment every two years. If all older workers experiencing age discrimination were to complain, we would expect around 440,724 claims per year, just from workers aged 50–64. In practice, there were only 422 age discrimination complaints received in 2018–19 in Australia, across all statutory agencies, all areas, and all age groups. Actual complaints received were therefore less than 0.09 per cent of the possible figure.

In the UK in November 2019, there were projected to be 10,618,882 older workers aged 50 and over.[123] In the 2017–18 British survey of prejudice, 26 per cent of respondents reported experiencing age discrimination (though this was not confined to the workplace).[124] This would equate to around 2,760,909 workers over the age of 50 experiencing age discrimination each year. This compares with 2,303 early conciliation notifications received by Acas in 2018–19, representing 0.08 per cent of potential claims.

It is not just equality agencies who rarely see age discrimination complaints: from September 2018 to September 2019, a women's industrial advocacy centre in an Australian jurisdiction received sixty-three client contacts relating to age discrimination, representing 0.9 per cent of all client contacts. Over a third (twenty-four) of those clients were also disabled; twelve were culturally and linguistically diverse, and six identified as ATSI. From these contacts, the centre conducted casework for only seven clients with age discrimination matters (1.06 per cent of all casework conducted). Even in the community, where assistance may be more approachable and accessible, age discrimination represents only a minute proportion of complaints and caseload.

This may be compared with statistics from JobWatch, a specialist employment rights CLC in Victoria. Older people (aged 45 and over) represented 31.1 per cent of callers to JobWatch's telephone service in 2010–11, up from 14.3 per cent in 1999–2000.[125] From 1999 to 2011, women were slightly over-represented in this group of callers (52.4 per cent of callers aged 45 and over), though this is similar to

[122] Australian Bureau of Statistics, *6291.0.55.001 Labour Force, Australia, Detailed* (November 2019) <https://www.abs.gov.au/AUSSTATS/abs@.nsf/DetailsPage/6291.0.55.001Nov%202019?OpenDocument> accessed 23 March 2021.

[123] Office for National Statistics, 'Employment in the UK' (18 February 2020) <https://www.ons.gov.uk/employmentandlabourmarket/peopleinwork/employmentandemployeetypes/bulletins/employmentintheuk/february2020> accessed 23 March 2021.

[124] Dominic Abrams, Hannah Swift, and Diane Houston, 'Developing a National Barometer of Prejudice and Discrimination in Britain' (2018) Research Report 119, 22, 24.

[125] JobWatch, 'Grey Areas: Age Barriers to Work in Commonwealth Laws, Submission to the Australian Law Reform Commission Issues Paper' (2012) 5 <https://www.alrc.gov.au/wp-content/uploads/2019/08/25._jobwatch.pdf> accessed 25 August 2020.

the gender split across all callers to JobWatch.[126] The majority of older callers were in permanent full-time work (61.2 per cent), or permanent part-time work (18.5 per cent); those employed on fixed-term contracts (1.4 per cent), in casual work (13.2 per cent), and working as independent contractors (3.4 per cent) were less likely to contact JobWatch.[127] Age discrimination was not recorded as one of the top ten enquiries received from this cohort; however, qualitative analysis of callers' workplace issues revealed age discrimination to be a key barrier to older callers participating in work.[128]

In the advocate survey, respondents who had not been involved in any work-related age discrimination matters in 2018 and 2019 were asked why they thought they had not been involved in these matters: responses focused on the lack of claiming in this area, and the under-utilization of age discrimination law generally: as one practitioner noted, 'The accepted norm is to not pursue such matters'.

The question, then, is *why* individuals choose not to pursue their rights under age discrimination law—and, conversely, what can be done to address it. While there are clear barriers to enforcement for all protected grounds, age discrimination law is relatively under-enforced even compared to other grounds.[129] The sections that follow consider in more detail the factors that might deter claiming, or direct disputes away from statutory agencies; and what can be done to address these barriers to justice.

A. Internal Dispute Resolution

Age discrimination complaints might be resolved internally within organizations, without recourse to statutory agencies.[130] Individuals who experience age discrimination may adopt a prosocial approach that seeks to repair and maintain relationships,[131] without recourse to legal processes. This could mean, then, that age discrimination complaints are not being recorded in agency data but are still being resolved successfully.

For expert respondents in this study, resolving complaints informally 'has to be the first line of defence'.[132] Directly approaching an employer, and attempting direct negotiation, was seen by advocates as an easier process than filing a claim,[133]

[126] ibid 6.
[127] ibid.
[128] ibid 7–10.
[129] UK79.
[130] UK97; A100; A104; A103; A111; A153; UK162.
[131] Laura Smart Richman and Mark R Leary, 'Reactions to Discrimination, Stigmatization, Ostracism, and Other Forms of Interpersonal Rejection: A Multimotive Model' (2009) 116 Psychological Review 365, 368.
[132] UK97.
[133] A100.

especially if matters involved a large employer with a dedicated human resource function.[134] In these cases, employers often made a business decision to negotiate directly.[135] Resolving a complaint early and informally can prevent a matter from escalating, help to maintain the employment relationship, and achieve creative solutions that support both parties.[136] Where a claim was resolved in this way, it was often accompanied by a deed of settlement with a confidentiality clause, meaning these matters are rarely seen in the public sphere.[137] Matters are also sometimes settled without agency assistance, including after agency conciliation has failed.[138] People armed with advice from equality agencies may be able to resolve a matter informally, especially if advice is obtained early, and before a discriminatory act has crystallized.[139] It is difficult to assess how common this is in practice.[140]

Informal, local resolution of disputes may be the best option for many claimants; resolving a matter locally—on the shop floor—was also the aim of union activists.[141] However, union respondents doubted the extent to which informal workplace resolution was addressing age discrimination in practice.[142] Local resolution is unlikely to deal with systemic issues, or to be negotiated by delegates who understand the intricacies of age discrimination law.[143]

The extent to which age discrimination is being effectively addressed at the local level is therefore questionable.[144] In the AHRC's *National Prevalence Survey*, for example, 14 per cent of respondents who had experienced age discrimination at work in the last two years raised the issue with the organization. This was nearly three times the number who raised the issue with an external organization (5 per cent). However, 58 per cent of those who had experienced age discrimination said their issue had not been resolved.[145] Of those who 'resolved' their issue in whole or part (42 per cent, n = 131), most achieved this through avoidance or withdrawal: by quitting their job (17 per cent), looking for another job or finding another job (12 per cent), moving on or ignoring the issue (14 per cent), or dismissing the behaviour as not an issue or a joke (13 per cent). More substantive 'resolution' was achieved in fewer cases: 8 per cent kept their job; 5 per cent discussed the issue with those involved; 5 per cent were retrained; 3 per cent received flexible work arrangements; and 3 per cent received an apology (respondents could select multiple

[134] ibid.

[135] ibid.

[136] UK162. That said, even filing a workplace grievance or calling behaviour 'discrimination' or 'bullying' can serve to escalate a matter: UK162; 'they're sort of heavy words to throw around': A111.

[137] A100.

[138] A103.

[139] UK97.

[140] ibid.

[141] A111.

[142] A154.

[143] A111.

[144] ibid.

[145] AHRC, 'National Prevalence Survey' (n 25) 71.

options).[146] Thus, informal dispute resolution at the workplace level does not appear to be dealing with many instances of age discrimination in a meaningful way.

This is consistent with the findings of the 2004 Unrepresented Worker Survey of 501 low-paid, non-unionized UK workers who had experienced problems at work in the previous three years. In that survey, 17.8 per cent of respondents (eighty-nine) had experienced discrimination at work in the last three years.[147] Age was the most common form of discrimination reported, being identified by 27.6 per cent of respondents (twenty-one) who reported discrimination, even though age discrimination was not unlawful at the time of the survey.[148] The vast majority (85.6 per cent) of workers with problems took action to try to resolve their problem;[149] indeed, 94.7 per cent of respondents took action in relation to discrimination, making discrimination the area most likely to lead to action.[150] The majority of respondents (69.3 per cent) made an informal approach to a line manager, and nearly half (42.7 per cent) made an informal approach to a senior manager;[151] formal workplace grievance procedures were used by only 11.6 per cent of respondents, and 2.4 per cent began ET proceedings.[152] Thus, most attempts to resolve a workplace issue occurred internally and informally within an organization. This does not, however, always lead to a satisfactory outcome: 47 per cent of respondents reported that there had been no conclusion to their problem;[153] of the 38 per cent who achieved a result, only half (49 per cent) were satisfied with the outcome.[154] Overall, then, only 16 per cent of vulnerable workers with problems at work and 18.6 per cent of those who tried to take steps to resolve them had a satisfactory outcome.[155] In the survey, 44 per cent of those who did not reach a satisfactory resolution had quit their job, compared to 29 per cent of those who achieved a satisfactory resolution.[156] 'Quit rates' were therefore 65 per cent higher for workers who did not achieve a satisfactory resolution.[157]

From an organizational perspective, too, internal complaints of discrimination appear rare: in an evaluation conducted of the EqA, which surveyed 1,811 organizations, only 171 organizations had dealt with one or more employee complaints about unequal treatment or discrimination in the three years prior to the survey,

[146] ibid 72.
[147] Pollert and Charlwood, 'The Vulnerable Worker in Britain and Problems at Work' (n 21) 350.
[148] Pollert and Charlwood, 'The Unorganised Worker' (n 23) 20.
[149] ibid 40.
[150] ibid 41.
[151] Pollert and Charlwood, 'The Vulnerable Worker in Britain and Problems at Work' (n 21) 351.
[152] ibid. This is consistent with the findings of the 2008 Fair Treatment at Work survey, where only 3 per cent of respondents made an application to an ET in an attempt to resolve their problem: Fevre and others (n 21) 136.
[153] Pollert and Charlwood, 'The Unorganised Worker' (n 23) 60.
[154] ibid.
[155] ibid.
[156] ibid 62.
[157] ibid.

Table 4.9 Reported outcomes of age discrimination matters relating to work, advocate survey

Outcome	Number of matters reported (all respondents)
Not pursued	37
Abandoned	4
Settled privately	31
Settled via statutory ADR	13
Settled via judicial mediation	10
Proceeded to court hearing	56
Settled during or after a hearing	3
Final judgment	15
Other (often ongoing)	14

across all protected characteristics.[158] Of the 144 resolved cases reported by organizations, twenty-eight were settled by way of a compromise contract (reached without the intervention of an ET or Acas),[159] thirty went to external mediation, and fourteen involved an ET.[160] However, organizational statistics are unlikely to capture informal approaches to line managers or senior managers, unless complaints are formalized.

In the advocate survey, more matters were reported as settling privately than through statutory ADR or judicial mediation (Table 4.9).[161] Of these matters settled privately, all resulted in monetary compensation; only two matters were reported as resulting in systemic change, two resulted in an apology, and none led to reinstatement. Thus, while a number of matters are settling without recourse to statutory agencies, this is not necessarily leading to broader change.[162]

It is impossible to assess the extent to which age discrimination matters are being resolved at the local level, with or without the support of unions. The evidence that is available, however, indicates that it is unlikely that informal or internal processes are resolving most issues.

[158] Kim Perren and others, 'Evaluation of the Implementation of the Equality Act 2010: Report 3: Disputes and Challenges' (2012) Centre for Research In Social Policy 621, 11.

[159] ibid 13.

[160] ibid.

[161] Understandably, given the involvement of legal practitioners and union officials, many of these matters proceeded to a court hearing; that said, few resulted in a final judgment.

[162] That said, of the matters resolved via statutory ADR, none were reported as leading to systemic change, meaning this is perhaps a systemic problem with ADR.

B. Displacement to Other Avenues of Redress

Age discrimination complaints may be uncommon because claimants pursue other avenues of redress, rather than making a claim on the basis of age. Some claims relating to age discrimination may also be argued as unfair dismissal, sex or gender discrimination, or race discrimination.

Age discrimination is less likely to be seen as a pressing issue than discrimination on the basis of other grounds.[163] This may be, in part, because people identify more strongly with other grounds than with their age:[164] our experience of age (and age discrimination) is shifting and constantly changing, whereas other grounds are comparatively more fixed.[165] Sex and race discrimination claims are more commonly pursued than age discrimination claims,[166] often being easier to prove,[167] and having a more substantial body of case law that offers more predictability in claiming. In the UK, too, unlike in relation to age discrimination, it is not possible to justify direct sex or race discrimination.[168]

Similarly, unfair dismissal claims are seen as being easier to prove[169] and, in Australia, offering a more efficient, timely, and less daunting machinery for enforcement (via the Fair Work Commission (FWC)),[170] being easier to navigate as a self-represented litigant[171] without the risk of costs.[172] For some practitioners, then, the limitations of discrimination law could often be overcome by using unfair dismissal law instead:[173] 'it is faster; it is simpler; it is cheaper.'[174]

Thus, claimants and their representatives may prefer to use legal avenues other than age discrimination law, if they are available; making a claim of discrimination is 'a last resort legal option',[175] and age is the least preferred ground on which to make a discrimination complaint. An age discrimination complaint 'kind of becomes that fallback. Like, if all these other things aren't there, is it something you could argue, to at least get a claim together and try to get someone some relief.'[176] While advisers frequently discuss discrimination law with their clients as a legal option, it is rarely pursued in practice.[177]

163 A156.
164 UK80.
165 ibid.
166 A99.
167 UK81.
168 ibid; UK82.
169 A107.
170 ibid; A115.
171 A107.
172 ibid.
173 A115; A169.
174 A115.
175 A107.
176 ibid.
177 A100.

Complaints may therefore be so unusual in the age jurisdiction because issues are displaced to other grounds and other claims. This is a self-replicating cycle, as no-one then wants to be 'a ground-breaking pioneer' by bringing a claim in this space.[178] Further, practitioners tend to favour legal areas that they are familiar with, especially in the community legal space: 'you're being bombarded [by cases], and so—I mean, you kind of just go with what you know will work, as opposed to exploring brand new options that will require a lot of extra effort.'[179] That said, as the statistics above show, it is not impossible or uncommon to make a complaint on the basis of age *and* other grounds;[180] or to pursue a claim of both unfair dismissal and age discrimination. In these cases, age claims often fall away as a claim progresses, being withdrawn or abandoned to focus on stronger claims:[181] in the UK, 'the uncertainties around justification really have played a big role in that'.[182]

C. The Cost of Complaining

Where age discrimination law is the only or best option for pursing a claim, formal complaints may be deterred by the significant costs associated with complaining. In the context of sexual harassment, Knapp and others argue that how people respond to experiencing harassment is strongly influenced by 'outcome expectancy'; that is, an assessment of the probable outcomes that will be achieved by taking various responses.[183] This sense-making process is informed by both individual and contextual variables (such as the individual's characteristics, power, the legal and economic environment, and work group and organizational characteristics).[184] Knapp and others argue that 'An individual considers possible actions that may be taken, weighs the expected costs and benefits, and then selects a strategy', considering the likely efficacy of the response, its ability to achieve a valued outcome (such as stopping the harassment or discrimination) and the potential risk of retaliation.[185]

Similarly, Wakefield and Uggen argue that claimants make a decision to file a complaint in a context shaped by macro-economic forces; legal structures and economic conditions will shape the attractiveness (or otherwise) of making a complaint compared with other strategies or options.[186] In the United States of America

[178] A107.
[179] ibid.
[180] ibid.
[181] UK81; UK82.
[182] UK82.
[183] Deborah Erdos Knapp and others, 'Determinants of Target Responses to Sexual Harassment: A Conceptual Framework' (1997) 22 The Academy of Management Review 687, 700.
[184] ibid.
[185] ibid.
[186] Sara Wakefield and Christopher Uggen, 'The Declining Significance of Race in Federal Civil Rights Law: The Social Structure of Employment Discrimination Claims' (2004) 74 Sociological Inquiry 128, 134.

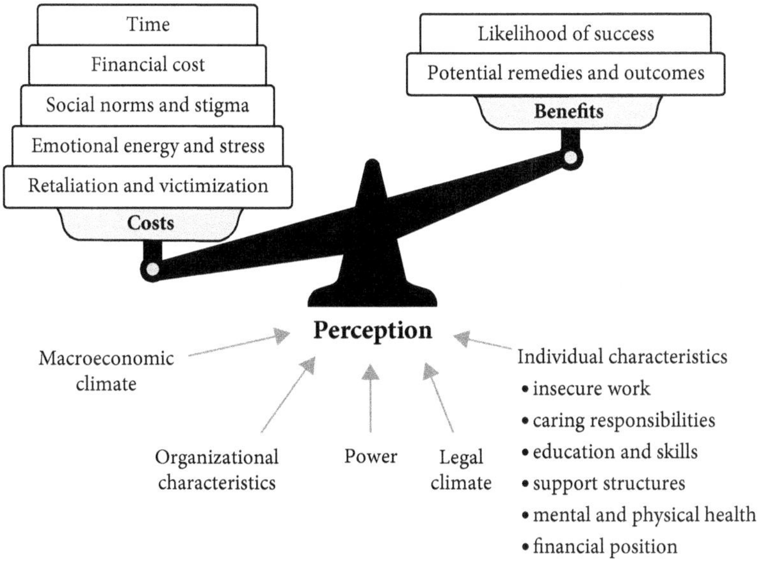

Figure 4.1 Balancing perceived costs and benefits of complaining

(USA), poor economic conditions and high unemployment may make a discrimination complaint more attractive, as exit becomes a less viable strategy.[187]

Macro-economic conditions may have different effects in other national contexts, such as Australia and the UK, where claiming is a less accepted and acceptable behaviour. Further, where the choice is not simply between exit and claiming—a third option is putting up with or 'lumping' it—poor macro-economic conditions may mean that individuals are less likely to actively address discrimination at all.

Overall, though, we can visualize this individual sense-making process as a balancing exercise between the perceived costs and benefits of bringing a complaint (Figure 4.1). These costs and benefits are influenced and overlaid by individual, organizational, economic, and legal factors.

1. Financial costs

In the UK, expert respondents frequently cited the financial costs of complaining as being a potential deterrent to claimants. Employment Tribunal (ET) fees in particular were seen as 'an absolute hammer-blow to the number of claims being brought'.[188] While fees are no longer charged, the legacy of the fee system has particularly affected the development of UK age discrimination law.[189] Even if

[187] ibid 135.
[188] UK78. See also UK80; UK84.
[189] UK84.

claimants are no longer required to pay ET fees, there are other financial costs involved in making a claim, such as the need to engage a lawyer:[190] changes to legal aid have made it more difficult to obtain affordable legal assistance.[191] The level of case management in ETs can also increase the cost of bringing a case.[192]

In Australia, claimants can also be deterred by the potential costs of claiming.[193] Discrimination claims are expensive, as the claimant is responsible for producing evidence of both discrimination and harm, though the respondent typically has control of relevant information.[194] Some complainants are deterred by the fear of having costs awarded against them, which is a particular risk in the federal jurisdiction.[195] Even a low risk of costs is a potential deterrent, especially where there are difficulties in proving discrimination.[196] State tribunals have made complainants aware that costs might be awarded against them if they proceed: 'that really scares people.... We've had a few people say, "Look, you know, we withdrew just on the basis of we were too scared about costs." '[197] Tribunals wielding the 'big stick'[198] of costs to encourage complainants to withdraw a claim is likely to have a substantial chilling effect on claiming behaviour. A fear of costs may also encourage some complainants to pursue a claim under the Fair Work Act 2009 (Cth) (FWA), rather than discrimination law, at the federal level.[199]

Conversely, the ability to obtain costs at the federal level might *encourage* law firms to take matters on in a pro bono capacity; cost recovery could incentivize firms to bring important test cases.[200] This poses a practical challenge for CLCs, particularly with other reductions in funding: while pursuing a costs jurisdiction is riskier, any benefit lies with the CLC (as it can potentially recover its costs); the risk lies with the client. There is therefore 'a bit of conflict of interest there'.[201]

Overall, though, the financial cost of making a claim was only infrequently raised by interview respondents,[202] perhaps because the initial stages of pursuing a complaint, and participating in conciliation, are comparatively low cost.[203] Instead, most of the 'costs' involved in claiming are non-financial.

[190] UK79.
[191] UK80.
[192] UK82.
[193] A4; A118. See AHRC, 'Willing to Work' (n 7) 322.
[194] A118.
[195] A4; A151. See AHRC, 'Willing to Work' (n 7) 322.
[196] A112.
[197] A102.
[198] ibid.
[199] A107.
[200] A118.
[201] A9. See also A10.
[202] UK79; UK82; A4; A111; A115; A118; A151.
[203] A4.

2. Non-financial costs

In the AHRC's *National Prevalence Survey*, for those who took no action after experiencing age discrimination (n = 133), the potential non-financial costs of complaining weighed heavily in their decision-making process: 16 per cent took no action because they thought the complaint process would be stressful, difficult, or embarrassing, or because it was easier to keep quiet; 6 per cent were afraid complaining would affect their career, or thought they might be dismissed; and 5 per cent were concerned about their reputation.[204] In the UK, these concerns were also prominent in evidence given to the WEC: when asked of the barriers to making an age discrimination claim, Christopher Brooks from Age UK noted that:

> It is actually incredibly stressful taking a claim, and it is not the kind of thing that most people would want to do, sometimes under any circumstances. For your personal wellbeing, it is much easier to put it behind you and move on, in many cases, even if that moving on means not working.[205]

A key non-financial cost is the emotional toll of a complaint,[206] and the stress and distress a claim causes,[207] including by requiring claimants to re-live their experience of discrimination.[208] Making a claim can be more stressful and debilitating than the event itself.[209] Claimants sometimes fear that making a claim can expose them—and their errors—to excessive and stressful scrutiny.[210] This reflects, too, the ways age discrimination and performance issues might be intertwined and overlapping.

Claimants may also be deterred by the time and energy involved in pursuing a claim,[211] and the opportunity cost when there is a need to—for example—find another job.[212] This is particularly acute for those with caring or family responsibilities[213] or who are in financial distress.[214] Pursuing a discrimination complaint requires a substantial emotional investment[215] for people who are already overburdened: 'a lot of our clients have so much else going on in their lives that it's not worth them battling that as well.'[216]

204 AHRC, 'National Prevalence Survey' (n 25) 70.
205 House of Commons (n 10) Q88.
206 A103; A150; A151; UK162. See AHRC, 'Willing to Work' (n 7) 323.
207 A7; A100; A108.
208 A151.
209 A7.
210 A108.
211 ibid; A151; A169; A7.
212 A98; A100; A102; A108; A112; A151.
213 A163.
214 A108.
215 A100.
216 A108.

Overall, then, making a claim is 'emotionally and physically draining and damaging':[217] 'It's not worth the risks, and it's also not worth the energy, and the time, and the drain on themselves ... it's tiring to fight something.... we have people just get exhausted.'[218] Many claimants feel '"It's too hard. Why would I do that to myself?"';[219] '"It's good to know it's there, but I just can't deal with this right now."'[220] These comments illustrate the substantial mental load of complaining: as one respondent noted,

> It's really tough [to bring a claim] ... The amount of stuff that you have to do, the information that you have to gather ... is horrendous.... there is a big issue around resilience, and what is mentally needed to be able to actually carry these loads.[221]

Bearing this mental load is especially difficult for claimants with caring responsibilities: 'if you've got care and responsibilities that's where your focus is. It's about getting through the day.'[222] Given women already bear a substantial and disproportionate mental load in heterosexual relationships,[223] and are more likely to have caring responsibilities, there will likely be gendered trends in who is able or willing to take on this additional mental load of claiming.

Bringing a claim may also exacerbate claimants' poor mental health:[224] some claimants become all consumed by the process and lose a sense of perspective or objectivity,[225] jeopardizing their health and relationships.[226] Indeed, all claimants—and all who experience discrimination—may experience some form of mental ill-health:[227]

[217] A100.

[218] A104. See also A7.

[219] A101. See also A105.

[220] A108. Indeed, experiencing discrimination can itself lead to exhaustion: Tiffany Trzebiatowski and María del Carmen Triana, 'Family Responsibility Discrimination, Power Distance, and Emotional Exhaustion: When and Why Are There Gender Differences in Work–Life Conflict?' (2020) 162 Journal of Business Ethics 15; Christian N Thoroughgood, Katina B Sawyer, and Jennica R Webster, 'Finding Calm in the Storm: A Daily Investigation of How Trait Mindfulness Buffers against Paranoid Cognition and Emotional Exhaustion Following Perceived Discrimination at Work' (2020) 159 Organizational Behavior and Human Decision Processes 49.

[221] UK97.

[222] UK84. See Belinda Smith, 'It's about Time: For a New Regulatory Approach to Equality' (2008) 36 Federal Law Review 117, 133.

[223] See, eg, Lindsey G Robertson and others, 'Mothers and Mental Labor: A Phenomenological Focus Group Study of Family-Related Thinking Work' (2019) 43 Psychology of Women Quarterly 184; Jocelyn M DeGroot and Tennley A Vik, '"The Weight of Our Household Rests on My Shoulders": Inequity in Family Work' (2020) 41 Journal of Family Issues 1258.

[224] UK97.

[225] ibid.

[226] A151.

[227] Angeline S Ferdinand, Yin Paradies, and Margaret Kelaher, 'Mental Health Impacts of Racial Discrimination in Australian Culturally and Linguistically Diverse Communities: A Cross-Sectional Survey' (2015) 15 BMC Public Health 401; Sylvanna M Vargas, Stanley J Huey Jr, and Jeanne Miranda, 'A Critical Review of Current Evidence on Multiple Types of Discrimination and Mental Health' (2020) 90 American Journal of Orthopsychiatry 374.

> people who have had excellent mental health [can] suddenly go to having really poor mental health, because of ... the way that discrimination makes you feel.... if you are being treated less favourably in the workplace, it will affect your mental health.[228]

This makes it especially complicated to navigate complex systems and the stress of conciliation.[229] There is little legal practitioners can do to reduce the load on claimants: even with legal representation and support, it is still demanding to be involved in the complaints process: 'that takes a huge toll on our clients.'[230]

3. Retribution or victimization

Claimants frequently fear retribution, victimization, or reputational damage for making a claim.[231] This fear persists, despite equality laws offering protection against victimization. Fear is particularly acute in small jurisdictions,[232] as people do not want to 'burn bridges'; where good jobs are hard to come by;[233] and in small industries, for fear of 'never getting employed in that industry again, for being a whinger.'[234]

Fear of retribution particularly affects those in precarious or insecure work,[235] or whose financial position is precarious (such as those with a low pension or superannuation balance).[236] In an insecure job market, speaking out to challenge discrimination 'singles you out regardless of whether you're speaking out for yourself or for a collective, so ... it's pretty hard to, you know, convince people that that's a good idea lot of the time'.[237] Speaking out is particularly difficult for those on zero-hours, variable hours, or casual contracts, as an employer can reduce working hours without discussion or notice, to the point where a worker is effectively dismissed.[238] Employers' absolute control of working time therefore enables retribution or victimization.

Relatedly, there is a fear that discrimination complaints will not help to repair a relationship; rather, that they will be perceived as antagonistic or an attempt to damage the employment relationship.[239] For one respondent, '[making a claim] is fundamentally incompatible with remaining in employment.... it's

228 UK117.
229 ibid.
230 A108.
231 UK78; UK84; A10; A99; A102; A104; A105; A115; A153; A154; A155. See AHRC, 'Willing to Work' (n 7) 325–26.
232 A99; A105; A110.
233 A154.
234 A104.
235 A154; A159; UK84. See Barnard, Ludlow, and Fraser Butlin (n 118) 241–43.
236 A104.
237 A154.
238 ibid.
239 Smart Richman and Leary (n 131) 368.

just ... untenable to be in conflict with your employer, and [make a claim to] an external body.' [240] Thus, if a complaint relates to promotion or a lack of training, for example, 'Are you going to bring a tribunal claim which is not going to please your employer? ... Suing people is not necessarily a good way of achieving those goals.'[241]

Complaints are therefore mostly raised after an employment relationship has ended.[242] In exceptional cases, where an external claim is made, but the employment relationship is maintained, this tends to reflect the merit of the complaint, and the way both parties manage and respond to the complaint.[243] Government agencies in particular are 'less likely to be personally offended by a complaint', allowing the relationship to be maintained.[244]

For older workers, a fear of experiencing age discrimination in recruitment for a new job can compound age discrimination in their current job: older employees are more likely to 'lump it' if they believe they will be unlikely to obtain a new job easily, including due to age discrimination.[245] As one respondent noted, '[older workers] are terrified of age discrimination and so that makes them less likely to complain if they want to stay in the workforce. Their fear of victimization is so high ... there's a terror out there which is tangible.'[246]

Conversely, for younger workers, who may obtain new employment more easily, the costs of exit are lower than the costs of complaining.[247] Younger workers may only raise an issue when they are ready to leave their current employment.[248] As one practitioner noted, young workers 'might be well aware that they're not being paid correctly but they're also well aware that the time to challenge it is when they want to move on. They can't fix it and remain. It can only be fixed when that relationship is going to end.'[249]

4. Social norms and stigma

Claiming may also be seen as costly if it breaches social norms. There are strong social and cultural norms in both Australia and the UK against claiming or challenging discrimination, or standing up for rights[250]—that is, causing a problem. Cultural norms lead to condemnation for being a 'whinger'[251] or a

[240] A115.
[241] UK78. This is despite (or perhaps because of) the fact that training is key for competitiveness in promotion, redundancy, and dismissal: Helen Meenan, 'Age: The Individual and the Law: Part 1' (2002) 10 Irish Law Times 154, 156.
[242] A115.
[243] ibid.
[244] ibid.
[245] UK84; A110.
[246] A99.
[247] A3; A153; A110; A160.
[248] A160.
[249] ibid.
[250] A3; UK166.
[251] A3; A104; A105.

'wuss',[252] not wanting to rock the boat[253] or be a troublemaker,[254] and 'a reluctance to speak out and make a fuss'.[255] A discrimination complaint runs counter to the strong egalitarian myth pervasive in Australian society;[256] this may increase reluctance to challenge discriminatory decisions or actions.[257]

Social norms are particularly problematic in relation to age discrimination: in addition to inhibiting 'naming' (Chapter 3), internalized age norms may mean that being discriminated against can 'feel humiliating' and evoke a sense of shame.[258] There may be stigma attached to making a claim for age discrimination:[259] making a claim is 'drawing attention to the fact that people think they're too old, and maybe they're starting to think they're too old themselves'.[260] Rather than wanting to challenge age discrimination, individuals may seek to bury it, to minimize their sense of shame[261] and rejection. Bringing a claim can be a source of shame in itself;[262] this may increase individual reluctance to bring a claim.[263]

Norms are both generational and gendered: 'generation[al] conditioning' and 'gender conditioning'[264] mean members of some age cohorts—particularly the oldest old—feel they should be grateful for what they have:[265] '"Oh no dear, we're fine. Someone else probably needs that package more than we do."'[266] Discrimination is a minor problem compared to, say, war: 'They've lived through a lot worse than that and that's just going to be water off a duck's back'.[267] Some may not identify with a 'claim culture';[268] this is particularly acute for older women, who have a 'level of tolerance and acceptance of behaviour that they've had to manage [and] negotiate on their way up through their careers'.[269] However, baby boomers may be better self-advocates than older generations,[270] meaning acceptance of age-based behaviour may not endure into the future, as future generations become more 'rights enabled' and 'rights literate',[271] and more willing to make a claim as

252 A99.
253 A109; UK80.
254 A7.
255 UK80. See also A154.
256 Colin Mcleay, 'Inventing Australia: A Critique of Recent Cultural Policy Rhetoric' (1997) 35 Australian Geographical Studies 40, 43; Hugh Mackay, *The Pleasing Myth of Egalitarian Australia* (South Australian Equal Opportunity Commission, 1997).
257 UK80.
258 A163.
259 UK84.
260 A4.
261 A163.
262 A6.
263 A4.
264 A109.
265 UK80; UK166.
266 A99.
267 UK88.
268 ibid; UK93.
269 A99.
270 ibid.
271 A105. See also A109; UK166.

an exercise of their rights.[272] Further, cultural norms against complaining may be less pervasive among younger workers: 'young people don't just stay silent about issues.'[273]

Generational differences in norms may cause tension between individuals of different ages if there is an expectation that individuals will not complain about the poor treatment and discrimination they experience:[274] 'if you try and call it out, you're seen as a bit of a pariah.'[275] Even individuals who are initially willing to stand up for their rights may be inhibited from claiming by an organizational culture against complaining.[276] In some organizations, those who complain are seen as 'snowflakes',[277] and excessively sensitive:

> the prevailing mindset ... is, suck it up.... one participant [in training] said, 'I don't believe in wrapping people in cotton wool', which is what most of us would call just decent, polite, respectful treatment, you know? ... So I have to say how some people are crystal, and crystal deserves cotton wool treatment. And would we, do we really want to do without crystal in our lives, even if it is a bit more hard to care for? Snowflakes are beautiful.[278]

Increasing the number of age discrimination complaints will therefore require a cultural shift,[279] the challenging of age norms,[280] and greater recognition of the need to value and treat all individuals with respect.[281] In part, this can be achieved by empowering individuals to feel like they can do something about age-based treatment,[282] and promoting the idea that making a complaint is a positive assertion of rights for the greater good, with broader significance.[283] However, it also requires societal recognition of the harm that discrimination can inflict, which is rarely well understood by those who have not experienced discrimination themselves.[284] This requires an empathetic understanding of how other people feel and experience discriminatory treatment.[285] Training and outreach programmes can help to build this understanding.[286]

272 A105.
273 A156. See also A105.
274 A156.
275 ibid.
276 A3.
277 A99.
278 ibid.
279 A101.
280 UK86.
281 A99.
282 UK86.
283 A105.
284 A99.
285 ibid.
286 ibid.

Reform 1: That age discrimination complaints be reframed as a positive assertion of rights with broader significance.

Reform 2: That equality agencies develop training and outreach programmes to promote empathy and understanding for those who are impacted by discrimination.

5. Chances of success

In weighing the likelihood of success, impressions of equality law can fundamentally influence individual willingness to claim and pursue rights. If claimants perceive that a court is likely to support or uphold their complaint, then they may be more likely to pursue formal legal avenues; conversely, if there is a perception that courts are unlikely to support a claimant, then their expectations of legal processes may be reduced, and they may be less likely to pursue a formal legal complaint.[287] Individuals are more likely to pursue a complaint if they are aware of someone else who has been successful, or if there are publicly available examples of success, as in case law. Conversely, individuals are less likely to file a complaint if they are aware of someone who has been unsuccessful, or if they are aware that many age discrimination cases fail: 'it's really powerful for workers to see someone lose and it has a big impact on other people not wanting to do anything else either';[288] 'word of mouth . . . is huge.'[289] The way discrimination and harassment complaints are resolved within organizations also influences how people respond when they experience age discrimination:

> the whole process is revictimizing for people—and young workers do know that—and they know that other people have been through a process. If they've been through it all and nothing has happened or, as is regularly the case, a settlement happens, no one knows about it, and all that is seen is the person who has experienced harassment is no longer in a workplace but the person who did the harassing still is and nothing is spoken of. Nothing changes.[290]

The use of non-disclosure agreements (NDAs) makes it difficult to communicate whether equality law has been 'successful'. Indeed, it is questionable whether a claim is 'successful' if the claimant leaves the organization, the harasser or discriminator remains, and there is no broader change or reform. This is likely to have an impact on individual willingness to make a claim.

These impressions of equality law also influence legal practitioners: age discrimination complaints may be uncommon due to a lack of case law, which may deter

[287] Barnard, Ludlow, and Fraser Butlin (n 118) 245–46.
[288] A154.
[289] A104.
[290] A160.

practitioners from advising their clients to pursue such a claim.[291] In the expert interviews, legal practitioners routinely noted that no age discrimination case had yet been successful under federal discrimination law in Australia. For some, this meant they could not in good conscience recommend that their clients pursue an age discrimination claim. Instead, claimants may pursue a disability discrimination claim, as there are good examples of success in the area.[292]

This is somewhat of a vicious cycle: cases are less likely because there are fewer complaints, and complaints are less likely because there are few examples of successful age discrimination cases. As noted by barrister Dee Masters in her evidence to the WEC: 'Once it's on people's agendas, they think about it more. It could well be that some sort of high-profile litigation around this would encourage people to come forward.'[293] There is therefore a need to better promote success stories when they occur,[294] and for equality agencies to support strategic claims in this area (Chapter 8).

> **Reform 3:** That equality agencies better promote successful age discrimination claims and cases.

6. Benefits

The costs of complaining can be balanced, at least to some extent, by the potential benefits of pursuing a claim. However, potential outcomes or remedies for an age discrimination claim are rarely adequate or sufficient to outweigh the costs of complaining: damages for discrimination complaints 'are very, very low',[295] 'a pittance',[296] and 'modest'.[297]

Further, remedies rarely align with what people who are impacted by discrimination actually want:[298] 'the thing that our clients want more than anything is not the financial results but ... [for] whoever ... has done the discrimination to understand that it's not okay and ... to make changes so that it doesn't happen again.'[299] Having a voice is an important driver for some claimants.[300] Others may want their job back,[301] to be offered the job in question,[302] or to obtain some sort of restitution 'or [a] way to walk away and say, "I'm no longer disadvantaged by what happened

[291] A111.
[292] A104.
[293] House of Commons (n 10) Q91.
[294] UK152.
[295] A99.
[296] A7; A100.
[297] UK97.
[298] A5; A104; A151.
[299] A100. See also AHRC, 'Willing to Work' (n 7) 327.
[300] A99; A101; A102.
[301] A5; A104.
[302] A98.

here"'.[303] Alternatively, claimants may want the respondent punished in some way[304] or some form of structural change.[305]

In practice, few of these outcomes are achievable via a discrimination claim. A lack of adequate and meaningful remedies is therefore a major deterrent to claiming: 'feeling that you're not going to get anything out of it is ... another one of the big reasons people don't want to pursue it.'[306] Individuals who feel that they cannot achieve structural change through a formal complaint process 'don't elect to participate in it'.[307]

7. A lopsided balance

Overall, then, the cost of complaining is so high that even when a complainant has a strong claim they will not necessarily pursue it.[308] Some advocates feel 'irresponsible' advising clients to pursue a complaint:[309] 'it's just so hard. It's such hard work and they are so emotionally and physically draining and damaging and I just feel like we have to be honest with people about what to expect.'[310] For many complainants, it is better to simply move on.[311] Time is better spent looking for other work:[312] 'they will just walk away ... dust themselves off and move onto the next job';[313] 'they want to go somewhere where their skills are valued, and their input is valued'.[314] A complaint is harder than finding the next job.[315] For those who are economically vulnerable, their focus is necessarily on immediate financial needs, such as paying the rent or finding a job, rather than pursuing a complaint.[316] Others will simply not want to waste their retirement[317] or finite time[318] dealing with these issues.

This starts to explain, then, the low numbers of age discrimination complaints across jurisdictions: not pursuing a claim may be a rational choice. Even claimants who are very conscious of their rights may choose not to pursue a claim;[319] this 'choice', however, is most often made by women.[320]

[303] A104.
[304] ibid.
[305] A100.
[306] A104.
[307] A100.
[308] ibid.
[309] ibid.
[310] A100. See also A154; A160; UK84.
[311] A100; A104; A112; A153; A160.
[312] A98; A100; A102; A108; A151.
[313] A100.
[314] A104. See also UK84. At least, assuming they have another job to go to, or have skills that are in demand: A104.
[315] A3.
[316] A108.
[317] A169.
[318] A7.
[319] A100; A108.
[320] A100; A108.

D. Difficulties in Claiming

Even where an individual is willing to bring a complaint, and bear the risks and costs of complaining, there are structural issues that may inhibit claiming, including around access to information and advice, access to statutory agencies, time limits, and proof.

1. Information and rights awareness

In the AHRC's *National Prevalence Survey*, only 5 per cent of those who did not take action said they did not know they could take action or did not how to take action.[321] Thus, at least for these respondents, a lack of information is not necessarily a major barrier to accessing justice. This is consistent with Dee Masters's evidence to the WEC: in her experience as a practitioner,

> I think people are aware that they have rights. I do not think that is the issue. I think the difficulty is that it is almost impossible, or at least very hard, for people to understand whether they have been discriminated against and whether they should bring claims. I think that is where the gap is.[322]

Thus, the issue is less about rights education, and more about information asymmetries between individuals and organizations.

That said, a lack of information and capacity might still inhibit claiming. In the expert interviews, nineteen respondents expressed concern that people were not adequately aware of their rights to be protected from age discrimination. While people have limited awareness of their rights generally,[323] this is a particular challenge in relation to age discrimination:[324] age as a protected ground is less well-known[325] and less understood than other areas of discrimination law,[326] and is seen as primarily focusing on older workers, not young people.[327] It is complicated to understand when age discrimination is legal or lawful, and when it can be challenged, given the extensive exceptions to age discrimination law.[328]

Rights awareness is not evenly distributed across people of different ages. Older claimants may not have 'access to the same information, knowledge, wherewithal' as younger claimants, meaning they may be less able to bring a claim.[329] Conversely,

321 AHRC, 'National Prevalence Survey' (n 25) 70.
322 House of Commons (n 10) Q46.
323 UK84; UK86; A9; A101; A102; A108; A160; A158; UK152; A153.
324 A98; UK80.
325 A163.
326 A1; A158; UK152.
327 UK79.
328 A160; A164.
329 A151.

older people may be *more* aware of their rights than young people;[330] those in middle age and the young-old in particular may have better rights awareness.[331] Thus, rights awareness may increase with time, as generations that are more 'rights enabled' age,[332] and there is more information literacy, including through the use of the internet.[333] Being in work may also increase access to information and rights awareness.[334] The obvious point, of course, is that not all individuals within an age cohort will have the same level of rights awareness; there is significant diversity *within* generations.

Even if claimants are aware of their rights, they may have limited understanding of the process by which they assert those rights, or where to bring a claim.[335] Awareness of equality agencies and their role is not always high: 'it's really easy for someone to bring [a claim] and come into the service, if they know we're here.... It's knowing we're here and that we're available.'[336] In Australia, this is compounded by the need to choose only one jurisdiction in which to pursue a claim.[337] Confusion also exists regarding the role of equality agencies: 'when people ring us ... what they really want is [for] the Commission to take this magic wand, and ... wave it in the direction of the respondent, and sort it all out.'[338] This is not typically what equality agencies are empowered to do (Chapter 8).

A lack of rights awareness could be addressed through outreach by equality agencies, including through structured training programmes for organizations,[339] education about workplace rights[340] (including in schools[341] and tertiary education[342]), producing fact sheets and information,[343] working with relevant groups in the community,[344] and co-locating legal advisers and equality agency officers in places frequented by vulnerable groups.[345] While there is already considerable activity happening in this space, there are still gaps in relation to age discrimination law, at least when compared to other protected characteristics.[346]

It is questionable, though, whether rights-based education is effective in the abstract; it is more likely to be impactful where an individual has a clear and

330 A110; A153. See also A160.
331 UK93.
332 A105. See also UK93.
333 A105.
334 A99.
335 A98; A101; A164; A153; A158; A159.
336 A101.
337 A158.
338 UK97.
339 A99; A102.
340 A102; A159; A160; UK167; UK84.
341 A164; A160; UK167.
342 A160.
343 A108.
344 A155.
345 A102; A108.
346 A103.

present need for assistance (ie, in this context, once they have experienced discrimination or a workplace issue).[347] Thus, any programme needs to be evidence-based.[348] Agencies have tried various forms of outreach—such as putting case studies of age discrimination on their website,[349] structured training programmes for organizations,[350] and advertising to young people on Facebook[351]—with sometimes limited success.[352] This may reflect a failure to pitch advertising in the most effective way: for example, advertising to older people (rather than young people) on Facebook may be far more successful.[353] For the agencies, there was a sense of frustration and struggle in reaching out to diverse communities:[354] limited resourcing significantly constrained agencies' outreach activities,[355] including in reaching out to relevant non-governmental organization (NGOs).[356] That said, statutory agencies and practitioners had observed a significant increase in the number of people accessing materials and resources on their websites;[357] web materials offer a solution and a legal framework for addressing problems and give people permission to seek further support.[358]

Reform 4: That equality agencies continue to build their evidence-based outreach and training activities in relation to age equality.

There is a concurrent need to promote and support advocacy organizations that enable people to understand and assert their rights.[359] While this clearly includes CLCs and Citizens Advice (CAB), community-led organizations could play a key role in this space by increasing rights awareness[360] and signposting other forms of support.[361] Austerity policies and funding cuts have increased funding pressure on third-sector organizations, limiting their capacity to assist in this way.[362] There is

[347] A8.
[348] ibid.
[349] A153.
[350] A99; A102.
[351] A101.
[352] ibid.
[353] David R Brake, 'The Social Implications of Teens Leaving Facebook' (*The Conversation*, 11 October 2018) <http://theconversation.com/the-social-implications-of-teens-leaving-facebook-99362> accessed 11 December 2020; Seoyeon Hong and Sookwang Klive Oh, 'Why People Don't Use Facebook Anymore? An Investigation into the Relationship Between the Big Five Personality Traits and the Motivation to Leave Facebook' (2020) 11 Frontiers in Psychology <https://www.frontiersin.org/articles/10.3389/fpsyg.2020.01497/full#B45> accessed 11 December 2020.
[354] A101.
[355] A155; UK97.
[356] UK97.
[357] A8.
[358] ibid.
[359] UK81.
[360] UK93.
[361] UK81.
[362] UK84; UK92.

a need for better support, funding, and recognition of third-sector work, which is often being done by volunteers.[363]

> **Reform 5:** That there be better support and funding of community organizations to advance age equality.

2. Access to legal advice

While individuals might have access to information through various telephone helplines,[364] they do not often have access to appropriate and quality legal advice. In the AHRC's *Willing to Work* inquiry, both individuals and organizations raised concerns about access to legal assistance.[365] In this study, twenty-two expert respondents raised this as a major barrier to justice.

Limited access to legal aid and cuts to CLCs have seriously inhibited the legal support on offer to claimants;[366] these services have been 'pretty much decimated'.[367] The UK has a number of 'advice deserts', where there are few local organizations that can give advice.[368] Few queries are received by EASS from these areas, implying that there is limited rights awareness in these regions. Unions were seen as often missing equality issues, and therefore being a limited source of advice and support.[369]

For CLCs, demand is 'killing us'.[370] In small jurisdictions, there might be only one community legal practitioner specializing in employment discrimination law.[371] If that practitioner runs a case, there is no other practitioner available to give advice on all other matters:[372] 'It's not like I can say "I don't have capacity, I can refer you on to this service", because there just isn't one in [this jurisdiction].'[373] Matters can therefore only be pursued if they have reasonable prospects of success.[374] It can also be difficult for claimants to find the right person to assist them with their case: word-of-mouth referrals are particularly important in small jurisdictions.[375]

While the advocate survey was specifically targeted at those working in this area, most advocates had worked on very few cases of age discrimination relating to work in the last two calendar years (that is, 2018 and 2019). Of fifty-four respondents answering this question, over 80 per cent had worked on five or fewer claims

363 UK92.
364 The helpfulness of telephone advice in GB was doubted: UK78.
365 AHRC, 'Willing to Work' (n 7) 321.
366 A9; A107; A115; UK78; UK79; UK80; UK82; UK161; UK162; UK84; UK97.
367 UK79.
368 UK161.
369 A101.
370 A8.
371 A108.
372 ibid.
373 ibid.
374 ibid.
375 ibid.

Table 4.10 Number of age discrimination matters at work involved in 2018 and 2019, advocate survey

Number of matters	Respondents reporting
0	12
1–5	32
6–10	5
11–20	3
21+	2
Total	54

in this period (Table 4.10). That said, some outlier practitioners were extremely active in this area, with one working on seventy-six matters, and another forty matters, over the two years. Advocates most commonly saw matters relating to dismissal (thirty-two matters reported) and redundancy (seventy-five matters); most cases related to older workers (210 matters) rather than younger workers (seven matters). Few practitioners are seeing age discrimination matters in their practice; as a result, few claimants are likely to be accessing expert legal advice.

A lack of affordable and accessible legal assistance has led to a rise of litigants in person in equality matters:[376] 'The tribunals are swamped with people having a go themselves.'[377] This creates its own challenges for courts and tribunals, who have to work harder to provide support to claimants and address power disparities between parties.[378] Unrepresented claimants may be at a substantial disadvantage in proceedings:[379] 'it's a hugely intimidating environment.'[380] It is difficult to pursue a claim to a court or tribunal without legal representation, due to the formality and complexity of the legal system, and the need to counter complex legal arguments.[381] There is a significant difference between an advocate, who is doing their job, and a claimant, who is talking about something that has happened to them and affected them deeply: 'they're just in completely different positions.'[382] In Australia, these difficulties are compounded by choice of jurisdiction;[383] having a choice is

376 UK78; UK82; UK97.
377 UK97.
378 ibid. See, eg, Gabrielle Garton Grimwood, 'Litigants in Person: The Rise of the Self-Represented Litigant in Civil and Family Cases in England and Wales' (2016) Commons Briefing papers SN07113 9–12 <http://researchbriefings.parliament.uk/ResearchBriefing/Summary/SN07113#fullreport> accessed 23 May 2017.
379 UK79; A115; UK97.
380 UK97.
381 A5; A10; A115.
382 A115.
383 A5.

only beneficial if claimants are supported by good advice.[384] Accessing advice—and quickly, within statutory time limits—is a clear potential barrier to claiming.[385]

Claimants who can afford legal representation are either very wealthy or backed by their union or household insurance.[386] This is a small class, especially as union membership declines;[387] many vulnerable claimants cannot afford legal representation.[388] While some vulnerable workers will be assisted by legal aid and CLCs, 'there's a big kind of gap in the middle, of people who can't afford a private lawyer, but aren't sufficiently disadvantaged for legal aid or a community legal centre'.[389] Any compensation awarded can be 'eaten up by legal fees';[390] in jurisdictions where parties typically bear their own costs, there is limited scope to recover legal fees, even if a claim is successful.[391]

Even where it can be afforded, private legal assistance is not always *quality* legal assistance:[392] this represents a 'massive gap'.[393] Few practitioners specialize or have expertise in equality law,[394] making it a struggle to find qualified legal representatives.[395] Practitioners and advocates do not always understand how discrimination law works:[396] there is limited understanding in the profession as to how to interpret equality law, the objects of the legislation, the case law, and the complexity of equality law.[397] As one Australian respondent noted,

> there's a real lack of expertise around the law.... [Lawyers] don't understand the policy framework or values that sit within it. They often come with work health frameworks or work industrial law frameworks. So legal expertise I find is a real barrier to the process.[398]

By contrast, in employment law, there is a sufficient volume of cases for practitioners to build expertise;[399] practitioners who specialize in employment law often prefer to bring a claim in that jurisdiction, even where discrimination law might be relevant. It appears, then, that this is a self-reinforcing process: few practitioners specializing in

384 A7.
385 A158.
386 UK78; UK97.
387 UK78.
388 A100.
389 A115.
390 UK97.
391 ibid.
392 A101.
393 A115.
394 UK161.
395 A100.
396 A7; A105; A115.
397 A105.
398 A99.
399 ibid.

equality law leads to few cases being brought; there are then too few cases for practitioners to build a practice and a specialism in this area.[400]

Practitioners have few financial incentives to take on discrimination cases: laims are generally low-paying,[401] but expensive to run.[402] In a no-costs jurisdiction, it is difficult for CLCs to recover their costs.[403] No-win no-fee arrangements are ill-suited to the complexity and preparation required in discrimination law;[404] here, 'the legislation is technical, complicated, difficult to intellectually navigate'.[405] Practitioners who attempt to proceed on a no-win no-fee basis may do a disservice to their clients;[406] indeed, without relevant expertise, lawyers can often make a case worse.[407]

This may explain, too, why so many age discrimination cases are struck out: cases run by specialist practitioners are rarely the subject of strikeout proceedings.[408] This may be attributable to the quality of legal representation, rather than anything inherent in the case itself: 'things running depend on, you know, whether you've got the right engineer to build the car that will sort of withstand the journey.'[409] While there are some excellent specialists in this area, that expertise is often costly,[410] and it is not unusual for specialists to face an opponent who has never undertaken a discrimination case before.[411] Overall, then, there is a clear difference between people who *practice* in discrimination law and those who have *expertise* in the area.[412]

Thus, while there is a growing legal culture in equality law, there is still limited skilled legal assistance available to most claimants. This has flow on effects, as few judges and tribunal members will have experience or expertise in equality law:[413] this has led to 'quite patchy court decision making'.[414] There is a need, then, to build expertise in this area more generally.[415]

Further, practitioners tend to focus on court processes, and what will happen once a claim proceeds to public hearing and judgment. For most discrimination complaints, however, there is a whole process that precedes that stage; this is rarely well understood by practitioners.[416] Distinguishing between conciliation and

400 ibid.
401 A100.
402 A118.
403 A9.
404 A118.
405 ibid. See also A7.
406 A118.
407 A10. Concern was also raised that these lawyers may not be the most scrupulous: A9.
408 A118.
409 ibid.
410 A101.
411 A115.
412 A118.
413 A105.
414 ibid.
415 ibid.
416 ibid.

court processes is important: while conciliation operates in the shadow of the law, strict legal rules and tests are not determinative of how conciliation will be resolved (Chapter 5). Recognizing these differences may encourage more advisers to recommend discrimination law as a path to their clients. Without this understanding, however, practitioners can be 'overly risk averse' in deciding whether to pursue an equality matter, even to conciliation.[417] This risk aversion is further compounded by the lack of case law in this area: practitioners who are unfamiliar with equality law may look at the number of cases that are dismissed and conclude that cases never succeed in this jurisdiction.[418] In reality, of course, many good cases are settling,[419] but those without a deep understanding of this jurisdiction would not be able to see that by looking at the case law alone.

Addressing gaps in legal support and advice would make a substantial difference in practice, even in tribunals where self-representation is theoretically possible.[420] Best practice in the provision of specialist equality advice is evident in the Australian state of Victoria, where Victoria Legal Aid has a specialist equality law programme, founded following the recommendations of the Gardner report.[421] While this equality work had been undertaken for a long time, the establishment of a specialist service has allowed for a more coordinated approach.[422] This service might still not be reaching those most in need,[423] and there is scope for additional, centralized advice about the different paths for taking action, to help claimants navigate the complex federal and industrial landscape in Australia.[424]

To improve the skills and familiarity of generalist legal practitioners with equality law, specialist assistance could be offered to practitioners in relation to particular cases, including via a phone line or email, or web-based tools and resources.[425] There is a need to re-examine the provision of legal aid and the 'undercutting of the advice sector', as part of a holistic understanding of the claim 'journey' and access to justice.[426] More fundamentally, too, equality law needs to be included as part of legal education and training: in many law courses, it forms just a small sliver of employment law, and studying employment law is generally optional.[427] This could explain the lack of qualified practitioners in this area.[428]

417 ibid; A101.
418 A105.
419 ibid.
420 UK78.
421 Department of Justice, *An Equality Act for a Fairer Victoria: Equal Opportunity Review Final Report* (2008) 79.
422 A5.
423 ibid.
424 A158.
425 UK79.
426 UK80.
427 UK167.
428 ibid.

Reform 6: That all jurisdictions establish a specialist equality law programme to assist claimants.

Reform 7: That equality law be part of legal education and ongoing professional training for law students, practitioners, judges, and tribunal members.

3. Accessibility

Access to justice can be inhibited by physical inaccessibility, especially for claimants with a disability.[429] In Australia, access to equality agencies is particularly difficult for those in rural or isolated areas, as agencies and tribunals are typically located in the city.[430] This is a major challenge in jurisdictions that cover large geographical areas:[431] 'there are some very real limitations in terms of geography.'[432] In some jurisdictions, the population has low literacy and numeracy,[433] making complaints, access to information, and written complaint forms especially difficult to navigate. Once a claimant comes to an equality agency, issues of access and language can generally be well navigated.[434] The issue, of course, is gaining access to the agency in the first place. Thus, accessibility affects different jurisdictions in varying ways, and this diversity needs to be recognized in both agency outreach activities and attempts at reform.

Assuming a level of knowledge or understanding of the way discrimination law works can be as big a barrier to justice as physical inaccessibility. Access can be limited by a lack of knowledge and understanding of the way agencies, courts and tribunals operate,[435] and by the formality of language used. This is especially problematic at tribunal, where the design and processes are designed to intimidate,[436] but also relates to the language used by equality agencies themselves.[437] Despite agencies' best efforts, they may still be relatively unapproachable.[438] Even relatively informal processes can be alienating and intimidating for younger workers[439] and for older workers as they age.[440] Equality agencies rarely have the time or capacity to explain this sort of basic information to claimants. This is likely to exacerbate some people's fears about engaging with government bureaucracy.[441]

Issues of access could be addressed by co-locating legal advisers in places likely to be frequented by people who are impacted by discrimination. For example, in

[429] UK81.
[430] A99; A163.
[431] A99.
[432] ibid.
[433] A102.
[434] A99.
[435] UK81; UK97.
[436] UK162.
[437] UK97.
[438] UK97; A99.
[439] A160; A99.
[440] A103.
[441] A105.

one jurisdiction, lawyers attended family and children centres, where women were receiving prenatal check-ups, to identify and assist in matters relating to pregnancy discrimination.[442] While this was a useful way to identify and refer matters, cases were not necessarily pursued following a referral;[443] those who have not specifically sought out legal advice may be unlikely to pursue a complaint.

It may also be possible to promote access by increasing transparency and allowing people to see and visit the space in which claims are addressed and resolved. Physically opening up equality agencies, so they can be seen and engaged with by the general public, may help to promote access.[444] This may be especially effective for young workers.[445]

Reform 8: That equality agencies, courts and tribunals continue to review the ways in which they promote access to justice, including through the use of accessible language, and by physically opening up premises to the public.

4. Time limits

Even at this early stage, complaints may be barred by statutory time limits. By the time a query is raised with EASS, for example, time limits may already have expired.[446] A more flexible approach to time limits would therefore be highly beneficial,[447] including to encourage claiming.

Reform 9: That equality legislation be amended to adopt a more flexible approach to time limits.

5. Proof and the nature of age discrimination

Difficulties of proof may limit claiming:[448] in the AHRC's *National Prevalence Survey*, of those who did not take action in response to experiencing age discrimination (n = 133), 23 per cent took no action because they thought that they would not be believed, or they did not have proof or evidence of the discrimination, or they thought that nothing could be done.[449] Issues of proof are fundamentally intertwined with the subtle nature of age discrimination, attributional ambiguity, the tensions in age discrimination law, and information asymmetries between parties. As Dee Masters argued in her evidence to the WEC,

442 A108.
443 ibid.
444 A160.
445 ibid.
446 UK161.
447 A101.
448 UK161; AHRC, 'Willing to Work' (n 7) 323–24.
449 AHRC, 'National Prevalence Survey' (n 25) 70.

> If you are an older person and you are being turned down for a job, how are you to understand that you have been turned down because of your age? How are you even to make an informed decision about whether it is worth bringing a discrimination case? One of the real problems with discrimination cases generally is what we call the asymmetry of information. If you are an external candidate, you often will not know why you have been rejected, and you might not know who made the decision, especially if there has been some sort of shortlisting on paper. You will not know who the other candidates are, you will not know their relative strengths and you might not even know who is ultimately successful. So, in those circumstances, how are you to understand and to make an informed decision?[450]

Evidential requirements are potentially less demanding at conciliation: 'if you have an argument of discrimination, we'll have a look at it and we'll try and engage with the respondent.'[451] Conciliation is 'absolutely flexible'.[452] Once a claim progresses to court, though, proof is essential,[453] and it is this (higher) standard that advisers often seek to meet, even for filing a complaint with an equality agency.[454] Thus, there may be gaps between the level of proof required for a complaint and to attempt conciliation, and what practitioners *perceive* is required for conciliation.[455] This is likely exacerbated by the number of practitioners giving advice in this area who do not have experience in the discrimination jurisdiction.

E. Weighing Barriers in Practice: The Advocate Survey

In the advocate survey, practitioners and union officials were asked to assess the impact of these various barriers on workers' decisions not to pursue an age discrimination claim. The most influential factors in deterring claiming, according to these respondents, related to difficulties of proof, limited prospects of success, and the financial cost of bringing a claim (Table 4.11).

Respondents noted the particular difficulty of proving claims relating to recruitment; the stress and anxiety of claiming; the restrictive nature of time limits and exceptions; and that people may not attribute their treatment to age. The legal process was described as 'a war of attrition', where 'big employers can outspend and scare off most older employees!'

450 House of Commons (n 10) Q43.
451 A101.
452 ibid.
453 AHRC, 'Willing to Work' (n 1006) 335.
454 A101.
455 ibid.

Table 4.11 Responses to the question 'If you represent claimants or workers, and your clients have chosen not to pursue potential age discrimination matters, to your knowledge what factors influenced their decision?', advocate survey

	n	Not at all influential	Somewhat influential	Fairly influential	Very influential	Determinative
Desired remedies not available	31	14	7	5	1	4
Desire to maintain the employment relationship	32	13	9	4	5	1
Potential reputational damage	31	10	12	6	2	1
Already moved on to another job	28	8	11	8	0	1
Risk of costs orders	31	8	8	6	7	2
Want to move on	31	4	10	13	3	1
Financial cost of claim	32	2	1	7	19	3
Limited prospect of success	33	1	4	5	17	6
Difficulties in proving age discrimination	33	1	4	7	15	6
Time required to resolve issues through legal proceedings	30	0	8	10	12	0

V. Conclusion: Strengthening the Claiming Process

Individual enforcement requires individuals to navigate the fraught process of 'naming, blaming, and claiming'. This chapter has illustrated the substantial barriers that may inhibit the claiming process, even if an individual identifies that they have been subjected to age discrimination. Difficulties include limited access to information and advice, costs of complaining outweighing the benefits, limited accessibility of legal processes, time limits, and issues of proof. These barriers likely affect all stages of the enforcement process, from claiming, to ADR, to hearing and judgment. While they may be less significant in relation to claiming—where processes are informal, financial costs are low, and technicalities and issues of proof are less pertinent—they are likely to progressively increase in significance as claims progress.

Even at this early stage of claiming, though, barriers often appear to be insurmountable. The very nature of age discrimination—which is ambivalent, beset by tensions, overlaid by strong social mores and norms, subtle and difficult to identify and prove—makes the process of naming, blaming, and claiming more complex than for other protected grounds. Understandably, then, there are relatively few claims of age discrimination.

This chapter shows that some individuals, at least, are able and willing to make a claim of age discrimination. Complaint data—where available—reveal some telling trends. First, claims appear fairly evenly weighted by gender, with women slightly more likely to make a complaint in state jurisdictions. However, women are slightly less likely than men to pursue a complaint in the 'high stakes' Australian federal jurisdiction. Second, complaints are far more likely to be raised by older workers, especially those over the age of 55. Equality agencies rarely receive complaints from younger workers, across all grounds of complaint. Third, complaints often relate to recruitment, and—to a lesser extent—harassment and dismissal. This is consistent with qualitative research, which has found age discrimination in recruitment to be widespread.[456] However, age discrimination in recruitment is likely to be difficult to prove; it is perhaps surprising that this has not deterred claiming further. Fourth, complaints are likely to be brought by those in secure work; casual workers are less likely to make a complaint. Of course, younger workers are far more likely to be employed insecurely, meaning it is difficult to disaggregate the impact of age from the impact of employment security on claiming behaviour. Fifth, and finally, intersectional or multiple complaints are common, across a range of other grounds, representing nearly half of complaints in SA and WA.

Thus, there are clear trends in complaint data, across gender, age, job security, substantive area, and intersectionality. This is cast into sharp relief by the survey of age discrimination case law in Chapter 6: by the time these complaints proceed to hearing and judgment, the vast majority relate to *dismissal*, not recruitment; and most are brought by older men. Thus, complaints relating to recruitment and complaints by women in particular disappear somewhere between the complaint stage and judgment. The analysis in Chapter 5 of ADR considers where these claims

[456] Sian Moore, '"No Matter What I Did I Would Still End up in the Same Position" Age as a Factor Defining Older Women's Experience of Labour Market Participation' (2009) 23 Work, Employment & Society 655. In New Zealand, see J Handy and D Davy, 'Gendered Ageism: Older Women's Experiences of Employment Agency Practices' (2007) 45 Asia Pacific Journal of Human Resources 85.

might be going. Even at this early stage of claiming, though, younger workers are already missing from formal legal processes. There are clear gaps in enforcement for those in younger age cohorts.

Overall, then, strengthening the claiming process requires renewed attention to how individuals access advice and support from equality agencies, CLCs, legal practitioners, legal aid, and community groups. Reform should focus on strengthening these forms of support. Further, it is clear that the claiming process is fundamentally beholden to the *perceived* costs and benefits of complaining. There is potential, then, to shift how discrimination law is perceived, including by equality agencies better communicating success stories, and increasing their outreach and communication activities. Agencies can also focus their attention on how they translate enquiries to complaints, given the number of queries that get lost in this initial process. Even with these reforms, there are still fundamental barriers to individual claiming, especially for younger workers, who are effectively missing from the claiming process. This chapter has therefore laid the groundwork for moving beyond individual enforcement of age discrimination law.

5
Negotiation and Alternative Dispute Resolution

I. Introduction

Chapter 4 has mapped the barriers inhibiting individual claiming. For many potential claimants, the perceived costs of making an age discrimination claim far outweigh the potential benefits. For those who *do* make a claim, most will be directed towards alternative dispute resolution (ADR), with conciliation conducted by Acas (the Advisory, Conciliation and Arbitration Service) in Great Britain (GB), the Labour Relations Agency (LRA) in Northern Ireland (NI), equality agencies and the Fair Work Commission (FWC) in Australia, and through judicial and tribunal mediation.

ADR is a long-standing feature of discrimination law in both Australia and the United Kingdom (UK).[1] ADR involves processes—outside a formal court hearing—in which a third party helps the parties to resolve a dispute, typically via settlement. In all Australian jurisdictions except Victoria, conciliation is compulsory before proceeding to a court or tribunal. In the UK, conciliation is not compulsory, but it is compulsory for claimants to notify Acas or the LRA before lodging a tribunal claim. In practice, ADR has become the primary mechanism for resolving age discrimination complaints; it is a key procedural aspect of the individual enforcement model. Most age discrimination claims settle;[2] few progress beyond ADR.

In this chapter, I consider the theoretical and practical impact of negotiation and ADR, as key components of the individual enforcement model. Focusing on empirical case studies of enforcement in the UK and Australia, I draw on statistics from agencies, tribunals, and courts; qualitative and quantitative content analysis of conciliation case files held by Australian equality agencies; qualitative expert interviews; and the advocate survey, to consider how ADR is shaping the process, outcomes, and general landscape of age discrimination law. While ADR offers important benefits to the parties involved, and to the justice system generally, the

[1] Alysia Blackham and Dominique Allen, 'Resolving Discrimination Claims Outside the Courts: Alternative Dispute Resolution in Australia and the United Kingdom' (2019) 31 Australian Journal of Labour Law 253.

[2] A158.

Reforming Age Discrimination Law. Alysia Blackham, Oxford University Press. © Alysia Blackham 2022.
DOI: 10.1093/oso/9780198859284.003.0005

degree to which it is directing age discrimination claims away from public forums is likely to limit legal development. I consider, then, how ADR processes could be improved to better balance these risks and benefits.

II. Advantages and Limits of ADR

A. Benefits for Parties

Compared with litigation, ADR is potentially less expensive, quicker, less formal and stressful, confidential, and flexible in terms of both process and outcome. It prevents claims from 'clogging the courts', and is better for parties' health than committing to a full legal process.[3] Conciliation is 'absolutely flexible':[4] processes can be adapted to the parties' needs, increasing the accessibility of discrimination law.[5] While conciliation is conducted in the shadow of the law, there is far more flexibility to achieve a result that is beneficial to both parties.[6] Conciliators are focused on 'solving the problem rather than through a technical legal framework, bringing parties together to understand what the nub of the dispute is and how that might be able to be resolved'.[7]

In some jurisdictions, at least at the start of the process, conciliation is complainant-friendly; quite a low threshold needs to be met for a complaint to be accepted.[8] Even a marginal complaint will be accepted, and an attempt made at conciliation.[9] The aim is to make the process as simple as possible, and not get too caught up on evidence. Proceedings can simultaneously be respondent-friendly: respondents may not be required to file a response to a claim prior to conciliation,[10] saving time and money, potentially avoiding the need for legal representation, preventing matters from escalating or becoming aggressive, and allowing conciliation to focus on finding a solution, rather than focusing on what did or did not happen.[11]

Both complainants and respondents therefore individually benefit from participating in ADR. Parties may settle to avoid investing the time and emotional energy involved in a court claim,[12] and to keep a claim confidential,[13] protecting

[3] A100.
[4] A101.
[5] ibid; A153.
[6] A101; A150.
[7] A150. That said, complex legal tests—including the comparator requirement—could filter down to the point of conciliation, being used to temper claimants' unrealistic expectations in conciliation: A151.
[8] A99; A106.
[9] A106.
[10] A99.
[11] ibid.
[12] A153.
[13] ibid.

the reputation of both parties. In some jurisdictions, a conciliation is typically listed within a six-week period,[14] meaning it is a fairly efficient process (and certainly if compared to court proceedings). While enforcement processes themselves can be 'really hard' for a claimant to navigate, the people employed within those processes are 'committed and supportive and passionate ... aware of the limitations of the process and keen to support people through it.'[15] Conciliators are 'incredibly skilful', including at resolving even marginal complaints.[16] The conciliation process is swift, thorough, and very engaged.[17]

B. Systemic Benefits

At a policy or systemic level, ADR may lead to more creative and systemic remedies than would be achieved in a court or tribunal,[18] including policy development,[19] education and training,[20] and culture change.[21] 'Committed' conciliation focuses on achieving conciliated outcomes that advance the substantive aims of equality law.[22] This requires the support of an active conciliator, who can suggest and guide the parties towards appropriate remedies.[23] Conciliators can be 'interventionist' in the sense that they encourage parties to think about 'the greater good' and structural change:[24] 'we're quite active in dispute resolution ... to bring in a systemic component ... or put it on the table for suggestion'.[25] Conciliators see themselves as 'advocate[s] for the legislation', if not advocates for a particular person.[26] Conciliation can lead to higher compensation than court or tribunal proceedings.[27] Agency respondents therefore felt conciliation was leading to 'really great conciliated outcomes':[28]

> We can help find the solution for the parties that they can't see themselves because we're outside of the issue. Just because we have the expertise, we may have learned from past matters things like, 'well, have you tried [this]?'[29]

14 A99.
15 A100.
16 A106.
17 A107.
18 A10; A101; A150; A153; A155.
19 A101; A150; A155.
20 A101; A153; A155.
21 A101.
22 Linda Dickens, 'The Road is Long: Thirty Years of Equality Legislation in Britain' (2007) 45 British Journal of Industrial Relations 463, 480.
23 A101.
24 A155.
25 A101.
26 A10.
27 A113; A163.
28 A150. See also A153; A99.
29 A99.

Active conciliators use ADR to ask questions of the respondent, probe their processes, and help respondents realize that their conduct may (even unwittingly or unintentionally) disadvantage certain groups: 'They probably don't even realise it themselves.... hopefully, during conciliation, they might go, "Oh, yes." ... "Didn't think about that." '[30] The conciliation process then becomes about both education and resolving individual complaints.[31]

While ADR *can* lead to flexible, systemic remedies, it is unclear how common this is in practice. In the advocate survey, respondents did not report any matters where systemic change was negotiated through statutory ADR. Similarly, in GB, the vast majority of Acas settlements achieved in the first year of early conciliation involved financial compensation (91 per cent, median payment of £1,200), and some involved a reference (25 per cent) and/or an apology (4 per cent); systemic remedies were not reported.[32] In Allen's study of conciliated discrimination claims in Queensland, most agreements featured individualized remedies, most commonly compensation (61 per cent), an apology (49 per cent) or a reference (26 per cent).[33] Systemic remedies were exceptional.

C. Maintaining Relationships

Where parties are in an ongoing employment relationship, ADR may help to maintain that relationship and sustain goodwill,[34] by 'not exacerbat[ing] the relational problems at the root of the individual problem'.[35] Menkel-Meadow argues that participatory ADR and settlement is consistent with values of consent, participation, empowerment, dignity, respect, empathy, equity, and access;[36] it is therefore also consistent with the participatory and transformative aims of equality law. Enabling a claimant to tell their story, and be listened to, can do more to remedy discrimination than compensation, and can be a sufficient remedy in and of itself.[37] Statutory agencies aim to achieve restorative justice:[38]

30 A102.

31 A10; A102; A150.

32 Matthew Downer and others, 'Evaluation of Acas Early Conciliation 2015' (Acas Research Paper 04/15) 69 <https://webarchive.nationalarchives.gov.uk/ukgwa/20210104113851mp_/https://archive.acas.org.uk/media/4335/Evaluation-of-Acas-Early-Conciliation-2015/pdf/Evaluation-of-Acas-Early-Conciliation-2015.pdf> accessed 24 March 2022.

33 Dominique Allen, 'In Defence of Settlement: Resolving Discrimination Complaints by Agreement' (2014) 14 International Journal of Discrimination and the Law 199.

34 Krista Mahoney, 'Mandatory Mediation: A Positive Development in Most Cases' (2014) 25 Australasian Dispute Resolution Journal 120, 125.

35 Annemarie Devereux, 'Human Rights by Agreement? A Case Study of the Human Rights and Equal Opportunity Commission's Use of Conciliation' (1996) 7 Australian Dispute Resolution Journal 280, 283.

36 Carrie Menkel-Meadow, 'Whose Dispute is it Anyway?: A Philosophical and Democratic Defense of Settlement (in Some Cases)' (1995) 83 Georgetown Law Journal 2663, 2669–70.

37 Dominique Allen, 'Behind the Conciliation Doors: Settling Discrimination Complaints in Victoria' (2009) 18 Griffith Law Review 778, 790.

38 A99; UK117.

> It's about identifying harms and how those harms can be repaired and relationships restored so that we can all move forward.... it's not about enforcing the law, it's about making tools and skills and a forum available to people to repair stuff. And especially in the workplace, that's so important because we know most people don't even complain, they quit or they just suck it up.[39]

Conciliation allows the parties to engage in this process of repair, unlike adversarial court processes. It allows for the repair of systemic issues, which would not otherwise be identified.[40]

In practice, though, ADR may not repair relationships: by the time a matter has proceeded to agency-based conciliation, animosity between the parties may be so intractable that it is not possible to actually repair the relationship.[41] Once a relationship has broken down, it is hard—if not impossible—to repair it.[42] The issue, too, is not so much that ADR cannot repair employment relationships; it is that, in some contexts, raising any form of employment dispute (or even just asking questions about employment entitlements) is enough to irreparably damage an employment relationship.[43] This is particularly the case for individuals who are vulnerable, and in workplaces that systemically and repeatedly exploit that vulnerability.[44]

D. Effective and Appropriate ADR

This flags the inherent risks of using ADR to resolve discrimination and employment disputes, where there are substantial power disparities between the parties; ADR may not always be effective and appropriate in this context.

First, ADR risks reinforcing power imbalances in the employment relationship, and may lead to lesser remedies than would be achieved at hearing.[45] Particularly in cases where one side has legal representation, and the other does not, ADR can replicate the challenges and power imbalances typical of courts in a new forum.[46]

[39] A99.
[40] UK117.
[41] ibid.
[42] A6.
[43] A160.
[44] ibid.
[45] A7; Margaret Thornton, 'Equivocations of Conciliation: The Resolution of Discrimination Complaints in Australia' (1989) 52 Modern Law Review 733, 742.
[46] A10.

Second, extensive use of ADR limits opportunities for courts to interpret and develop the law,[47] confining the scope for public interest litigation, systemic change, law reform,[48] and the educative function of court proceedings. Conciliation is 'disastrous' for public interest litigation.[49] Case law that does emerge tends to favour employers as 'repeat players',[50] as they have the resources and long-term interests to challenge unfavourable decisions.[51]

There is a public interest in having matters heard and decided in public.[52] It is not normatively desirable that all claims be settled; sufficient cases must progress to a public hearing to ensure the development of precedent, and to provide visible evidence that rights can and will be enforced. As the UK Supreme Court opined in *R (on the application of UNISON) v Lord Chancellor (UNISON)*:

> Every day in the courts and tribunals of this country, the names of people who brought cases in the past live on as shorthand for the legal rules and principles which their cases established. Their cases form the basis of the advice given to those whose cases are now before the courts, or who need to be advised as to the basis on which their claim might fairly be settled, or who need to be advised that their case is hopeless.... the value to society of the right of access to the courts is not confined to cases in which the courts decide questions of general importance. People and businesses need to know, on the one hand, that they will be able to enforce their rights if they have to do so, and, on the other hand, that if they fail to meet their obligations, there is likely to be a remedy against them. It is that knowledge which underpins everyday economic and social relations.[53]

As a system of resolving disputes, ADR is most effective when positioned against a backbone of a rights-based dispute resolution system—in this case, court-based litigation.[54] A lack of case law inevitably has an impact on conciliation processes:[55] even if ADR is not strictly bound by court decisions, cases will act as '*de facto* precedents' and influence the ways in which parties negotiate.[56] Litigated outcomes

47 Julian Gruin, 'The Rule of Law, Adjudication and Hard Cases: The Effect of Alternative Dispute Resolution on the Doctrine of Precedent' (2008) 19 Australasian Dispute Resolution Journal 206, 208. Though some of these cases may not have been brought at all without ADR: at 211.

48 Lola Akin Ojelabi, 'Community Legal Centres' Views on ADR as a Means of Improving Access to Justice—Part I' (2011) 22 Australasian Dispute Resolution Journal 111, 115.

49 A9.

50 Marc Galanter, 'Why the "Haves" Come out Ahead: Speculations on the Limits of Legal Change' (1974) 9 Law & Society Review 95, 98–103.

51 Beth Gaze, 'The Costs of Equal Opportunity' (2000) 25 Alternative Law Journal 125, 126.

52 A163.

53 *R (on the application of UNISON) v Lord Chancellor* [2017] UKSC 51, [2017] 3 WLR 409, [69]–[71].

54 Jeffrey Scott Wolfe, 'Across the Ripple of Time: The Future of Alternative (or, is it Appropriate) Dispute Resolution' (2000–01) 36 Tulsa Law Journal 785, 794.

55 A153; A158.

56 Thornton, 'Equivocations of Conciliation' (n 45) 756.

establish 'the parameters within which parties can seek to negotiate an outcome'.[57] Without this, ADR risks enabling 'anarchistic manipulations of situational morality—"whatever works"'.[58] A lack of case law—and resulting uncertainty—may encourage claimants to settle: 'if there's no case law about it imagine being at that precipice and certainly it's sensible on some occasions to consider that settlement offer as a very viable way of resolving the dispute.'[59] Conversely, respondents may be less likely to settle if the chance of success at court or tribunal is minimal, or if legal precedent is unclear.[60] ADR can therefore only work effectively if it is supported and under-girded by a strong system of legal precedent.

ADR should therefore be seen as a *complement* to court proceedings, not a way of displacing them entirely. Some cases will never resolve via ADR, no matter how skilfully a matter is conciliated:

> The great advantage of a judicial system is it will resolve those disputes. It may not do so very fairly. It may do so at a great personal and general cost but in the end, you will get an outcome in a way that you can't guarantee out of any other type of system.[61]

Negotiation will only be effective and fair if parties have the prospect of access to a court or tribunal if negotiation is unsuccessful.[62] As noted in *UNISON*,

> although it is often desirable that claims arising out of alleged breaches of employment rights should be resolved by negotiation or mediation, those procedures can only work fairly and properly if they are backed up by the knowledge on both sides that a fair and just system of adjudication will be available if they fail. Otherwise, the party in the stronger bargaining position will always prevail. It is thus the claims which are brought before an ET which enable legislation to have the deterrent and other effects which Parliament intended, provide authoritative guidance as to its meaning and application, and underpin alternative methods of dispute resolution.[63]

A system that solely enables the confidential conciliation of claims, *at the expense of* public court hearings and determinations, may undermine the effective enforcement of individual rights, and will fail to give effect to legislative aims. Barriers that

[57] Therese MacDermott, 'The Collective Dimension of Federal Anti-Discrimination Proceedings in Australia: Shifting the Burden from Individual Litigants' (2018) 18 International Journal of Discrimination and the Law 22.

[58] Wolfe (n 54) 794.

[59] A158. See also A150.

[60] A150; A158.

[61] UK78.

[62] *R (on the application of UNISON) v Lord Chancellor* [2017] UKSC 51, [2017] 3 WLR 409, [92].

[63] ibid [72].

prevent disputes progressing to court or tribunal following unsuccessful attempts at ADR must therefore be scrutinized carefully.

Third, ADR is unlikely to be sufficient for addressing and effecting change with repeat respondents. Restorative justice only works if the respondent has a sense of responsibility or accountability: 'our understanding of a restorative justice model is that there needs to be ... guilt or remorse on the behalf of one party. And that is not our experience in those conciliations.'[64] Some legal representatives are more skilled at ADR than others; some do not come to ADR with the right openness or willingness to conciliate, and some see ADR as a tool or a tactic, rather than an end in itself.[65] Without an openness to ADR, conciliation becomes more about an employer's capacity and willingness to pay than the merits of the matter.[66] Some 'cheque-book respondents' treat discrimination claims 'as a risk management issue in the organization.'[67] Restorative justice may also be inappropriate in cases of recruitment discrimination, as there is nothing to restore.[68] It is likely to be more appropriate, however, in the case of an ongoing employment relationship.[69]

Fourth, ADR's focus on individual feelings and emotions tends to ignore and underplay the role of systemic discrimination and disadvantage in these cases:[70]

> Women's complaints are so often attributed to women being emotional and reactive, rather than being structural inequalities, and when you're in a space where you're encouraged to talk about your feelings, as opposed to talking about structural inequalities and violence and the violations of the law, that's really problematic for me.... I think the damage that is caused by discrimination is not just about hurt feelings, and it's really important that that is acknowledged.[71]

There is therefore a need to discern when ADR may be appropriate, and when it may be fundamentally inappropriate, including due to the systemic nature of discrimination or power disparities. Conciliators need the skill and experience to determine where ADR is not appropriate, and to be empowered to direct those claims to other avenues. This might include, for example, directing claims to a tribunal, or empowering the agency to investigate a matter itself (Chapter 8).

The risks and benefits of ADR affect claimants differently. Women may be less likely to pursue their rights to hearing, and more likely to conciliate.[72] ADR, then, might disproportionately direct some groups of claimants away from public

[64] A100.
[65] A10.
[66] A7
[67] A99.
[68] A104.
[69] ibid.
[70] A100.
[71] ibid.
[72] A113.

hearings, regardless of the merits or strength of their claim. The extent to which this is occurring in practice is considered in Part III.

Overall, conciliation should not be seen as an inherently good or bad thing.[73] If a matter is appropriate for ADR, substantive change can be achieved, and a good news story can be crafted as a result, then conciliation can have a broader impact and has significant advantages over pursuing a matter to a court or tribunal.[74] The issue, of course, is that good news stories rarely emerge: secrecy is embedded in ADR (see Part F).

E. Light-Touch and Intensive Conciliation

Further, while we might talk broadly about 'conciliation', much turns on how ADR is conducted in practice, and whether statutory bodies adopt a light-touch or intensive approach to ADR. To address the inherent risks and power disparities of ADR, conciliators must level the playing field.[75] A skilled mediator should challenge and reality test proposed settlement outcomes, to prevent a weaker party being 'railroaded' into an agreement.[76] Conciliators who are time-poor, or conducting conciliation via phone or email, may be unable to fulfil this role.[77]

Effective conciliation therefore takes both time and skill.[78] Discrimination complaints are highly emotive, not black and white, and often have claimants in challenging circumstances.[79] They cannot be resolved quickly,[80] 'but if you do dig a bit deeper and you do spend the time, you can actually get there, which is the benefit of [conciliation]'.[81] Effectively addressing parties' grievances requires a conciliator who is willing—if necessary—to challenge the parties, and work actively to identify relevant issues, especially where discrimination is subtle or cloaked.[82] It takes a skilled, knowledgeable, and sympathetic conciliator to navigate these competing demands and tensions.

Without a skilled conciliator, respondents may resist settling due to the stigma of discrimination.[83] Employers can be devastated when they receive a complaint;

[73] A9.
[74] ibid.
[75] A164.
[76] Gay R Clarke and Iyla T Davies, 'Mediation: When is it Not an Appropriate Dispute Resolution Process?' (1992) 3 Australian Dispute Resolution Journal 70, 74.
[77] Maria Hudson and others, 'Race Discrimination Claims: Unrepresented Claimants' and Employers' Views on Acas' Conciliation in Employment Tribunal Cases' (2007) Advisory, Conciliation and Arbitration Service (ACAS) 10, 11.
[78] Rosemary Hunter and Alice Leonard, 'Sex Discrimination and Alternative Dispute Resolution: British Proposals in the Light of International Experience' (1997) 42 Public Law 298, 311, 313.
[79] A151.
[80] A6.
[81] A107.
[82] A104.
[83] A100.

the challenge, then, is to shift their mindset, to see complaints as a tool that help to identify problems and how to address them.[84] Successful conciliation is partly about 'getting people out of that retributory mindset into a restorative mindset',[85] and moving away from a 'victim villain model'.[86] For some employers, a claim infringes upon their 'personal fiefdom', creating resistance to conciliation and settlement;[87] 'people don't like scrutiny, so even if probably what is alleged is true, people just don't want scrutiny of their operations.'[88] Even in a confidential conciliation, respondents will rarely admit to anything; a statement of regret—without admission—is the closest to an apology a claimant is likely to achieve.[89]

Thus, achieving the posited benefits of conciliation requires that (1) sufficient time be committed to each matter, (2) conciliators be skilful and committed, and (3) parties be open to, and willing to participate in, a meaningful ADR process.

Not all conciliation processes are designed in this way: conciliation conducted by Acas and the FWC is far more perfunctory than that conducted by Australian statutory equality agencies.[90] In GB, individual conciliation is typically conducted on the phone or via email, not in person.[91] This gives facilitators less opportunity to meaningfully engage with parties, and non-verbal cues might be missed or eliminated.[92] While discrimination claims are typically assigned a senior Acas conciliator, conciliation is conducted via shuttle negotiation;[93] parties are rarely brought into the same room for individual complaints.[94]

Acas has resisted adopting a rights-based approach to conciliation, instead emphasizing the benefits of its 'objective' and problem-solving approach to resolving matters.[95] Hands-off or laissez-faire conciliation of this nature is not likely to achieve the social policy objectives underlying discrimination law: as Dickens argues,

> ACAS conciliation officers do not take a view as to the reasonableness, sufficiency or fairness of any settlement judged by any external standard. ACAS's concern for (and interpretation of) its impartiality prevents conciliation officers acting as guardians of fairness or promoters of equality within the ET system.... There is a

[84] A99.
[85] ibid.
[86] ibid.
[87] A115.
[88] ibid.
[89] A153.
[90] UK78; UK162.
[91] By contrast, collective conciliation is conducted in person: UK117. See Michael Legg, 'The Future of Dispute Resolution: Online ADR and Online Courts' (2016) 27 Australasian Dispute Resolution Journal 227.
[92] Wolfe (n 54) 803.
[93] UK119.
[94] ibid.
[95] Dickens, 'The Road is Long' (n 22) 480.

> conflict between the search for compromise, which is at the centre of conciliation, and the pursuit of rights.[96]

In practice, the intensive conciliation offered by Australian equality agencies is prohibitive for Acas, given the sheer number of claims received each year.[97] While Acas aims to identify cases that would benefit from intensive, in-person conciliation, and offer it as an exceptional service, 'as workloads have got up and up, there is less and less of that happening'.[98]

That said, light-touch conciliation is comparatively ineffective at resolving disputes, being effectively 'pointless',[99] and representing a 'mass production approach to dispute resolution', or a 'sausage factory ... [an] abbreviated process for the sake of convenience':[100] 'if people had the skills to resolve [these matters] they wouldn't come to us'.[101] In-person conciliation would be more efficient at resolving disputes, especially in more complex matters.[102] This may explain, then, the low conciliation success rate for Acas conciliation (see Part III.A).

If governments are determined to re-direct matters away from the Employment Tribunal (ET) system, offering more intensive Acas conciliation would be one obvious solution. That said, as many Acas conciliators have been recruited into a model of limited in-person conciliation, there would need to be a cultural shift *within* Acas for a renewed focus on intensive, in-person conciliation.[103]

Reform 10: That governments increase funding for Acas, to facilitate intensive conciliation in appropriate discrimination matters.

In Australia, the way conciliation is conducted varies dramatically from jurisdiction to jurisdiction. Unlike conciliation conducted by statutory equality agencies, FWC conciliation is more focused on efficiency and bargaining than therapeutic styles.[104] At the FWC, conciliation is concluded within ninety minutes; statutory equality agencies offer around three hours per matter.[105] Equality agencies 'work from a much more strategic perspective' to attempt to achieve systemic outcomes,[106] whereas the FWC has 'more that churn effect.... there's a high volume of matters that come through and it's more about meeting timeframes ... than about

[96] ibid 479.
[97] UK119.
[98] ibid.
[99] A169.
[100] A10.
[101] ibid.
[102] UK119.
[103] ibid.
[104] Susan S Silbey and Sally E Merry, 'Mediator Settlement Strategies' (1986) 8 Law & Policy 7, 19–20.
[105] A115.
[106] A99.

an outcome'.[107] FWC conciliation 'happens quickly',[108] with claims often resolved within four to six weeks.[109] By comparison, equality agencies 'have [a] pretty good success rate of getting things done within six months'.[110]

For some practitioners and parties, the FWC's approach is a major strength of the federal industrial relations system. Complaints are resolved efficiently, quickly,[111] and with a minimum of fuss: 'it is good for a kind of positional bargaining, banging of heads, for a relatively simple cash [transaction] that is about settling for dollars';[112] 'Unions love to go to Fair Work';[113] 'that churn method works, to an extent. They resolve heaps of things.'[114] FWC conciliation is 'a bargain … It's just paying some money to have it go [away]';[115] 'I would say that's not conciliation. That's a settlement negotiation, which is a very different thing.'[116]

The risk, of course, is that this leads to unfair outcomes in individual cases.[117] Further, this approach to 'conciliation' fails to address the deeper and often systemic nature of discrimination, or the individual emotional harm experienced by complainants. By contrast,

> statutory [conciliation] has that restorative approach of being heard, valued, acknowledged, even if they deny [the claim]. . . . they're here in the room, that's some acknowledgement that they're taking you seriously.[118]

Thus, FWC conciliation is often not appropriate for dealing with discrimination claims.[119]

There is a trade-off, though, between the speed of FWC conciliation and the restorative benefit of equality agency conciliation. Some respondents reported waiting seven months for a conciliation at the Australian Human Rights Commission (AHRC): 'so that's probably one of the other reasons we don't go [the] discrimination route, it's just time, especially if you're talking international students, they may not be here in eight or nine months.'[120] The AHRC prioritizes claims by those currently in employment, expediting matters where an employment relationship might be salvaged.[121] Even if processes are now more efficient,

107 ibid.
108 A100. See also A107.
109 A100; A107.
110 A99.
111 A100; A107.
112 A115.
113 A101.
114 A115.
115 A101.
116 A108.
117 A157.
118 A101. See also A115.
119 A108.
120 A107.
121 A108.

or more efficient in particular matters, 'there's that idea that they take forever'.[122] Equality agencies need to grapple with both the reality and the *perception* of delay, in what is essentially a public relations exercise with claimants and their representatives:[123] 'word of mouth is . . . is huge'.[124]

The important thing, then, is to choose the right forum—and the most appropriate form of conciliation—for a particular client or matter. Even if FWC conciliations are a 'less suitable vehicle for discrimination type claims',[125] they might suit other matters.[126] The advantage of the Australian system is that claimants (and their representatives) can choose between the efficiency of FWC conciliation, and the more therapeutic and intensive conciliation offered by statutory equality agencies. For a skilled legal practitioner, then, choice of jurisdiction allows a nuanced selection of the 'right' (or most appropriate) type of conciliation for a particular dispute.

Unfortunately, though, the system does not cater for those who desire both speed *and* restorative benefit. Further, choosing the most appropriate jurisdiction requires a detailed understanding of equality law and different jurisdictional approaches to conciliation. Given most practitioners are not equality law specialists, the choice between conciliation models may be illusory; individuals without legal representation are almost certainly unable to make an informed choice. Other factors—like the risk of costs and time limits—may be more influential in the choice of jurisdiction than the quality of conciliation on offer. That said, even a limited choice may be better than no choice at all (as in the UK).

Even with intensive conciliation, complainants do not necessarily obtain what they want from conciliation. Some claimants desire a more proactive, hands-on conciliator, who will make an independent assessment of whether there was discrimination;[127] an objective conciliator is not necessarily going to offer the vindication and support that complainants desire or expect. According to one industrial advocate,

> what people are looking for is, I want someone to tell them they are wrong, I want them to understand they can't do this and it's against the law and that doesn't really happen in a conciliation.[128]

Vulnerable claimants may be confused or intimidated by an 'impartial' conciliator, or may feel that the conciliator is biased towards the employer,[129] exacerbating

[122] ibid.
[123] A104; A108.
[124] A104.
[125] A115.
[126] A108; A115.
[127] A100; A104.
[128] A100.
[129] Nicole Busby and Morag Mcdermont, 'Workers, Marginalised Voices and the Employment Tribunal System: Some Preliminary Findings' (2012) 41 Industrial Law Journal 166, 180.

feelings of powerlessness.[130] That said, parties may have a positive view of the conciliation process so long as they feel that a conciliator has listened to them and responded to their experience, even if they are not happy with the actual outcome.[131]

F. Secrecy

A key attraction of ADR for parties is its confidentiality, which allows parties to communicate freely, knowing discussions cannot be produced at trial.[132] Parties may be more prepared to reveal their 'true interests' in the 'safe haven' of conciliation,[133] promoting effective dispute resolution. The confidentiality of conciliation processes is increased by the confidentiality of conciliated outcomes: non-disclosure agreements (NDAs) are 'an integral part of ADR'[134] and ubiquitous in settlements; according to one practitioner, 'I would really struggle to think of a settlement without a confidentiality clause that I've seen in the last 15 years.'[135]

Confidentiality may encourage claimants to file a complaint, as there is less risk of reputational damage from claiming.[136] Similarly, confidentiality is a key benefit of settlement for respondents,[137] allowing them to avoid the 'stigma' of a court or tribunal decision branding them a discriminator.[138] This makes confidentiality a key 'bargaining chip' and form of power for claimants;[139] respondents often 'pay a premium' to settle a matter.[140] Confidentiality is a key reason matters settle, which often has nothing to do with the merit of a claim;[141] without confidentiality, 'matters just wouldn't settle'.[142] Thus, confidentiality has practical benefits for both claimants and respondents, and may facilitate the effective resolution of disputes.

While the confidentiality of ADR may benefit parties, it has a number of systemic disadvantages. Confidentiality exacerbates the other risks and limitations of ADR,

130 ibid 179; Andrew Boon, Peter Urwin, and Valeriya Karuk, 'What Difference Does it Make? Facilitative Judicial Mediation of Discrimination Cases in Employment Tribunals' (2011) 40 Industrial Law Journal 45, 78.

131 Hudson and others (n 77) 74.

132 See, eg, Equal Opportunity Act 2010 (Vic) s 117; Anti-Discrimination Act 1991 (Qld) s 164AA; Enterprise and Regulatory Reform Act 2013, s 10; Trade Union and Labour Relations (Consolidation) Act 1992, s 251B.

133 Clarke and Davies (n 76) 74.

134 A115.

135 ibid.

136 A118; UK162.

137 A115.

138 A118; Thornton, 'Equivocations of Conciliation' (n 45) 740.

139 A115; A153.

140 A118.

141 A153.

142 A115.

limiting legal development,[143] preventing success stories from entering the public sphere, and making it harder for non-specialists to bring discrimination claims. The enforcement of discrimination law appears opaque to non-specialists: as one practitioner noted, 'when everything's happening in private, it's hard to properly advise people on their prospects, in going down that route'.[144] Confidential settlement has therefore become a major barrier to the enforcement of age discrimination law.[145]

More fundamentally, too, confidential conciliation relegates matters to the private sphere:[146] through confidential ADR, discrimination law is reframed as a system of private transgressions,[147] rather than a 'project of cultural transformation'.[148] Experiences of discrimination are individualized, and enforcement is privatized,[149] with a focus on individual solutions.[150] Confidential conciliation hides systemic issues, and hinders societal change;[151] complaints resolved via a private deed are rarely the subject of a full investigation, even where a statutory agency has that power.[152] Confidentiality therefore 'causes silence … [and] while there is silence around these issues there can't be structural change.… People's voices need to be heard'.[153] Secrecy also inhibits group empowerment and collective approaches to achieving systemic change.[154]

At a systemic level, confidentiality makes it difficult to evaluate the broader impact of discrimination law, and the degree to which it is achieving social change.[155] In some jurisdictions, for example, the progressive framing of equality statutes is seen as having little impact; this is because those sections are typically utilized in confidential conciliation, rather than in the public sphere. Scholars and others might under-appreciate the extent to which progressive legislation can have an impact in practice, as it is mostly used behind closed doors.[156]

Thus, while secrecy and confidentiality are entirely consistent with an individual enforcement model, they do not advance the broad programme of social and

[143] A113.
[144] A107.
[145] A100.
[146] Margaret Thornton, 'The Public/Private Dichotomy: Gendered and Discriminatory' (1991) 18 Journal of Law and Society 448, 450.
[147] Margaret Thornton, *The Liberal Promise: Anti-Discrimination Legislation in Australia* (OUP 1990) 144–45.
[148] Andrew Koppelman, *Antidiscrimination Law and Social Equality* (Yale University Press 1996) 5.
[149] Anna Pollert, 'The Unorganised Worker: The Decline in Collectivism and New Hurdles to Individual Employment Rights' (2005) 34 Industrial Law Journal 217, 226–27; Trevor Colling, 'No Claim, No Pain? The Privatization of Dispute Resolution in Britain' (2004) 25 Economic and Industrial Democracy 555.
[150] Thornton, *The Liberal Promise* (n 147) 151.
[151] A3.
[152] A6.
[153] A100.
[154] Thornton, 'Equivocations of Conciliation' (n 45) 741.
[155] Dominique Allen and Alysia Blackham, 'Under Wraps: Secrecy, Confidentiality and the Enforcement of Equality Law in Australia and the UK' (2019) 43 Melbourne University Law Review 384.
[156] A99.

cultural change at the heart of discrimination law. Confidentiality reflects a tension between individual interests—to confidentiality, privacy, and achieving a quick settlement—and structural or systemic interests in achieving broader change.[157] Equality law is trapped in this tension between a desire for confidentiality and a desire for transparency: both have distinct advantages and limitations.[158]

The use and misuse of NDAs is under increased scrutiny, particularly in the context of sexual harassment.[159] In the absence of legislative reform to make certain NDAs void, the Equality and Human Rights Commission (EHRC) has issued guidance for organizations about the use of confidentiality agreements.[160] Even without legislative change, equality agencies can work proactively to promote transparency of conciliated outcomes. Some conciliators encourage parties to have no confidentiality clause in settlement terms:[161] 'we say, "no, what do you need it for? What are you trying to achieve?" '[162] Despite this prompting, 'if you looked at a dozen agreements here, you'd probably see ten with [NDAs] in, because people do insist'.[163]

> **Reform 11:** That governments more closely regulate the use of NDAs in discrimination cases, including through legislative change.

An alternative approach is evident in NI: the Equality Commission for Northern Ireland (ECNI) actively offers claimants legal support, through applications to its Legal Funding Committee (LFC). In exchange for this support, the ECNI asks claimants to participate in publicity around their claim, and to refuse confidentiality clauses in settlement deeds. This has enabled the ECNI to develop a substantial public database of successfully conciliated outcomes,[164] and a significant public media presence in NI.[165] Matters are more likely to be reported in the media if there is a story attached;[166] conversely, de-identified claims are unlikely to receive publicity, making it more difficult to '[get] that message out there'.[167] In recent years,

[157] A153; Thornton, 'Equivocations of Conciliation' (n 45) 735.
[158] A99.
[159] Equality and Human Rights Commission, 'Turning the Tables: Ending Sexual Harassment at Work' (2018) 16–17 <https://www.equalityhumanrights.com/sites/default/files/ending-sexual-harassment-at-work.pdf> accessed 3 May 2018.
[160] EHRC, 'The Use of Confidentiality Agreements in Discrimination Cases' (2019) <https://www.equalityhumanrights.com/sites/default/files/guidance-confidentiality-agreements-in-discrimination-cases.pdf> accessed 15 April 2021.
[161] UK119.
[162] ibid.
[163] ibid.
[164] ECNI, 'Legal Case Decisions and Settlements' (2021) <https://www.equalityni.org/cases> accessed 20 April 2021.
[165] See, eg, ECNI, 'Arts Council NI Chief Executive Settles Age Discrimination Case' (5 July 2019) <https://www.equalityni.org/Footer-Links/News/Individuals/Arts-Council-Chief-Executive-settles-Age-Discrimin> accessed 20 April 2021. This story was picked up by news outlets including the BBC, *Belfast Telegraph*, *The Stage*, *Irish News*, and *Arts Industry*.
[166] UK97.
[167] ibid.

respondent lawyers have sought to bypass this publicity requirement, by offering claimants substantially more money to settle with an NDA: an offer of £12,000, for example, escalates to £30,000, so long as there is a confidentiality clause.[168] It would be unusual for a claimant to be able to resist this sort of offer;[169] the claimant might then withdraw their application for assistance and settle the matter without the agency's assistance.[170] On the whole, though, offering direct assistance to claimants promotes transparency in some settlement outcomes.

III. Negotiation and ADR in Practice

Recognizing the potential risks and benefits of ADR, we can turn to how negotiation is occurring in practice. Are the risks and benefits of ADR being realized? Are systemic outcomes being achieved? Are certain demographic groups—like women—more likely to conciliate? This demands empirical consideration of complaints that are being conciliated (and not conciliated), the outcomes that are being achieved, and any issues that may exacerbate power differentials, such as unequal access to legal representation.

A. Conciliations Conducted

At the AHRC, around a third of finalized age discrimination complaints are conciliated each year (Table 5.1).[171] Many complaints are withdrawn, closed, or terminated without being subject to conciliation.

This is consistent with state conciliation data. Of ninety-six complaints in Western Australia (WA), only nineteen proceeded to conciliation; twenty-four were dismissed under s 89(1) of the Equal Opportunity Act 1984 (WA) as misconceived or lacking in substance, thirty-three were withdrawn (often following a conversation with the Commission about the potential merits of the claim or statutory provisions), seventeen lapsed under s 83A(2), and four were referred on to the State Administrative Tribunal (WASAT) (one by the Commissioner, which subsequently settled at mediation; three by the complainant themselves). Two complaints had not yet been resolved.[172]

Similarly, in the 2010–14 South Australian (SA) data, of sixty-seven complaints, thirty-four were accepted, twenty-two were not accepted, and eleven were

[168] ibid.
[169] ibid.
[170] ibid.
[171] These figures relate to age discrimination complaints generally, and not those specifically related to work.
[172] These numbers do not add to ninety-six, as one complaint can be both conciliated and referred.

Table 5.1 Outcomes of age discrimination complaints, AHRC, 2016–17 to 2019–20

	2016–17	2017–18	2018–19	2019–20
Age complaints	155*	174*	138*	168
Finalized	144	173	160	117
Still open	0	0	10	dns
Deferred	0	0	4	dns
Conciliated	49	73	48	34
Did not wish to participate	21	28	38	dns
Terminated	24	20	17	27
Withdrawn	50	41	17	14
Upfront termination	1	5	2	1
Admin closure	10	7	2	4
% Conciliated (of finalized)	34.0	42.2	30.0	29.0

Source: AHRC
Table notes:
* = numbers differ from annual report due to time of reporting
dns = did not specify

undetermined. Only fourteen complaints proceeded to conciliation. For claims that were not conciliated, twenty-five were withdrawn, lost contact, or did not want to proceed; twelve were outside jurisdiction; three were lacking in substance; nine had no ground or area link; and one was covered by an exemption.[173] In the 2014–20 data, sixty-three complaints were received. Of these, eight were not initiated (ie, not in jurisdiction), sixteen were declined (ie, engaged the Act, but were declined for other reasons), and thirteen were withdrawn; one was still being assessed. Only eighteen complaints were conciliated, and seven were referred to the SA Civil and Administrative Tribunal (SACAT).

In the UK, parties may opt out of conciliation. At Acas, take-up of conciliation is substantially higher in age discrimination matters than for all notifications (Table 5.2).

Few Acas conciliations lead to settlements: COT3 settlements[174] are achieved in only 15 to 18 per cent of age discrimination matters each year; this is similar to all matters (Table 5.3). Between 28 and 35 per cent of age discrimination matters progress to ETs each year; this is higher than for all matters,[175] and significantly higher

[173] These were not mutually exclusive.
[174] That is, settlements with Acas's involvement.
[175] cf Downer and others (n 32) 93.

Table 5.2 Take-up of early conciliation (per cent), age, and all notifications, Acas, 2014–15 to 2018–19

	Age discrimination notifications (%)	All notifications (%)
2014–15	82	73.2
2015–16	80	67.3
2016–17	83	64.6
2017–18	85	59
2018–19	77	53.9

Source: Acas

than the comparable (3–4 per cent) figure in Australia. Most disputes do not proceed to an ET or reach a conciliated settlement.

Conciliation success rates are relatively low in GB, especially when compared with Australia. In 2018–19, for example, conciliation was taken up in 77 per cent of age discrimination notifications, yet only 16 per cent of age discrimination matters resulted in a COT3 settlement. As a rough estimate, then, about 20.7 per cent of conciliated age discrimination matters reached a COT3 settlement. By contrast, the AHRC in 2018–19 successfully conciliated 30.0 per cent of age discrimination complaints. This may reflect the practical difference between 'light-touch' and intensive conciliation in achieving settlements.

Claims filed in the ET can be referred back to Acas for conciliation (Table 5.4). The number of claims referred declined significantly with the introduction of early conciliation, but is again increasing over time.

In NI, early conciliation came into effect on 27 January 2020.[176] Even prior to this, the LRA was dealing with only a small proportion of the complaints it received each year (Table 5.5). In the LRA's 2018–19 Annual Report, it reported carrying over 43,847 employment cases and 1,833 equality cases to 2019–20;[177] the number of employment cases carried over more than doubled from 2017–18 to 2018–19. This high outstanding case load reflects an agency under significant pressure, including from budget cuts and staff departures. The introduction of early conciliation will only exacerbate these workload issues.

[176] The Industrial Tribunals and Fair Employment Tribunal (Early Conciliation: Exemptions and Rules of Procedure) Regulations (Northern Ireland) 2020 (NI).

[177] NI Labour Relations Agency, 'Annual Report and Accounts 2018–19' (2019) 28 <https://www.lra.org.uk/sites/default/files/2019-07/Labour-Relations-Agency-annual-report-2018-19.pdf> accessed 25 March 2021.

Table 5.3 Outcome of matters (per cent), age, and all matters, GB, 2014–15 to 2018–19

	Age discrimination matters (%)			All matters (%)			
	Progressed to ET	Did not progress to ET	COT3 settlement		Progressed to ET	Did not progress to ET	COT3 settlement
2014–15	31	54	16	*April–Dec 2014*	22	63	15
2015–16	28	56	15	*2015*	19	65	16
2016–17	28	54	18	*2016*	19	63	18
2017–18	35	48	17	*2017*	28	56	16
2018–19	35	49	16	*2018*	27	63	10

Source: Acas

Table 5.4 ET1 cases received by Acas for conciliation from the ET Service, age and total, 2010–11 to 2019–20

	Age	Total
2010–11	2,686	74,620
2011–12	2,796	72,075
2012–13	2,235	67,825
2013–14	1,473	40,938
2014–15	844	18,830
2015–16	850	20,074
2016–17	dns	18,647
2017–18	1,056	26,012
2018–19	1,633	36,531
2019–20	2,286	40,978

Source: Acas Annual Reports
Table notes:
dns = did not specify

Table 5.5 Complaints received and dealt with, age and total, NI LRA, 2016–17 to 2018–19

	2016–17		2017–18		2018–19	
	Received	*Dealt with*	*Received*	*Dealt with*	*Received*	*Dealt with*
Age	226	86	128	75	93	106
Total	10,180	6,195	38,294	5,027	26,815	4,365

Source: LRA Annual Reports

Of age claims that are 'dealt' with by the LRA, many are withdrawn (Table 5.6). This is not the case for all matters (Table 5.7): age claims are far more likely to be withdrawn, and less likely to be settled or referred to a tribunal, than all claims. Overall, though, the LRA's settlement rate for age discrimination matters is similar to—or even higher than—that at the AHRC. It remains to be seen how these statistics are affected by early conciliation.

Table 5.6 Age claims received and dealt with, by outcome, LRA, 2005–06 to 2018–19

	Received	Dealt with	Settled	Withdrawn	Referred to tribunal
2005–06	0	0	0	0	0
2006–07	24	0	0	0	0
2007–08	65	36	17	17	2
2008–09	76	65	21	37	7
2009–10	137	103	34	57	12
2010–11	95	117	38	62	17
2011–12	189	109	51	40	18
2012–13	199	158	48	95	15
2013–14	80	106	33	54	19
2014–15	114	182	48	117	17
2015–16	104	120	43	66	9
2016–17	226	86	36	44	6
2017–18	128	75	37	30	8
2018–19	93	106	50	43	13

Source: LRA Annual Reports

B. Conciliated Outcomes

Confidentiality tends to limit public data on conciliated outcomes. The AHRC's online conciliation register provides a public sample of 'selected' conciliations.[178] Given the register is 'curated' by the AHRC, and has no precedential weight, its usefulness for practitioners is questionable.[179] However, the register could be useful for claimants, especially if better publicized so individuals could see successful outcomes in the federal jurisdiction.[180] Transparency of this nature might encourage more claiming.[181]

> **Reform 12:** That jurisdictions develop and publicize a register of conciliated outcomes to inform and educate potential claimants.

[178] A115.
[179] A115.
[180] A106.
[181] A112.

Table 5.7 Age and total claims dealt with, by outcome, LRA, 2015–16 to 2018–19

	2015–16			2016–17			2017–18			2018–19		
	Age (n = 118)		All (n = 7,009)	Age (n = 86)		All (n = 6,195)	Age (n = 75)		All (n = 5,027)	Age (n = 106)		All (n = 4,365)
	n	%	%	n	%	%	n	%	%	n	%	%
Settled	43	36.44	53.03	36	41.86	66.91	37	49.33	53.83	50	47.17	63.67
Withdrawn	66	55.93	29.48	44	51.16	21.81	30	40	32.07	43	40.57	22.66
Referred	9	7.63	17.49	6	6.98	11.28	8	10.67	12.25	13	12.26	12.26

Source: LRA Annual Reports

Table 5.8 Age claims conciliated, AHRC, 2010–11 to 2018–19

	Age claims All areas			Age claims Employment	
	Conciliated claims	Conciliation success rate (%)	Claims successfully conciliated (n, approx.)	n	% all age complaints
2010–11	78	66	51	195	66
2011–12	102	69	70	134	68
2012–13	78	76	59	103	66
2013–14	75	74	56	128	70
2014–15	65	70	46	103	69
2015–16	81	80	65	105	65
2016–17	47	73	34	100	65
2017–18	58	81	47	105	61
2018–19	71	83	59	83	61
Total			**487**	**1056**	**66**

Source: AHRC Annual Reports and author's own calculations

On 13 April 2020, there were only thirty-nine conciliated age discrimination claims on the register that related to employment,[182] dating from 2011 to 2018. No conciliations from 2013 or 2019 had been published. Assuming age discrimination claims relating to employment are successfully conciliated at similar rates to age claims relating to all areas (Table 5.8),[183] we would expect around 321 claims to have been successfully conciliated over this period. As a rough estimate, then, approximately 12 per cent of all conciliated age discrimination complaints that relate to work are published on the register. It is unclear how the AHRC selects conciliated outcomes to include on the register: these may be the 'best' outcomes negotiated (however that is judged), or could be representative of trends. This is not specified on the register itself.

Reform 13: That jurisdictions publicly state how matters are selected for inclusion on the register of conciliated outcomes.

[182] In my search of the register, I removed one conciliation that did not have an age complaint, and two duplicate entries.

[183] The AHRC does not report the conciliation rate or conciliation success rate for age discrimination complaints relating to employment.

Table 5.9 Outcomes of age discrimination conciliations, AHRC conciliation register, 2011–19

Outcome	Number of conciliations
Apology	12
Compensation	26
Other opportunity	3
Revised terms	2
Statement of service or reference	11
Policy change	7
Training	4

However selective, the AHRC's register provides some illustration of conciliated outcomes (Table 5.9). Of the thirty-nine conciliations, twenty-six resulted in some form of compensation, ranging from \$75 to \$55,000, with a median amount of \$6,750 and average payment of \$13,183.92. The next most common remedy was a statement of service or reference (eleven conciliations). Some conciliations led to more creative remedies, such as offering the claimant an opportunity (eg, contacting the claimant for future work opportunities (two conciliations), or approving the claimant's transfer to another work location), or changing terms or conditions of employment (such as by holding weekly meetings to address any of the claimant's concerns, and a pay-rise subject to business performance; and changing the frequency with which the complainant had to have credentials renewed). Systemic changes—such as changes to policies, or training—were achieved eighteen times across seventeen conciliations (one resulted in both policy change and training), meaning systemic changes were achieved in 43.6 per cent of conciliations reported.

These conciliations were not particularly effective at repairing or maintaining relationships: of the twenty-eight conciliations relating to existing employees, relationships between the parties were noted as being maintained in five conciliated outcomes. The relationship between the parties had clearly ended in twenty-three conciliation reports (82.1 per cent). This may be because many claims related to dismissal (eight), retirement (six), or redundancy (four), where relationships will be difficult to maintain or re-enliven.

A more comprehensive picture of conciliated outcomes emerges from state and FWC data (Table 5.10). Compensation is the primary remedy in all jurisdictions. Comparatively few complaints are successfully conciliated.

Table 5.10 Conciliated outcomes, age complaints, Queensland, WA, SA, FWC

	Qld	WA	SA	SA	FWC
	1/2009–7/2019	2014–19	7/2010–6/2014	7/2014–6/2020	7/2012–6/2020
Complaints	387	96	67	63	605[ii]
Referred to tribunal	54	4	3	7	41 (arbitration) 156 (certificates issued)
Withdrawn	33	33	25	13	
Dismissed/lapsed	128	41	25	24	
Not yet resolved	8	2		1	
Conciliated	145	19	14	18	605
Unconciliable	19		3		197
Private settlement	1	3	1		
Remedy recorded	96		10		381
Compensation	69	8	5	9	306
Mean	$8,906.65	$2,470		$4,071.25	
Median	$5,000	$2,000		$3,500	
Minimum	$100	$350		$2,500	
Maximum	$78,000	$5,000[i]		$12,093.55	
Apology or statement of regret	26	6	6		
Explanation		5			
Reinstatement	3				
Systemic outcomes	19	Policy change (1) Education/training (2)	Policy change (3) Training (1)		
Statement of service or reference	19				
Other remedy	13	Reconsidered for a job (1) Transfer (1) Job offer (1) Undertaking to cease action (1)	Employment options improved (5)		

Continued

Table 5.10 *Continued*

	Qld	WA	SA	SA	FWC
	1/2009–7/2019	2014–19	7/2010–6/2014	7/2014–6/2020	7/2012–6/2020
Non-monetary award					241

Source: QHRC, WAEOC, SAEOC, FWC, SA Attorney-General's Department, Discrimination Complaints and Enquiries (2015) <https://data.sa.gov.au/data/dataset/aff12383-bb28-4a97-9c75-fbbcf9eeec7e> and author's own calculations

Table notes:

[i] One claim settled at SAT mediation for $8,000.

[ii] General protections applications involving dismissal where age was identified as a ground; these data do not purport to completely and accurately record all applications received.

Qld = Queensland

Blank = not reported or discernible

Table 5.11 Outcomes achieved, claims with legal assistance (all grounds), ECNI, 2011–12 to 2018–19

Year	Claims granted assistance	Number of settlements	Total settlement compensation	Number of tribunal cases
2011–12	85	50	£360,000	66
2012–13	83	62	*	6
2013–14	110	50	£235,125	11
2014–15	59	20	*	7
2015–16	71	38	£293,200	*
2016–17	59	41	£343,500	6
2017–18	52	26	*	3
2018–19	67	38	£950,000	2

Source: ECNI Legal Services Reports

Table notes:

* = not reported

There is no publicly available data in GB about the outcomes achieved in COT3 settlements. However, the ECNI reports on settlements achieved with its legal assistance across all protected grounds (Table 5.11). In 2018–19 the ECNI reported two settlements relating to age discrimination at work; one had a settlement of £14,000.

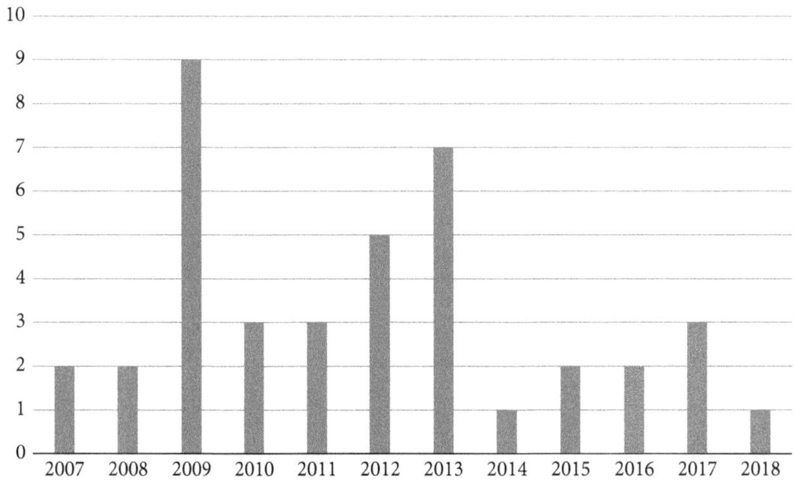

Figure 5.1 Age discrimination claims supported by year of resolution, ECNI

According to the ECNI's records (provided for this research), from 2007 until mid-2019 legal assistance was granted to forty-one claimants in relation to age discrimination at work. The highest number of claims resolved was in 2009 (nine claims); fewer claims have been supported in recent years (Figure 5.1).

The majority (thirty-three or 80 per cent) of supported claims settled; only eight were resolved at tribunal.[184] The ECNI supported a similar number of men (20) and women (21) claimants over this time. In claims resolved since 2014, however, women were supported in eight claims, while only one man was supported; this may reflect a concerted focus on supporting women age discrimination claimants in recent years.

Most supported claimants alleged they were perceived as too old (thirty-six); only four matters related to claimants who were perceived to be too young. Where age was specified (thirty-six claims), the youngest claimant was aged 20, and the oldest was aged 72; the mean age for supported claimants was 53.97, and the median was 58. The majority of supported claimants (twenty-two) were aged between 50 and 65. A number of complaints also raised issues of sex discrimination (fifteen), disability discrimination (five), race discrimination (two), religious discrimination (two), and political opinion discrimination (one). The most common substantive area of complaint was the end of the employment relationship, whether due to dismissal (eleven cases) or redundancy (nine). Other

[184] One claim was the subject of a tribunal judgment at first instance, but settled on appeal.

common areas of complaint were recruitment (thirteen), promotion (five), and harassment (five).

The majority of successful claims (thirty-seven) resulted in monetary compensation.[185] These awards ranged in value from £500 to £70,000,[186] with a mean of £13,571 and median of £9,275. Two claims resulted in an apology or statement of regret, and four led to a letter of reference. Policy change was achieved in four settlements; and in twenty-eight settlements respondents agreed to meet or liaise with the ECNI to ensure their policies, procedures, and practices complied with equality law, and to make recommended changes.

The matters supported by the ECNI are notable for four key reasons. First, many claims achieved low levels of monetary compensation, especially those relating to recruitment, where it is difficult to quantify loss. For claimants without agency support, the costs of pursuing such a matter will typically outweigh any monetary benefit (Chapter 4). Thus, it is likely that the ECNI's legal assistance is supporting claims that would not otherwise be pursued to the point of settlement or hearing.

Second, these settlements are notable for their potential to achieve systemic change. By requiring respondents to meet or liaise with the ECNI as part of the terms of settlement, it is possible for the agency to identify and support non-compliant employers and achieve systemic change to policies and practices. Offering legal assistance to individual claimants is therefore an effective way for the ECNI to identify employers who require agency intervention or support, and to help direct its other functions (Chapter 8).

Third, and relatedly, these claims highlight the holistic way in which the ECNI exercises its functions as a statutory agency. Claimants who approach the ECNI's advice line for assistance are, where appropriate, directed to apply for legal assistance. Through the provision of legal assistance, the ECNI can identify employers in need of structured agency support or intervention, and can build these interventions into terms of settlement for individual claims. While the provision of legal assistance is not cheap, the ECNI can leverage individual claims to achieve systemic and societal outcomes. Key to this, however, is making publicity a condition of the provision of legal support. Publicizing settlement outcomes can help educate and raise public awareness of age discrimination. Given that the vast majority of ECNI-supported age discrimination claims settle, transparency is essential to achieve broader societal change.

Fourth, even with the provision of early legal assistance, very few employment relationships were maintained or salvaged through these claims. This is not surprising for the claims that related to recruitment. For those relating to

[185] For those four claims where monetary compensation was not awarded, in one claim, compensation was not sought; in another, the relationship was maintained and the respondent agreed to meet with the ECNI; one tribunal claim failed because it was beyond the scope of the Regulations; and one tribunal claim failed where a retirement age was held to be objectively justified.

[186] This was a remedy settlement following a tribunal decision.

dismissal or redundancy, though, not one resulted in the claimant being reinstated. Relationships were only maintained in three claims; all of these related to promotion. This indicates that, even with proper legal support, it is difficult to maintain employment relationships once discrimination is alleged; conciliation and settlement do not necessary help to facilitate future relationships, though they may help to repair past harm.

C. Legal Representation

Given the risk of power disparities in ADR, legal representation—and, more specifically, disparities in parties' legal representation—might influence conciliated outcomes. The data from Australian jurisdictions offers two conclusions. First, representation appears to be limited for both complainants and respondents at conciliation. Second, though, there is limited evidence that represented complainants achieve better conciliated outcomes. Thus, legal representation does not appear to be influencing outcomes at conciliation, perhaps because representation in ADR remains exceptional.

In WA, only one complaint noted that the complainant was represented by a solicitor. However, other complainants were represented by trade unions (three complaints), family members (two), and a community legal centre (CLC) (one). Complainants were unrepresented in sixty-three complaints, and data was not collected for twenty-six complaints (those from 2014–15). This is similar to the representation rate for respondents: legal representation was recorded in only six complaints, and respondents were unrepresented in sixty-four complaints. Again, this data was not collected for twenty-six complaints from 2014–15. Thus, complainants and respondents were represented at similar rates in WA. The difference, though, is that respondents were more likely to be represented by a solicitor, while complainants were typically represented by family or trade unions.

This sample offers limited evidence that representation leads to better outcomes for complainants. The claim supported by a CLC was dismissed as lacking in substance; the complaint with a private solicitor was resolved with a privately negotiated settlement, with the complainant receiving performance bonus shares (the value of which was not specified). For the complaints supported by trade unions, one was resolved privately, one was still under investigation, and another was dismissed as lacking in substance.

In Queensland, only nine conciliation files noted that the complainant was legally represented; by contrast, sixty-seven files noted that a complainant was not legally represented. Respondent representation was not recorded. Of the nine conciliations where claimants were legally represented, conciliated outcomes were noted in seven files: two complaints were resolved with a statement of service or written reference; the other five complaints achieved damages of AU$15,000,

AU$10,000 (plus a transfer of employment), AU$8,000, AU$6,500, and AU$5,000. These represented claimants achieved average compensation of AU$8,900 and a median of AU$6,500; this is comparable to what was achieved across conciliations as a whole (mean of AU$8,906.65 and median of AU$5,000). There is therefore no evidence from this limited sample that represented complainants do better at conciliation than unrepresented complainants, though the small number of represented complainants makes comparison difficult.

D. Outcomes by Gender

Conciliation may be more aligned with women's values and 'moral voice' than adversarial litigation,[187] meaning women may be more likely to participate in ADR than court proceedings.[188] However, as Thornton warns, assuming that women are innately more attracted to conciliation ignores prevailing power structures and structural barriers to women accessing formal court proceedings:

> rather than to hastily assume the existence of an innate sex-based homology between the respective modes, culturally-imposed imperatives, such as the cost of formal litigation, which favour white, middle class men and reflect their relative superiority in the labour market, should not be dismissed.[189]

Thus, even if women are more likely to conciliate their claims, this reflects structural power and resource disparities, rather than any innate preference for a particular form of dispute resolution.

In Queensland, the recorded pronouns or gender of the complainant were discernible in 310 of 387 complaints; women (161 complaints) were slightly more likely to bring complaints than men (149 complaints). Complaint outcomes were fairly evenly distributed by gender (Table 5.12), though women were less likely to withdraw their complaint than men.

Where recorded, negotiated compensation appeared similar for men and women (Table 5.13): if anything, women negotiated slightly higher compensation than men. The challenge, though, is that this analysis does not capture the complaints in which gender was not discernible.

In WA, where all complaints were coded by gender, the trends are markedly different. Again, women were slightly more likely to bring a claim than men,

[187] Janet Rifkin, 'Mediation from a Feminist Perspective: Promise and Problems' (1984) 2 Law and Inequality: A Journal of Theory and Practice 21; though see Susan Hekman, 'Moral Voices, Moral Selves: About Getting it Right in Moral Theory' (1993) 16 Human Studies 143 who questions whether women have a singular 'moral voice'.

[188] A113.

[189] Thornton, 'Equivocations of Conciliation' (n 45) 753.

Table 5.12 Outcome by gender, age complaints, Queensland, 2009–19

	All complaints	Women	Men	Women % total discernible
Referred	54	20	21	48.8
Conciliated	145	65	57	53.3
Rejected	4	2	1	66.7
Not under Act	116	50	38	56.8
Lapsed	3	2	1	66.7
Lost contact	5	2	2	50.0
Withdrawn	33	7	16	30.4
Unconciliable	19	10	8	55.6
Not yet resolved	8	3	5	37.5
Total	387	161	149	51.9

Source: QHRC and author's own calculations

Table 5.13 Conciliated compensation ($), age complaints, by gender, Queensland, 2009–19

	Men	Women
n	22	27
Average	7,811.36	12,018.11
Median	5,000.00	5,451.99
Max	61,279.03	78,000.00
Min	100.00	300.00

Source: QHRC and author's own calculations

representing 55.2 per cent of all complaints. However, women represented only 36.8 per cent of those who conciliated (Table 5.14). Women were far more likely than men to withdraw their claim, and slightly more likely to let their claim lapse. Women often withdrew complaints following correspondence with the equality agency, after being asked to demonstrate a causative link or to substantiate a complaint.[190] Thus, issues of causation and proof appear to be deterring some women

[190] This was not just due to the subject matter of the claim: women were slightly *less* likely to bring a claim about recruitment than men (such claims being notoriously hard to prove): women brought 17 (42%) complaints about recruitment; men brought 19.

Table 5.14 Outcomes of age complaints by gender, WA, 2014–19

	Women	Men	Total	Women % of total
Dismissed	12	12	24	50
Withdrawn	21	12	33	63.6
Conciliation	7	12	19	36.8
Lapsed	10	7	17	58.8
Mediation	1	0	1	
Not yet resolved	2	0	2	
Total	53	43	96	55.2

Source: WAEOC and author's own calculations

from progressing to conciliation. The quantum of only one monetary settlement (of $2,000) was noted for a woman complainant (one other woman complainant received $8,000 at a mediation settlement).

Given the gendered nature of complaint withdrawals in WA, further action should be taken by equality agencies to monitor complaint outcomes by gender, and to consider how complainants can be encouraged (rather than discouraged) to progress their complaints to conciliation; withdrawal does not necessarily mean that issues have been resolved.

In SA, too, there is some evidence that conciliated outcomes are gendered: in 2014–20 conciliations (n = eighteen), matters with women claimants were less likely than those with men claimants to include compensation in conciliated outcomes. Out of ten conciliations involving women, only four resulted in compensation (40 per cent); whereas 62.5 per cent of conciliations involving men resulted in compensation. Where compensation was awarded, women achieved both the highest sums ($12,093.55, $10,000, $10,000) and the lowest amount ($2,500). These gendered trends need to be actively monitored by equality agencies.

Reform 14: That equality agencies monitor complaint outcomes by gender.

Reform 15: That equality agencies consider how complainants can be encouraged to progress their claims to conciliation.

E. Court and Tribunal Mediation

Courts and tribunals also refer matters to their own ADR processes. Reliance on ADR by courts and tribunals varies across jurisdictions. In GB, for example,

Table 5.15 Matters heard and resolved at ADR, human rights list, VCAT, 2011–12 to 2018–19

	Compulsory conference		Mediation		Total resolved (% of all heard)
	Heard	Resolved	Heard	Resolved	
2011–12	27	18	73	56	74.00
2012–13	40	28	56	31	61.46
2013–14	42	23	52	25	51.06
2014–15	74	43	67	40	58.87
2015–16	75	47	34	15	56.88
2016–17	64	40	54	42	69.49
2017–18	92	58	89	54	61.88
2018–19	119	88	50	38	74.56

Source: VCAT Annual Reports and author's own calculations

judicial mediation is 'far more intensive' than conciliation conducted by Acas, in part because it is conducted in person.[191] By contrast, in most Australian jurisdictions, matters have already undergone intensive conciliation by the time they proceed to a court or tribunal. Despite this, many complaints are resolved via court or tribunal-based ADR in Australia.

At the Victorian Civil and Administrative Tribunal (VCAT), for example, there is a substantial emphasis on using ADR to resolve claims.[192] In 2018–19, though, only 2,516 cases at VCAT were listed for a compulsory conference or mediation (ie, around 3 per cent of all cases finalized in that year).[193] For the human rights list specifically, though, 455 cases were lodged in 2018–19, and 169 (37.14 per cent) were heard at a compulsory conference or mediation.[194] The majority of cases heard in compulsory conference or mediation are resolved (Table 5.15). Similar trends apply to *Equal Opportunity Act 2010* (Vic) (EO Act) cases specifically (Table 5.16):[195] in 2017–18, over 20 per cent of EO Act applications were resolved via compulsory conference or mediation.

191 UK78.
192 VCAT, 'Annual Report 2018–19' (2019) 25.
193 ibid 8.
194 ibid 25.
195 This table combines data on cases filed under the EO Act from VCAT's Annual Reports, with ADR data for the EO Act specifically, sourced from VCAT, and published in Dominique Allen, 'Addressing Discrimination Through Individual Enforcement: A Case Study of Victoria' (2019) 11 <https://www.monash.edu/__data/assets/pdf_file/0005/1898996/Addressing-Discrimination-Through-Individual-Enforcement_D-Allen_Aug-2019.pdf> accessed 24 March 2022.

Table 5.16 Matters referred and resolved at ADR, EO Act Applications, VCAT, 2013–14 to 2017–18

	Applications	Compulsory conference		Mediation		All applications		
	n	Referred (n)	Resolved (% of referred)	Referred (n)	Resolved (% of referred)	Referred (%)	Resolved (% of referred)	Resolved (% of total)
2013–14	232	18	45	40	33	25.00	36.72	9.18
2014–15	223	61	54	61	50	54.71	52.00	28.45
2015–16	162	68	67	34	55	62.96	63.00	39.67
2016–17	201	54	57	48	62	50.75	59.35	30.12
2017–18	310	83	39	72	48	50.00	43.18	21.59

Source: Allen (2019), VCAT Annual Reports and author's own calculations

Table 5.17 Human rights list matters resolved by ADR and adjudication, WASAT, 2015–16 to 2018–19

	Resolved by ADR (%)	Resolved by Adjudication (%)
2015–16	67.0	33.0
2016–17	31.0	31.0
2017–18	27.0	24.0
2018–19	33.3	45.5

Source: WASAT Annual Reports

Similarly, in WA, a sizeable proportion of complaints received by the WA State Administrative Tribunal (WASAT) in the human rights list are resolved via ADR each year, either through mediation or a compulsory conference (Table 5.17). The proportion of complaints resolved by ADR can exceed the proportion resolved by adjudication.

In the Australian Capital Territory (ACT), few discrimination complaints are referred and finalized at the ACT Civil and Administrative Tribunal (ACAT) each year. Of those that are referred, however, most are resolved prior to a full hearing (Table 5.18).

At the federal level, the Federal Circuit Court of Australia (FCCA) relies heavily on mediation to resolve discrimination disputes. In 2018–19, 48.84 per cent of all human rights matters filed were referred to mediation (Table 5.19);[196] this was eight times the referral rate for all matters (5.94 per cent of filings).[197] Similarly, for employment and industrial relations matters, 504 of 1,291 FCCA filings in 2018–19 were referred for mediation (39.04 per cent).[198] Of thirty-six finalized mediation referrals in 2018–19 in the Human Rights List, twenty-six matters were resolved (72 per cent); of 472 finalized referrals in the Fair Work jurisdiction, 304 matters were resolved, and four were resolved in part (65 per cent).[199]

The Federal Court of Australia (FCA), by contrast, appears less reliant on ADR: in the administrative law, constitutional law, and human rights list, between 10 and 20 per cent of applications are referred to mediation each year. For

[196] Federal Circuit Court of Australia, 'Annual Report 2018–2019' (2019) 47.
[197] ibid.
[198] ibid.
[199] ibid 48.

Table 5.18 Discrimination complaints at ACAT by manner resolved, 2016–17 to 2018–19

	Complaints finalized	Referred to mediation	Resolved at ADR	Resolved after ADR	Proceeded to hearing
2016–17	8	3	3	0	0
2017–18	9	4	2	0	2
2018–19	24	15	7	5	3

Source: ACAT Annual Reports

Table 5.19 Applications, referrals to mediation and judgments, human rights list, FCCA, 2013–14 to 2018–19

	Applications filed	Applications finalized	Referrals to mediation	Judgments finalized
2013–14	79	dns	63	23
2014–15	87	79	43	17
2015–16	75	77	50	23
2016–17	58	70	28	28
2017–18	60	57	39	14
2018–19	86	85	42	18

Source: FCCA Annual Reports
Table notes:

dns = did not specify

Table 5.20 Matters finalized by outcome, employment and industrial relations matters, FCA, 2015–16 to 2019–20

	Matters finalized	Mediation	Judgment	Other*	Mediation (% of matters finalized)
2015–16	185	33	53	99	17.8
2016–17	199	51	48	100	25.6
2017–18	180	32	61	87	17.8
2018–19	205	62	44	99	30.2
2019–20	216	57	62	97	26.4

Source: Bromberg (2020) and author's own calculations
Table notes:

*Other includes matters withdrawn, discontinued, finalized by consent, and transferred to another court

employment and industrial relations matters, though, mediation resolves between 17.8 and 30.2 per cent of all matters finalized (Table 5.20).[200]

In GB, ETs offer judicial mediation. An initial pilot found that women claimants were statistically more likely to take up the offer of judicial mediation.[201] However, there was no statistically significant association between participating in judicial mediation and settling or avoiding a hearing.[202] That said, parties may derive other benefits from participating in judicial mediation.[203] In 2018, ETs in England and Wales conducted 525 judicial mediations, with a success rate of 70.9 per cent.[204] Judicial mediation in Scottish ETs also has a success rate of around 70 per cent.[205]

It is intriguing that so many matters settle at court or tribunal-facilitated ADR. In the UK, this may be because judicial mediation is more intensive than conciliation offered by Acas or the LRA. In Australia, though, most claims will have already undergone intensive conciliation at an equality agency. It is possible that the moral authority of a judicial mediator exceeds that of a statutory equality agency, encouraging parties to resolve their disputes.[206] It is also possible that, as court and tribunal costs mount, parties become more amenable to resolving their claims.

IV. Strengthening ADR Through Transparency

A recurring theme through this discussion has been the substantial difficulties with ensuring transparency and accountability, and overcoming secrecy, in relation to ADR. In an area characterized by confidentiality, transparency becomes positively radical. Given the sheer number of claims resolved via ADR (or withdrawn or abandoned during ADR processes), transparency is essential to strengthen the individual and systemic outcomes achieved via conciliation.

First, ADR processes could be strengthened through more comprehensive and systematic data collection by statutory agencies and more transparency regarding the claims that are made. This is key to strengthening other forms of

[200] Mordy Bromberg, 'Review of E&IR Filings, Outcomes and Other Statistics' (3 December 2020) <https://www.fedcourt.gov.au/digital-law-library/judges-speeches/justice-bromberg/bromberg-j-2020-12-3> accessed 12 June 2021.

[201] Peter Urwin and others, 'Evaluating the Use of Judicial Mediation in Employment Tribunals' (2010) Ministry of Justice Research Series 7/10 29; Peter Urwin, Paul L Latreille, and Valeriya Karuk, 'Quantitative Evidence in the Evaluation of ADR: The Case of Judicial Mediation in UK Employment Tribunals' (2012) 23 International Journal of Human Resource Management 567.

[202] Urwin and others (n 201) 57.

[203] Boon, Urwin, and Karuk (n 130).

[204] Senior President of Tribunals, 'Senior President of Tribunals' Annual Report: 2019' (2019) 57 <https://www.judiciary.uk/wp-content/uploads/2019/10/6.5845_The-Senior-President-of-Tribunals-Annual-Report-2019_Print_NoCrops.pdf> accessed 25 March 2021.

[205] Senior President of Tribunals, 'Senior President of Tribunals' Annual Report: 2020' (2020) 63 <https://www.judiciary.uk/wp-content/uploads/2020/07/6.6755_The-Senior-President-of-Tribunals-Annual-Report-2020_WEB-CS-amend-1.pdf> accessed 25 March 2021.

[206] Busby and Mcdermont (n 129) 177.

enforcement.[207] At present, agencies themselves largely determine their level of public accountability for how ADR is conducted; it is up to equality agencies to determine how much (or how little) data they report on conciliations and their outcomes.[208] Statutory secrecy provisions may have had a chilling effect on equality agencies, limiting their willingness to release information publicly. There is a strong argument, then, that statutory secrecy provisions should be clarified or even repealed, given there is already protection for personal information afforded by privacy law.[209]

Reform 16: That statutory secrecy provisions in equality law be clarified or repealed.

Regardless, statutory agencies could release further, de-identified information about complaints, while still complying with their statutory secrecy obligations.[210] Agencies could release de-identified case studies of successful conciliations and the remedies that have been achieved.[211] As the AHRC conciliation register shows, though, it is important to be transparent about how these case studies are selected, and the degree to which they are representative of all conciliations. Further, producing de-identified data in a way that preserves confidentiality is 'hugely resource intensive',[212] even if an agency turns its mind to the issue. Reporting may therefore be limited where agencies lack time or resources.[213]

Ideally, then, transparency would be supported by a comprehensive data system that allows de-identified reports to be produced in a non-labour intensive way.[214] This was not yet the case in any jurisdiction: data is still partial, inconsistent, difficult to extract, and often unreliable. That said, Acas is working to improve its data management, having introduced a case management system (using the Microsoft Dynamics platform) in 2019.[215] Tailoring the system to Acas's needs has entailed 'lots and lots of work, lots of design work to make it do what we need it to do' and the use of internal and external technical consultants.[216] After a fifteen-month 'journey', 'decent data' has been available for about two months.[217]

Improving data capture and analysis is therefore a long-term, resource intensive process. The potential improvements offered by these systems, though, are substantial: for example, they could automatically allocate cases to conciliators, rather

207 A105.
208 Thornton, 'Equivocations of Conciliation' (n 45) 740.
209 Allen and Blackham (n 155).
210 ibid.
211 A113.
212 A153.
213 A113.
214 A153.
215 UK119.
216 ibid.
217 ibid.

than all allocations occurring manually.[218] Systems could give parties access to updates on their claim, to check on progress, rather than having to seek such information from a conciliator.[219]

Reform 17: That governments provide statutory agencies with targeted funding to improve data collection and reporting.

Reform 18: That statutory agencies adopt comprehensive data management systems that facilitate data extraction and reporting.

Second, beyond information collected by statutory agencies, individual practitioners can promote transparency by seeking to narrow the scope of confidentiality provisions in conciliated settlements,[220] though some lawyers may be resistant to this.[221] Conciliators can assist this process by offering examples of less restrictive confidentiality provisions or encouraging parties to settle without an NDA.[222] This reflects Leonard and Hunter's argument that confidentiality should apply to the mediation *process*, but not to mediated *settlements*.[223]

Reform 19: That practitioners seek to limit the scope of NDAs.

Reform 20: That conciliators encourage parties to settle without an NDA.

Third, transparency could be promoted via broader data collection in relation to age. As Dee Masters argued to the House of Commons Women and Equalities Committee (WEC): 'there is a lack of openness, and statistics in particular, about age decisions.... improving transparency might encourage people to hold organizations to account.'[224] Thus, increased transparency might support individual claiming. This form of strategic transparency could be modelled on gender pay gap reporting or the transparency requirements embedded in positive duties.[225]

Reform 21: That governments extend or adopt transparency requirements that include age as a protected characteristic.

[218] ibid.
[219] ibid.
[220] A9.
[221] A160.
[222] UK119. Indeed, equality agencies should be monitoring instances where organizations are signing a lot of NDAs: UK162.
[223] Hunter and Leonard (n 78) 313.
[224] House of Commons, 'Oral Evidence: Older People and Employment' (2018) HC 359 Q44 <http://data.parliament.uk/writtenevidence/committeeevidence.svc/evidencedocument/women-and-equalities-committee/older-people-and-employment/oral/76656.html> accessed 24 March 2022.
[225] Alysia Blackham, 'Positive Equality Duties: The Future of Equality and Transparency?' (2021) 37(2) Law in Context 98.

Fourth, transparency would be supported through the reinstatement of the questionnaire procedure in the UK,[226] and its adoption in Australia, to improve workplace communication and transparency.[227] For practitioners, obtaining information through the questionnaire procedure 'makes a huge difference'[228]—without it, all the power and information remains with the employer.[229] Requiring more transparency at an early stage, prior to conciliation, may encourage claims to achieve an early resolution.[230] While the questionnaire procedure was abolished as it was seen as too onerous for employers,[231] with claimants asking too many questions, this could be addressed by the EHRC providing standard (more limited) questionnaire templates.[232]

Reform 22: That the questionnaire procedure be reinstated in the UK, and adopted in Australia.

Fifth, transparency requires a sufficient flow of cases to progress to hearing and judgment: not all claims should be resolved via confidential conciliation. This is key to ensuring the development of legal precedent, and recognizes that some claims are ill-suited to privatized dispute resolution. Statutory agencies should therefore have referral powers allowing them to direct matters to a tribunal or court where claims do not resolve at ADR, or where issues are of legal or systemic importance.[233] Further, claimants must be supported where matters are referred;[234] this is taken up in Chapter 8.

V. Conclusion

In theory, ADR offers substantial benefits to parties over adversarial court proceedings, avoiding the time, cost, stress, rigidity, and publicity of a hearing. In practice, though, it is debatable whether these benefits are being realized, in part due to a lack of transparency in conciliated processes and outcomes.

It is unclear whether ADR is resolving *disputes*, rather than just resolving *claims*. Most claims are withdrawn or abandoned, many prior to participating in

[226] Formerly Equality Act 2010, s 138.
[227] House of Commons (n 224) Q45.
[228] UK162.
[229] ibid; A112.
[230] A112; House of Commons (n 224) Q97.
[231] Government Equalities Office, *Equality Act 2010: Employment Tribunals' Power to Make Wider Recommendations in Discrimination Cases and Obtaining Information Procedure: Government Response to the Consultation* (2012).
[232] UK162.
[233] Blackham and Allen (n 1).
[234] ibid.

conciliation. Few claims are successfully settled, and the terms of settlement can be limited. Relationships are rarely saved through ADR processes; this may be because there was nothing to save (as in cases of recruitment), because claims are rarely made in ongoing employment relationships, or because making a claim in and of itself is seen as undermining the relationship.

Achieving systemic outcomes requires active and intensive conciliation by conciliators who are experienced and skilled and have sufficient time to dig into the issues; this is not always the approach taken. Each statutory agency adopts a slightly different approach to ADR. Some, such as Acas and the FWC, are more hands-off,[235] in part due to their heavy workload; others are more interventionist, suggesting systemic remedies, making rights-based interventions,[236] redressing power imbalances between parties,[237] and challenging behaviour that risks perpetuating discrimination. Adopting a deep and nuanced approach to conciliation takes time and funding; with insufficient staffing, delays in progressing to conciliation can deter parties from pursuing their rights. Key to meaningful ADR, then, is adequate funding and resourcing of statutory agencies. This is considered further in Chapter 8.

ADR is most effective when positioned against a backbone of court-based litigation[238] as a complement to court proceedings. Negotiation can only be effective and fair if parties have the prospect of access to a court or tribunal.[239] Thus, barriers that prevent disputes progressing further must be scrutinized carefully: this is taken up in Chapter 6.

[235] Dickens, 'The Road is Long' (n 22) 480.

[236] Rosalie Poole, 'Facilitating Systemic Outcomes through Anti-Discrimination Conciliation and the Role of the Conciliator in This Quest' (2016) 47 Australasian Dispute Resolution Journal 49, 57.

[237] Hunter and Leonard (n 78) 311.

[238] Wolfe (n 54) 794.

[239] *R (on the application of UNISON) v Lord Chancellor* [2017] UKSC 51, [2017] 3 WLR 409, [92].

6

Hearing and Judgment

I. Introduction

Chapter 5 has demonstrated the fundamental importance of alternative dispute resolution (ADR) in redirecting age discrimination claims away from formal court and tribunal proceedings; most claims are settled, withdrawn, or abandoned during the ADR process. Few claims are subsequently filed with courts or tribunals; even fewer progress to hearing or judgment. This is having a systemic impact on the development of age discrimination law: there is a lack of case law in the age discrimination jurisdiction,[1] and the case law that exists is relatively underdeveloped.[2] Given that good cases settle,[3] the cases that tend to proceed to hearing and judgment can be disproportionately weak,[4] hopeless,[5] or lacking merit;[6] hard[7] or complex;[8] against public bodies;[9] or 'the slightly crazy ones'.[10]

Case law may therefore misrepresent the many positive outcomes that can and are being achieved at conciliation.[11] Without a strong body of precedent, claimants and their legal representatives may be deterred from pursuing a complaint,[12] as it is unclear how a court or tribunal will respond.[13] Practitioners generally start from the case law; if there is limited case law, and a practitioner is not familiar with the area, they are unlikely to feel confident advising their clients to pursue such a matter.[14] Unsympathetic or 'disappointing' decisions raise concerns about how specific courts or tribunals will engage with a claim;[15] there is therefore greater

[1] A5; A102; A108; A111; A151; A163; A169; UK79.
[2] A105; UK79; UK84.
[3] A3; A5; A105; A118; A153; UK78; UK162.
[4] UK78.
[5] UK162.
[6] A3.
[7] UK78.
[8] A3.
[9] UK162.
[10] A105. This raises challenges for judges and tribunal members: a series of weak cases may condition judges to expect cases to be weak: 'when the exception comes along, are you attuned enough to see it?': UK78. A constant stream of weak or hard cases also increases judicial workload and judicial stress: UK78.
[11] A102; A107; A113.
[12] A163.
[13] A3; A108.
[14] A105; A107; A111; A163.
[15] A3; A5.

Reforming Age Discrimination Law. Alysia Blackham, Oxford University Press. © Alysia Blackham 2022.
DOI: 10.1093/oso/9780198859284.003.0006

certainty and predictability in bringing a claim in jurisdictions with a more developed body of case law.[16]

Conversely, examples of successful claims may encourage more complaints, and encourage the early settlement of disputes.[17] High profile successful claims can act as 'a lightning rod', leading to more complaints, and increasing practitioners' willingness to use a particular jurisdiction.[18] Two such 'lightning rod' age discrimination cases emerged in this study: *O'Reilly v BBC*,[19] and *Fair Work Ombudsman v Theravanish Investments Pty Ltd*.[20] Cases can have systemic 'ripple effects',[21] raising awareness of equality legislation through publicity, using remedies as preventative measures,[22] changing discriminatory practices, and enabling follow-up by equality agencies[23] (Chapter 8). There is a public interest, then, in having some matters determined in the public sphere.[24] That said, few cases make a big difference;[25] to do so, a case must be accompanied by significant publicity, involve a 'perfect' claimant (who is popular with the general public), and be a strong legal case.[26] Even then, the process can have negative impacts on the claimant themselves.[27]

The question, then, is why so little case law has developed in the age discrimination jurisdiction specifically. The vast majority of *all* discrimination complaints are settled or abandoned prior to hearing; this is not unique to age.[28] Barriers to and costs of pursuing a claim affect all protected characteristics. That said, age discrimination law was introduced comparatively recently when compared to other grounds;[29] given that some legal issues have already been ironed out in cases relating to other protected characteristics, respondents are now less likely to try to defend 'extreme cases'.[30] In Great Britain (GB), too, Employment Tribunal (ET) fees were introduced at a critical time in the development of age discrimination law, inhibiting its development.[31] Further, statutory agencies like the Equality and Human Rights Commission (EHRC) have reviewed and limited their support for

16 UK82.
17 A111; A163.
18 A111.
19 [2011] UKET 2200423/2010.
20 [2014] FCCA 1170.
21 UK97.
22 Women and Equalities Committee, *Enforcing the Equality Act: The Law and the Role of the Equality and Human Rights Commission* (2017–19 HC 1470) 60–61 [217]–[220].
23 UK97.
24 A163.
25 UK162.
26 ibid.
27 ibid.
28 UK97; Alysia Blackham and Dominique Allen, 'Resolving Discrimination Claims Outside the Courts: Alternative Dispute Resolution in Australia and the United Kingdom' (2019) 31 Australian Journal of Labour Law 253.
29 A151.
30 UK82.
31 UK84.

test cases, particularly in relation to age discrimination: 'because age is still sort of barely walking, its impact may be more pronounced in that area.'[32]

This chapter critically analyses the court hearing and judgment stage of the individual enforcement of age discrimination law. Focusing on empirical case studies of enforcement in the United Kingdom (UK) and Australia, it draws on qualitative and quantitative content analysis of Australian case law and UK tribunal decisions on age discrimination in employment; statistics from tribunals and courts; qualitative expert interviews; and the survey of advocates, to consider doctrinal and jurisdictional hurdles to individual enforcement. It interrogates who is able to pursue a claim to hearing and judgment and the issues that arise in advancing a claim to court.

II. The Costs of Pursuing a Claim This Far

Pursuing a claim to a court or tribunal involves all of the initial costs of filing a complaint (Chapter 4). However, these costs escalate once a claimant is required to engage with the more formal processes of a court or tribunal. Pursuing a claim to a tribunal or court is an emotionally costly process and, for some claimants, can be an all-consuming 'personal disaster'[33] that is 'inherently harmful'[34] and 'traumatic'.[35]

While conciliation allows for a flexible application of legal tests and principles, that is not the case at hearing or in court. This means, in practice, that recurring issues like proof became particularly acute at the hearing stage.[36] Significant costs orders can be made against claimants in discrimination cases, especially in the Australian federal jurisdiction.[37] As financial costs escalate, the combined effects of time limits, a lack of legal assistance (or costly legal assistance), the burden of proof, and the risk of costs orders make age discrimination claims unlikely.[38]

Court and tribunal proceedings also tend to be more time consuming and 'lengthy'[39] than participating in ADR; pursuing a discrimination complaint is a 'long, drawn-out process'.[40] While tribunal processes are improving and becoming more expeditious in some jurisdictions,[41] in other jurisdictions it can take years to resolve a matter at a court or tribunal:[42] 'when it gets to the tribunal, the timeframes just go out the window.'[43] The time that litigation takes is therefore a substantial

32 UK82.
33 UK97.
34 UK78.
35 UK84.
36 A158.
37 ibid.
38 ibid.
39 A102.
40 A107.
41 A99.
42 A102; A151.
43 A102.

barrier to claiming:[44] claimants do not want to engage in a process that is 'drawn out'[45] but want an 'instant result'.[46]

Pursuing a discrimination complaint this far is therefore 'a last resort legal option'[47] for many people. Younger workers in particular do not want to take the risk or the time to pursue a complaint to a court or tribunal: 'they don't really care about being a ground-breaking pioneer for the next three years.'[48] This reflects a tension at the heart of public interest litigation: while it might be in the public interest or a practitioner's interest to be a 'pioneer', this is rarely what a client would prefer: 'everyone chooses the easiest, quickest, less stressful option, which is their right to do.'[49]

This is also a tension for agency enforcement: while an agency like the Fair Work Ombudsman (FWO) might have the power to pursue a matter to court, this will result in substantial delays for the individual claimant:

> putting a poor individual through a year-long investigation, another year waiting for it to get to court, then the court hearing, then three or four months waiting for an outcome; against referring them to a state anti-discrimination commission, and having a hearing within months, and some sort of a settlement or a reward.[50]

This trade-off between the public interest and individual interests may limit the use of agency enforcement powers for individual matters (Chapter 8).

A further cost is posed by the transparency and public accessibility of legal proceedings. Unlike conciliation, which is confidential, court records are in the public sphere. In GB, online publishing of ET decisions means that employers can easily check prospective employees' legal history.[51] Individuals may have very real concerns about challenging discriminatory behaviour in a public forum. With ET decisions being published online, there is a risk that individuals will not pursue their rights due to fear of reputational damage. Thus, again, it is perhaps surprising that as many claims progress as far as they do, particularly once matters proceed to a court or tribunal.

[44] A115; A107.
[45] A100.
[46] A104. On timeliness in ETs, see Alysia Blackham, 'Enforcing Rights in Employment Tribunals: Insights from Age Discrimination Claims in a New "Dataset"' (2021) 41 Legal Studies 390.
[47] A107.
[48] ibid.
[49] ibid.
[50] A110.
[51] See, eg, the discussion of anonymity orders in *Kirkham v United Kingdom Research and Innovation* [2019] UKET 2501482/2018. See further Zoe Adams, Abi Adams-Prassl, and Jeremias Adams-Prassl, 'Online Tribunal Judgments and the Limits of Open Justice' (2022) 42 Legal Studies 42.

III. Who Proceeds to Hearing and Judgment?

A. Court and Tribunal Statistics

In Australia, few complaints received by statutory agencies progress to a court or tribunal. In the federal jurisdiction, the Australian Human Rights Commission (AHRC) estimates that around 3 per cent of discrimination complaints proceed to court.[52] Complaints that proceed are often withdrawn prior to hearing:[53] around two-thirds of complaints filed with a tribunal may not be pursued,[54] and the other third are typically subject to court-ordered mediation[55] (Chapter 5). Claims are often withdrawn once a claimant comes to understand how the tribunal operates: 'they don't realise what the process is until they get into it, and then it becomes, "Whoa.".'[56]

Australian courts and tribunals rarely collect or publish disaggregated statistics on age discrimination claims.[57] It is difficult to track how many claims are filed, withdrawn, or abandoned.[58] This represents a substantial gap in the Australian data. Compiling data from the annual reports of tribunals and courts, it is possible to build a general picture of discrimination applications across all grounds (Table 6.1). Jurisdictions variously publish data on *applications*; *referrals* (typically from the statutory equality agency); and *proceedings*, meaning statistics are not easily comparable across jurisdictions. Federal courts only publish statistics for broader case lists, not discrimination claims specifically.[59] At best, then, these figures offer only a general guide.[60]

[52] AHRC, '2015–16 Complaint Statistics' (2016) 2 <http://www.humanrights.gov.au/our-work/commission-general/publications/annual-report-2015-2016> accessed 17 July 2017.

[53] A102.

[54] A101.

[55] ibid.

[56] A102.

[57] A101; Alysia Blackham, 'When Law and Data Collide: The Methodological Challenge of Conducting Mixed Methods Research in Law' (2022) 49 Journal of Law and Society (forthcoming). See also Dominique Allen, 'Addressing Discrimination Through Individual Enforcement: A Case Study of Victoria' (2019) 3 <https://www.monash.edu/__data/assets/pdf_file/0005/1898996/Addressing-Discrimination-Through-Individual-Enforcement_D-Allen_Aug-2019.pdf> accessed 24 March 2022.

[58] Though the Australian Capital Territory Civil and Administrative Tribunal (ACAT) reports the number of referrals received that relate to age: the maximum number received in any given year was two, in 2013–14. Other years had one or no referrals on the basis of age.

[59] Federal courts record some statistics on employment and industrial relations matters filed: in 2019–20, eighty-five general protections matters and one discrimination matter were filed in the Federal Court of Australia (FCA): Mordy Bromberg, 'Review of E&IR Filings, Outcomes and Other Statistics' (3 December 2020) <https://www.fedcourt.gov.au/digital-law-library/judges-speeches/justice-bromberg/bromberg-j-2020-12-3> accessed 12 June 2021. In 2019–20, 642 general protections applications were filed in the Federal Circuit Court of Australia (FCCA): Alister McNab, 'E&IR the Federal Circuit Court of Australia' (3 December 2020) <https://www.fedcourt.gov.au/digital-law-library/judges-speeches/justice-bromberg/bromberg-j-2020-12-3> accessed 12 June 2021.

[60] Note, too, that statistics in South Australia (SA) are variable, given the shift from the Equal Opportunity Tribunal (SAEOT) to the Employment Tribunal (SAET) over this period. It is difficult to determine what is being reported in the SA Equal Opportunity Commission's (SAEOC) annual report in any given year.

Table 6.1 Discrimination applications, referrals, and proceedings, all grounds, Australian first instance courts and tribunals, 2009–10 to 2018–19

	Applications							Referrals					Proceedings	Total
	VCAT	NCAT	QCAT	QIRC	WASAT	FCCA*	FCA#	SAET (complaints)	SAET (inquiries)	SAEOT	TADT	ACAT	NTCAT	
2009–10	351	152	105		65	105				8	6	9		801
2010–11	352	128	151			94				18	9	30		782
2011–12	316	175	147		65	81				13	10	19		826
2012–13	264	112	108		57	105	304	34		63	11	17		1,075
2013–14	232		114		50	79	330	43	9	34	12	12		915
2014–15	223	139	108		42	87	315	36	5	38	11	7	0	1,011
2015–16	162	142	104			75	228	18	1	12	10	11	5	768
2016–17	201	94	107	9	22	58	266	13	0	13	15	13	7	818
2017–18	310	89	52	108	34	60	247	66	0		10	17	5	998
2018–19	316	97	57	114	24	86	286	20	1		14	24	8	1,047

Source: Court, Tribunal and Equality Agency Annual Reports and author's own calculations
Table notes:

* Human Rights List

Administrative and Constitutional Law & Human Rights List

Blank = not reported

VCAT = Victorian Civil and Administrative Tribunal

NCAT = New South Wales Civil and Administrative Tribunal

QCAT = Queensland Civil and Administrative Tribunal

QIRC = Queensland Industrial Relations Commission

WASAT = WA State Administrative Tribunal

FCCA = Federal Circuit Court of Australia

FCA = Federal Court of Australia

SAET = South Australia Employment Tribunal

SAEOT = South Australia Equal Opportunity Tribunal

TADT = Tasmania Anti-Discrimination Tribunal

ACAT = Australian Capital Territory Civil and Administrative Tribunal

NTCAT = Northern Territory Civil and Administrative Tribunal

Table 6.2 GB ET jurisdictional complaints received, age and total, 2013–19

	Total claims accepted	Total jurisdictional complaints	Age complaints	Age complaints (% of total jurisdictional complaints)
2013	158,551	291,335	2,203	0.76
2014	51,940	112,856	1,470	1.30
2015	74,068	154,681	12,654	8.18
2016	86,622	167,886	7,498	4.47
2017	115,334	171,630	6,704	3.91
2018	118,348	193,595	2,465	1.27
2019	108,606	174,036	1,938	1.11

Source: Ministry of Justice, Management Information on ET Receipts, Annex C Table 2 (2020) and author's own calculations

In GB, ETs collect and publish more comprehensive data about age discrimination complaints specifically. Compared to Australia, a comparatively large number of age discrimination complaints progress to GB ETs each year (Table 6.2) though this represents a small proportion of all jurisdictional complaints.[61]

Few of these complaints progress to hearing or judgment. From 2007–08 to 2018–19, an average of 2,448 age discrimination complaints were disposed of each year (Table 6.3). Acas (Advisory, Conciliation and Arbitration Service) settlements account for a large proportion of age discrimination disposals (between 18 per cent and 45 per cent), and many claims are withdrawn (23 per cent to 63 per cent). Few complaints are successful at hearing (between 1 per cent and 4 per cent). Outcomes likely to be unfavourable to complainants[62] account for between 52 per cent and 80 per cent of disposals each year.[63]

These figures for age discrimination complaints differ markedly to those for all jurisdictions and grounds. Age discrimination complaints are significantly less likely than all claims to be successful at hearing, more likely to be withdrawn, and less likely to be resolved by a default judgment; though, in some years, they are also more likely to be subject to Acas conciliated settlements (Table 6.3). While it is not

[61] The exception was in in 2015, when age discrimination complaints represented 8.18 per cent of all jurisdictional complaints. This was the year in which a challenge to the transitional provisions in the Judicial Pensions Regulations 2015 was filed by 210 UK judges; and a challenge to transitional provisions in the Firefighters Pension Scheme 2015 was filed by over 5,000 firefighters. This will have distorted the overall complaint statistics in 2015.

[62] Withdrawn, unsuccessful at hearing, struck out (not at a hearing), dismissed at a preliminary hearing, dismissed rule 27, dismissed upon withdrawal, case discontinued.

[63] That said, claims may be withdrawn when a non-Acas conciliated settlement is reached; this could, then, be a positive outcome for a complainant.

Table 6.3 GB ET disposals for all claims and age discrimination claims, by year, 2007–08 to 2018–19

	2007–08		2008–09		2009–10		2010–11		2011–12		2012–13		2013–14		2014–15		2015–16		2016–17		2017–18		2018–19	
	All	Age	All	Age	All	Age	All	Age	All	Age	All	Age	All	Age	All	Age	All	Age	All	Age	All	Age	All	Age
Annual Total	157,493	1,778	172,944	2,472	226,968	3,873	243,952	3,651	229,968	3,820	225,896	2,674	275,561	4,259	386,465	1,528	102,551	865	88,922	806	86,664	1,732	94,332	1,917
Acas conciliated settlements (%)	29	45	32	40	31	39	29	35	33	33	33	43	21	19	8	28	31	35	27	35	24	18	25	21
Successful at hearing (%)	13	3	13	2	13	2	12	2	12	1	11	4	7	2	3	2	6	2	6	2	10	1	9	1
Default judgment (%)	4	1	4	1	7	1	6	1	6	1	6	1	3	0	1	0	3	0	4	0	4	0	5	0
Withdrawn (%)	33	35	33	32	32	39	32	40	27	42	28	32	48	63	16	42	24	23	20	24	12	27	24	49
Unsuccessful at hearing (%)	7	8	8	10	6	9	9	9	7	8	7	11	5	7	2	12	6	13	6	13	6	6	6	5
Struck out (not at a hearing) (%)	11	4	7	10	9	7	10	10	13	13	12	6	9	4	67	6	14	12	11	4	18	7	12	9
Dismissed at a preliminary hearing (%)	2	5	2	5	2	3	2	3	2	3	3	4	2	2	0	2	1	1	1	2	1	1	1	1

Continued

Table 6.3 Continued

	2007–08		2008–09		2009–10		2010–11		2011–12		2012–13		2013–14		2014–15		2015–16		2016–17		2017–18		2018–19	
	All	Age	All	Age	All	Age	All	Age	All	Age	All	Age	All	Age	All	Age	All	Age	All	Age	All	Age	All	Age
Dismissed rule 27 (%)													0	0	0	0	0	0	0	0	0	0	0	0
Dismissed upon withdrawal (%)													5	4	4	8	14	12	24	19	24	38	16	12
Case discontinued (%)													0	0	0	0	0	0	0	0	1	1	2	1
'Negative outcome' total (%)	53	52	50	57	49	58	53	62	49	66	50	53	69	80	89	70	59	61	62	62	62	80	61	77

Source: Ministry of Justice, Tribunal Statistics, Main Tables, Table ET3 (2020) and author's own calculations

uncommon for ET claims generally to be withdrawn through settlement[64] or abandonment, this appears to be a particular challenge in relation to age discrimination complaints. Uncertainty around justification may explain why age claims are commonly withdrawn.[65]

In Northern Ireland (NI), tribunals do not publish statistics about age discrimination complaints specifically. In 2019–20, across all jurisdictions, the Labour Relations Agency (LRA) recorded sixty-eight tribunal cases; twenty-five cases were upheld in whole or part, twenty-one were struck out, and twenty-two were dismissed.

B. Survey of Case Law

Overall, then, few cases filed proceed to hearing and judgment. Court and tribunal data tells us little about the nature of age discrimination complaints, or the demographics of those pursuing these claims. Insight into cases that *are* proceeding to courts and tribunals (or, at least, those with a published judgment)[66] can be gleaned from a survey of Australian and UK case law (Table 6.4).[67] While these surveys considered different case samples and time periods, the differences between the jurisdictions are illuminating.

In the UK, the number of withdrawn claims in my sample is higher than in ET statistics (2016–17: 24 per cent, 2017–18: 27 per cent; 2018–19: 49 per cent). This may be attributable to three key reasons. First, the period I studied does not align neatly with the period reported in ET statistics; it is possible that more claims were withdrawn at certain times of year, distorting my figures. Second, some decisions relating to withdrawn age discrimination claims noted that the parties had settled their disputes, including with Acas's assistance; these may be counted as '*Acas Conciliated Settlements*' in ET statistics, rather than withdrawn. Third, uploading decisions to the ET website appears to be a manual process, dependent on individual tribunal registries. There can be substantial delays in uploading decisions, and not all decisions are necessarily recorded in writing or uploaded. This may limit the comprehensiveness and reliability of the ET decision website for analysing these sorts of statistics.[68] Despite these methodological limitations, the case survey reveals key insights into claims that are progressing to courts and tribunals.

[64] UK82.
[65] ibid.
[66] In one Australian jurisdiction, some tribunal decisions are not being reported or published in the public domain: A102.
[67] I have written in detail about the findings of this study elsewhere: in Australia, see Alysia Blackham, 'Why Do Employment Age Discrimination Cases Fail? An Analysis of Australian Case Law' (2020) 42 Sydney Law Review 1; in the UK, see Blackham, 'Enforcing Rights in Employment Tribunals' (n 46).
[68] Adams, Adams-Prassl, and Adams-Prassl (n 51).

Table 6.4 Findings from the case sample, Australia and the UK

	Australia (up to 31 December 2017)	UK (February 2017 to 17 April 2019)
Case total	108	1,208[1]
Nature		
Substantive	64	244
Procedural	44	162
Withdrawn		804[2]
Substance of claim		
Dismissal	63	165
Recruitment	33	23
Claimant demographics		
Men	81	664
Women	28	573
Too old	99	136
Too young	6	20
Legal representation	53	187
Outcome		
Successful at hearing	12	43
Compensation (median)		8,800

Table notes:

[1] There were 1,208 age discrimination cases with 1,563 published decisions.

[2] In an additional thirty-four cases, the age claim disappeared—most likely having been withdrawn or abandoned over the course of proceedings, though it was not possible to tell definitively.

1. Substance of complaints

Claims relating to dismissal were over-represented in both jurisdictions. In Australia, for example, of 108 cases in the sample, the majority (sixty-three) related to dismissal (including twelve relating to retirement and ten to redundancy).[69] A substantial number (thirty-three) related to recruitment.

This differs from complaints being received by equality agencies, where recruitment was the most common area of complaint in both Queensland (ninety-four of

[69] Other areas included: training (six), promotion (five), demotion (four), working time (eight), harassment (ten), benefits (five), performance (two), and other (five). As cases can relate to multiple areas, these numbers do not add up to 108.

387 complaints, or 24 per cent) and Western Australia (WA) (thirty-six of ninety-six complaints, or 37.5 per cent). Complaints about dismissal represented only 9 per cent of total complaints in WA (nine complaints). Dismissal complaints are therefore over-represented in the case law, and recruitment complaints are under-represented, compared to the complaints received by equality bodies. Further, in Queensland, many agency complaints (eighty-seven or 22 per cent) related to harassment or age-based treatment, including 'everyday ageism'; these issues appear less frequently in the case law.

In the UK, where possible to discern, many cases related to dismissal (127), retirement (five), and redundancy (thirty-three); that is, the end of the working relationship. Claims relating to matters during or at the commencement of the employment relationship were less common, including harassment (twenty-nine); recruitment (twenty-three), training (three), promotion (eight), demotion (three), working time (twenty-three), benefits (fifteen), and performance processes (eighteen).[70]

Overall, age discrimination cases, with their heavy focus on dismissal, are unrepresentative of how age discrimination is generally experienced by older workers.[71] Dismissal cases are the most damaging and high value claims:[72] 'big issues like retirement or pensions where there's an awful lot at stake ... will be pursued and will be fought really hard.'[73] Given the costs of claiming, only the most serious cases are pursued to a public hearing.

2. Claimant demographics

The case sample illuminates which claimants are likely to pursue a matter to hearing and judgment. In relation to gender, eighty-one Australian cases had claimants who were men (75 per cent), and only twenty-eight had claimants who were women.[74] By comparison, in complaints received by equality agencies, the gender balance was slightly skewed *towards* women in Queensland and WA, and only slightly towards men at the AHRC. The absence of complaints by women in courts and tribunals may be attributable to what is occurring at agency level: in WA, for example, women were more likely than men to withdraw their complaint or let it lapse at the agency level, and less likely to conciliate or achieve an outcome

70 This is consistent with Irving's earlier study: LD Irving, 'Challenging Ageism in Employment: An Analysis of the Implementation of Age Discrimination Legislation in England and Wales' (Coventry University 2012) 88 <https://curve.coventry.ac.uk/open/file/ffc88163-6994-4400-bead-121298f52bd1/1/Irving%202012.pdf> accessed 2 April 2015.

71 AHRC, 'National Prevalence Survey of Age Discrimination in the Workplace: The Prevalence, Nature and Impact of Workplace Age Discrimination amongst the Australian Population Aged 50 Years and Older' (2015) 38.

72 UK78.

73 UK82.

74 One case included both a man and woman claimant, meaning these numbers add to 109, not 108.

Table 6.5 Gender and age group of claimants in age discrimination tribunal cases, WA and Queensland, case sample

	Cases total	Gender		Age group	
		Men	Women	Older	Younger
Queensland	11	9	2	11	0
WA	3	2	1	3	0

Table 6.6 Cases and case withdrawals by gender, UK age discrimination case sample, February 2017 to April 2019

	Total	Men		Women	
	n	n	% (of total)	n	% (of total)
All cases	1,237	664	53.7	573	46.3
Not withdrawn	391	218	55.7	173	44.2

through ADR. In Queensland, though, similar numbers of complaints were referred to tribunal for men (twenty-one) and women (twenty). While women represented 48.8 per cent of referred complaints where gender was discernible, they represented only 18 per cent of complainants in reported cases (Table 6.5). It appears, then, that women in Australia are less likely to pursue an age discrimination claim to hearing and judgment, though they are no less likely to make a complaint to an equality agency.

The UK sample included 664 men and 573 women as claimants;[75] men were slightly more likely to bring a claim than women.[76] Table 6.6 analyses withdrawal rates by gender across the sample; women appear more likely to withdraw their claim than men.

Older workers were over-represented in case samples in both jurisdictions. In Australia, over 90 per cent of cases (ninety-nine) related to claimants who alleged they were regarded as too old; only six related to claimants who were allegedly too

[75] This was determined based on claimants' titles: Mr, Ms, Mrs, or—in the case of Dr—pronouns used in the decision itself. Some cases involved multiple claimants; where possible, the gender of each individual claimant was added to this analysis, meaning the numbers exceed 1,208. For some cases, the full gender breakdown was not possible to discern; this was analysed as one man, and one woman, though the actual numbers will likely be higher. In some claims (ten), the gender of the claimant was not specified or possible to discern; these cases were omitted from the analysis.

[76] This difference was less substantial than in Irving's study: in that study, of the 3,944 judgments where claimant gender was identifiable, 2,555 claimants (64.8 per cent) were men, and only 1,389 (35.2 per cent) were women: Irving (n 70) 98.

young.[77] In the UK, where the age or age range of the claimant was specified (138 cases),[78] claimants had a median age of 57.[79] Most cases (138) involved claimants alleging they were seen as 'too old'; only twenty-one claims had claimants who were 'too young'.[80]

The majority of claimants in Australian (seventy-three claimants or 68 per cent) and UK cases (86 of 172 discernible claimants or 50 per cent) were men bringing a claim on the basis that they were perceived as being too old. There appear to be particular barriers facing women and younger workers in proceeding to a court or tribunal.

3. Respondent demographics

Some organizations are 'repeat respondents', being subject to multiple claims over time. In the United States of America (USA), Nazarov and von Schrader found that the strongest predictor of an establishment receiving an Age Discrimination in Employment Act of 1967 (ADEA) charge in this current year was receiving an ADEA charge in the past, independent of any industry-level or environmental differences between employers.[81] Past claims may increase rights awareness among the workforce, or indicate that organizations struggle with (perceived) age discrimination; organizational culture, leadership, and systems may cultivate or enable discrimination; and, in the USA at least, internal structures and mandatory arbitration agreements may limit external claiming.[82] For Thornton, though, repeat respondents undermine the 'simple-minded model of social change' underlying discrimination law, whereby a claim is made, conciliated, and thereafter 'the discriminator will not err again once politely informed of the error of his or her ways'.[83] Repeat respondents illuminate the limits of discrimination law in changing organizational behaviour.

[77] Though, of course, someone can be 'too old' at any age. Cases do not always specify a claimant's age, making more detailed analysis difficult.

[78] It is perhaps surprising that age is specified in so few decisions, given age could be assumed to be integral to an age discrimination claim; however, Irving similarly found that claimant age was specified in only 436 age discrimination folio reports, out of 4,001 judgments: Irving (n 70) 95.

[79] Where the claimant's age was expressed as an age range (eg 60+, under 35), this was analysed as the specified age (eg 60, 35 respectively). This is a blunt tool, which is why the *median* age is used for this analysis, not the mean. This analysis does not necessarily accurately capture the age of multiple claimants to a claim. Where multiple claimants were involved in a decision, the lead claimant's age was used for analysis. Typically, though, multiple claimants fell within a similar age range.

[80] This is consistent with Irving's study, where those who were perceived to be 'too old' represented 91.1 per cent of complainants (565 of 620 cases where identifiable): Irving (n 70) 90.

[81] Zafar Nazarov and Sarah von Schrader, 'A Longitudinal Analysis of the Relationship between Employer Characteristics and Age Discrimination Charge Filings' (2020) 32 Employee Responsibilities and Rights Journal 33, 42.

[82] ibid, 36.

[83] Margaret Thornton, *The Liberal Promise: Anti-Discrimination Legislation in Australia* (OUP 1990) 146.

In the Australian case sample, four cases were brought against both the Commonwealth Department of Defence and the New South Wales (NSW) Department of Education. Supermarket chain Woolworths and Australia Post were respondents in two cases each. In the UK case sample, repeat respondents included Birmingham City Council (twenty-five), BT (eight), Sainsbury's supermarket (seven), IBM, British Airways, and Royal Mail (six). These organizations may have high unionization rates or many older staff, increasing the likelihood of claims.[84] Complaints may also be associated with large-scale workforce change measures, such as mass redundancies or restructuring.[85] Industries with more employees—as opposed to independent contractors—may experience higher numbers of age discrimination complaints given the scope of discrimination law.[86]

At a sectoral level, a substantial number of UK cases were brought against NHS trusts (forty-eight), local councils (seventy-four), the police (eighteen), universities (thirty-three), and government departments and ministers (forty-six). Colleges, schools, academies, nurseries, and out of school services were respondents in sixty cases, and public transport providers, such as those operating the underground, trains, coaches, and buses were frequent respondents (thirty-one). Cases against power and water utility companies were less common (ten); against banks (thirty) and supermarkets (twenty-four) more so.

Repeat respondents and sectors typically have internal 'machinery [that] is too vast' to facilitate timely participation in conciliation.[87] In some cases, organizations need an external body's approval to make a compensation payment[88] or have a policy of not settling: '"we don't engage in trying to settle cases, we wait for a judicial determination."'[89] Thus, respondent demographics may reflect the matters that are unlikely to settle, rather than an over-representation of claiming in some organizations and sectors.

4. Representation

Where discernible in the Australian case sample, claimants were represented in fifty-three cases (49 per cent); fifty cases had litigants in person. Three cases were

[84] Though unions might both mobilize and increase the number of claims, and/or direct claims away from external processes: Sara Wakefield and Christopher Uggen, 'The Declining Significance of Race in Federal Civil Rights Law: The Social Structure of Employment Discrimination Claims' (2004) 74 Sociological Inquiry 128, 152.

[85] Birmingham City Council, for example, made 8,769 staff redundant between 2010–11 and 2017–18, equating to half its workforce: Patrick Butler, 'Redundancies Have Cost English Councils £4bn since 2010: Study' *The Guardian* (13 September 2018) <http://www.theguardian.com/society/2018/sep/13/councils-in-england-spend-4bn-on-220000-redundancies-since-2010> accessed 13 May 2021.

[86] See, eg, Alysia Blackham, '"We Are All Entrepreneurs Now": Options and New Approaches for Adapting Equality Law for the "Gig Economy"' (2018) 34 International Journal of Comparative Labour Law and Industrial Relations 413.

[87] UK119.

[88] ibid.

[89] ibid.

unclear regarding representation; in two cases the claimant did not appear. Most representatives were solicitors or barristers; unions acted as representatives in only two cases. This is a higher rate of representation than at conciliation (Chapter 5); claimants may be more likely to seek legal representation when pursuing their claim to court or tribunal or, perhaps, represented claimants may be more likely to advance to a court or tribunal.

In the UK case sample, claimant representation was specified in 538 cases. Nearly half (259 claimants or 48.1 per cent) appeared in person, though 187 (34.7 per cent) were legally represented.[90] Eighty-four claimants had some other form of representation or assistance, by a friend, spouse, parent, or—infrequently—a union representative, and twenty-eight did not appear. For respondents, where representation was specified (541 cases), only twenty-eight appeared in person; 446 were legally represented (82.4 per cent), and forty-eight had some other form of representation. Twenty-two respondents did not appear, and one attended to observe only.

In the UK, then, claimants were unlikely to be legally represented, but often faced a respondent who was legally represented.[91] This may mean claimants are disadvantaged in practice in putting forward their case.

5. Outcomes

While successful claims are exceptional across all grounds of discrimination,[92] age discrimination claims have notably low success rates (Table 6.3). Unsurprisingly, then, success was exceptional in both the UK and Australian case samples. In Australia, claimants were successful in only twelve substantive decisions, a success rate of 18.75 per cent. Successful substantive cases had one common factor: compelling and explicit evidence of age discrimination. The question, of course, is why these claims did not settle at conciliation.[93] Successful claimants were no more likely to be legally represented (67 per cent legally represented) than unsuccessful claimants (61 per cent).[94]

In GB ETs, between 1 per cent and 4 per cent of age discrimination complaints are successful at hearing each year (Table 6.3). In the UK case sample, of 215 substantive cases that dealt with an age discrimination claim, only forty-three (20 per

[90] Parties may have more than one type of representation, for example, over two separate hearings, or two days of hearing, or appearing in person with assistance.

[91] *Angeli v The Orthopaedic Footwear Company Ltd* [2019] UKET 2201663/2018 was a rare case where the claimant was represented, but the respondent was not; that said, the claimant only briefed counsel one week prior to the hearing.

[92] Linda Dickens, 'The Road is Long: Thirty Years of Equality Legislation in Britain' (2007) 45 British Journal of Industrial Relations 463, 480.

[93] In *Fair Work Ombudsman v Theravanish Investments Pty Ltd* [2014] FCCA 1170, the respondent conceded liability; the decision solely related to penalty.

[94] For borderline cases, though, good legal representation could be key to success: A5.

cent) were successful for the age discrimination claim specifically;[95] in seven cases the outcome was unclear. Overall, only 3.56 per cent of 1,208 cases were successful at hearing.[96]

The median age of claimants in successful claims where age was specified (twenty-two cases) was 59.5, higher than the general claimant population (57). Twenty-four successful cases involved claimants who alleged they were seen as 'too old'; only six involved claimants who alleged they were 'too young'.[97] The majority of successful claimants (thirty-one) were men; only seventeen successful claimants were women.[98] Most successful claims (twenty-five) related to dismissal. Some successful claims were potentially intersectional, with remedies addressing both age and other grounds of discrimination.[99] In twenty successful cases the claimant was legally represented (46.5 per cent), a substantially higher rate than for the general case sample (34.7 per cent) and for substantive cases where the claimant was not successful (36.4 per cent) (Table 6.7).[100]

Ten successful cases (23.2 per cent) were decided under rule 21 (ie, the respondent failed to file a response in time, or the claim was uncontested).[101] Six successful claims were against respondents in liquidation or administration. Seventeen successful cases had no full record of the ET's reasons online, including eight decisions under rule 21.

[95] 'Success', here, includes later success or failure in the Employment Appeal Tribunal (EAT) or Court of Appeal within the time period of study. In this case sample, three cases progressed on appeal in the time period in question: *Lord Chancellor v McCloud* [2018] EWCA Civ 2844 (20 December 2018), [2019] WLR(D) 1 (jointly heard with the appeal of *Sargeant v London Fire and Emergency Planning Authority* [2017] UKET 2202235/2015); *Heskett v Secretary of State for Justice* [2020] EWCA Civ 1487, [2020] WLR(D) 603. After the review period, the decision in *Ryan v South West Ambulance Services NHS Trust* [2019] UKET 1400628/2018 was successfully appealed to the EAT: *Ryan v South West Ambulance Services NHS Trust* [2020] UKEAT/0213/19/VP; and the decision in *Uddin v London Borough of Ealing* [2019] UKET 2206904/2017 was successfully appealed to the EAT on the unfair dismissal point only: *Uddin v London Borough of Ealing* [2020] UKEAT/0165/19/RN. The orders in *Ryan* had not been published in May 2021, but likely add one 'success' to these case statistics.

[96] This is lower than the success rate in Irving's earlier study: Irving found success rates of 3.2 per cent, or 124 of 3,904 cases; plus 2.7 per cent or 104 cases that resulted in a default judgment for the claimant: Irving (n 70) 113. My statistic *includes* default judgments.

[97] One of these cases involved a claimant who was classified as both too old and too young (where a young person also associated with an older colleague).

[98] These numbers do not add to forty-three given the multiple claimants in *Lord Chancellor v McCloud* [2018] EWCA Civ 2844 (20 December 2018); [2019] WLR(D) 1.

[99] *Jolly v Royal Berkshire NHS Foundation Trust* [2019] UKET 3324869/2017 (disability); *Amu v Department for Work and Pensions* [2018] UKET 1600465/2017 (race); *Fogarty v Colman Greaves Fabrications Ltd* [2019] UKET 2410534/2018 (sex).

[100] This is consistent with Rosenthal and Budjanovcanin's study of ET sexual harassment cases, which found that legal representation was a significant predictor of a case's outcome: Patrice Rosenthal and Alexandra Budjanovcanin, 'Sexual Harassment Judgments by British Employment Tribunals 1995–2005: Implications for Claimants and Their Advocates' (2011) 49 British Journal of Industrial Relations s236, s250. It is also consistent with Irving's earlier study of ET age discrimination decisions, where claimants with legal representation were nearly twice as likely to be successful in their claim: Irving (n 70) 133.

[101] The Employment Tribunals (Constitution and Rules of Procedure) Regulations 2013, SI 2013/1237, sch 1, r 21. In one case a default judgment was later revoked. In Irving's earlier study of 3,904 cases, 104 successful claims (2.7 per cent of the sample) were default judgments for the claimant: Irving (n 70) 113.

Table 6.7 Success and claimant legal representation, UK age discrimination case sample, February 2017 to April 2019

	n	Claimants represented	% Represented
All cases	538	187	34.7
Successful substantive claims	43	20	46.5
Unsuccessful substantive claims	165	60	36.4

Overall, then, in the UK sample, claimants were far more likely to be successful if they were legally represented, the respondent did not participate, or the respondent was in liquidation or administration. Essentially, success was correlated with claims not being meaningfully contested.

6. Remedies

Despite some courts and tribunals having broader remedial powers,[102] remedies for successful age discrimination claims typically reflect the individualized model of discrimination law, emphasizing compensation for individual harm rather than structural or behavioural change.[103] Compensation in discrimination cases is 'very, very low',[104] 'a pittance'[105] and 'modest'.[106] This may disincentivize claiming,[107] especially where damages can be entirely consumed by legal fees.[108] Low compensation means complaints can be regarded as just a cost of doing business,[109] doing little to achieve systemic change or deter repeat respondents.[110]

In GB, annual compensation statistics are published for ETs, and are broken down for age discrimination claims specifically (Table 6.8). However, this depicts compensation *per claim*, not per jurisdiction; compensation awarded in different jurisdictions is not disaggregated. Compensation is allocated to the lead

[102] See, eg, Fair Work Act 2009 (Cth) s 545 (hereafter FWA); Australian Human Rights Commission Act 1986 (Cth) s 46PO(4). ET powers are more limited: Equality Act 2010, s 124(2) (hereafter EqA).

[103] Dickens, 'The Road is Long' (n 92) 480.

[104] A99.

[105] A7; A100.

[106] UK97.

[107] A112.

[108] UK97; Women and Equalities Committee, *The Use of Non-Disclosure Agreements in Discrimination Cases* (2017–19 HC 1720) [65].

[109] A99.

[110] ibid; A107; A155.

Table 6.8 Compensation by band, ET age discrimination claims, 2007–08 to 2018–19

	2007–08	2008–09	2009–10	2010–11	2011–12	2012–13	2013–14	2014–15	2015–16	2016–17	2017–18	2018–19
<£500	2	–	–	–	1	–	1	–	0	0	0	0
£500–£999	2	3	–	–	1	–	2	1	0	1	0	0
£1,000–£1,999	11	3	5	6	2	3	2	–	0	1	0	1
£2,000–£2,999	1	3	–	1	–	2	4	1	0	0	0	1
£3,000–£3,999	–	4	2	–	3	3	1	–	1	1	0	0
£4,000–£4,999	2	1	3	1	1	5	–	2	0	0	1	1
£5,000–£5,999	–	–	4	2	1	2	2	–	1	1	0	0
£6,000–£6,999	–	2	1	–	3	2	3	–	0	1	3	1
£7,000–£7,999	–	1	2	–	1	2	1	1	0	0	1	0
£8,000–£8,999	–	2	1	1	1	1	–	–	0	0	0	0
£9,000–£9,999	–	2	1	–	–	–	1	–	0	0	0	1

£10,000–£12,499	4	–	1	2	1	2	2	–	1	1	1	1
£12,500–£14,999	–	–	2	1	1	1	–	1	0	0	0	3
£15,000–£19,999	–	1	2	2	1	–	2	1	1	2	0	0
£20,000–£29,999	–	–	1	2	1	–	–	2	0	1	0	1
£30,000–£39,999	–	–	1	2	1	–	1	–	0	1	0	0
£40,000–£49,999	–	–	2	2	1	–	1	–	0	1	0	1
£50,000+	–	1	–	4	3	1	2	–	0	3	0	1
All	22	23	28	26	23	24	25	9	4	14	6	12
Maximum award	£12,124	£90,031	£48,710	£144,100	£144,100	£72,500	£137,000	£28,428	£16,263	£154,309	£10,432	£172,070
Median award	£1,526	£3,816	£5,868	£12,697	£6,065	£4,499	£6,000	£7,500	£8,417	£15,198	£6,184	£12,365
Mean award	£3,334	£8,430	£10,931	£30,289	£19,327	£8,079	£18,801	£11,211	£9,025	£35,663	£6,796	£26,148

Source: Ministry of Justice, Employment Tribunal and Employment Appeals Tribunal Annual Tables, Table E9 (2019)

Table 6.9 Compensation awarded (£), age discrimination jurisdiction, UK case sample

Compensation (£)	Number of cases
< 5,000	6
5,000—9,999	11
10,000—99,999	11
≥ 100,000	2

jurisdiction only; where age discrimination is a subsidiary or non-lead claim, any compensation awarded will not appear in these tables.

The UK case sample therefore offers a more complete picture of remedies awarded. Of the forty-three successful claims, a remedy was discernable in thirty cases.[111] The primary (and generally sole) remedy was compensation, awarded in all thirty cases. The median award for the age discrimination claim was £8,800, with a minimum of £1,000 and maximum of £386,059.73 (Table 6.9).[112] Only two decisions included non-compensatory remedies.[113]

In nineteen cases, the claimant was successful in multiple jurisdictions (not just on the basis of age discrimination). In these cases, age discrimination compensation ranged from 10 per cent to 97 per cent of the total award, typically reflecting whether loss of earnings was awarded in the age discrimination jurisdiction or not. Where specified, most cases (twenty-two) included awards for injury to feelings[114] though the highest awards were typically for loss of earnings (awarded in the age discrimination jurisdiction in eleven cases).[115] Overall, compensation for successful claims is low; the House of Commons Women and Equalities Committee (WEC) has advocated for awarding higher compensation, including through the award of exemplary or punitive damages, and increasing the *Vento* bands.[116]

[111] At the original date of analysis, a remedy was discernible in twenty-nine cases; in twelve cases, the remedy had not yet been determined; in two claims the remedy was agreed or settled privately. Given the number of cases with outstanding remedy decisions, these data were again updated on 17 August 2020, to identify any additional remedy decisions. Over this period, remedies were determined in two additional cases: *McCloud v The Lord Chancellor* [2020] UKET 2201483/2015 (10 January 2020) and *Amu v Department for Work and Pensions* [2018] UKET 1600465/2017 (22 February 2020). These cases have been included in the following statistics for comprehensiveness, though the compensatory remedy in *McCloud* had not yet been determined.

[112] These calculations use gross figures.

[113] *McCloud v The Lord Chancellor* [2020] UKET 2201483/2015 (10 January 2020); *Amu v Department for Work and Pensions* [2018] UKET 1600465/2017 (22 February 2020).

[114] The exception was *Fogarty v Colman Greaves Fabrications Ltd* [2019] UKET 2410534/2018, where the claimant did not seek an award for injury to feelings.

[115] cf *Shirin v Wilson Barca LLP* [2019] UKET 2208035/2016, where £46,908.38 was awarded for injury to feelings and aggravated damages; the claimant sought over £1 million.

[116] Women and Equalities Committee, *Enforcing the Equality Act* (n 22) 62–63.

Claimants may not actually receive any compensation awarded: in the 2018 Survey of Employment Tribunal Applications, only 72 per cent of claimants said their award had been paid.[117] In England and Wales, enforcement requires claimants to pursue their award in the county courts or via a High Court enforcement officer;[118] it can require highly technical examinations of company law, especially if the respondent is trading while insolvent, there is a breach of directors' duties, or phoenix activity.[119] Pursuing these matters is often beyond the capacity of an individual complainant.[120]

7. Costs

Costs orders can be a substantial deterrent to claiming,[121] particularly in 'risky' cases. Claimants may feel pressured to settle for fear of becoming liable for the other party's costs;[122] respondents' legal tactics play on this risk.[123] That said, costs orders are not the norm; the *fear* of costs may have a broader and disproportionate impact.

In Australia, for example, in the states and territories and under the Fair Work Act 2009 (Cth) (FWA), parties typically bear their own costs;[124] at the federal level, though, costs generally follow the event.[125] In the Australian case sample, costs were rarely raised as an issue; costs were flagged in only one successful case,[126] though it is possible that costs were negotiated in other cases after the event. Still, reducing the risk of cost orders,[127] moving to no-cost jurisdictions,[128] or allowing only claimants to recover costs[129] would significantly support claiming.

In UK tribunals parties generally bear their own costs;[130] cost orders in the ET are 'rare'.[131] In this sample, forty-five cases addressed the issue of costs; costs were

[117] 'Survey of Employment Tribunal Applications: Findings from the 2018 Survey' (2020) BEIS Research Paper Number 2020/007, 65–66.
[118] ibid.
[119] UK78; Jasper Hedges and others, 'The Potential Economic Gains from Increasing Public Law Enforcement against Illegal Phoenix Activity' (2018) 44 Monash University Law Review 267.
[120] UK78.
[121] Women and Equalities Committee, *Enforcing the Equality Act* (n 22) 58, [208].
[122] ibid, 59–60 [213].
[123] ibid.
[124] See, eg, Victorian Civil and Administrative Tribunal Act 1998 (Vic) s 109(1); *Federal Circuit Court of Australia Act 1999* (Cth) s 79(1); Federal Court of Australia Act 1976 (Cth) s 43(1)(b); FWA (n 102) s 570(2).
[125] Federal Circuit Court of Australia Act 1999 (Cth) s 79; Federal Court of Australia Act 1976 (Cth) s 43.
[126] *Carr v Blade Repairs Australia Pty Ltd (No 2)* [2010] FCA 688.
[127] A158.
[128] A115.
[129] A112.
[130] The Employment Tribunals (Constitution and Rules of Procedure) Regulations 2013, sch 1, reg 76. See also provision for wasted costs orders against representatives: reg 80–82. In NI, see similarly The Industrial Tribunals and Fair Employment Tribunal (Constitution and Rules of Procedure) Regulations (Northern Ireland) 2020, sch 1, reg 73.
[131] Women and Equalities Committee, *Enforcing the Equality Act* (n 22) 58 [209].

Table 6.10 Costs orders by recipient, UK case sample

	In favour of claimants	In favour of respondents
Number	8[1]	27
Median (£)	622.50	4,000
Minimum (£)	160	230
Maximum (£)	2,138.40	20,000

Table notes:

[1] Includes one preparation time award.

awarded in thirty-five cases (Table 6.10). Costs were mostly awarded in favour of respondents, and for higher monetary values, reflecting higher rates of legal representation among respondents; awards in favour of claimants might only cover ET fees or issue fees. Preparation time awards were particularly low in value: in *Kendall v Newark*,[132] the award was £185. That said, cost awards may represent a fraction of a respondent's actual expenses: in *Galloway v Barnet Enfield & Haringey Mental Health Trust*,[133] for example, the claimant was ordered to pay the respondent's 'costs' of £4,000, about 9 per cent of the respondent's actual costs (£45,000).

Awarding costs may therefore deter claiming, and disproportionately affect claimants in practice. That said, requiring parties to bear their own costs may mean legal expenses wipe out any compensation awarded: in *Hodgkiss v Travis Perkins Trading Company Ltd*,[134] for example, the claimant's legal fees were £14,004, 33.6 per cent of the total compensation awarded. The claimant's application for costs was dismissed. An alternative approach, then, would be to allow costs to be recovered by claimants only, in the event their claim is successful (ie, a form of qualified, one-way costs shifting).[135]

Reform 23: That governments consider introducing qualified, one-way costs shifting, allowing costs to be recovered by claimants only.

IV. Points of Contention and Barriers to Success

Age discrimination claims are therefore less likely to be successful at court or tribunal than claims on other grounds. What are the barriers to success at hearing and judgment, and how (if at all) do they particularly affect age claims?

132 [2017] UKET 3200503/2017.
133 [2019] UKET 3325473/2017.
134 [2019] UKET 2411659/2018.
135 Women and Equalities Committee, *The Use of Non-Disclosure Agreements* (n 108) [61].

I have considered elsewhere the general barriers to age discrimination claims in Australia,[136] and the impact of time limits and delays in the UK context.[137] In this part, I focus on issues flagged in earlier chapters as particular costs of and barriers to bringing a complaint of age discrimination: the burden of proof; intersectionality; and justification.

A. Burden of Proof

Proof, and a lack of proof, was a recurring issue throughout this study, being a major barrier to claiming[138] and limiting success at hearing. Issues of proof are intertwined with the nature of age discrimination, which tends to be subtle and rarely blatant[139] (Chapters 1 and 2). While overt age discrimination is rare, these are the only cases that tend to be successfully pursued:[140] proving a case otherwise is 'very, very difficult'.[141]

While there is a shifting burden of proof in the UK,[142] only the FWA in Australia makes provision for the burden of proof to shift (Chapter 3).[143] This exacerbates issues of proof in Australian jurisdictions;[144] a lack of evidence was raised in thirty-two of the 108 Australian cases.

One obvious reform, then, would be to shift the burden of proof in discrimination claims in Australia.[145] This could be 'incredibly beneficial' to claimants.[146] That said, despite the FWA's shifting burden of proof, courts have remained highly deferential to employers' evidence:[147] the FWA's reverse burden of proof has become a 'façade'.[148] Shifting the burden of proof could have perverse effects if courts are unsympathetic to discrimination claims; it means 'the whole culture of the trial process would be shifted and it would actually turn the focus around to the respondent', potentially generating sympathy for the respondent: 'The

136 Blackham, 'Why Do Employment Age Discrimination Cases Fail?' (n 67).

137 Blackham, 'Enforcing Rights in Employment Tribunals' (n 46).

138 A3; A5; A103; A107; A108; A109; A112; A113; A115; A118; A150; A155; A158; A160; A164; UK80; UK161; UK84.

139 A100; A101; A102; A103; A113; A150; A153; UK78. cf UK80.

140 A109; A110; A113; UK167; UK78.

141 A109.

142 EqA (n 102) s 136, Employment Equality (Age) Regulations (Northern Ireland) 2006 (NI) reg 42(2); Council Directive 2000/78/EC of 27 November 2000 establishing a general framework for equal treatment in employment and occupation [2000] OJ L303/16, art 10 (hereafter Framework Directive).

143 FWA (n 102) s 361(1).

144 A158.

145 A71; A106; A112; A113.

146 A112. See also A113.

147 A5.

148 A5. See, eg, Anna Chapman, Kathleen Love, and Beth Gaze, 'The Reverse Onus of Proof Then and Now: The Barclay Case and the History of the Fair Work Act's Union Victimisation and Freedom of Association' (2014) 37 University of New South Wales Law Journal 471.

poor respondent being put in this situation where they have to justify [their behaviour].'[149]

With a shifting burden of proof, a claimant must still establish a prima facie case;[150] some claims will not even meet this hurdle.[151] In the UK case sample, a lack of evidence was raised in eighty-seven cases. In many claims, a prima facie case could not be established: the burden of proof was explicitly held to not shift to the respondent in twenty-eight cases.[152] Other cases did not even progress this far due to a complete lack of evidence: the claimant's evidence was unreliable;[153] the claim was merely speculative or an 'assertion' without evidentiary backing,[154] or was not particularized or actively pursued.[155]

149 A153.

150 A115. See *Igen Ltd v Wong* [2005] EWCA Civ 142, [2005] ICR 931; *Royal Mail Group Ltd v Efobi* [2021] UKSC 33, [2021] 1 WLR 3863.

151 UK97.

152 *Waterloo v National Library of Scotland* [2019] UKET S/4105348/17; *Wallace v The Student Loans Company Ltd* [2018] UKET S/4100769/2017, [118]; *Cameron v LEM Europe GmbH* [2019] UKET 2410407/2018, [44]; *Richards v Vodafone Ltd* [2017] UKET 4106119/2015; *Fitzpatrick v The Scottish Ministers* [2018] UKET 4101694/2017, [91]; *McDougall v LGSS Law Ltd* [2018] UKET 3400373/2017, [6.1]; *Atkins v Mason* [2018] UKET 3328241/2017, [66], [67]; *Mubayiwa v Cygnet Health Care Ltd* [2017] UKET 3324515/2017, [49]; *Harman v TMD Technologies Ltd* [2017] UKET 3324348/2016, [10]; *Rana v Royal Mail Group Ltd* [2019] UKET 3304619/2018, [62]; *Heydon v LB Europe Ltd* [2018] UKET 2403553/2017, [57], [58]; *Nwokedi v Wondrwall Ltd* [2018] UKET 2403163/2018; *Niba v Platt and Hill Ltd* [2017] UKET 2401612/2017, [28]; *Mhlanga v Kendrick* [2017] UKET 2300280/2017, [37]; *Wallace v KPI Bridge Oil London Ltd* [2017] UKET 227596/2016; *Jouhari v London Mayfair Hotel Ltd* [2017] UKET 2207752/2016; *Cheney v MS Amlin Corporate Services Ltd* [2017] UKET 2207640/2016; *Rawlinson v TLC Care Management Ltd* [2019] UKET 1807107/2017; *Morrison v JSB Healthcare Ltd* [2018] UKET 1600440/2017; *Sharp v Plympton Academy* [2018] UKET 1400688/2017; *Wood v Liz Earle Beauty Co Ltd* [2019] UKET 1400079/2017; *Jabbar v West Midlands Travel Ltd* [2017] UKET 1300288/2016; *Toner v L F Fasthouse Ltd* [2019] NIFET 06955/18IT, [88], [91]; *Taheri v Perry Motor Sales Ltd* [2019] UKET 3304326/2018, [48], [50]; *Rose v Nightingale Hammerson Trustee Company Ltd* [2017] UKET 2302852/2016, [145]; *Jabbar v West Midlands Travel Ltd* [2017] UKET 1300288/2016, [3.11]; *Aslam v Tees Esk and Wear Valleys NHS Foundation Trust* [2018] UKET 2501009/2017, [42].

153 *Atkins v Mason* [2018] UKET 3328241/2017, [60], [63]; *Bassi v London Borough of Hillingdon* [2017] UKET 3323899/2016, [25.1]; *Ahmed v Autism Consulting Ltd* [2017] UKET 3322728/2016, [10.9]; *Limer v Baker* [2017] UKET 2600994/2016, [19]; *Stewart v Loughborough Specsavers Ltd* [2018] UKET 2600760/2017, [17]; *Aslam v Tees Esk and Wear Valleys NHS Foundation Trust* [2018] UKET 2501009/2017, [41]; *Fairclough v Allen* [2018] UKET 2403288/2017; *Nwokedi v Wondrwall Ltd* [2018] UKET 2403163/2018, [39]; *Kidd v Wates Living Space* [2018] UKET 2302180/2017, [29]; *Wallace v KPI Bridge Oil London Ltd* [2017] UKET 227596/2016, [102]; *Littlewood v Aviva Employment Services Ltd* [2018] UKET 1801611/2017, [3.14]; *Wood v Liz Earle Beauty Co Ltd* [2019] UKET 1400079/2017, [78.15]; *Hughes v Aktrion Group Ltd* [2017] UKET 1301951/2016, [10]; *Toner v L F Fasthouse Ltd* [2019] NIFET 06955/18IT, [18]; *Ballentine v The Board of Governors, Lismore Comprehensive School* [2019] NIIT 00051/18IT; 01014/17IT; 02819/16IT, [69].

154 *Wallace v The Student Loans Company Ltd* [2018] UKET S/4100769/2017, [118]; *Patton v Secretary of State for Justice* [2017] UKET 1302702/2016, [175]; *Mokrani v Jaguar Land Rover Ltd* [2017] UKET 1300662/2017, [31]; *Ballentine v The Board of Governors, Lismore Comprehensive School* [2019] NIIT 00051/18IT; 01014/17IT; 02819/16IT, [68].

155 *Gee v Santander UK plc* [2017] UKET 3400309/2016; *Atkins v Mason* [2018] UKET 3328241/2017; *Harman v TMD Technologies Ltd* [2017] UKET 3324348/2016; *Abberley v Royal Opera House Covent Garden Foundation* [2017] UKET 2200067/2017; *Taylor v Dr Kelpie and Partners (A Partnership)* [2017]

A shifting burden of proof is therefore only likely to be determinative in finely balanced cases with very particular fact scenarios.[156] That said, in some cases in the sample, the burden of proof shifted, and this was key to the success of the claim.[157] In *James v Coedffranc Community Council*,[158] for example, the claimant argued that he had been discriminated against on the basis of age in recruitment for a role as a park attendant. The claimant brought evidence of: comments relating to age made in the job interview by one Councillor; interview notes recording the ages of the two oldest job applicants, and which circled the age of the successful (younger) candidate; and that this Councillor's lower mark for the claimant 'was a game changer in the decision to appoint' the younger candidate: the claimant had scored top marks with the other two interviewers.[159] The circling of the age of the successful (younger) candidate in particular allowed the ET to:

> properly infer that the age of the claimant was a matter that [the Councillor] bore in mind when making her decision. We also note that she was concerned about the length of time the claimant would be able to undertake the role, given the role would require training for which the council would incur a cost.[160]

The respondent did not subsequently discharge its burden of proof, and the ET could not conclude that the decision 'had nothing to do with the claimant's age'.[161]

In *Khan v Roadrunners GB Ltd*,[162] the claimant's employment as a taxi-cab controller ended after a meeting with two of the respondent's managers. One manager (Mr Hussain) failed to give evidence at hearing.[163] The claimant and the other manager (Mr Foster) gave conflicting accounts of the meeting: the claimant said he was dismissed; the other manager said the claimant had 'agreed mutually' to retire.[164] The claimant's evidence was preferred to that of the second manager: it was 'simply not credible that the Claimant was summoned to a meeting without

UKET 1401375/2016; *Richardson v B&Q plc* [2017] UKET 1401373/2016; *Nixon v Staffordshire South West Citizens Advice* [2018] UKET 1301395/2017.

156 UK78.
157 See, eg, *James v Coedffranc Community Council* [2018] UKET 1600068/2018; *Amu v Department for Work and Pensions* [2018] UKET 1600465/2017; *Khan v Roadrunners GB Ltd* [2019] UKET 2302696/2017.
158 [2018] UKET 16000/68.
159 ibid, [47]–[49].
160 ibid, [47].
161 ibid, [50].
162 [2019] UKET 2302696/2017.
163 ibid, [1].
164 ibid, [11].

being given any information about the subject matter of that meeting in advance, and then simply agreed to retire immediately', especially when he was not yet able to draw a pension.[165] The claimant also told his colleague that he had been fired immediately after the meeting.[166] Given the respondent had given evidence that retirement was discussed at the meeting, that was sufficient to establish a prima facie case.[167] The respondent could not discharge its burden of proof, and the age discrimination claim succeeded. Thus, while a shifting burden of proof will not resolve all issues of proof and evidence, it may substantially assist particular claimants and claims.

> **Reform 24:** That a shifting burden of proof be adopted in Australian discrimination law.

B. Intersectional or Dual Discrimination

There is limited provision for intersectional, multiple, or dual discrimination in the UK and Australia (Chapter 3).[168] While this does not necessarily *prevent* intersectional claims from being raised, especially in jurisdictions with no comparator requirement,[169] there are few legal signposts that *encourage* such claims. For claimants, recognizing intersectionality in law 'allows us to talk about the person's whole experience rather than break it down to that sort of granular level';[170] it allows claims to be 'a more coherent representation of their experience than trying to narrow it down to one or the other [ground]'.[171] For respondents, treating protected grounds in the same way, with unified legislation, provides a clearer set of requirements for fair treatment, making compliance with equality law a 'much more straightforward task'.[172] Thus, there is a need to re-examine how intersectionality is provided for in the law[173] for the benefit of both claimants and respondents; given

[165] ibid, [14].
[166] ibid, [15].
[167] ibid, [20].
[168] Alysia Blackham and Jeromey Temple, 'Intersectional Discrimination in Australia: An Empirical Critique of the Legal Framework' (2020) 43 University of New South Wales Law Journal 773. See EqA (n 102) s 14, which has not commenced.
[169] A112; BA Hepple, *Equality: The Legal Framework* (2nd edn, Hart Publishing 2014) 78; cf Iyiola Solanke, 'Infusing the Silos in the Equality Act 2010 with Synergy' (2011) 40 Industrial Law Journal 336, 340–41; Shreya Atrey, *Intersectional Discrimination* (OUP 2019).
[170] A105.
[171] ibid; Tessa Wright, Hazel Conley, and Sian Moore, 'Addressing Discrimination in the Workplace on Multiple Grounds: The Experience of Trade Union Equality Representatives' (2011) 40 Industrial Law Journal 460, 462.
[172] A4.
[173] UK80.

Table 6.11 Count of jurisdictions in complaints, age discrimination ECAs and ET1s, 2018–19

Count of jurisdictions	% of age discrimination ECAs	% age discrimination ET1s
1	26	11
2	38	26
3	22	25
4	9	18
5+	5	20

Source: Acas

few legal practitioners are familiar with equality law, it is essential that statutes be clarified on this point.[174] This may demand a full reconsideration of the framing and nature of discrimination law.[175]

Reform 25: That there be explicit recognition of intersectional discrimination in UK and Australian discrimination law.

While there is limited statutory recognition of intersectionality, multiple claims are common at complaint stage (Chapter 4) and in tribunals. According to Acas, in 2018–19, only around a quarter of age discrimination early conciliation notifications (ECAs) solely related to age discrimination; most raised at least one other ground (Table 6.11). Of matters that proceeded to an ET claim via an ET1 form, 89 per cent raised at least one issue other than age discrimination, and the majority raised three or more issues.

In half of complaints, the other jurisdiction raised was unfair dismissal, followed by discrimination on the grounds of sex, race, and disability and—for ET1s—religion or belief (Table 6.12). This implies some degree of overlap between different grounds of discrimination; many complaints potentially involve intersectional or multiple discrimination.

This is consistent with the UK case sample: of the 1,208 cases, most involved multiple jurisdictions, most commonly unfair dismissal (764); breach of contract (337); disability discrimination (284); sex discrimination (267); race discrimination (245); and unlawful deduction from wages (282). Most successful substantive cases initially raised at least two grounds of claim (Table 6.13), but this was most

174 A112.
175 Atrey (n 169).

Table 6.12 Top ten other jurisdictions raised, age discrimination ECAs and ET1s, 2018–19

Jurisdiction	% of age discrimination ECAs	% of age discrimination ET1s
Unfair dismissal	50	62
Sex discrimination	26	24
Race discrimination	21	25
Disability discrimination	20	27
Wages Act	13	27
Breach of contract	13	27
Public interest disclosure	8	9
Working Time Regulations/annual leave	5	17
Unfair dismissal for exercising a statutory right	2	
Equal pay	2	
Religion and/or belief discrimination		8
Redundancy payment		9

Source: Acas

Table 6.13 Successful age discrimination cases by number of jurisdictions raised, UK case sample

Number of jurisdictions	Successful cases	% of successful cases
1	6	13.95
2	13	30.23
3	8	18.60
4	13	30.23
5	2	4.65
6	1	2.33

commonly unfair dismissal (twenty-two cases), breach of contract (fifteen), sex discrimination (eight), and unlawful deduction from wages (eight); other grounds of discrimination were less common.

Where claims are brought in multiple discrimination jurisdictions, they are not necessarily argued or decided as *intersectional* claims. Different grounds of discrimination may be addressed as separate and distinct issues. In this sample, though, some successful UK cases were potentially intersectional, with remedies addressing both age and other forms of discrimination.[176] In *Jolly v Royal Berkshire NHS Foundation Trust*,[177] for example, the ET considered age and disability discrimination claims concurrently: the treatment of the claimant was related to her perceived 'frailty', which arose due to both her age and disability.[178] The remedy (by consent) did not distinguish between the discrimination claims. In *Amu v Department for Work and Pensions*,[179] though, claims of race, sex, and age discrimination were considered separately; allegations of race and age discrimination were held to be established. In assessing the injury to feelings award, however, the ET did not seek to assess separately the injury to feelings caused by each act of discrimination: to do so would be 'artificial'. Instead, the ET 'had in mind all of the acts of discrimination and the impact that they collectively had upon the Claimant throughout the period'.[180] Thus, ETs may recognize the way grounds of discrimination intersect, interact, and compound, but this is not consistent or uniform in tribunal decision-making.

C. Justification

It is not possible to justify direct age discrimination in Australia. In the UK, however, it is possible to objectively justify direct age discrimination as a proportionate means of achieving a legitimate aim.[181] This distinguishes age from all other protected grounds, freezing the development of age discrimination law at a particular point in its development.[182] The possibility of justification means that drawing the line between acceptable and unacceptable discrimination sits at the heart of age discrimination law,[183] requiring complex, fact-driven normative judgements about the instrumental utility of age discrimination, and when it should give way to the principle of equality.[184]

176 *Jolly v Royal Berkshire NHS Foundation Trust* [2019] UKET 3324869/2017 (disability); *Amu v Department for Work and Pensions* [2018] UKET 1600465/2017 (race); *Fogarty v Colman Greaves Fabrications Ltd* [2019] UKET 2410534/2018 (sex).

177 [2019] UKET 3324869/2017.

178 ibid, [94.4]–[94.9]. In *Fogarty v Colman Greaves Fabrications Ltd* [2019] UKET 2410534/2018, a decision under rule 21, the claims of age and sex discrimination also appear to have been considered together: the claimant would not have been dismissed if she was 'a man of her same age or a considerably older woman who was not seen ... as having presented a threat': at [12].

179 [2018] UKET 1600465/2017.

180 [2019] UKET 1600465/2017, [88].

181 See Framework Directive (n 142) art 6(1); EqA (n 102) s 13(2); The Employment Equality (Age) Regulations (Northern Ireland) 2006, reg 3(1).

182 UK82.

183 Sandra Fredman, *Discrimination Law* (2nd edn, OUP 2011) 101.

184 Or, if reframing to take individual rights as a starting point, the question should be: when should the principle of equality give way to the instrumental benefits of discrimination? See Malcolm

Justification could be a major area of contention in age discrimination law, and is well canvassed in superior case law[185] and academic scholarship, particularly in the contexts of mandatory retirement,[186]pensions,[187] and redundancy pay.[188] In practice, though, employers now rarely adopt directly age discriminatory practices,[189] perhaps due to a perception that age-based measures are difficult to justify.[190]

Few cases in the ET sample related to the justification of direct age discrimination. Indeed, justification—for both direct and indirect age discrimination—was raised in only eighteen cases;[191] in three of these cases it was not ultimately necessary to consider justification.[192] In cases relating to direct age discrimination,

Sargeant, 'The Employment Equality (Age) Regulations 2006: A Legitimisation of Age Discrimination in Employment' (2006) 35 Industrial Law Journal 209, 218. On the complexity of this task, see Elaine Dewhurst, 'Proportionality Assessments of Mandatory Retirement Measures: Uncovering Guidance for National Courts in Age Discrimination Cases' (2016) 45 Industrial Law Journal 60.

185 See, eg, *Seldon v Clarkson Wright and Jakes (A Partnership)* [2012] UKSC 16 (25 April 2012), [2012] 2 CMLR 50; *Lockwood v Department of Work and Pensions* [2013] EWCA Civ 1195 (11 October 2013), [2014] ICR 1257.

186 See, eg, Elaine Dewhurst, 'Intergenerational Balance, Mandatory Retirement and Age Discrimination in Europe: How Can the ECJ Better Support National Courts in Finding a Balance between the Generations?' (2013) 50 Common Market Law Review 1333; Dewhurst, 'Proportionality Assessments of Mandatory Retirement Measures' (n 184); Alysia Blackham, 'Interrogating the "Dignity" Argument for Mandatory Retirement: An Undignified Development?' (2019) 48 Industrial Law Journal 377; Lucy Vickers and Simonetta Manfredi, 'Age Equality and Retirement: Squaring the Circle' (2013) 42 Industrial Law Journal 61; Catherine Barnard and Simon Deakin, 'Age Discrimination and Labour Law in the UK: Managing Ageing' in Ann Numhauser-Henning and Mia Rönnmar (eds), *Age Discrimination and Labour Law: Comparative and Conceptual Perspectives in the EU and beyond* (Kluwer Law International 2015); Ann Numhauser-Henning, 'The EU Ban on Age-Discrimination and Older Workers: Potentials and Pitfalls' (2013) 29 International Journal of Comparative Labour Law and Industrial Relations 391.

187 See, eg, Lydia Seymour, 'The Courts, Non-Discrimination and Systemic Change in UK Public Sector Pension Scheme' in Sinéad Agnew, Paul S Davies and Charles Mitchell (eds), *Pensions: Law, Policy and Practice* (Hart Publishing 2020).

188 See, eg, Malcolm Sargeant, 'Age Discrimination, Redundancy Payments and Length of Service' (2009) 72 Modern Law Review 628; Alysia Blackham, 'Falling on Their Feet: Young Workers, Employment and Age Discrimination' (2015) 44 Industrial Law Journal 246.

189 House of Commons, 'Oral Evidence: Older People and Employment' (2018) HC 359 Q64 <http://data.parliament.uk/writtenevidence/committeeevidence.svc/evidencedocument/women-and-equalities-committee/older-people-and-employment/oral/76656.html> accessed 24 March 2022.

190 ibid, Q65.

191 *Jenkins v Tesco Stores Limited* [2018] UKET 3401288/2016; *Neiman v British Airways plc* [2018] UKET 3346924/2016; *Haslam v London Borough of Waltham Forest* [2017] UKET 3200580/2016; *Gibson v Newcastle upon Tyne Hospitals NHS Foundation Trust* [2018] UKET 2500035/2017; *Peckham v Magnox Ltd* [2017] UKET 2301637/2016; *Heskett v Secretary of State for Justice* [2017] UKET 2300295/2016; *Mhlanga v Kendrick* [2017] UKET 2300280/2017; *Uddin v London Borough of Ealing* [2019] UKET 2206904/2017; *Sargeant v London Fire and Emergency Planning Authority* [2017] UKET 2202235/2015; *McCloud v The Lord Chancellor* [2017] UKET 2201483/2015; *Leinhardt v Harrogate and District NHS Foundation Trust* [2019] UKET 1806833/2018; *Mundin v Beal Developments Ltd* [2017] UKET 1800455/2017; *Ryan v South West Ambulance Services NHS Trust* [2019] UKET 1400628/2018; *Cook v Beckford Silk Limited* [2018] UKET 1400279/2017; *Mawhinney v Chief Constable of the Police Service of Northern Ireland* [2018] NIIT 04119/17IT; 04120/17IT; *Robinson v Schivo NI Ltd (In Liquidation)* [2018] NIFET 00013/16FET; *Wright v Schivo NI Ltd (In Liquidation)* [2018] NIFET 00012/16FET, 00270/16IT; *Barlow v Gallagher Ltd* [2017] NIIT 00924/15IT.

192 *Mhlanga v Kendrick* [2017] UKET 2300280/2017; *Haslam v London Borough of Waltham Forest* [2017] UKET 3200580/2016; *Cook v Beckford Silk Limited* [2018] UKET 1400279/2017.

justification was successfully argued in only one of the seven cases where justification was considered. In *Uddin v London Borough of Ealing*,[193] the claimant (age 43) was dismissed for gross misconduct after being accused of 'inappropriate sexual behaviour' with a social work student (age 26). The alleged age discrimination was that the investigator referred to the claimant's age in the report of the incident. This was held to be justified: the ET held that: 'In assessing the seriousness of an alleged assault, it was not irrelevant to take account of age, and the risk of abuse of seniority meant it was to be considered; control of such abuse is a legitimate aim, and it was proportionate to mention it.'[194] Of course, the report could have referred to differences in seniority and power, rather than age.

Even if an exception is rarely used, it 'does make a difference'[195] and can have a broader symbolic impact on the way age discrimination law is perceived and regarded.[196] The ability to justify direct age discrimination 'demotes it . . . automatically from the start'[197] to be a weaker form of legislative protection.[198] The possibility of justification means claimants are less willing to bring a claim of age discrimination, and more likely to abandon or withdraw their claim pre-hearing;[199] indeed, raising age as a ground of claim may dilute protection in intersectional claims.[200] While employers might feel empowered by the possibility of justification,[201] it can cause difficulties: employers may believe their conduct is justified, yet have an ET disagree.[202]

Given the limited use of justification provisions in practice, then, it is timely to reconsider whether direct age discrimination should be able to be objectively justified. We must address the devaluing of age as a protected characteristic[203] by removing age-based exceptions that no longer reflect contemporary views of age and ageing.[204] It is time for a narrowing of this broad exception; instead, if deemed necessary, allowance could be made for objectively justifying specific employment practices, such as retirement ages and differences in pension provision.

193 [2019] UKET 2206904/2017.
194 ibid, [73].
195 UK97.
196 Alysia Blackham, 'A Compromised Balance? A Comparative Examination of Exceptions to Age Discrimination Law in Australia and the UK' (2018) 41 Melbourne University Law Review 1085.
197 UK79.
198 UK82.
199 ibid.
200 Judy Fudge and Ania Zbyszewska, 'An Intersectional Approach to Age Discrimination in the European Union: Bridging Dignity and Distribution?' in Ann Numhauser-Henning and Mia Rönnmar (eds), *Age Discrimination and Labour Law: Comparative and Conceptual Perspectives in the EU and Beyond* (Kluwer Law International 2015) 152.
201 UK161.
202 UK117.
203 A98; Sargeant, 'The Employment Equality (Age) Regulations 2006' (n 184) 219; Malcolm Sargeant, 'Age Discrimination' in Malcolm Sargeant (ed), *The Law on Age Discrimination in the EU* (Kluwer Law International 2008) 3; Malcolm Sargeant, 'The European Court of Justice and Age Discrimination' [2011] Journal of Business Law 144, 148.
204 A98; A99; A103.

Reform 26: That the ability to objectively justify direct age discrimination in the UK be removed and replaced by more specific exceptions if required.

V. Strengthening Courts and Decision-Making

There are substantial barriers to pursuing a claim to a court or tribunal. The initial costs of claiming—financial, personal, reputational, and relational—are amplified as claims progress. Even where claimants file a court or tribunal claim, there is substantial attrition during these processes; few cases are ultimately successful at hearing. In Australia, for example, if roughly 3 per cent of those who experience age discrimination approach an external body; 3 per cent of formal complaints proceed to court; and less than 20 per cent of cases are successful, then less than 0.018 per cent of those experiencing age discrimination might be successful in a court or tribunal. Barriers to claiming are disproportionately affecting women, young people, and claims that do not relate to dismissal.

We might question, then, how well age discrimination law is operating in practice. In the advocate survey, respondents were sharply divided on whether the legal system appropriately supports claimants and respondents (Table 6.14). There was consensus, though, that ADR effectively resolves complaints; and that age discrimination at work remains problematic.

For some respondents, equality law has become outdated and not kept pace with changing social norms. The strict divide between direct and indirect discrimination is 'inadequate' for 'captur[ing] the actual effects of discrimination' and obscures how discrimination manifests on a broader and systemic scale.[205] Some jurisdictions require a broad legislative overhaul[206] of statutory frameworks that are 'clunky and from another time'.[207] Without political will, change is impossible,[208] and equality legislation is left to 'atrophy';[209] being politically contentious, 'no one wants to touch it'.[210] Equally, though, this means that 'nobody has been tampering with it of either political persuasion';[211] reform is not always helpful or progressive. Legislative change—where it occurs—tends to be piecemeal, haphazard,[212] and incremental;[213] anything 'too lofty',[214] radical, or ambitious might

205 A111.
206 A10; A71; A155.
207 A71.
208 A10.
209 A71.
210 A10.
211 A71.
212 A10.
213 A71.
214 ibid.

Table 6.14 Responses to the question, 'Please indicate your level of agreement with each statement', advocate survey

	n	% agree
The legal system supports claimants bringing age discrimination complaints	38	52.63
The legal system supports respondents to age discrimination complaints	37	59.46
The enforcement mechanisms available for age discrimination law are appropriately designed to meet claimants' needs	38	36.84
The enforcement mechanisms available for age discrimination law are appropriately designed to meet respondents' needs	37	54.05
ADR offers an effective means for resolving age discrimination complaints	36	80.56
Age discrimination law is helping to address ageism at work	38	47.37
Age discrimination at work is a problem	37	89.19

scare off legislators.[215] While some jurisdictions have managed to overhaul their equality laws, with strong political will driving comprehensive processes of review, inquiry, and consultation,[216] this is exceptional. Further, broad reform projects might be wound back by later governments,[217] and constant inquiries, reports, and consultation exercises risk creating consultation fatigue and a sense that little is being achieved.[218] It is understandable, then, that legal regulation might fail to reflect contemporary understandings of (in)equality.

While the legal framework matters, there needs to be a whole infrastructure in place for law to achieve change.[219] Progressive statutes do not necessarily encourage people to make a complaint or to persevere with their complaint,[220] though some issues might fit within the statutory framework where they would not otherwise.[221]

215 ibid. For example, respondents cited the attempt to consolidate Australian federal discrimination laws as an example of how an attempt at radical overhaul might fail: A9; A10; A150.

216 See, eg, Department of Justice, *An Equality Act for a Fairer Victoria: Equal Opportunity Review Final Report* (2008); Department for Communities and Local Government, *Discrimination Law Review. A Framework for Fairness: Proposals for a Single Equality Bill for Great Britain. A Consultation Paper* (2007).

217 This may take the form of amending legislation (as in Victoria and GB), limited statutory instruments (as in GB), or a failure to commence legislative provisions (as in GB).

218 UK92.

219 UK93.

220 A100; A104; A154.

221 A100.

Gaps in enforcement are not necessarily attributable to the legislative framework itself:[222] as one advocate in the survey summarized:

> The system of determining age discrimination claims is simply too complex and costly for the citizen who is not a millionaire—and most clients are not. These are not novel reasons but well-known and documented by legal scholars—and yet nothing much ever changes.

A more pertinent question, then, is how to reframe discrimination law to ensure effective enforcement. This is taken up in Chapters 7, 8, and 9, which consider enforcement mechanisms beyond individual claims. A focus on law reform should also not come at the expense of measures that make a tangible difference, such as attitudinal change.[223] There is a need 'to tackle [age discrimination] from the bottom up and the top down'.[224]

That said, individual claims are likely to remain an important part of any enforcement model.[225] Individual rights have an important role to play.[226] Complaints can and do have an impact,[227] and can change organizational practices, though this is infrequent and exceptional.[228] Complaints can also inform other forms of enforcement.[229] Our focus should therefore be on creating favourable precedents which might lead to broader change; generating a 'critical mass' of cases to promote a culture of compliance;[230] and achieving systemic change through individual litigation.

We need, then, to strengthen individual enforcement, and address barriers to claiming in public forums. The reforms highlighted in the parts above seek to simplify and modernize discrimination law, to make it easier to navigate and bring a claim.[231] Building on the findings of previous chapters, we must better support individual claimants through hearing and judgment, including by addressing power disparities in the enforcement process;[232] ensuring individuals are better informed of their rights, and have the capacity and confidence to exercise them;[233] offering practical support through proceedings,[234] such as from a dedicated legal advocate;[235] improving the quality of legal representation, and making it more

222 A108.
223 A150.
224 ibid.
225 Women and Equalities Committee, *Enforcing the Equality Act* (n 22) 55 [192].
226 A104; A105.
227 A101.
228 UK162.
229 A105.
230 Women and Equalities Committee, *Enforcing the Equality Act* (n 22) 55 [192].
231 A102; A112; A153.
232 A164.
233 A101; UK86.
234 A103.
235 A102.

accessible;[236] and focusing on making court and tribunal proceedings faster and simpler.[237] There may be scope, too, to make proceedings less adversarial,[238] perhaps by adopting an inquisitorial model with appropriate judicial training.[239]

While recognizing the difficulties of legal change, the sections that follow consider specific legal reforms that could improve mechanisms for addressing age discrimination at work, including by reference to Canadian law.

A. Reasonable Accommodations on the Basis of Age

In Canada and the Northern Territory (NT), reasonable accommodations are required for all protected grounds, not just disability. Adopting this in other jurisdictions could strengthen age discrimination law, change perceptions of ageing and older age, and encourage workers to ask for adjustments.[240]

While the Canadian duty is an affirmative *defence* rather than an affirmative *duty* (Chapter 3),[241] in the NT the obligation is broader. Section 24 of the Anti-Discrimination Act 1992 (NT) says:

> A person shall not fail or refuse to accommodate a special need that another person has because of an attribute.

This includes making inadequate or inappropriate provision to accommodate a special need, and unreasonably failing to provide for a special need.[242] Determining whether a failure to accommodate is unreasonable will depend on all relevant circumstances, including the nature of the special need; the cost and disruption of accommodation; the person's financial circumstances; the number of people who will benefit or be disadvantaged; and any benefit or detriment to all concerned.[243] Reasonable accommodation is also an affirmative defence: under s 35(1)(b)(ii), discrimination at work is lawful if based: 'on the other person's inability to adequately perform the inherent requirements of the work *even where the special need of the other person has been or were to be accommodated*' (emphasis added). Requiring reasonable accommodations for all protected grounds has significant potential to promote more inclusive work practices.

[236] A118.
[237] A115.
[238] A164; UK162.
[239] UK162.
[240] UK152.
[241] Pnina Alon-Shenker, 'Legal Barriers to Age Discrimination in Hiring Complaints' (2016) 39 Dalhousie Law Journal 289, 317.
[242] Anti-Discrimination Act 1992 (NT) s 24(2).
[243] ibid, s 24(3). See also s 58.

Reform 27: That reasonable accommodations be required for all grounds, including age.

B. Equality Rights as Human Rights

The enforcement of age discrimination law could be strengthened by reframing equality rights as human rights and adopting a human rights framework[244] as an 'umbrella' for other legislation 'so everything is read through that lens'.[245] Reframing equality rights as human rights changes the whole legal framework;[246] it creates a different rhetoric and framework for discussions of (in)equality,[247] representing a more authentic approach to equality consistent with individual lived experience.[248] Linking equality obligations with human rights obligations encourages a focus on socio-economic rights and substantive inequalities,[249] facilitating a shift away from a siloed view of equality based on individual grounds.[250] A rights-based approach therefore encourages recognition of intersectionality and individual needs.[251] Including equality rights as constitutional rights, which can be further developed in specific equality statutes, reinforces the public nature of (in)equality, emphasizing that 'this is about society, not just about individuals'.[252]

For enforcement, a human rights approach could reframe individual complaints under equality law as a positive exercise of rights, rather than a negative complaint-based process.[253] Individuals may be more likely to complain and pursue their rights if complaints are cast as positive assertions of rights for the greater good, with broader significance.[254] This framing may 'drive and motivate' individuals to start examining equality issues in their workplaces 'and obviously that has a flow on effect elsewhere'.[255]

Unlike in Canada, age equality law in the UK and Australia has limited grounding in human rights. In the UK, while age discrimination is regulated by the European Convention on Human Rights (at least in relation to Convention rights),[256] these provisions have rarely been used in relation to age discrimination

244 A99.
245 A105.
246 A2.
247 A10.
248 A105.
249 UK94.
250 A105.
251 UK94.
252 UK81.
253 A105.
254 ibid.
255 A99.
256 Convention for the Protection of Human Rights and Fundamental Freedoms (European Convention on Human Rights, as amended) (hereafter ECHR) art 14. See also Human Rights Act 1998.

at work.[257] In Australia, Victoria,[258] the Australian Capital Territory (ACT)[259] and Queensland[260] have adopted human rights instruments, which offer protection from discrimination on the ground of age. However, equality rights in the Victorian Charter can only be enforced as a 'piggyback' claim, with no right to individual damages. While this is a limited mechanism for enacting equality rights as human rights, even this limited approach is influencing how courts and tribunals interpret equality rights;[261] practitioners are making Charter-based arguments in their advocacy (Chapter 7).[262]

A focus on equality rights as human rights could be strengthened by the adoption of a United Nations (UN) Convention on the rights of older persons.[263] This would provide a valuable base on which to shift and change domestic law;[264] Brynes notes 'the importance of a focused treaty framework to analysis, advocacy and action around ageing issues'.[265] While there is already a UN Convention on the rights of the child,[266] this is limited to those under the age of 18; young people are excluded from this rights discourse.[267] Thus, a stronger rights framework would assist both older and younger people. That said, bottom-up empowerment is potentially just as important as a UN Convention.[268]

Reform 28: That Australian jurisdictions adopt a human rights framework, including equality rights.

Reform 29: That governments and non-governmental organizations actively support the adoption of a UN Convention on the rights of older persons, and consider how UN conventions could better advance the rights of young people.

See further the Charter of Fundamental Rights of the European Union, art 21 (which relates to EU institutions and bodies, and Member States when implementing EU law).

[257] Though see the discussion of pensions in Alysia Blackham, 'Age Discrimination beyond Employment' (2019) 52 Kobe University Law Review 1.
[258] Charter of Human Rights and Responsibilities Act 2006 (Vic) s 8(3)–(4).
[259] Human Rights Act 2004 (ACT) s 8(3).
[260] Human Rights Act 2019 (Qld) s 15.
[261] A5.
[262] ibid.
[263] UK94. See, eg, Annie Herro, 'The Human Rights of Older Persons: The Politics and Substance of the UN Open-Ended Working Group on Ageing' (2017) 23 Australian Journal of Human Rights 90.
[264] UK152.
[265] Andrew Byrnes, 'Human Rights Unbound: An Unrepentant Call for a More Complete Application of Human Rights in Relation to Older Persons—and Beyond' (2020) 39 Australasian Journal on Ageing 91, 95.
[266] *Convention on the Rights of the Child*, 1577 UNTS 3 (entered into force 2 September 1990).
[267] UK94.
[268] A2.

C. Purposive Interpretation

One way to strengthen court and tribunal decision-making is to encourage a more purposive and sympathetic application of age equality statutes.[269] Australian courts and tribunals tend to adopt an unsympathetic or conservative interpretation of legal requirements in discrimination complaints,[270] though this depends on the individual judge or tribunal member.[271] In the UK, while judges have not traditionally interpreted equality statutes purposively,[272] this has shifted to a more purposive approach over time, including due to the case law of the Court of Justice of the European Union (CJEU) and the need to interpret UK law in light of European directives.[273] This has two important consequences: first, judicial approaches to interpretation can change, meaning a more purposive approach is possible in Australia. Second, though, the UK shift was at least partly driven by external factors and European Union (EU) law; it is unclear what would have happened without this external 'irritation', and what will happen now the UK is no longer bound by EU law.

In Australia, a purposive approach could be supported by adopting a domestic human rights framework and an international UN Convention on the rights of older persons. However, we also need to address factors that may encourage an unsympathetic interpretation of age discrimination law. Unsympathetic decision-making may reflect a lack of judicial experience in discrimination law;[274] some Australian jurisprudence is 'disappointing', with FWA case law 'amplifying some of the worst shortcomings of anti-discrimination law'.[275] While neither jurisdiction has specialist discrimination tribunals, ET judges are given extensive training on how to deal with discrimination matters.[276] Such training would also be beneficial in the Australian context.

Reform 30: That Australian jurisdictions provide judges and tribunal members with training on how to deal with discrimination matters.

[269] Beth Gaze, 'Context and Interpretation in Anti-Discrimination Law' (2002) 26 Melbourne University Law Review 325.

[270] A5; A102; Alysia Blackham, 'Defining "Discrimination" in UK and Australian Age Discrimination Law' (2018) 43 Monash University Law Review 760; Blackham, 'Why Do Employment Age Discrimination Cases Fail?' (n 67).

[271] A5.

[272] Dickens, 'The Road is Long' (n 92) 477.

[273] ibid.

[274] A5; A118; Anna Chapman, Beth Gaze, and Adriana Orifici, 'Substantive Equality at Work: Still Elusive under Australia's Fair Work Act' (2017) 30 Australian Journal of Labour Law 214, 221, 233, 235.

[275] Chapman, Gaze, and Orifici (n 274) 223–24. Also A105.

[276] Dickens, 'The Road is Long' (n 92) 477.

Cultural factors and the biases of decision-makers may also influence how decisions are made. This affects all grounds, not just age, and tribunal members are generally very conscious of their own limits and biases.[277] That said, age discrimination is often seen as less serious than other forms of discrimination; this social ambivalence may affect court and tribunal decision-making. In the UK, this ambivalence is embedded in age discrimination law itself, through the ability to justify direct age discrimination. While the justification principle does not often determine the outcomes of cases, it may introduce an ambivalence into the legal framework that affects the way the law is applied by courts and tribunals. Unsympathetic interpretation could therefore be attributable to the limits of age discrimination law itself.[278] Finally, courts and tribunals may be reluctant to find that discrimination has occurred due to the social stigma surrounding a finding of discrimination.[279] Even under the FWA, then, where there is a shifting burden of proof, courts may be excessively deferential to employers' evidence.[280] Thus, encouraging a more purposive approach requires addressing social stigma around discrimination and age; building judicial and tribunal expertise in this area; and reviewing the specific limits of age discrimination legislation itself. Again, it may be time to limit or remove the ability to objectively justify direct age discrimination in the UK.

D. Increasing the Systemic Impact of Individual Enforcement

While individual enforcement can achieve systemic outcomes,[281] increasing this systemic impact requires a focus on remedies. Remedies need to address the issue in dispute, including where that issue is systemic or has broader implications. In the UK, this could be achieved by, for example, reinstating ET powers to make broader recommendations, beyond those that affect the individual claimant.[282] More generally, though, to encourage higher rates of claiming, remedies need to be focused on what claimants want or need.[283] Claimants rarely want financial compensation; compensation is simply a proxy for the harm caused. Instead, remedies should focus on addressing or remedying the *actual* harm caused wherever possible; this might entail reinstatement, an apology, policy or procedural change, access to a job, training, or promotion opportunities, or other creative measures. While Australian courts and tribunals already have broad remedial powers, these are rarely exercised in practice. Increasing the systemic impact of individual enforcement therefore

277 UK78.
278 UK82.
279 A105; A153; Loretta de Plevitz, 'The Briginshaw "Standard of Proof" in Anti-Discrimination Law: "Pointing with a Wavering Finger"' (2003) 27 Melbourne University Law Review 308.
280 A5; Chapman, Gaze, and Orifici (n 274) 224–26.
281 UK97.
282 House of Commons (n 189) Q85.
283 UK94.

requires a more purposive and creative application of existing statutes by judges and tribunal members. It also requires greater expertise on the part of legal practitioners to develop and put forward creative remedial solutions.

VI. Conclusion

In critically analysing the court hearing and judgment stage of the individual enforcement of age discrimination law, this chapter has outlined the many and varied ways in which the process of hearing and judgment might inhibit individual claims. It has identified key areas in which law reform is both necessary and desirable. However, even if legal change is practically possible, much depends on how decision-makers and advocates use and interpret these legal provisions. A purposive approach to equality law should be encouraged and promoted, and would be supported by framing equality rights as human rights.

Law reform is also only effective if people actually use the law, including by making complaints: 'if people don't bring claims, then it doesn't matter what the law says.... it's not just about having the laws but using them and enforcing them.'[284] Legal mechanisms are rarely utilized to address age discrimination, and those who appear best able to use the law to assert their rights are older men. This does not reflect or capture the way age interacts with gender, ethnicity, disability, and other protected grounds; other claimants need to be supported to assert their legal rights.[285] While a range of reforms can and should be made to the process of individual enforcement, these systems are operating in a workplace context that is likely to inhibit claiming. Growing work precarity and unemployment, and declining job and employment security, mean the costs of complaining far exceed any individual benefit.[286] Changing these systemic workplace trends is 'going to be a long fight'.[287]

The question, then, is what alternative measures can be used to ensure the effective enforcement of age discrimination law, while this fight is ongoing? How can we move beyond individual enforcement? These questions are taken up in the chapters that follow.

[284] A111.
[285] UK81.
[286] A154.
[287] ibid.

PART III

BEYOND INDIVIDUAL ENFORCEMENT

It is clear, then, that individual enforcement cannot and will not address age discrimination at work. There will likely always be substantial gaps in claiming. Reliance on individual enforcement is misplaced as a social change strategy.[1] Recognizing the rationale and justification for age discrimination law, and its fundamental importance for ensuring access to a range of social goods (Chapter 2), it is essential that we move beyond individual enforcement.

This study identifies four key areas of reform for improving the enforcement of age discrimination law. Necessary improvements to the individual enforcement model have been discussed in the preceding chapters. Moving beyond individual enforcement, the following chapters advocate for strengthening positive duties (Chapter 7); bolstering the roles of statutory agencies (Chapter 8); and enhancing collective enforcement, whether by trade unions, groups of individuals, or the third sector (Chapter 9).

These reforms work best together—they are mutually reinforcing and mutually supportive. For example, supporting individual claiming will strengthen agency enforcement; agency enforcement and collective action are key to effective positive duties; and positive duties can help individuals who are impacted by discrimination.[2] Thus, these reforms should be seen as a fourfold model of reform, with each change working together and in conjunction with other areas.

[1] UK78; A99.
[2] A112.

7

Positive Duties

I. Introduction

Positive duties mark a step change in equality law, creating a legal framework that requires organizations to develop their own solutions to equality issues.[3] Rather than relying on individual enforcement,[4] positive equality duties promote a proactive approach to the implementation of equality law.[5] Proactive approaches of this nature sit at the intersection of law and politics;[6] positive duties give legal force and status to policy-led approaches like mainstreaming[7] that aim to make equality issues central to organizational processes.[8] Positive duties therefore offer a more specific and legally enforceable form to proactive approaches for achieving equality.

Adopting and strengthening positive duties may help address the limits of the individual enforcement model. Positive duties are an increasingly prominent part of United Kingdom (UK) equality law: Northern Ireland (NI) pioneered the use of positive duties in the UK;[9] in Great Britain (GB), a patchwork of duties under different discrimination statutes was consolidated in the Equality Act 2010 (EqA) with the introduction of a Public Sector Equality Duty (PSED) for all protected characteristics.[10] Comparatively, positive duties have not typically been a feature of Australian discrimination law, though limited duties exist in some Australian states and territories; and duties in Canada do not extend to age as a protected characteristic.[11] These duties are framed in different ways, and have had differing

[3] Sandra Fredman, 'The Public Sector Equality Duty' (2011) 40 Industrial Law Journal 405, 419.

[4] Sandra Fredman and Sarah Spencer, 'Delivering Equality: Towards an Outcome-Focused Positive Duty: Submission to the Cabinet Office Equality Review and to the Discrimination Law Review' (2006) 6–7; Sandra Fredman, 'Breaking the Mold: Equality as a Proactive Duty' (2012) 60 American Journal of Comparative Law 265, 266.

[5] Colm O'Cinneide, 'Positive Duties and Gender Equality' (2005) 8 International Journal of Discrimination and the Law 91.

[6] Sandra Fredman, *Human Rights Transformed: Positive Rights and Positive Duties* (OUP 2008) 191.

[7] ibid.

[8] Christopher McCrudden, 'Equality' in Colin J Harvey (ed), *Human Rights, Equality and Democratic Renewal in Northern Ireland* (Hart Publishing 2001) 110–11.

[9] ibid.

[10] Bob Hepple, 'Enforcing Equality Law: Two Steps Forward and Two Steps Backwards for Reflexive Regulation' (2011) 40 Industrial Law Journal 315.

[11] The Employment Equity Act (SC 1995, c. 44) extends to women, Aboriginal peoples, persons with disabilities, and members of visible minorities, but does not apply to age. It is arguable that s 15 of the Charter creates a positive duty, though the Supreme Court has retreated from this view in later cases: see Fredman, *Human Rights Transformed* (n 4) 184–86.

Reforming Age Discrimination Law. Alysia Blackham, Oxford University Press. © Alysia Blackham 2022.
DOI: 10.1093/oso/9780198859284.003.0007

degrees of success at advancing equality. The question, then, is how positive duties can be made most meaningful and impactful in practice, in a way that is least dependent on political will for success.[12]

In this chapter I critically analyse the extent to which positive duties might offer a viable alternative or addition to the individual enforcement of age discrimination law. In Part II, drawing on a theoretical model grounded in reflexive law and regulatory theory (Chapter 1), I consider the theoretical potential of positive duties to enhance discrimination law, and identify key criteria that should be considered in their framing. Part III maps existing positive duties in the UK and Australia; these duties are critiqued in Part IV using this theoretical model. I argue that positive duties do not yet meet the requirements for effective second-generation regulation, and propose reforms to strengthen existing provisions.

II. The Potential of Positive Duties

A. Radically Reconfiguring Equality Law

Positive duties have the potential to markedly reconfigure[13] and change 'the whole landscape of discrimination law',[14] through a 'radical strategy for tackling deep-seated discrimination'[15] and a shift away from individual enforcement. Positive duties seek to achieve cultural change, to make equality part of an organization's 'core business'.[16] Positive duties are therefore key to achieving substantive equality at work: 'without a positive duty to promote equality, patterns of discrimination and social exclusion will remain unchanged.'[17]

Positive duties pose five radical challenges to the individual enforcement model. First, they recognize that discrimination is not confined to individual acts:[18] rather, it is systemic and structural.[19] Positive duties shift organizational thinking to focus on the structural and systemic causes of individual behaviour,[20] rather than individualizing and personalizing acts of discrimination.[21] This compares markedly to the individual enforcement model.[22]

12 Fredman, *Human Rights Transformed* (n 4) 192–93.
13 Sandra Fredman, *Discrimination Law* (2nd edn, OUP 2011) 230.
14 Fredman, 'Breaking the Mold' (n 2) 271.
15 Anne CL Davies, *Perspectives on Labour Law* (2nd edn, CUP 2009) 135.
16 Department for Communities and Local Government, *Discrimination Law Review. A Framework for Fairness: Proposals for a Single Equality Bill for Great Britain. A Consultation Paper* (2007) 79, [5.3].
17 Fredman, *Human Rights Transformed* (n 4) 175.
18 Sandra Fredman, 'Equality: A New Generation?' (2001) 30 Industrial Law Journal 145, 164.
19 Susan Sturm, 'Second Generation Employment Discrimination: A Structural Approach' (2001) 101 Columbia Law Review 45.
20 Fredman, *Discrimination Law* (n 11) 299.
21 A99.
22 ibid.

Second, rather than seeking to remedy harm via a tort-based model, positive duties seek to restructure institutions towards a more proactive, preventative model that prevents harm from occurring.[23] Positive duties have the potential to fundamentally reshape equality law to become more proactive, responsive, pre-emptive, and transformative, by focusing on organizational responses to the equality framework.[24] Without positive duties, there is little that forces organizations to be proactive.[25]

Third, and relatedly, positive duties shift responsibility to organizations to detect and address unlawful discrimination, whether or not an individual complaint has been received.[26] The duty-bearer is the organization which is in the best place to address inequality, even if it did not create the problem.[27] Positive duties encourage organizational change to accommodate individual needs, rather than forcing individuals to fit existing structures.[28] They therefore represent a shift from a *fault*-based model to a *capacity*-based model of regulation;[29] and from a 'dispute resolution' model to one of 'structural reform',[30] taking the burden of enforcement off the individual[31] to try to change the system.[32] Without positive duties, individual complaints still largely drive organizational responses:[33] conciliation is being used to seek systemic remedies that might be included as part of a positive duty, such as action plans, training, and policy change.[34]

Fourth, in shifting responsibility away from individuals, positive duties aim to prompt organizations to internally scrutinize their own operations, and proactively respond to their findings,[35] including through improved data collection and analysis, transparency, and active monitoring.[36] Positive duties provide an important framework within which organizations can scrutinize their own behaviour and start to ask the right questions.[37] Targeted transparency can then create an

[23] Fredman, *Discrimination Law* (n 11) 230, 299.

[24] Linda Dickens, 'Equality and Work-Life Balance: What's Happening at the Workplace' (2006) 35 Industrial Law Journal 445, 447; Linda Dickens, 'The Road is Long: Thirty Years of Equality Legislation in Britain' (2007) 45 British Journal of Industrial Relations 463, 474; Fredman, 'Breaking the Mold' (n 2) 271.

[25] A71.

[26] A164; Fredman, 'Breaking the Mold' (n 2) 266.

[27] Fredman, *Discrimination Law* (n 11) 230, 299.

[28] Dickens, 'The Road is Long' (n 22) 472.

[29] Sandra Fredman, 'Changing the Norm: Positive Duties in Equal Treatment Legislation' (2005) 12 Maastricht Journal of European and Comparative Law 369; Belinda Smith and Dominique Allen, 'Whose Fault is it?: Asking the Right Question to Address Discrimination' (2012) 37 Alternative Law Journal 31, 31. Though individual enforcement models can focus on capacity, as in Canada: see further ibid 31, 33–34.

[30] Owen Fiss, 'The Forms of Justice' (1979) 93 Harvard Law Review 1, 16–28.

[31] Fredman, 'Breaking the Mold' (n 2) 270–71.

[32] A3.

[33] A99.

[34] A106.

[35] Hepple, 'Enforcing Equality Law' (n 8) 326.

[36] A110; A164.

[37] A99.

'action cycle' of engagement by information users (such as consumers, investors, and employees),[38] generating market-based, organizational, and political pressure for change.[39] Through transparency, positive duties can assist statutory agencies with monitoring and targeted enforcement,[40] using a policy and legal approach to question and enforce compliance as a 'persuasive tactic';[41] and empower non-governmental organizations (NGOs) to scrutinize organizations and government policy-making.[42] Given the pervasiveness of secrecy and confidentiality in equality law,[43] transparency and data collection are radical features of positive duties.[44]

Fifth, positive duties can be social goods in and of themselves, by promoting participation in organizational decision-making and involvement in public life.[45] Positive duties are not static: they require a continuous process of identifying an issue and potential responses, monitoring and modifying.[46] They represent a dynamic and inclusive approach to addressing inequality and promoting equality: 'the very process of achieving equality becomes a democratic one.'[47]

Overall, then, positive equality duties mark a transformative change in equality law,[48] which:

> constitutes a shift away from legislative reliance on a retrospective, individualized victim-centred complaints approach towards pro-active, pre-emptive action by power-holders. It is a move away from 'non-discrimination' towards promoting equality, thus targeting inequality and disadvantage—and not only that arising from discrimination—rather than attempting neutrality.[49]

Positive duties have significant potential to reframe the structure and orientation of equality law, as a new 'generation' of equality law.[50]

[38] Archon Fung, Mary Graham, and David Weil, *Full Disclosure: The Perils and Promise of Transparency* (CUP 2007) 48.

[39] ibid 49. See Alysia Blackham, 'Positive Equality Duties: The Future of Equality and Transparency?' (2021) 37(2) Law in Context 98. For example, pairing workforce data with comparative benchmarking and the business case for employing an age-diverse workforce can be particularly effective at prompting organizational change: A110.

[40] A110; UK167.

[41] UK167. See also UK90.

[42] UK95.

[43] Dominique Allen and Alysia Blackham, 'Under Wraps: Secrecy, Confidentiality and the Enforcement of Equality Law in Australia and the UK' (2019) 43 Melbourne University Law Review 384.

[44] Blackham, 'Positive Equality Duties: The Future of Equality and Transparency?' (n 37).

[45] Fredman, 'Equality' (n 16) 164.

[46] ibid.

[47] ibid.

[48] UK81.

[49] Dickens, 'The Road is Long' (n 22) 473.

[50] Fredman, *Discrimination Law* (n 11) 299–302. See also Fredman, *Human Rights Transformed* (n 4) ch 7.

B. Framing Positive Duties

The question, though, is how positive duties should best be structured and framed to advance these ambitious ends. Expert respondents in this study—especially those in Australia—supported the *idea* of positive duties,[51] but expressed concern as to how they would be implemented in practice[52] and their likely effectiveness.[53] Organizations cannot be relied on to advance equality voluntarily: there is a need for a legislative 'standard' to effect change.[54] The issue is therefore not *whether* positive duties should be introduced, but *how* they should best be framed and implemented; how we answer these practical questions depends on the theoretical framing and rationale driving our approach to positive duties.

First, positive duties are only likely to be effective if they are aimed at achieving particular targeted outcomes.[55] The view of 'equality' that is embedded in the PSED is complex and contested, and the result of years of campaigning, reviews, and political machinations.[56] In developing the PSED, the *Discrimination Law Review* adopted the four 'dimensions of equality' advocated by Fredman and Spencer;[57] that is:

- Addressing disadvantage;
- Promoting respect for the equal worth of different groups, and fostering good relations within and between groups;
- Meeting different needs while promoting shared values; and
- Promoting equal participation.[58]

The PSED therefore adopts a 'comprehensive' notion of equality that includes recognition, dignity, redistribution, redressing disadvantage, participation, and inclusion.[59]

Second, positive duties embed a form of second-generation regulation,[60] which focuses on shifting the internal operations of an organization.[61] Some of the aims underlying the PSED are aspirational; enforcement is therefore less about 'coercive court proceedings' and more about 'achiev[ing] a culture of compliance'.[62]

[51] A100; A104; A105; A106; A108; A10; A115; A150; A164.
[52] A10; A71; A108; A100.
[53] A71; A115.
[54] A104.
[55] Fredman, 'Equality' (n 16) 164–65.
[56] Simonetta Manfredi, Lucy Vickers, and Kate Clayton-Hathway, 'The Public Sector Equality Duty: Enforcing Equality Rights Through Second-Generation Regulation' (2018) 47 Industrial Law Journal 365, 368–69.
[57] Fredman and Spencer (n 2) 5–6.
[58] Department for Communities and Local Government (n 14) 87.
[59] Manfredi, Vickers, and Clayton-Hathway (n 54) 369–70.
[60] ibid 370.
[61] ibid 371.
[62] ibid 370.

Law should structure and influence organizational decision-making to focus on equality, so that it is not necessary to dictate substantive outcomes.[63] In the language of systems theory, law is an *irritation* that prompts the internal systems of organizations to consider and integrate equality in internal processes.[64] Second-generation regulation achieves this through a focus on self-regulation, self-scrutiny, and problem-solving, including through setting, review, and reporting against goals. This is supported by external scrutiny by the state, interested stakeholders, and interest groups, through information, consultation, and engagement.[65] This creates a triangular relationship between those who are being regulated (ie, organizations), those who are affected (such as workers or consumers), and the enforcement agency.[66]

Third, consistent with this regulatory focus, positive duties must reflect and accommodate the diverse needs of different employers and sectors.[67] Positive duties need to be sufficiently flexible to give public authorities scope and 'freedom to genuinely mainstream equality',[68] allowing legal rules to be translated into organizational processes. For example, rules around data and reporting make limited sense for very small organizations, or risk identifying individuals;[69] in organizations with low declaration rates, data may be unreliable.[70] Rules around quotas may be highly effective, but best target organizations of a certain size or with a certain level of turnover.[71] Larger organizations may be more readily able to offer training and redeployment opportunities for older workers.[72] This is where second-generation regulation is particularly apt, as strategies can be tailored to local conditions and needs. Positive duties should therefore be framed as flexible tools focused on 'the end, not the means',[73] yet contain enough specificity and clarity to help organizations comply with their responsibilities.[74]

[63] ibid 371.
[64] ibid 372.
[65] Hepple, 'Enforcing Equality Law' (n 8) 321.
[66] ibid.
[67] UK167.
[68] Government Equalities Office, *Equality Bill: Making it Work. Policy Proposals for Specific Duties* (2010) 6.
[69] A104; UK167.
[70] UK167.
[71] A106.
[72] UK84.
[73] Government Equalities Office, *Equality Bill* (n 66) 6.
[74] Martin Mitchell and others, 'Review of the Public Sector Equality Duty (PSED) in Wales' (2014) 18–19.

III. Existing Positive Duties

A. UK

The GB PSED[75] requires public authorities or people exercising public functions to, in the exercise of their functions, have 'due regard' to the need to:

- Eliminate discrimination, harassment, victimization, and conduct prohibited by the EqA;
- Advance equality of opportunity between persons who share and do not share a protected characteristic; and
- Foster good relations between persons who share and do not share a relevant protected characteristic.[76]

The general PSED is complemented by specific duties, designed to facilitate compliance; specific duties are more comprehensive and onerous in Scotland and Wales than in England.[77] A duty regarding socio-economic inequalities[78] has been implemented in Scotland[79] and Wales[80] but not England; this may encourage a focus on intersectionality,[81] increasing the efficacy of the duties overall.[82] The PSED is enforced via individual judicial review (JR) proceedings and the Equality and Human Rights Commission (EHRC).[83]

In NI, there is a statutory duty on public authorities to have due regard to the need to promote equality of opportunity between persons of different ages.[84] The

[75] It is arguable that s 14 of the Convention for the Protection of Human Rights and Fundamental Freedoms (European Convention on Human Rights, as amended) (hereafter ECHR) also creates a positive duty, at least in relation to the exercise of Convention rights. This is rarely enforced in relation to age or employment specifically.

[76] Equality Act 2010, s 149 (hereafter EqA). This may be compared with s 6 of the Human Rights Act 1998, which includes no consideration requirements, but merely requires compliance. See Melanie Schleiger, 'One Size Fits All: The Obligation of Public Authorities to Consider Human Rights under the Victorian Charter' (2011) 19 Australian Journal of Administrative Law 17.

[77] EqA (n 74) ss 153, 154. See Government of Wales Act 2006, s 77, 35; Scotland Act 1998, sch 5, L2.

[78] EqA (n 74) s 2(4); Wales Act 2017, s 45. On positive duties for socio-economic rights, see Fredman, *Human Rights Transformed* (n 4).

[79] The Equality Act 2010 (Authorities subject to the Socio-economic Inequality Duty) (Scotland) Regulations 2018.

[80] The Equality Act 2010 (Authorities subject to a duty regarding Socio-economic Inequalities) (Wales) Regulations 2021, SI 295(W72)/2021.

[81] UK87; UK94.

[82] Belinda Smith, 'What Kind of Equality Can We Expect from the "Fair Work Act"?' (2011) 35 Melbourne University Law Review 545, 546–47.

[83] EqA (n 74) s 156; Equality Act 2006, s 31, 32 (hereafter EqA 2006).

[84] Northern Ireland Act 1998, s 75 (hereafter NI Act). Public authorities must also have regard to the desirability of promoting good relations between persons of different religious beliefs, political opinions, or racial groups in carrying out their functions: s 75(2). Duties continue to operate in NI under the Disability Discrimination Act 1995, s 49A and Race Relations (Northern Ireland) Order 1997, SI 1997/869, art 67.

'due regard' standard under the Northern Ireland Act 1998 is similar to that under the EqA.

The PSED extends to public authorities when acting as employers. According to the Government Equalities Office, the PSED:

> requires public authorities to consider taking proactive steps to root out discrimination and harassment and advance equality of opportunity in relation to their functions ... [including in] their capacity as employers. The duties require public authorities to integrate equality considerations into all areas of a public authority's work and to give consideration to taking positive steps to dismantle barriers. The advancing equality of opportunity limb reflects the fact that in order to ensure full equality in practice, this may necessitate a difference in treatment, rather than the same treatment.[85]

Thus, in theory at least, public authorities are expected to *proactively* address equality issues relating to their workforce, even prior to or in the absence of an individual complaint.

It may be practically difficult to evaluate the impact of positive duties:[86] O'Cinneide argues that:

> rarely will these duties drive forward change by themselves, but at a minimum their existence can act as a focus and legal basis for equality initiatives, and provide support to those within public sector organisations pushing for more action to promote equality of opportunity.[87]

The nature and aims of positive duties may therefore make evaluation problematic. At the same time, though, evidence-based policy-making is needed both to evaluate the effectiveness of existing measures and inform the future development of positive duties.[88]

Key theoretical benefits of positive duties are being realized in practice in the UK, though outcomes are generally mixed. A 2004 study of the Welsh Assembly's statutory equality duty[89] found it had 'initiated equality reforms that would either not have taken place, or would have taken much longer to be implemented', and had been used to overcome resistance to equality reforms.[90] Thus, Chaney

[85] Government Equalities Office, Submission No 169 to the Joint Committee on Human Rights, *26th Report*, 12 November 2009, HC 736/HL paper 169, ev 52, [261].

[86] O'Cinneide, 'Positive Duties and Gender Equality' (n 3) 101–02.

[87] ibid 102.

[88] Paul Chaney and Teresa Lesley Rees, 'The Northern Ireland Section 75 Equality Duty: An International Perspective' in Eithne McLaughlin and Neil Faris (eds), *The Northern Ireland Section 75 Equality Duty: An Operational Review* (Northern Ireland Office 2004) 29.

[89] Government of Wales Act 1998, s 120. Now Government of Wales Act 2006, s 35(2), 77.

[90] Paul Chaney, 'The Post-Devolution Equality Agenda: The Case of the Welsh Assembly's Statutory Duty to Promote Equality of Opportunity' (2004) 32 Policy & Politics 63, 73.

concludes that the 'duty is having a significant impact on the equality agenda in Wales and beyond'.[91]

In NI, the initial implementation of the s 75 duty was limited by a lack of funding, a rushed timeframe for implementation, and the complexity of operationalizing such a comprehensive duty.[92] However, Chaney and Rees argue that these initial difficulties should not constrain the long-term positive impact of the duty:

> Whilst acknowledging the problems involved in the comparatively rapid drafting, implementation and 'bedding-in' of the duty, it is likely that in future years the unified yet multi-faceted approach to mainstreaming equality that is underpinned by s.75 will prove to have greater effectiveness than many contemporary approaches operating around the globe.[93]

In 2018, the NI Equality Coalition still identified 'significant patterns of non-compliance' with the s 75 duty: 'Section 75 duties are regularly flouted to the extent the duties are currently ineffective in key policy areas.'[94] Despite these problems, Coalition members identified key benefits of the duty, with 'the very existence of the duties providing an important "way in" to discuss equality issues'.[95] The duty can and does work, if operationalized effectively:[96] 's 75 is flawed, and it's limited, but it's still . . . a very valuable tool.'[97] The issue, then, is around implementation and enforcement.

In relation to the PSED, a 2013 review (conducted to evaluate whether it was 'operating as intended')[98] concluded it was premature to make any firm assessments of its impact. The general duty commenced in April 2011, specific duties commenced in England in September 2011, and the review was announced in May 2012; evidence of impact gathered in 2013 was—understandably—'inconclusive'.[99] Examining evidence presented to the review, though, Manfredi and others identify three positive impacts of the PSED. First, public authorities reported that they had improved their data collection and monitoring systems.[100] Second, there were multiple examples of good practice in relation to consultation. Third, and relatedly, this participative dimension helped to empower NGOs to hold government authorities

[91] ibid 74.
[92] Chaney and Rees (n 86) 30–34.
[93] ibid 38.
[94] Equality Coalition, 'Equal to the Task? Investigative Powers and Effective Enforcement of the "Section 75" Equality Duty' (2018) 2 <https://www.equalitycoalition.net/wp-content/uploads/2018/01/Equal-to-the-Task-Jan-2018.pdf> accessed 26 March 2021.
[95] ibid 52.
[96] ibid 53–54.
[97] UK95.
[98] Government Equalities Office, *Review of the Public Sector Equality Duty: Report of the Independent Steering Group* (2013) 9, [10].
[99] ibid 11, [15].
[100] Manfredi, Vickers, and Clayton-Hathway (n 54) 381.

to account.[101] Thus, the PSED appears to be having a positive impact in practice, though the review expressed concerns that public authorities were 'gold plating' and 'over-complying' in their response to the duty.[102]

B. Australia

Positive duties are not generally a feature of Australian anti-discrimination law.[103] In Victoria, the Australian Capital Territory (ACT), and Queensland, positive duties that include age arise under human rights legislation; in Victoria and Tasmania, duties are in place under equality legislation.[104] The Australian Human Rights Commission's (AHRC) *Willing to Work* report recommended that the federal government consider a federal positive duty to promote substantive equality or eliminate discrimination,[105] and adopt sector-wide and agency-specific employment targets for older workers, based on workforce data; integrate performance against these targets into performance management systems; and report on progress annually.[106] These recommendations have not been adopted.

1. Victoria

In Victoria, those who have a duty not to discriminate under the *Equal Opportunity Act 2010* (Vic) (including employers) 'must take reasonable and proportionate measures to eliminate that discrimination, sexual harassment or victimisation as far as possible'.[107] What is 'reasonable and proportionate' depends on:

- The size of the business;
- The nature and circumstances of the business;
- Available resources;
- Business and operational priorities; and
- Practicability and the cost of the measures.[108]

The duty is not subject to individual enforcement:[109] where a claimant tried to argue a breach of the duty in *Collins v Smith*,[110] the Victorian Civil and

[101] ibid 379–81.
[102] Government Equalities Office, *Review of the Public Sector Equality Duty* (n 96) 16, 31, 32.
[103] Neil Rees, Simon Rice, and Dominique Allen, *Australian Anti-Discrimination Law* (2nd edn, Federation Press 2014) 7.
[104] Gender reporting obligations are in place at the federal level: see *Workplace Gender Equality Act 2012* (Cth) ss 3, 13; *Workplace Gender Equality (Matters in Relation to Gender Equality Indicators) Instrument 2013 (No 1)* (Cth). These do not relate to age equality.
[105] AHRC, 'Willing to Work: National Inquiry into Employment Discrimination Against Older Australians and Australians with Disability' (2016) 21.
[106] ibid 16.
[107] Equal Opportunity Act 2010 (Vic) s 15(2).
[108] ibid s 15(6).
[109] ibid s 15(3).
[110] [2015] VCAT 1029 (10 July 2015).

Administrative Tribunal (VCAT) held that it did not have jurisdiction to hear such an application.[111]

Following a change of government in Victoria, and a watering down of its enforcement powers,[112] the Victorian Equal Opportunity and Human Rights Commission (VEOHRC) no longer has the power to conduct a public inquiry into a possible failure to comply with the duty,[113] issue a compliance notice, or enter an enforceable undertaking.[114] Enforcement of the duty now depends on the VEOHRC conducting an investigation:[115] the VEOHRC may subsequently take any action it sees fit, including reporting the matter to Parliament.[116]

With minimal enforcement, it appears that the Victorian duty is having limited impact on employers' behaviour. While organizations may make a voluntary equality action plan, this is very rarely done.[117] At the same time, the duty might be used as a 'stick' in conciliation,[118] asking organizations to provide evidence of training and other mechanisms that might support the duty.[119] However, this depends on individuals bringing a complaint, so that the duty can be raised in conciliation.[120] In areas such as age discrimination, where complaints are rare, 'if we're not seeing the problem, then we're not going to be approaching those duty holders.'[121] This does not reflect the proactive, preventative approach that might be desired of a positive duty: 'our positive duty isn't really what . . . had been envisaged. And so it hasn't been as effective [as] we would've liked.'[122]

Victorian public authorities are also subject to a duty under s 38(1) of the Charter of Human Rights and Responsibilities Act 2006 (Vic) (the Victorian Charter), which makes it 'unlawful for a public authority to act in a way that is incompatible with a human right or, in making a decision, to fail to give proper consideration to a relevant human right'. The human rights protected by the Victorian Charter include the right to: enjoyment of human rights without discrimination,[123] equal protection of the law without discrimination, and equal and effective protection against discrimination.[124] 'Discrimination' is defined as that within the scope of the Equal Opportunity Act 2010 (Vic).[125] The Victorian Charter duty does not

[111] ibid [46].
[112] Rees, Rice, and Allen (n 101) 7.
[113] ibid 177–78. See also Equal Opportunity Amendment Act 2011 (Vic) s 6.
[114] See Paul Harpur, 'A Proactive Duty to Eliminate Discrimination in Victoria' (2012) 19 Australian Journal of Administrative Law 180, 182.
[115] Equal Opportunity Act 2010 (Vic) s 15(4).
[116] ibid ss 139–43.
[117] A101.
[118] A3.
[119] A3; A101; A105.
[120] A101.
[121] ibid.
[122] ibid.
[123] Charter of Human Rights and Responsibilities Act 2006 (Vic) s 8(2).
[124] ibid s 8(3).
[125] ibid s 3(1).

apply if: the public authority could not reasonably have acted differently or made a different decision due to a statutory provision;[126] it is an act or decision of a private nature;[127] or it would impede a religious body.[128]

The Victorian Charter is aimed at changing the culture of government, rather than enforcement and litigation.[129] The duty cannot be pursued independently as a cause of action, and a breach does not sound in damages.[130] However, there is standing to make a complaint for breach of the Victorian Charter if linked with another complaint for the same relief via a non-Charter cause of action.[131]

The Victorian Charter seeks to mainstream human rights, and to be preventative;[132] thus, it is more focused on achieving dialogue about human rights,[133] and compelling decision-makers to think and act in a way that respects rights,[134] than enforcement. The Victorian Charter duty requires public authorities to justify their decision-making, rather than seeking to overturn their decisions.[135] Thus, the Victorian Charter provides an incentive for public authorities to think and act transparently in way that respects human rights;[136] increased transparency is hoped to increase public satisfaction with the work of government.[137]

A 2015 VEOHRC review questioned the effectiveness of this approach, describing the remedies available under the Victorian Charter as 'inaccessible and inadequate'.[138] The structure of the duty has led to: few consequences for its breach; a focus on government administration rather than remedies; limited accessibility of government actions, as claims need to be raised in a superior court; and convoluted litigation, due to the need to 'piggyback' Charter claims onto another cause of action.[139] The review recommended that individuals be allowed to enforce s 38 in VCAT or any other legal proceedings;[140] that VCAT be given the power to grant any remedy it considers just and appropriate; and that it be made clear that individuals can seek JR without any other claim.[141] These recommendations have not been adopted.

126 ibid s 38(2).
127 ibid s 38(3).
128 ibid s 38(4).
129 George Williams, 'The Victorian Charter of Human Rights and Responsibilities: Origins and Scope' (2006) 30 Melbourne University Law Review 880, 899.
130 Charter of Human Rights and Responsibilities Act 2006 (Vic) s 39(3).
131 ibid s 39(1).
132 Williams (n 127) 893.
133 ibid 901–02.
134 Schleiger (n 74) 30.
135 ibid 31.
136 ibid.
137 ibid.
138 VEOHRC, 'Eight-Year Charter Review–Position Paper: Legal Proceedings and Remedies' (2015) 1.
139 Michael Brett Young, 'From Commitment to Culture: The 2015 Review of the Charter of Human Rights and Responsibilities Act 2006–Summary Report' (2015) 11.
140 See similarly Human Rights Act 2004 (ACT) s 40C.
141 Brett Young (n 137) 11.

2. ACT

In the ACT, s 40B(1) of the Human Rights Act 2004 (ACT) makes it unlawful for a public authority:

(a) to act in a way that is incompatible with a human right; or
(b) in making a decision, to fail to give proper consideration to a relevant human right.

Human rights include 'the right to equal and effective protection against discrimination on any ground.'[142] Unlike in Victoria, individuals may start Supreme Court proceedings against a public authority if they would be a 'victim' of the contravention of the duty, or rely on their rights in other legal proceedings.[143] The Supreme Court may grant any appropriate relief except damages.[144] As in Victoria, the duty might be used instrumentally in conciliation, though its impact is limited to instances where individual complaints are made.[145]

The ACT duty straddles both the Human Rights Act 2004 (ACT) and the Discrimination Act 1991 (ACT)[146] and is therefore not 'a proper positive duty'.[147] Implementation and enforcement are easier where a duty is specifically included in equality legislation (rather than in human rights legislation), and applies to all organizations, not just the public sector.[148] The Victorian duty is clearer and easier to communicate than that in the ACT.[149] Even as it stands, though, the ACT duty is important for both its practical and procedural impact, and for what it symbolizes:

> the positive duty is actually an expression of community value in legislation. So the government is saying 'this is the community we want to be and we want everyone to take steps to eliminate discrimination.' … that's actually a commitment that our community has put into legislation and put onto the books.[150]

3. Queensland

A similar duty is imposed in Queensland: s 58(1) of the Human Rights Act 2019 (Qld) makes it unlawful for a public entity

142 Human Rights Act 2004 (ACT) s 8(3).
143 ibid s 40C.
144 ibid s 40C(4). The time limit on such claims is a year, unless the Court orders otherwise: s 40C(3).
145 A108.
146 A105; A106.
147 A106.
148 A105.
149 ibid.
150 ibid.

(a) to act or make a decision in a way that is not compatible with human rights; or
(b) in making a decision, to fail to give proper consideration to a human right relevant to the decision.

The Act specifies that 'giving proper consideration' to a human right includes (but is not limited to) identifying human rights that may be affected by the decision, and considering whether the decision would be compatible with those human rights.[151] Human rights include the enjoyment of human rights without discrimination; the equal protection of the law without discrimination; and equal and effective protection against discrimination.[152]

Failure to comply with s 58(1) does not render a decision invalid or constitute an offence.[153] As in Victoria, the duty cannot be pursued independently as a cause of action, and a breach does not sound in damages;[154] complaints may only be pursued if linked with another cause of action.[155]

4. Tasmania

A positive duty is imposed on Tasmanian organizations by s 104 of the Anti-Discrimination Act 1998 (Tas). An organization must 'take reasonable steps to ensure that no member, officer, employee or agent of the organization engages in discrimination or prohibited conduct'.[156] Organizations must ensure that their members, officers, employees, and agents are aware of conduct prohibited by the Act, notified of any tribunal order resulting from an inquiry, and do not engage in, repeat, or continue such conduct.[157]

Failure to comply with the duty means an organization is liable for any contravention of the Act committed by its members, officers, employees, and agents.[158] The duty has led to a number of organizations implementing training for their workforce;[159] this is not always 'heartfelt' or 'genuine',[160] but a tick box approach to limiting and mitigating legal exposure.[161]

[151] Human Rights Act 2019 (Qld) s 58(5).
[152] ibid s 15(2)–(4).
[153] ibid s 58(6).
[154] ibid s 59.
[155] ibid s 59(1).
[156] Anti-Discrimination Act 1998 (Tas) s 104(2).
[157] ibid s 104(1). It is unclear whether this latter requirement only relates to the conduct which is the subject of a tribunal order.
[158] ibid s 104(3). This presumably relaxes the requirement for a claimant to establish vicarious liability and/or agency.
[159] A102.
[160] ibid.
[161] ibid.

IV. Limits of Positive Duties

While positive duties have significant potential to advance age equality, at present, they have more *potential* than actual *impact*.[162] Positive duties are rarely used to advance age equality specifically;[163] instead, 'people are very focussed on gender, disability and race, and to a lesser extent [sexuality]', to the exclusion of age.[164] That said, most organizations already hold data on age for their employees,[165] providing an evidence base for evaluation and action. A key issue in the implementation of positive duties is therefore how to elevate and better prioritize age equality.

It can be difficult to assess the impact of positive duties, including due to a lack of consistency in reporting and data collection.[166] The question, then, is how positive duties and their enforcement mechanisms are operating in practice, and how they can be enhanced and reformed as a form of 'second generation' regulation.[167] This study identifies four interlocking limitations of existing positive duties: they have not effectively prompted self-regulation and internal scrutiny; they do not adequately integrate consultation and engagement; there is insufficient state-based or central scrutiny; and individual enforcement is highly problematic. Thus, positive duties are not yet realizing their potential as a form of second-generation regulation.

A. Self-Regulation and Internal Scrutiny

Self-regulation is fundamental to the success of positive duties; it is the key means by which enforcement should occur.[168] Positive duties aim 'to achieve a culture of compliance, rather than relying on coercive court proceedings'.[169] Being grounded in 'responsive proceduralized self-regulation', positive duties achieve compliance by developing organizational capacity[170] and changing organizations' internal operations to advance equality.[171] The success of positive duties is therefore measured not by the outcomes of cases, but whether a culture of mainstreaming has

[162] UK167.
[163] UK152.
[164] ibid.
[165] UK167.
[166] ibid.
[167] I have written elsewhere about the setting of goals, reporting, and transparency that might be achieved through positive duties: Blackham, 'Positive Equality Duties: The Future of Equality and Transparency?' (n 37).
[168] Fredman, *Discrimination Law* (n 11) 322.
[169] Manfredi, Vickers, and Clayton-Hathway (n 54) 370.
[170] ibid 371.
[171] ibid.

developed,[172] and how duties are being implemented by organizations on a day-to-day basis.[173]

The PSED is helping to mainstream equality in some organizations. In a 2014 review of the PSED in Wales, for example, organizations reported that it had helped to mainstream equality issues in decision-making,[174] raise the profile and level of commitment to equality, and give equality initiatives a better structure and focus.[175] Similarly, examining submissions to the review of the PSED, Manfredi and others conclude 'that self-regulation is taking place and leading to the mainstreaming of equality',[176] at least in some organizations, and in some contexts:[177] the authors did not attempt to measure the prevalence of these practices.[178]

At an organizational level, the effective implementation of positive duties requires 'visible, committed and coordinated leadership', equalities expertise, and a commitment to training.[179] Self-regulation depends on there being an internal impetus for change, and 'voluntary and motivated compliance'; without this, 'these models will not achieve their aim of ultimately transforming the organizational culture'.[180] Conversely, positive duties will be difficult to implement in organizations without institutional buy-in,[181] including among senior executives;[182] where equality training is difficult to roll out;[183] or that lack capacity or confidence in advancing equality.[184] This may explain the success of the PSED in prompting mainstreaming and self-regulation in some organizations but not others.

A lack of organizational capacity is one of the key challenges facing the implementation of positive equality duties. Ineffective implementation is often not intentional, but reflects a lack of education, training, and resourcing.[185] Even large government departments and agencies may lack an understanding of positive duties and equality law.[186] While a lot of guidance has been issued around the PSED, and the PSED has been in place for some time,[187] organizations are still not

[172] Lucy Vickers, 'Promoting Equality or Fostering Resentment? The Public Sector Equality Duty and Religion and Belief' (2011) 31 Legal Studies 135, 137.
[173] ibid 156.
[174] Mitchell and others (n 72) 17.
[175] ibid.
[176] Manfredi, Vickers, and Clayton-Hathway (n 54) 383.
[177] ibid.
[178] ibid 378.
[179] ibid 395. Policy-led mainstreaming is rarely effective without political will: Fredman, *Discrimination Law* (n 11) 321. See Fiona Mackay and Kate Bilton, 'Learning from Experience: Lessons in Mainstreaming Equal Opportunities' (2003) 2, 5, 6, 10.
[180] Fredman, *Discrimination Law* (n 11) 322.
[181] UK78.
[182] UK167.
[183] UK78.
[184] John Braithwaite, 'The Essence of Responsive Regulation' (2011) 44 University of British Columbia Law Review 475, 498–99.
[185] UK95.
[186] UK93.
[187] UK167.

sure what they are meant to do to comply with the duty;[188] perhaps there is now too much guidance, meaning the general equality duty gets forgotten, and organizations get caught in the mechanics of the specific duties.[189] Uncertainty, 'timidity', and 'fear' mean some authorities 'retreat' into a narrow interpretation of the 'due regard' standard, focusing on 'due regard' rather than outcomes.[190] The loss of key staff can also undermine progress,[191] especially where organizational equalities expertise is thin. Organizations then '[run] out of steam' when the person responsible for advancing equality leaves.[192]

That even government departments are struggling to effectively implement positive duties reveals broader challenges with relying on self-regulation to advance equality: 'when you have government departments not really implementing that what's the chances of other people in society implementing it, if they're not taking it seriously?'[193] Governments have a 'duty to model best practice';[194] there is therefore a need to 'shift the culture of non-compliance with the equality duty by public authorities'.[195] In part, this requires a cultural change in public entities and a different approach to failure that embraces the risks of innovation.[196] Making mistakes and having to revisit or revoke a policy may have political repercussions for ministers and policy-makers; there may be a reluctance to admit that a mistake has been made, or that a positive duty has not been complied with.[197] Organizations may be hesitant to take risks and unwilling to innovate: 'the cultural shock will be so big they won't want to do it.'[198]

As they are currently framed, positive duties are too weak to overcome these organizational limits and hesitancies. In GB, the 'due regard' standard is 'too flimsy' to prompt mainstreaming and organizational change,[199] or to encourage organizations to develop their own solutions to equality issues.[200] As it has been developed in the case law, the PSED imposes a very low bar on public authorities,[201] does not demand detailed consideration of equality issues in decision-making, or necessitate organizational problem-solving.

[188] ibid; UK93.
[189] UK167.
[190] UK81.
[191] Mackay and Bilton (n 177) 5.
[192] UK167.
[193] UK93.
[194] A104.
[195] UK95.
[196] UK85; Mackay and Bilton (n 177) 5.
[197] UK95.
[198] UK85.
[199] Fredman and Spencer (n 2) 9; Dickens, 'The Road is Long' (n 22) 473; Fredman, 'The Public Sector Equality Duty' (n 1) 419; Fredman, 'Breaking the Mold' (n 2) 266.
[200] Fredman, 'The Public Sector Equality Duty' (n 1) 419.
[201] See, eg, *R (on the application of Staff Side of the Police Negotiating Board) v Secretary of State for Work and Pensions* [2011] EWHC 3175 (Admin) (2 December 2011), [2012] Pens LR 31. See Fredman, 'The Public Sector Equality Duty' (n 1); Fredman, 'Breaking the Mold' (n 2).

In Victoria, Queensland, and the ACT, mainstreaming is embedded in positive duties making it unlawful for public authorities 'to fail to give proper consideration' to equality in their decision-making.[202] In the Victorian case of *Castles v Secretary of the Department of Justice*,[203] Emerton J held that:

> proper consideration will involve understanding in general terms which of the rights of the person affected by the decision may be relevant and whether, and if so how, those rights will be interfered with by the decision that is made.... proper consideration will involve balancing competing private and public interests. There is no formula for such an exercise, and it should not be scrutinised over-zealously by the courts.
>
> ... it will be sufficient in most circumstances that there is some evidence that shows the decision-maker seriously turned his or her mind to the possible impact of the decision on a person's human rights and the implications thereof for the affected person, and that the countervailing interests or obligations were identified.[204]

At first glance, this appears to be a relatively weak standard of review. However, courts have emphasized that this 'consideration' must be serious and 'genuine, not formulaic';[205] it is not sufficient to 'merely invoke the Charter like a mantra',[206] and the requirement is 'an obligation of some stringency'.[207] While 'proper consideration' does not demand a 'sophisticated legal exercise',[208] it does require that decision-makers consider who is potentially affected by their decision and its impact on their rights, and identify and balance any competing interests and obligations.[209] This approach has also been adopted in the ACT.[210] Thus, 'proper consideration' may represent a stronger standard than 'due regard'.

In Victoria, too, this is strengthened by the need to take 'reasonable and proportionate measures' to eliminate discrimination.[211] Imposing a duty to take action avoids the 'risk of proceduralism' inherent in the PSED;[212] a focus on substantive outcomes ensures positive duties are more than just a neoliberal smokescreen for

[202] Charter of Human Rights and Responsibilities Act 2006 (Vic) s 38(1); Human Rights Act 2004 (ACT) s 40B(1); Human Rights Act 2019 (Qld) s 58(1).

[203] (2010) 28 VR 141.

[204] ibid [185]–[186]. See also *Loielo v Giles* [2020] VSC 722, [255]–[260].

[205] *Minogue v Thompson* [2021] VSC 56, [46].

[206] *Castles v Secretary of the Department of Justice* (2010) 28 VR 141, [186].

[207] *Minogue v Thompson* (n 203) [46].

[208] ibid [46].

[209] ibid.

[210] *Little v Commissioner for Social Housing (Administrative Review)* [2017] ACAT 11, [127]; *Miller v Commissioner for Social Housing (Administrative Review)* [2017] ACAT 10, [118], [120].

[211] Equal Opportunity Act 2010 (Vic) s 15(2). This could also be framed as a duty 'to achieve employment equality or fair participation'; this would require clarification of what 'equality' and 'fair' mean in this context: Fredman, 'Breaking the Mold' (n 2) 271.

[212] Fredman, 'The Public Sector Equality Duty' (n 1) 427.

concealing inaction at addressing inequality.[213] Requiring both meaningful consideration of equality issues, and the taking of proportionate action, offers an important route for strengthening positive duties.

Reform 31: That positive duties be strengthened to require both proper consideration and proportionate action to eliminate discrimination and advance equality of opportunity.

The primary role of enforcement agencies in relation to positive duties should be to develop the capabilities of those being regulated[214] to address any lack of organizational capacity. This can have a substantial and sustained impact on how organizations approach their equality duties.[215] Statutory agencies should work closely with organizations to help set equality outcomes and measures, offer examples of successful practices, mainstream equality in decision-making, and gain management buy-in.[216] The issue, though, is that this 'hand-holding' is labour-intensive, and can only be targeted at certain organizations (often the worst or least compliant).[217] The challenge is how to roll out this support to a wider pool of organizations, to improve compliance more generally; the EHRC cannot intensively support 300 individual public authorities.[218] Public authorities themselves therefore need to also take ownership of driving reform;[219] achieving this requires a renewed focus on engagement and consultation.

Reform 32: That statutory agencies re-emphasize their role in organizational capacity building, to better support the implementation of positive duties.

B. Engagement and Consultation

Engagement,[220] consultation, and collective organizing are critical to the success of second-generation regulation in three ways. First, they add a participative

[213] Manfredi, Vickers and Clayton-Hathway (n 54) 389.
[214] Hepple, 'Enforcing Equality Law' (n 8) 334.
[215] UK167.
[216] UK167; UK85.
[217] UK167.
[218] ibid. This is consistent with Fredman's argument that the successful strategies deployed by the ECNI cannot necessarily be scaled up to the sheer number of public authorities in GB without substantial additional resourcing: Fredman, *Discrimination Law* (n 11) 323–24, 328–30.
[219] UK167.
[220] For Hepple, 'engagement' involves the exchange of information, mutual learning, and persuasion, with a view to ultimately reaching agreement: Hepple, 'Enforcing Equality Law' (n 8) 322–23. This goes beyond the passivity of 'consultation', where those consulted typically only respond to proposals that have already been formulated. Hepple argues that engagement must uphold certain values, such as dignity, eliminating discrimination, advancing equality of opportunity, and fostering good relations; that is, values consistent with deliberative democracy.

dimension to decision-making, which is a public good and equality outcome in itself.[221] Through engagement and consultation, the decision-making process becomes as important as other equality outcomes:[222]

> … if equality is understood less as to do with formal equality and same treatment, and more as a notion involving inclusion and participation in public life, then the very process of consultation with disadvantaged groups achieves these aims.[223]

Second, engagement is key for identifying appropriate equality objectives and developing workable plans for action.[224] Including those affected in the process of making and implementing a decision improves the quality of regulation.[225] A decision made in a consultative way is more likely to be 'right' or appropriate: 'If you're talking to people, you'll get it right and if you don't talk to them, you'll get it wrong.'[226] Participative processes thereby increase the legitimacy and reach of equality law: younger and older workers should be involved in decision-making.[227]

Third, engagement and consultation are essential for the effective monitoring and enforcement of positive duties: Hepple argues that the most important function of positive duties is to facilitate internal scrutiny by and with stakeholders.[228] Consultation is key to challenging organizational assumptions and approaches, promoting effective problem-solving,[229] and ensuring that positive duties become more than a 'tick box' exercise.[230]

Consultation and involvement were originally seen as being 'of fundamental importance' to the PSED's success;[231] previous duties relating to race, gender, and disability all included some provision for engagement. However, the Conservative government viewed transparency and democratic accountability as supplanting any need for consultation or engagement.[232] The English specific duties therefore include no provision for consultation; engagement is essentially voluntary.[233]

[221] Manfredi, Vickers, and Clayton-Hathway (n 54) 390.
[222] Fredman, *Discrimination Law* (n 11) 317.
[223] Manfredi, Vickers, and Clayton-Hathway (n 54) 391.
[224] Department for Communities and Local Government (n 14) 92, [5.44].
[225] Bob Hepple, Mary Coussey, and Tufyal Choudhury, *Equality: A New Framework–Report of the Independent Review of the Enforcement of UK Anti-Discrimination Legislation* (Hart Publishing 2000) 57.
[226] UK87.
[227] A164; Fredman, *Discrimination Law* (n 11) 318.
[228] BA Hepple, *Equality: The Legal Framework* (2nd edn, Hart Publishing 2014) 167.
[229] A157; Christopher McCrudden, 'Equality Legislation and Reflexive Regulation: A Response to the Discrimination Law Review's Consultative Paper' (2007) 36 Industrial Law Journal 255, 265.
[230] UK167.
[231] Government Equalities Office, *Equality Bill* (n 66) 15.
[232] Government Equalities Office, *Equality Act 2010: The Public Sector Equality Duty. Promoting Equality through Transparency: A Consultation* (2010) 22, [6.4].
[233] Hepple, 'Enforcing Equality Law' (n 8) 331–32.

However, transparency and democratic accountability are insufficient for promoting equality. Transparency alone does not achieve change; there must be an 'action cycle' to accompany transparency and reporting, which includes engagement.[234] A focus on transparency—at the expense of engagement—is therefore misguided.

Further, employers are unlikely to adopt consultative mechanisms without a formal requirement to do so.[235] That said, Manfredi and others, examining evidence presented to the review of the PSED, found some positive examples of consultation, even if it was not required by the specific duties in England.[236] Consultation, where it is occurring, embodies one of the key aims of the PSED; that is, the pursuit of a transformative model of equality, grounded in the idea of inclusion.[237] The processes created by the PSED, particularly as they relate to consultation, therefore achieve the inclusion aims of the PSED in and of themselves.[238] It is therefore critical that consultation be built into and embedded within the English specific duties, to extend its reach beyond these 'best practice' organizations.

Consultation is already embedded in the specific duties in other nations. In Wales, for example, consultation lies at the heart of the Welsh approach to governance,[239] and the specific duties extend that to equality issues.[240] Public authorities must comply with engagement provisions in developing equality objectives,[241] identifying relevant information for publication,[242] carrying out an assessment,[243] and making or revising a Strategic Equality Plan.[244] In the 2014 review of the PSED in Wales, organizations reported that consultation and engagement was both more frequent and more thorough than what had been in place prior to the PSED.[245] In Scotland, public authorities must take reasonable steps to include those with protected characteristics in developing equality outcomes;[246] and consider relevant evidence from those with protected characteristics in making or reviewing policies.[247] Consultation is also built into the NI duty: authorities must consult on[248]

234 Blackham, 'Positive Equality Duties: The Future of Equality and Transparency?' (n 37).

235 A157; UK167. Though see the examples of good practice in Manfredi, Vickers, and Clayton-Hathway (n 54) 379–81.

236 Manfredi, Vickers, and Clayton-Hathway (n 54) 379–81.

237 ibid 390.

238 ibid 391.

239 These provisions are like those that were in the original draft of the English regulations: see Hepple, 'Enforcing Equality Law' (n 8) 326–27.

240 Deborah Foster, 'Devolution and Disabled Workers: The Experiences of Union Equality Representatives in Wales: Devolution, Disabled Workers and Equality Representatives' (2015) 46 Industrial Relations Journal 153, 156.

241 Equality Act 2010 (Statutory Duties) (Wales) Regulations 2011 (Wales), SI 1064/2011 (W155) reg 4.

242 ibid reg 7.

243 ibid reg 8.

244 ibid reg 15.

245 Mitchell and others (n 72) 23–24.

246 The Equality Act 2010 (Specific Duties) (Scotland) Regulations 2012 (Scotland), SI 162/2012, reg 4(2)(a).

247 ibid reg 5(2).

248 NI Act (n 82) sch 9, s 5.

the scheme for fulfilling their duty obligations,[249] and include information in that scheme on how they will consult on equality matters.[250] Thus, consultation and engagement can and should be integrated into specific duties.

Positive duties in Australia do not require consultation or engagement. The Victorian Charter, for example, 'promotes a dialogue between the three arms of the government—the Parliament, the executive and the courts—while giving Parliament the final say'.[251] This dialogue does not extend beyond government. Consultation *is* required, however, by positive duties relating to gender. For example, consultation is required when preparing a Gender Equality Action Plan under the Gender Equality Act 2020 (Vic);[252] and the Workplace Gender Equality Act 2012 (Cth) includes consultation as a gender equality indicator. Extending consultation requirements to age equality duties is therefore possible and desirable.

Reform 33: That English and Australian positive duties be amended to require consultation and engagement.

The quality of consultation also matters: it must have both reach and depth, be meaningful, participatory,[253] and focus on deliberation and openness.[254] Quality consultation requires the identification and inclusion of key stakeholders (which is more straightforward when dealing with workplace issues), and the adoption of measures to address inequalities of bargaining power.[255] Participative mechanisms often assume that groups have a high degree of collective organization, knowledge of government processes, a commitment to equality, and the necessary resources to be involved in extensive consultation processes;[256] this is rarely the case in relation to age equality (Chapter 9). There is therefore a need to protect individuals and groups against 'engagement fatigue', including through the better sharing of information across public authorities.[257]

The quality of consultation might be limited—intentionally or unwittingly—in practice. Some public authorities undertake 'informal' consultations, so they do not need to report on the results:[258] 'They're under no obligation to comply with the results, or take them on board, whereas if it was a formal consultation process, they would be subject to those.'[259] In other situations, 'consultation' is conducted

249 ibid sch 9, s 2(1), 4(1).
250 ibid sch 9, s 4(2).
251 Victoria, Parliamentary Debates, Legislative Assembly, 4 May 2006, 1290 (Robert Hulls).
252 Gender Equality Act 2020 (Vic) s 10(2)(b).
253 'Participation' can be achieved through the provision of information; co-decision-making; discussion, and debate to develop and refine goals; facilitating voice of excluded groups; and policy implementation: Fredman, *Discrimination Law* (n 11) 319.
254 Manfredi, Vickers, and Clayton-Hathway (n 54) 398.
255 ibid 375.
256 Fredman, *Discrimination Law* (n 11) 320.
257 Mitchell and others (n 72) 46.
258 UK95.
259 ibid.

online via a proforma survey with a few closed questions.[260] This might particularly exclude older people from participating, as they do not wish to engage in this 'impersonal' way.[261] In some cases, public authorities undertake consultative activities, but do not communicate how that is translating to policy-making: 'I think generally speaking, we're pretty good at engaging and then we create our policy and plans, but finding the point that connects the two can be quite hard to do.'[262] In sum, then, positive duties need to be explicit about the need for consultation and engagement, and provide general principles for how engagement processes should be conducted.

Reform 34: That positive duties include general principles for how engagement processes should be conducted.

C. State and Central Scrutiny

While the enforcement of positive duties should primarily occur through self-regulation and engagement,[263] equality agencies are an essential back-up for securing compliance and imposing sanctions where self-regulation fails.[264] The success of self-regulation depends on the perceived *inevitability* of escalation.[265] As Hepple explains: 'The choice is not between voluntarism and legal sanctions. In many cases, voluntarism can work only if there is the possibility of gradual escalation of sanctions by the regulator.'[266] Consistent with the enforcement pyramid and a reflexive law framework,[267] statutory agencies should initially focus on capacity building, information and training, and encouragement and support, to secure compliance without the need for adversarial proceedings.[268] Where this fails, agencies can proceed to negotiation and discussion, then progressively escalate to an order to comply, fines, or other judicial sanctions.[269] As Manfredi and others argue: 'Formal enforcement may not be used very often, but the potential for its use is necessary for the more indirect forms of regulation to operate effectively.'[270]

At present, statutory agencies have only limited capacity to escalate matters where self-regulation fails. In GB, the EHRC may: assess the extent to which the

260 UK166.
261 ibid.
262 UK87.
263 At present, though, these processes are unlikely to be working effectively.
264 Hepple, 'Enforcing Equality Law' (n 8) 321.
265 John Braithwaite, *Restorative Justice and Responsive Regulation* (OUP 2002) 34.
266 Hepple, 'Enforcing Equality Law' (n 8) 322.
267 ibid 321–22.
268 Fredman, *Discrimination Law* (n 11) 323.
269 ibid.
270 Manfredi, Vickers, and Clayton-Hathway (n 54) 396.

PSED has been complied with;[271] issue a compliance notice;[272] and institute or intervene in JR proceedings[273] (Chapter 8). These powers are more limited than what was originally envisaged,[274] and the EHRC's capacity to use these powers has been 'weakened by under-funding'.[275] This poses significant risks to the implementation of the PSED: a lack of enforcement can lead to a lack of compliance,[276] especially where resilient self-enforcement mechanisms are not in place.[277] While specific duties are more 'rigorous'[278] in Scotland and Wales than in England, enforcement depends on the GB EHRC, and is subject to EHRC funding arrangements: 'There is a tension there.'[279]

Consistent with regulatory theory, the EHRC has prioritized enforcement activity at the base of the enforcement pyramid. This informal approach is quicker and easier than taking court action, and a better use of public funds.[280] Most issues are resolved following an approach by the EHRC:[281] organizations are very receptive to resolving matters informally, so compliance notices do not need to be issued.[282] The threat of enforcement is sufficient.[283] The EHRC did not issue any compliance notices between 5 April 2011, when the PSED came into force, and March 2016.[284] To target its activities, the EHRC continuously monitors equality impact assessments (EIAs) that are published, approaching organizations where an EIA is missing or incomplete.[285] The EHRC has also undertaken systemic reviews of compliance, including of information published by public authorities,[286] and intervened in cases relating to the PSED.[287] The challenge with an informal approach, though, is that the EHRC's enforcement actions are not visible;[288] this may have implications for institutional legitimacy (Chapter 8).

EHRC enforcement aims to be forward-looking and strategic,[289] as not all matters can be addressed. The aim, then, is to give individuals the tools they need to

271 EqA 2006 (n 81) s 31.
272 ibid s 32.
273 ibid s 30.
274 Hepple, 'Enforcing Equality Law' (n 8).
275 Manfredi, Vickers, and Clayton-Hathway (n 54) 396. See also Hepple, 'Enforcing Equality Law' (n 8) 319.
276 Manfredi, Vickers, and Clayton-Hathway (n 54) 396.
277 UK87; UK95.
278 UK90.
279 UK87.
280 UK167.
281 ibid.
282 ibid.
283 ibid.
284 Email from Markus Piscapore-Caruana (EHRC) to Peter Williams, regarding *Freedom of Information Request*, 24 March 2016, available at <https://www.whatdotheyknow.com/request/compliance_notices_issued_by_the> accessed 25 March 2022.
285 UK167. That said, there is no legal requirement to publish an EIA in England.
286 EHRC, 'Publishing Equality Information: Commitment, Engagement and Transparency' (2012) 4.
287 See, eg, *Ward v The London Borough of Hillingdon* [2019] EWCA Civ 692, [2019] WLR(D) 244.
288 UK167.
289 ibid.

enforce matters themselves.[290] Both statutory agencies and third sector organizations have produced tools and guidance to empower individuals and NGOs to challenge government decision-making,[291] with the aim of achieving broader cultural change and improving compliance with positive duties.[292] These initiatives will be most successful where there is a thriving third sector that is able and willing to challenge government decision-making. This presents a particular challenge in relation to age equality, where collective action is limited (Chapter 9). In effect, the weight of enforcement has—again—fallen back on individuals.

This may be compared with enforcement in NI: where an authority fails to comply with the NI duty, a person who claims to have been directly affected by the failure must first raise the issue with the public authority,[293] then make a complaint to the Equality Commission for Northern Ireland (ECNI), which will either investigate or give reasons for not investigating.[294] The ECNI may also conduct an investigation of its own initiative.[295] If a public authority does not respond to the ECNI's recommendations for action within a reasonable time, the matter may be referred to the Secretary of State, who may give directions to the public authority.[296] This process of enforcement operates entirely beyond the court system. It offers the prospect of strong central review of organizational actions. However, complaints can take up to twelve months to be investigated and resolved, even where the issues are relatively straightforward.[297] Statutory enforcement is therefore very limited in practice, undermining the potential of the NI duty: 'these duties are going to become obsolete if they're not enforced.... [yet] if they rigorously enforced this, then you would see public authorities slowly shifting.'[298]

In Australia, equality agencies have very limited powers to escalate the enforcement of positive duties. For example, the VEOHRC no longer has the power to conduct a public inquiry,[299] issue a compliance notice or enter an enforceable undertaking.[300] Enforcement of the duty depends on the VEOHRC conducting an investigation:[301] the VEOHRC has never exercised this power. Without appropriate powers and funding,[302] equality agencies can 'engage' with organizations in relation to the duty, but cannot do much more.[303] Even that engagement is limited,

290 ibid.
291 UK85; UK95.
292 UK95.
293 NI Act (n 82) sch 9, s 10(4).
294 ibid sch 9, s 10.
295 ibid sch 9, s 11(1).
296 ibid sch 9, s 11(3).
297 UK95; Equality Coalition (n 92) 103.
298 UK95.
299 Rees, Rice and Allen (n 101) 177–78. See also Equal Opportunity Amendment Act 2011 (Vic) s 6.
300 See Harpur (n 112) 182.
301 Equal Opportunity Act 2010 (Vic) s 15(4).
302 A3; A5; A101.
303 A101.

as matters cannot be escalated.[304] The Victorian positive duty is therefore far less effective than what was originally envisaged: 'there was a vision and it was implemented and then it was sort of carved out. And it's . . . obstructing the way in which we can deal with a lot of those more systemic issues.'[305] Without effective enforcement, the Victorian duty has had limited impact in practice;[306] it is more aspirational than practical.[307] Chapter 8 considers in detail how the powers of statutory agencies might best be reformed.

D. Individual Enforcement

Second-generation regulation is specifically intended to *move beyond* individual enforcement. That said, courts can be central actors in experimentalist regulation. In hearing cases, courts are both a 'catalyst and backstop' for organizational reform, incentivizing employers to adopt their own problem-solving processes; specifying general norms; assessing the effectiveness of internal problem-solving mechanisms;[308] ensuring organizational accountability; and imposing sanctions where problem-solving fails.[309] The role of the courts should be to 'advance accountability, deliberative democracy, and participative equality', by requiring decisions to be justified, exposing reasons to scrutiny and debate, and improving deliberative decision-making.[310]

The PSED creates no cause of action at private law.[311] Instead, it may be enforced in public law via JR proceedings. In practice, the weight of enforcement has fallen on JR proceedings.[312]

JR is not well suited to the enforcement of positive duties. In an experimentalist framework, the success of positive duties is measured by the extent to which they encourage effective organizational problem-solving. This is impossible to evaluate via JR. Instead, JR focuses on the *process* of the PSED.[313] This focus on process—not outcome[314]—may exacerbate a 'box ticking' mentality to the PSED,[315] with organizations going through the procedural motions of compliance[316] with

304 ibid.
305 ibid.
306 A3.
307 A7.
308 Sturm (n 17) 479–82.
309 ibid 483.
310 Fredman, *Human Rights Transformed* (n 4) 181.
311 EqA (n 74) s 156.
312 Fredman, 'Breaking the Mold' (n 2) 270.
313 Manfredi, Vickers, and Clayton-Hathway (n 54) 386.
314 UK78; UK80; UK167; Fredman, 'Breaking the Mold' (n 2) 275.
315 A102; A108; UK78; UK80; UK167; UK95; Manfredi, Vickers, and Clayton-Hathway (n 54) 374–75.
316 Fredman, 'The Public Sector Equality Duty' (n 1) 420; Fredman, 'Breaking the Mold' (n 2) 276.

'tokenistic lip service',[317] while resisting actual change.[318] The 2013 review of the PSED found public authorities to be risk averse,[319] with 'box ticking' in relation to procurement[320] and widespread use of 'often formulaic' EIAs.[321] In the Steering Group Chair's view, the specific duties added a 'layer of unnecessary bureaucracy' for public authorities.[322] Similar concerns about 'box ticking' have emerged in the context of the Welsh specific duties.[323]

Courts may struggle to 'penetrate' or 'see through' these bureaucratic responses.[324] The 'due regard' standard subjects authorities to a very low level of scrutiny;[325] is overly deferential,[326] does not require concerted action to achieve equality,[327] and tends to be 'amorphous and difficult to pin down', increasing the risk of bureaucratic responses.[328] Courts apply the standard in unpredictable ways, so 'instead of facilitating deliberation, judicial review has become the first rather than the last resort'.[329] Proceduralism driven by the 'due regard' standard may have exacerbated the regulatory limits of command and control regulation,[330] inhibiting effective organizational problem-solving.[331] Fredman therefore argues that there is a paradox at the heart of using JR to enforce compliance with the PSED:

> On the one hand, the role of courts is to supply a stable set of principles capable of guiding decision-making without resort to litigation. On the other hand, the more settled the principles, the more scope there is for mere procedural compliance and the less space is left for flexible decision-making.[332]

On a practical level, JR is slow and more difficult to pursue than an Employment Tribunal (ET) claim. It is difficult to explain to individuals that all they can challenge is the decision-making *process*, not the impact of the decision itself.[333] JR remedies can be particularly disheartening for claimants: government decisions

[317] UK80. See also UK93.
[318] Fredman, 'Breaking the Mold' (n 2) 276.
[319] Government Equalities Office, *Review of the Public Sector Equality Duty* (n 96) 11.
[320] ibid 13.
[321] ibid 14. If done well, though, EIAs 'are a really important way of getting it right in the first place . . . to get things right the first time': UK85.
[322] Government Equalities Office, *Review of the Public Sector Equality Duty* (n 96) 15.
[323] Foster (n 238) 161.
[324] Samuel Bagenstos, 'The Structural Turn and the Limits of Antidiscrimination Law' (2006) 94 California Law Review 1, 20–21, 25–26.
[325] Manfredi, Vickers, and Clayton-Hathway (n 54) 386.
[326] Fredman, 'Breaking the Mold' (n 2) 271–72.
[327] Fredman, *Discrimination Law* (n 11) 308–10.
[328] ibid 330.
[329] Fredman, 'Breaking the Mold' (n 2) 266.
[330] ibid 281.
[331] Lizzie Barmes, *Bullying and Behavioural Conflict at Work: The Duality of Individual Rights* (OUP 2016) 9, 212.
[332] Fredman, 'Breaking the Mold' (n 2) 276–77.
[333] UK95.

are rarely overturned;[334] the remedy may simply be a declaration that the duty has not been complied with.[335] Requiring reconsideration of a decision can lead to the same result:[336] 'It's frustrating, right? It's, like, two steps forward, one step back.'[337] That said, even these limited remedies may have an educative and sensitizing effect on public authorities.[338] While remedies may help with 'moving the dial slightly', they are unsatisfying for individual claimants.[339] This is unlikely to encourage claiming.[340]

Individuals are therefore unlikely to use the PSED to challenge public authority decision-making; this is a route more often pursued by NGOs.[341] Indeed, it is inappropriate to rely on individuals to identify and challenge systemic procedural issues, like a lack of effective mainstreaming.[342] The cultural shift required to mainstream equality will not be achieved by JR alone.[343]

Other jurisdictions have de-centred individual litigation for enforcing positive duties. In NI, complaints under s 75 must first be raised with the public authority,[344] before proceeding to the ECNI.[345] This may encourage the early and efficient resolution of disputes and avoid escalating issues unnecessarily. However, few issues are resolved in this way, as public authorities are often reluctant to admit that there is a problem.[346]

In Victoria and Queensland, individual enforcement of positive duties is restricted.[347] In Victoria, for example, remedies are available for a breach of s 38(1) of the Victorian Charter in JR proceedings[348] and, through the 'piggyback' enforcement provisions, Victorian Charter rights can be raised in any legal proceeding in which they are relevant, not just JR proceedings.[349] However, this depends on

[334] Manfredi, Vickers, and Clayton-Hathway (n 54) 386.

[335] UK167. See, eg, *R (on the application of Bapio Action Ltd) v Secretary of State for the Home Department* [2007] EWHC 199 (QB) (9 February 2007); *R (on the application of Hottak) v Secretary of State for Foreign and Commonwealth Affairs* [2015] EWHC 1953 (Admin), [2015] IRLR 827.

[336] UK95.

[337] ibid.

[338] Manfredi, Vickers, and Clayton-Hathway (n 54) 386–87.

[339] UK95.

[340] ibid; UK167.

[341] UK95.

[342] UK80.

[343] Fredman, 'Breaking the Mold' (n 2) 281.

[344] NI Act (n 82) sch 9, s 10(4).

[345] ibid sch 9, s 10.

[346] UK95.

[347] Equal Opportunity Act 2010 (Vic) s 15(3); Charter of Human Rights and Responsibilities Act 2006 (Vic) s 39; Human Rights Act 2019 (Qld) s 59.

[348] Supreme Court (General Civil Procedure) Rules 2015 (Vic) Order 56. See, eg, *Haigh v Ryan* [2018] VSC 474, [100].

[349] Brett Young (n 137) 126. Note, though, that assessing the Charter lawfulness of a decision or action must be pursued through JR in the Supreme Court: *Director of Housing v Sudi* [2011] VSCA 266; *Commissioner for Social Housing in the ACT & Massey (Residential Tenancies)* [2013] ACAT 41. See further Louis Schetzer, 'Queensland's Human Rights Act: Perhaps Not Such a Great Step Forward?' (2020) 45 Alternative Law Journal 12, 14.

claimants having some other claim; breach of a positive duty does not create an independent cause of action.

By contrast, the ACT duty has a direct right of action: individuals may commence Supreme Court proceedings against a public authority if they would be a 'victim' of the contravention of the duty, or rely on their rights in other legal proceedings.[350] The Supreme Court may grant any appropriate relief except damages.[351] The direct right of action was introduced[352] with the express intention of increasing human rights litigation in the ACT:

> the government looks forward to the growth in the number of cases and the depth of argument on the issues. In due course, we may see the trickle of human rights case law turn into a stream. This stream will be the evidence of the growing awareness of human rights in this jurisdiction and the strength of the underlying legal principles.[353]

However, the direct right of action 'remains under-utilised',[354] in part due to the lack of monetary compensation, and the inaccessibility of the Supreme Court:[355]

> The removal of monetary compensation as a remedy may deter genuine litigants who can incur significant costs (and a risk an adverse costs order if unsuccessful) in commencing Supreme Court proceedings, and removes an incentive for private law firms to take on human rights cases for impecunious litigants on a pro bono or 'no win, no fee basis'.[356]
>
> … the Supreme Court remains an inaccessible avenue for many ordinary people aggrieved by a breach of their human rights.[357]

Building on the ACT provisions, a 2015 review of the Victorian Charter recommended adopting a direct cause of action to VCAT, modelled on the jurisdiction conferred by the *Equal Opportunity Act 2010* (Vic).[358] Individuals could also rely on Victorian Charter rights in other legal proceedings.[359] The

[350] Human Rights Act 2004 (ACT) s 40C.
[351] ibid s 40C(4). The time limit on such claims is a year, unless the Court orders otherwise: s 40C(3).
[352] Human Rights Amendment Act 2008 (ACT).
[353] ACT, Parliamentary Debates, Legislative Assembly, 6 December 2007, 4031 (Simon Corbell).
[354] ACT Human Rights and Discrimination Commissioner, 'Look Who's Talking: A Snapshot of Ten Years of Dialogue Under the Human Rights Act 2004 by the ACT Human Rights and Discrimination Commissioner' (2014) 6 <https://hrc.act.gov.au/wp-content/uploads/2015/03/HRA-10-yr-snapshot-HRDC-webversion.pdf> accessed 4 June 2021.
[355] Helen Watchirs and Gabrielle McKinnon, 'Five Years' Experience of the Human Rights Act 2004 (ACT): Insights for Human Rights Protection in Australia' (2010) 33 University of New South Wales Law Journal 136, 158–59, 170.
[356] ibid 158–59.
[357] ibid 170.
[358] Brett Young (n 137) 129. Gans recommends the same: Jeremy Gans, 'The Charter's Irremediable Remedies Provision' (2009) 33 Melbourne University Law Review 105.
[359] Brett Young (n 137) 126.

Review did not recommend that damages be made available, at least until 'the direct cause of action is established and there is experience of it in operation'.[360] While this model offers a more accessible avenue for claims (VCAT, not the Supreme Court), it does not address issues arising from a lack of monetary compensation.

To encourage better use of the ACT provisions, Watchirs and McKinnon recommend funding community legal centres (CLCs) and advocacy organizations to support individual claimants and run test cases, and that the equality agency be granted a complaint-handling function, allowing complaints to be resolved using the existing discrimination conciliation model (Chapter 5).[361] A complaint-handling function of this nature has been introduced in Queensland: a human rights complaint about a contravention of s 58(1) may be made to the Commissioner by someone who is the subject of the contravention,[362] so long as the complaint is first raised with the public entity.[363] The Commissioner may take 'reasonable action the commissioner considers appropriate to try to resolve the complaint',[364] conduct a conciliation conference,[365] and prepare a report with recommendations if the complaint is not successfully conciliated.[366] The Commissioner has no power to direct a public entity to address the issues raised in the complaint, or to provide a claimant with a remedy.[367] Without an effective remedy, claimants and respondents may be unwilling to engage in this process;[368] as in NI, few issues may be resolved via this route.[369] Conciliation is more effective if claims can be escalated (Chapter 5); thus, complaint-handling should be paired with a direct cause of action to the relevant tribunal. This offers a more accessible option than reliance on JR.

Reform 35: That positive duties be enforceable by a direct cause of action to the relevant tribunal, with the possibility of damages, in a similar jurisdiction to that established under discrimination laws.

Reform 36: That equality agencies be given statutory powers to receive and conciliate complaints relating to positive duties.

360 ibid 131.
361 Watchirs and McKinnon (n 353) 170.
362 Human Rights Act 2019 (Qld) s 64(1).
363 ibid s 65.
364 ibid s 77.
365 ibid s 79.
366 ibid s 88.
367 Schetzer (n 347) 16.
368 ibid.
369 UK95.

V. Conclusion: Enhancing Positive Duties

Positive duties are innovative tools for enhancing the effectiveness of equality legislation. As O'Cinneide argues: 'it is important not to underestimate the symbolic and educative impact of the positive duties.'[370] As currently framed, positive duties have serious limitations as a form of 'second-generation regulation'. It is challenging to make age equality a priority for those implementing positive duties, and difficult to structure duties around fundamental rights 'without reverting to individualized complaints mechanisms with all their inbuilt weaknesses'.[371] That said, this chapter puts forward practical reforms to extend and modify positive duties to improve their operation. We can be optimistic about the radical potential of positive duties to effect organizational change.[372]

At present, though, there are clear gaps in the coverage of positive duties. In Canada, duties do not extend to age equality; in Australia, duties are entirely absent in most states and territories and at the federal level; and in the UK and Australia, duties are mostly confined to the public sector, on the assumption they would be 'unfairly onerous' on private organizations.[373] It is potentially unfair and practically problematic to distinguish between the public and private sectors in this way;[374] the line between public and private is already blurred, as duties encompass private bodies undertaking public functions.[375] Equality duties 'harness the energies' of employers, who are in the best position to promote equality and achieve structural change;[376] the private sector has 'potential strategic importance' in addressing inequality, given it employs the vast majority of the workforce in the UK and Australia.[377] To be most effective, then, positive duties should encompass both the public and private sectors in their role as employers.[378]

Reform 37: That positive duties be adopted in all Australian states and territories, and federally.

Reform 38: That positive duties apply to both the public and private sectors in their role as employers.

370 O'Cinneide, 'Positive Duties and Gender Equality' (n 3) 107.
371 Fredman, *Human Rights Transformed* (n 4) 189.
372 O'Cinneide, 'Positive Duties and Gender Equality' (n 3) 107.
373 Fredman, *Discrimination Law* (n 11) 178. cf the duties in the Equal Opportunity Act 2010 (Vic) s 15(6) and Anti-Discrimination Act 1998 (Tas) s 104, which apply to both the public and private sector.
374 Fredman, *Discrimination Law* (n 11) 178.
375 ibid 304–05.
376 ibid 176.
377 Fredman and Spencer (n 2) 8. See also Dickens, 'The Road is Long' (n 22) 474.
378 Hepple, Coussey, and Choudhury (n 223) 59–65, 69–72. Indeed, in the 2014 review of the PSED in Wales, some non-listed bodies were already modelling their approach to equality on the PSED, as it matched with their corporate ethos, they wanted to emulate best practice, or they were seeking to align their activities and approach with that of listed bodies: Mitchell and others (n 72) 19–20.

While positive duties may be effective tools for facilitating mainstreaming and encouraging organizational problem-solving, they must be supported by a robust institutional architecture. Enforcement of positive duties is best achieved through an integrated model of individual, agency, and self-regulation, supported by meaningful consultation and engagement. To achieve this, we need to strengthen the powers of statutory agencies to act as an effective backstop where self-regulation fails and support capacity building within organizations[379] (Chapter 8); and bolster collective action in the area of age equality (Chapter 9). In Chapter 8, I consider how we might strengthen the position of statutory agencies to achieve this end.

[379] Hepple, 'Enforcing Equality Law' (n 8) 334.

8
Agency Enforcement

I. Introduction

The success of second-generation regulation fundamentally depends on strong agency enforcement. Statutory agencies play a key role in assisting, building capacity, and addressing instances where self-regulation fails;[1] they are an essential back-up for securing compliance.[2] In this chapter, I critically analyse the role of statutory agencies in moving beyond the individual enforcement of age discrimination law. Critiquing legal provisions in the United Kingdom (UK), Canada, and Australia, I consider how agency powers have been used in practice, and propose reforms to strengthen agency enforcement of age discrimination law.

II. Existing Statutory Agencies and their Powers

The UK, Canada, and Australia each have at least one specialist agency responsible for the enforcement of equality law. Agency powers and functions differ markedly across jurisdictions, reflecting the political and regulatory choices and compromises inherent in the enforcement of equality law. Focusing on Britain, McCrudden identifies four regulatory approaches to the role of statutory equality agencies: enforcing collective regulation; command and control regulation; responsive or reflexive regulation; and assisting individual enforcement.[3] This fourth approach—assisting individual enforcement—is in addition or complementary to the other three approaches.[4]

UK equality agencies have, over time, increasingly moved towards a model of responsive or reflexive regulation, where the agency fulfils a 'back up' role if internal scrutiny and consultation fail.[5] In this model, the agency is 'the guardian of the public interest'.[6] This model is most effective if accompanied by positive duties

[1] Bob Hepple, 'Enforcing Equality Law: Two Steps Forward and Two Steps Backwards for Reflexive Regulation' (2011) 40 Industrial Law Journal 315, 321.
[2] ibid.
[3] Christopher McCrudden, 'Equality Legislation and Reflexive Regulation: A Response to the Discrimination Law Review's Consultative Paper' (2007) 36 Industrial Law Journal 255, 257–59.
[4] Bob Hepple, 'Agency Enforcement of Workplace Equality' in Linda Dickens (ed), *Making Employment Rights Effective: Issues of Enforcement and Compliance* (Hart Publishing 2012) 50.
[5] ibid 55.
[6] ibid.

Reforming Age Discrimination Law. Alysia Blackham, Oxford University Press. © Alysia Blackham 2022.
DOI: 10.1093/oso/9780198859284.003.0008

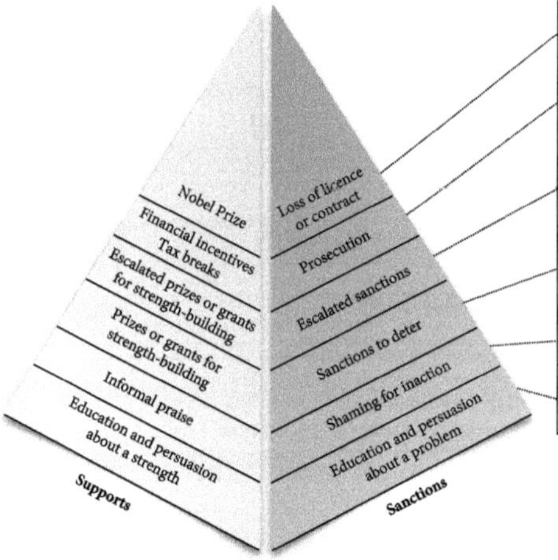

EHRC	FWO
n/a	n/a
Contempt of court Injunction Order to comply	Court proceedings Represent employees Order to comply with undertaking Penalties Injunction, contempt
Unlawful act notice Agreements Action plan	Enforceable undertakings Compliance notice (not for adverse action)
Investigation or inquiry PSED assessment PSED compliance notice Voluntary agreements	Investigation or inquiry Assessment or contravention letter Voluntary agreements
Benchmarking Naming and shaming	Benchmarking Naming and shaming
Information and advice Codes of practice Advise	Information and advice Best practice guides

Figure 8.1 Pyramid of supports and sanctions, EHRC and FWO

on the public and private sector, and deterrent sanctions, such as through contracts and subsidies.[7] A similar shift towards reflexive law can be seen in Australia, particularly in the federal industrial relations jurisdiction. Despite this shift, the Equality and Human Rights Commission's (EHRC) powers 'still seem locked into command and control regulation', except as they relate to positive duties.[8] Figure 8.1 maps the powers of equality agencies (focusing on the EHRC and Fair Work Ombudsman (FWO)) against the pyramid of supports and pyramid of sanctions (Chapter 1);[9] these powers are discussed in more detail in the sections that follow.

A. UK

In Great Britain (GB), the EHRC is tasked with promoting understanding and awareness and encouraging good practice in relation to equality; promoting equality of opportunity; enforcing the Equality Act 2010 (EqA); and working towards the elimination of unlawful discrimination and unlawful harassment.[10] To achieve this, the EHRC has a range of powers: it can provide information, advice, education, and training;[11] issue codes of practice and other guidance;[12] conduct

[7] ibid.
[8] ibid 59.
[9] For further description, see Hepple, 'Enforcing Equality Law' (n 1); Dominique Allen, 'Barking and Biting: The Equal Opportunity Commission as an Enforcement Agency' (2016) 44 Federal Law Review 311.
[10] Equality Act 2006, s 8 (hereafter EqA 2006).
[11] ibid s 13.
[12] ibid ss 14, 15.

inquiries;[13] and advise government on the law.[14] It is empowered to take enforcement action, spanning investigations, unlawful act notices, action plans, agreements, and applications for injunctions to restrain and orders to comply.[15] The EHRC can assist individuals to bring complaints, including through legal assistance.[16] It may also conduct assessments[17] and issue compliance notices relating to the Public Sector Equality Duty (PSED),[18] and can institute or intervene in legal proceedings.[19]

These powers are rarely exercised in practice,[20] particularly in relation to age discrimination: significant budget and staffing cuts have limited the EHRC's efficacy.[21] From 2010 to 2019, EHRC staff numbers declined by 61 per cent (from 530 to 206 staff), and its budget was reduced by 73.6 per cent from 2007 to 2019 (from £70.3 million to £18.55 million).[22] In the EHRC's 2019–20 accounts, this further declined to 199 full-time equivalent (FTE) staff and a budget of £17.4 million.[23] Even accounting for the outsourcing of some of the EHRC's functions, its budget has been reduced by over £42 million since 2007.[24]

While the EHRC is the specialist equality body in GB, other agencies could undertake enforcement action in this space, including the Health and Safety Executive,[25] Employment Agency Standards Inspectorate, Gangmasters and Labour Abuse Authority, and Her Majesty's Revenue and Customs (HMRC),[26] potentially under the auspices of a new single labour market enforcement body.[27] These bodies are subject to the PSED and the EqA, and should have due regard

[13] ibid s 16.
[14] ibid s 11.
[15] ibid ss 20–24. See also s 32(8).
[16] ibid s 28.
[17] ibid s 31.
[18] ibid s 32.
[19] ibid s 30.
[20] Historically, see Linda Dickens, 'Road Blocks on the Route to Equality: The Failure of Sex Discrimination Legislation in Britain' (1991) 18 Melbourne University Law Review 277, 285–86.
[21] UK Parliament, *Budget for Equality and Human Rights Commission, Early Day Motion* 382 (21 July 2016), 2016–17 session.
[22] Women and Equalities Committee, *Enforcing the Equality Act: The Law and the Role of the Equality and Human Rights Commission* (2017–19 HC 1470) 25 [76]. Though £10.2 million of this reduction is attributable to the EHRC's functions—like the helpline—being outsourced.
[23] EHRC, 'Annual Report and Accounts 2019–20' (2020) HC 491 51, 57.
[24] Women and Equalities Committee, *Enforcing the Equality Act* (n 22) 25, [76].
[25] See, eg, Belinda Smith, Melanie Schleiger, and Liam Elphick, 'Preventing Sexual Harassment in Work: Exploring the Promise of Work Health and Safety Laws' (2019) 32 Australian Journal of Labour Law 219.
[26] See Women and Equalities Committee, *Enforcing the Equality Act* (n 22) ch 4.
[27] Department for Business, Energy and Industrial Strategy, 'Good Work Plan: Establishing a New Single Enforcement Body for Employment Rights—Consultation' (2019) <https://assets.publishing.service.gov.uk/government/uploads/system/uploads/attachment_data/file/817359/single-enforcement-body-employment-rights-consultation.pdf> accessed 30 October 2020; Department for Business, Energy and Industrial Strategy, 'UK Labour Market Enforcement Strategy 2019/20: Government Response' (2020) <https://www.gov.uk/government/publications/labour-market-enforcement-strategy-2019-to-2020-government-response> accessed 30 October 2020.

to the general equality duty in exercising their regulatory and enforcement functions.[28] The EHRC could, then, prioritize enforcement action against other regulatory bodies when they fail to meet their equality duties.[29] This requires the EHRC to work closely with other bodies to clarify and negotiate overlapping roles and responsibilities for enforcement.[30]

In Northern Ireland (NI), the Equality Commission for Northern Ireland (ECNI) has broadly similar aims and powers to the EHRC, including undertaking education and research activities, issuing codes of practice, and assisting individual claimants,[31] though its role in relation to positive duties is far more extensive (Chapter 7).[32] Responsibility for human rights oversight in NI lies with the Northern Ireland Human Rights Commission (NIHRC); in GB this also sits with the EHRC. While the ECNI has historically been well-funded,[33] it is also experiencing significant budgetary and staffing challenges: from 2009–10 to 2019–20, ECNI staff numbers declined by 48.6 per cent, from 138 to 71 FTE.[34]

B. Australian Federal Industrial Law

Industrial bodies like the FWO have extensive enforcement powers, including in relation to age discrimination law.[35] The FWO supports the Fair Work Act 2009 (Cth) (FWA) regime as a statutory authority tasked with ensuring compliance with federal workplace laws. The FWO is empowered with a broad range of functions, including:

- Promoting compliance with the FWA through education, assistance, and advice and producing best practice guides;
- Monitoring compliance;
- Inquiring into, and investigating, contraventions of the FWA;
- Commencing court or Fair Work Commission (FWC) proceedings to enforce the FWA;
- Referring matters to relevant authorities; and

[28] See Women and Equalities Committee, *Enforcing the Equality Act* (n 22) ch 4.
[29] ibid 37.
[30] ibid.
[31] Employment Equality (Age) Regulations (Northern Ireland) 2006, regs 37–39, 47; Northern Ireland Act 1998 (UK) ss 73–74.
[32] Northern Ireland Act 1998 (UK) s 74, sch 9.
[33] Dominique Allen, 'Strategic Enforcement of Antidiscrimination Law: A New Role for Australia's Equality Commissions' (2010) 36 Monash University Law Review 103.
[34] ECNI, 'Annual Report and Accounts 2019–2020' (2020) HC 591 15, 16.
[35] Therese MacDermott, 'Affirming Age: Making Federal Anti-Discrimination Regulation Work for Older Australians' (2013) 26 Australian Journal of Labour Law 141, 150–51; Therese MacDermott, 'Challenging Age Discrimination in Australian Workplaces: From Anti-Discrimination Legislation to Industrial Regulation' (2011) 34 University of New South Wales Law Journal 182, 206–07.

- Representing employees who are party to proceedings.[36]

The FWO also has powers as a workplace inspector, with the ability to enter[37] and inspect premises and documents,[38] require the production of documents,[39] ask for a person's name and address,[40] and apply to the Administrative Appeals Tribunal for notices that require the production of evidence or attendance at the FWO for questioning.[41] The FWO may accept written undertakings, and seek their enforcement in court,[42] and issue compliance notices.[43] These powers closely map the enforcement pyramid (Figure 8.1).[44]

C. Australian Discrimination Law

The powers of Australian equality agencies are more limited. At the federal level, the Australian Human Rights Commission (AHRC) is tasked with inquiring into, and attempting to conciliate, discrimination complaints.[45] The AHRC is also tasked with:

- Promoting understanding and acceptance of, and compliance with, the Age Discrimination Act 2004 (Cth) (ADA);
- Conducting research and education programmes;
- Examining legislation for compliance;
- Reporting to the Minister on laws or action that should be made or taken;
- Publishing guidelines; and
- Intervening in proceedings, with the leave of the court.[46]

The AHRC may hold inquiries to perform its functions,[47] and may obtain information and documents[48] and examine witnesses.[49]

36 Fair Work Act 2009 (Cth) s 682 (hereafter FWA).
37 ibid s 708.
38 ibid s 709.
39 ibid s 712.
40 ibid s 711.
41 ibid s 712AA.
42 ibid s 715.
43 ibid s 716.
44 See Hepple, 'Enforcing Equality Law' (n 1).
45 Australian Human Rights Commission Act 1986 (Cth) ss 11(aa), 31(b).
46 Age Discrimination Act 2004 (Cth) s 53 (hereafter ADA); Australian Human Rights Commission Act 1986 (Cth) ss 11, 31.
47 Australian Human Rights Commission Act 1986 (Cth) s 14.
48 ibid s 21.
49 ibid s 22.

Powers of state and territory equality agencies differ somewhat to those at the federal level: in Victoria, for example, the Victorian Equal Opportunity and Human Rights Commission (VEOHRC) is tasked with:

- Preparing, consulting on, and issuing (non-legally binding)[50] practice guidelines;[51]
- On request, reviewing and advising on compliance;[52]
- Advising on, setting requirements for, and keeping a register of action plans to improve compliance;[53]
- Offering dispute resolution services;[54]
- Conducting investigations, if a matter:
  - o relates to the Act;
  - o is 'serious in nature';
  - o affects a class or group;
  - o 'cannot reasonably be expected to be resolved' through conciliation or a tribunal application;
  - o there are reasonable grounds to believe a contravention of the Act has occurred; and
  - o the investigation would advance the Act's objectives.[55]
- After conducting an investigation, taking any action the VEOHRC 'thinks fit', such as entering into an agreement, referring the matter to the tribunal, or reporting to the Attorney-General or Parliament.[56]

While powers differ across jurisdictions, all Australian equality agencies are primarily tasked with a complaint-handling function, acting as gatekeepers before a claim can progress to a court or tribunal.[57] Agencies are therefore tasked with both conciliating individual disputes *and* supporting the enforcement of equality law. By contrast, this gatekeeping function is performed by Acas (the Advisory, Conciliation and Arbitration Service) in GB, the Labour Relations Agency (LRA) in NI, and the FWC in Australian federal industrial law.

[50] Equal Opportunity Act 2010 (Vic) s 149(a). Note, however, that a court or tribunal may consider compliance with the guidelines if relevant: s 149(b).

[51] ibid s 148.

[52] ibid s 151.

[53] ibid ss 152, 153. A search on 2 June 2020 identified only two action plans on the VEOHRC's website; both were issued by the Commission itself.

[54] ibid s 111.

[55] ibid s 127.

[56] ibid s 139. These powers are more confined than what was originally envisaged: see Equal Opportunity Amendment Act 2011 (Vic).

[57] Allen, 'Strategic Enforcement of Anti-Discrimination Law' (n 33) 105. The exception is in Victoria, where complaints may be filed directly with the Victorian Civil and Administrative Tribunal (VCAT).

As both enforcers and (objective) conciliators, Australian equality agencies straddle two potentially competing roles; this may limit the extent to which agencies use their assistance functions to support individual claimants.[58] More likely, though, these dual roles are mutually supportive, enhancing agency operations. In resolving individual disputes, a conciliator from the statutory regulator may support restorative justice, as the 'spectre of punishment in the background'[59] supports and encourages parties to resolve the matter. Equality agencies can have a substantial impact in the way they conduct conciliation, helping to restore relationships, act as advocates for equality or for the legal framework, suggest systemic remedies, and prompt broader change (Chapter 5). A purposive approach to conciliation, informed by the agency's regulatory role, can therefore significantly improve the individual and systemic outcomes of conciliation. At a systemic level, too, equality agencies use their gatekeeping role to inform their compliance activities, through collection and analysis of claim data to inform strategic decision-making.

D. Canada

The Canadian Human Rights Commission also occupies this dual role, responsible for the administration of the Canadian Human Rights Act (RSC, 1985, c H-6) and receiving complaints under Part III of the Act. It is also given functions under s 27(1)–(3) to:

- Develop and conduct information programmes to foster public understanding of the Act and equality;
- Undertake or sponsor research programmes;
- Liaise with similar bodies or authorities in the provinces, and conduct functions for those bodies by agreement;
- Produce reports, including on recommendations, suggestions, and requests concerning human rights; studies concerning human rights and freedoms as referred to it by the Minister of Justice; reviews of regulations, rules, orders, by-laws, and other instruments made pursuant to an Act of Parliament;
- Try to discourage and reduce discriminatory practices, by persuasion, publicity, or any other means considered appropriate; and
- Issue guidelines (binding on the Commission) setting out how, in its opinion, any provision of the Act applies in a class of cases.[60]

58 ibid 111–12.
59 John Braithwaite, *Restorative Justice and Responsive Regulation* (OUP 2002) 35.
60 The Age Guidelines (SI/78-165) only apply to goods, services, and facilities.

III. Optimizing the Role of Equality Agencies

Strong agency enforcement depends on three requirements. First, the body must have sufficient legal powers to operate effectively in this space, consistent with the demands of a reflexive regulatory approach and the enforcement pyramid. These powers must be drafted (and interpreted) in a way that does not unnecessarily constrain the agency's ability to take action.[61] Second, the agency must have adequate resourcing to exercise those powers effectively. Third, the agency must exercise those powers, and use their resources, strategically, to maximize the impact and effectiveness of their operations in advancing equality.

A. Adequate Legal Powers

1. The base of the pyramid: supporting self-regulation

Statutory equality agencies are tasked with multiple responsibilities at the base of the enforcement pyramid, around education, capacity building,[62] and promoting dialogue and understanding. Agencies offer organizations examples of what works[63] through 'an accessible and respectful process',[64] educating through training, compliance publications (such as guidelines, good practice guides or explanatory materials), the process and outcome of public inquiries, litigation reports, conciliation of disputes,[65] and responding to queries. Many educational initiatives and programmes run for a fixed period (say, a year) and are then shelved when funding runs out or other priorities emerge;[66] this makes it difficult to build and consolidate on progress.

Effective education, capacity building, and dialogue hinge on active communication between agencies, organizations, and the general public. This communication can be direct, as in Australia and NI, where equality agencies field enquiries and provide information to individuals and organizations via email, phone, or online (Chapter 4). However, direct communication can be resource intensive and difficult to manage with a small team:[67] while a lot of information is available online, people increasingly want to talk to someone,[68] and personalized assistance is often the most effective tool for helping people navigate the legal framework.[69] The

[61] See, eg, Linda Dickens, 'The Road is Long: Thirty Years of Equality Legislation in Britain' (2007) 45 British Journal of Industrial Relations 463, 475–76.

[62] Hepple, 'Enforcing Equality Law' (n 1) 321.

[63] UK85.

[64] A105.

[65] Belinda Smith, 'Not the Baby and the Bathwater: Regulatory Reform for Equality Laws to Address Work-Family Conflict' (2006) 28 Sydney Law Review 689, 718.

[66] UK79.

[67] UK97.

[68] ibid.

[69] ibid.

challenge, then, is how to sustainably offer this support to an entire population, particularly as agency resources decline.[70]

In England and Wales, discrimination enquiries have been outsourced to the Equality Advisory and Support Service (EASS) since 2012[71] to provide 'significantly better value for money' than the previous EHRC helpline.[72] It is unlikely that EASS can offer the same quality of advice as the EHRC.[73] EASS steers away from giving advice about the merits of a claim, instead focusing on its referral function.[74] Thus, while the cost 'per case' (from initial enquiry to final action) has been reduced from £28 for the EHRC helpline to £10 per call for the EASS,[75] this more likely reflects a reduction in the support offered:[76] 'the telephone line at the moment is just not working, not for people who need advice.'[77]

Removing the EHRC's helpline function has severely curtailed one communication avenue between statutory enforcement agencies and the public.[78] Fielding enquiries helps agencies to get a 'feel' for what is going on in practice;[79] without access to that data, it is difficult to link agency work with community need.[80] The outsourcing of enquiries has therefore constrained the EHRC's ability to monitor, consider, and inform its enforcement work using real-life complaints and queries,[81] creating a 'disconnect' between the EHRC and the community, and limiting the early resolution of cases:[82] 'We are in a situation where we do not have the evidence base to enable those sorts of systemic enforcement actions.'[83]

Information flows between the EHRC and EASS are also limited and problematic: the EHRC has 'had considerable difficulty in accessing sufficient information about the inquiries coming into [EASS]'[84] and 'expressed concerns the data

70 ibid.

71 GOV.UK, 'New Equality Advisory and Support Service Is Launched' (15 November 2012) <https://www.gov.uk/government/news/new-equality-advisory-and-support-service-is-launched> accessed 25 May 2020.

72 ibid.

73 Hepple, 'Agency Enforcement of Workplace Equality' (n 4) 63.

74 Select Committee on the Equality Act 2010 and Disability, *The Equality Act 2010: The Impact on Disabled People* (HL 2015–16, 117) [149]–[150].

75 ibid [153].

76 In the cases sampled in this study, one case noted that incomplete advice had been received from EASS: *O'Neill v Jaeger Retail Ltd* [2019] UKET 4103815/2018. The claimant contacted EASS, which reportedly 'gave her general advice but nothing about Employment Tribunals or time limits': at [16].

77 UK81.

78 UK79.

79 UK161.

80 UK97.

81 UK79.

82 Select Committee on the Equality Act 2010 and Disability (n 74) [146].

83 Elizabeth Prochaska, then Legal Director of the EHRC, in her evidence to the WEC: House of Commons, 'Oral Evidence: Older People and Employment' (2018) HC 359 Q82 <http://data.parliament.uk/writtenevidence/committeeevidence.svc/evidencedocument/women-and-equalities-committee/older-people-and-employment/oral/76656.html> accessed 25 March 2022.

84 Select Committee on the Equality Act 2010 and Disability (n 74) [147].

it receives from the helpline is of poor quality'.[85] While the bodies meet regularly and work closely together,[86] the colour and detail of individual enquiries is lost when presenting information in aggregate, leaving 'very, very basic information'.[87] Strategic case referrals are not emerging from EASS; attempts to improve the quality and flow of information have not been successful.[88] The EHRC received 112 strategic referrals from EASS in 2014, and 333 in 2015; only fifty-two of these 445 referrals were assessed by the EHRC as being of strategic value; none were the subject of strategic litigation. The House of Lords Select Committee on the Equality Act 2010 and Disability therefore concluded that the EASS should be returned to the EHRC 'to embed the helpline into its role as a strategic regulator'.[89]

Reform 39: That the equality helpline be insourced and returned to the EHRC.

Handling enquiries is only one means of communicating with the public. The House of Commons Women and Equalities Committee (WEC) has argued that the EHRC needs a broader strategy and approach to intelligence gathering, encompassing other sources and forms of information beyond a helpline.[90] For example, one Australian jurisdiction has adopted informal 'Report It' forms, allowing issues to be reported to the agency, and included in data collection, even if a complaint will not be pursued.[91] There is space on the form for a person to indicate if they want to be contacted by the agency.[92] The FWO also has an anonymous 'tipoff' form on its website.[93]

Reform 40: That equality agencies enable anonymous reporting of issues via their website to facilitate intelligence gathering, allowing people to indicate on the form if they want to be contacted.

Communication between agencies, organizations, and the public can also be indirect, through the media and social media. At present, much of the 'persuasion' work done by equality agencies is communicated poorly, limiting its broader

[85] National Audit Office, 'Briefing for the Women and Equalities Committee' (2017) <https://www.nao.org.uk/wp-content/uploads/2017/01/Briefing-for-the-Women-and-Equalities-Committee.pdf> accessed 25 May 2020.
[86] UK117.
[87] UK79.
[88] Select Committee on the Equality Act 2010 and Disability (n 74) [147].
[89] ibid [154]–[156]. While this report focused on the experiences of those with a disability, its findings are arguably relevant to all protected characteristics.
[90] Women and Equalities Committee, *Enforcing the Equality Act* (n 22) 19–21.
[91] A102.
[92] ibid.
[93] FWO, 'Report an Issue Anonymously' <https://www.fairwork.gov.au/workplace-problems/fixing-a-workplace-problem/report-an-issue-anonymously> accessed 25 March 2022.

impact. For example, the EHRC focuses primarily on 'pre-enforcement' work, including by writing letters to organizations and threatening to take action. This informal approach typically resolves around 350 matters each year 'quickly and easily';[94] however, 'the vast majority of those 350 cases will have received little or no publicity'.[95] Informal action is typically 'quiet'[96] and not well publicized, in part due to a lack of resources. That said, addressing a matter informally can lead to public messaging and awareness raising, if the agency chooses.[97] While the EHRC has a website that describes its pre-enforcement work, when accessed on 11 June 2021, that website was more than three years out of date.[98] Agencies therefore need to reprioritize public communication and messaging, to better support self-regulation through the management and communication of information.

The gathering and communication of information therefore can and should become a key function of equality agencies at the base of the enforcement pyramid. Statutory agencies hold a wealth of data about compliance, enforcement activity, training, enquiries, complaints, and conciliations. Particularly where positive duties are in place, equality agencies can play a pivotal role in the centralized aggregation, analysis, and reporting of data across organizations and industries, enabling effective benchmarking and the public scrutiny of information.[99] The AHRC's *Willing to Work* report, for example, recommended expanding the remit of the Australian Workplace Gender Equality Agency (WGEA), to become the Workplace Gender Equality and Diversity Agency (WGEDA),[100] enabling it to collect diversity data and engage collaboratively with employers and business to promote equality across all grounds.[101] In this way, the progress made through data and reporting in relation to gender equality could be extended to support older workers.[102]

The question, though, is how the information held by statutory agencies should best be managed, used, and communicated in practice, and to what end. For example, 'naming and shaming' could be used for a 'general deterrence type purpose',[103] identifying organizations that are non-compliant, or who have been subject to enforcement activity. In many cases, though, data becomes dated quickly: one agency, for example, contemplated creating a map of those who had

[94] Women and Equalities Committee, *Enforcing the Equality Act* (n 22) 15–16.
[95] ibid 16.
[96] UK81.
[97] ibid.
[98] Last updated on 11 December 2017: Equality and Human Rights Commission, 'Pre-Enforcement Work' (11 December 2017) <https://www.equalityhumanrights.com/en/legal-casework/pre-enforcement-work> accessed 11 June 2021.
[99] Alysia Blackham, 'Positive Equality Duties: The Future of Equality and Transparency?' (2021) 37(2) Law in Context 98.
[100] AHRC, 'Willing to Work: National Inquiry into Employment Discrimination Against Older Australians and Australians with Disability' (2016) 14.
[101] ibid.
[102] ibid 109.
[103] A110.

breached legislative requirements, but found that many organizations went bankrupt, 'phoenixing' to become new companies.[104] A map, then, would be minimally informative, instead being a historical artefact of previous corporate entities. Equally, if most small businesses fail, there is no point creating a list of best practice employers, especially if that list is not relatively stable.[105] This flags some of the fundamental challenges in regulating small businesses through these sorts of persuasive techniques.

Managing data and achieving transparency is complex where resources are limited: 'it's hugely resource intensive' to de-identify information and make it public.[106] Where resources are limited, transparency and information publishing often decline.[107] This flags the need for adequate resourcing of equality agencies (Part B).

Reform 41: That statutory equality agencies review and reprioritize strategic public messaging and the gathering and communication of data.

2. Escalating enforcement

Equality agencies should be empowered to escalate enforcement action in the event of non-compliance. Even if these powers are used infrequently, they remain important tools in an agency's arsenal:[108] just the threat or possibility of enforcement can increase compliance.[109] Action at the base of the enforcement pyramid will therefore be more successful where there is capacity to escalate.[110]

Enforcement must be selective: agencies cannot pursue all matters or issues with limited budgets and staff.[111] Powers should be used strategically and selectively, to maximize their impact.[112] For example, investigations are an important tool for 'deterrence messaging' where there is systemic or blatant exploitation on the basis of age;[113] conducting an investigation can raise awareness and escalate an issue on the political agenda.[114] In determining what enforcement is 'strategic', agencies can draw on both consultation and engagement,[115] and regulatory theory, including

[104] ibid.
[105] ibid.
[106] A153.
[107] ibid; A113.
[108] Dickens, 'The Road is Long' (n 61) 476.
[109] Smith, 'Not the Baby and the Bathwater' (n 65) 706. See also Women and Equalities Committee, *Enforcing the Equality Act* (n 22) 15–16.
[110] Smith, 'Not the Baby and the Bathwater' (n 65) 714.
[111] Tess Hardy, John Howe, and Sean Cooney, 'Less Energetic but More Enlightened? Exploring the Fair Work Ombudsman's Use of Litigation in Regulatory Enforcement' (2013) 35 Sydney Law Review 565, 568.
[112] UK81; UK86.
[113] A6.
[114] UK79.
[115] UK86.

the enforcement pyramid,[116] which offers a strategic guide for when to punish and when to persuade.[117]

It is critical, though, that threats of enforcement are not perceived to be empty threats: agencies must *use* their powers to promote compliance. The exercise of coercive enforcement powers is resource intensive, and rarely has specific funding;[118] if equality agencies are not adequately resourced, these powers will be exercised infrequently, if ever.[119] Investigations and inquiries are particularly demanding,[120] often requiring one to two dedicated full-time staff;[121] this is beyond the capacity of some agencies.[122] The combined impact of statutory hurdles,[123] fear of political repercussions,[124] and a lack of resourcing[125] mean the exercise of these powers has become impracticable. Without dedicated additional funding and the buy-in of the organization being investigated,[126] 'it would have to be a really significant problem for them to do anything'.[127]

In GB, for example, the EHRC has powers to escalate enforcement at least partway up the enforcement pyramid (Figure 8.1), though these powers could be strengthened at the pyramid's upper levels.[128] While there are already many regulatory players in the UK,[129] there is still a need for a labour law enforcement body, similar to the Australian FWO.[130] HMRC can be 'absolutely terrifying' when they 'aggressively pursue things', but they are not consistently enforcing labour laws.[131] It makes sense, then, to give these stronger and broader enforcement powers to the EHRC, which is the specialist equality agency.[132]

To do this, though, demands a fundamental rethink about how the EHRC is funded and structured.[133] Cuts to funding and judicial review (JR) decisions

[116] A110. See Hardy, Howe, and Cooney's study of litigation activity by the FWO: Hardy, Howe, and Cooney (n 111). Weil's concept of 'strategic enforcement' uses four principles to guide an enforcement policy: prioritization (based on risk); deterrence; sustainability; and systemic effects: David Weil, 'Creating a Strategic Enforcement Approach to Address Wage Theft: One Academic's Journey in Organizational Change' (2018) 60 Journal of Industrial Relations 437.
[117] Smith, 'Not the Baby and the Bathwater' (n 65) 714.
[118] A71.
[119] ibid; A105; UK87.
[120] A71; A101; A102.
[121] A71.
[122] A102.
[123] A113.
[124] A71.
[125] UK87.
[126] A71.
[127] A115.
[128] UK81. See, eg, Hepple, 'Enforcing Equality Law' (n 1).
[129] UK167.
[130] UK78. Department for Business, Energy and Industrial Strategy, 'Good Work Plan: Establishing a New Single Enforcement Body for Employment Rights–Consultation' (n 27); Department for Business, Energy and Industrial Strategy, 'UK Labour Market Enforcement Strategy 2019/20: Government Response' (n 27).
[131] UK78.
[132] ibid.
[133] ibid.

curbing the EHRC's powers[134] mean even existing enforcement powers are used rarely;[135] some of the EHRC's 'unique' powers have not been used.[136] From April 2010 to March 2018, the EHRC's least exercised powers included the issuing of compliance notices (never used); applying for injunctions (used six times); conducting formal investigations (used once); conducting inquiries (used four times); and assessments of compliance with the PSED (never used).[137] The EHRC rarely 'shouts' about its enforcement work, and does not routinely publish data on enforcement action,[138] inhibiting its ability to use communication as a 'tool for change'.[139] The WEC has therefore recommended that the EHRC 'significantly increase the volume, transparency and publicity of its enforcement work by making much greater use of its unique enforcement powers, publicising that work and reducing its reliance on individual complainants',[140] including by publishing data and case studies on formal and informal enforcement and compliance activity.[141]

Australian equality agencies have powers that are 'flat and rectangular, rather than pyramidal',[142] with few powers to 'escalate' enforcement. This risks undermining activity at the base of the enforcement pyramid.[143] The legislative framing of enforcement powers can also make their use impracticable. In Victoria, for example, the VEOHRC can conduct an investigation, but can do little with the results of that investigation.[144] In other jurisdictions, requiring approval from both the Attorney-General and a tribunal prior to the exercise of own motion powers mean those powers are rarely exercised.[145] Australian equality agencies should therefore be given expanded and enhanced powers, consistent with reflexive law and the enforcement pyramid.[146] Failing to give equality agencies powers comparable to other statutory regulators devalues equality and the enforcement of discrimination law.[147]

The FWO has some capacity to escalate enforcement, by launching investigations, accepting enforceable undertakings,[148] pursuing litigation, and seeking civil penalties.[149] That said, even the FWO cannot impose penalties for adverse action

[134] Dickens, 'The Road is Long' (n 61) 475–76.
[135] UK81; Women and Equalities Committee, *Enforcing the Equality Act* (n 22) 11–12.
[136] Women and Equalities Committee, *Enforcing the Equality Act* (n 22) 14.
[137] ibid.
[138] ibid 18.
[139] ibid.
[140] ibid 19.
[141] ibid.
[142] Allen, 'Barking and Biting' (n 9) 321.
[143] Smith, 'Not the Baby and the Bathwater' (n 65) 714.
[144] A101; A112.
[145] A113.
[146] A115; Smith, 'Not the Baby and the Bathwater' (n 65) 723.
[147] A105.
[148] Smith, 'Not the Baby and the Bathwater' (n 65) 715.
[149] FWA (n 36) ss 539 Item 11, 546. See, eg, *Fair Work Ombudsman v Theravanish Investments Pty Ltd* [2014] FCCA 1170.

without a court order, and it has only limited capacity to pursue criminal penalties;[150] civil litigation has therefore become 'a critical component of the [FWO's] overall compliance and enforcement strategy'.[151] Hardy, Howe, and Cooney therefore argue that the 'tip' of the enforcement pyramid is too blunt, even for the FWO, including due to a lack of incapacitation measures.[152] Further, while the FWO does conduct civil litigation in relation to equality and discrimination matters,[153] most cases tend to focus on under-payment of wages and entitlements.[154] The FWO is more likely to litigate in cases of repeat or deliberate non-compliance; exploitation of vulnerable workers; failure to cooperate with the FWO; or against parties with a prior history of contraventions.[155] Thus, it is not just that enforcement powers must be available and be used: they must also be used in the area of age equality.

Reform 42: That equality agencies be given more extensive powers to escalate enforcement in the event of non-compliance.

Reform 43: That equality agencies be given adequate funding to enable the strategic exercise of their enforcement powers.

3. Assisting individual claimants

Regulatory theory does not fully capture the importance of litigation for enforcement. Litigation is key for clarifying the law, building public knowledge, generating public attention and debate,[156] and strengthening normative pressures to comply:[157] 'A critical mass of cases is needed to build a culture where compliance ... is the norm.'[158] Individual litigation is therefore an important complement to responsive or reflexive regulation (Chapter 1) but there are substantial barriers to individuals asserting and enforcing their rights (Chapters 3–6). Targeted advice and assistance for individual claimants could help address these barriers, promoting access to justice, developing the law and legal precedent, raising the profile of discrimination law, and using the threat of litigation as a deterrent.[159] Statutory agencies can therefore play a key role in enforcement by assisting individual claimants.[160]

150 Hardy, Howe, and Cooney (n 111) 573.
151 ibid 574.
152 ibid 594–95.
153 See, eg, *Fair Work Ombudsman v Tiger Telco Pty Ltd (in liq)* [2012] FCA 479; *Fair Work Ombudsman v Rocky Holdings Pty Ltd* [2013] FCCA 1549.
154 Hardy, Howe, and Cooney (n 111) 582.
155 FWO, 'Compliance and Enforcement Policy' (2020) 10.
156 Hardy, Howe, and Cooney (n 111) 576.
157 ibid.
158 Women and Equalities Committee, *Enforcing the Equality Act* (n 22) 64.
159 Allen, 'Strategic Enforcement of Anti-Discrimination Law' (n 33) 124–32.
160 Hepple, 'Agency Enforcement of Workplace Equality' (n 4) 50.

UK equality agencies can assist and fund individual litigation,[161] and the EHRC may institute or intervene in legal proceedings.[162] These powers have been used to develop the law, achieve systemic remedies, and challenge unfavourable decisions.[163] Support for individual claimants is therefore important and often very effective.[164] Publicizing the outcomes of supported cases (including those that settle) promotes transparency in equality law and can create 'lightning rod' settlements (Chapter 6). The ECNI, for example, generally asks claimants who receive legal assistance to not sign a confidentiality agreement, and to participate in publicity if their claim is successful. The ECNI's policy for the provision of legal assistance states:

> The Commission will normally publicise decisions and settlements secured under its auspices with the aim of educating potential applicants and respondents as to their respective rights and responsibilities.[165]

However, supporting individual claimants—potentially at the expense of broader enforcement action—represents a 'piece by piece approach [which] is insufficient in the face of the systemic and routine discrimination'.[166] Individual claims can consume substantial agency resources: the EHRC estimates the costs of funding a case as between £4,000 and £80,000, with a mean of £28,000.[167] Thus, few cases are supported each year.[168] The EHRC's online legal case database[169] included only forty-nine cases on 18 June 2021, fourteen of which involved legal assistance. Of eight cases relating to age, only one had the EHRC providing legal assistance.[170] In NI, less than a third of applications received by the ECNI's Legal Funding Committee (LFC) are granted assistance each year (Table 8.1).[171]

Powers to assist individual claimants are therefore exercised selectively, giving priority to cases that clarify points of law, establish broader legal precedent,[172] raise questions of principle, have a broader impact, raise public awareness,[173] or target

[161] EqA 2006 (n 10) s 28; Employment Equality (Age) Regulations (Northern Ireland) 2006 (NI) s 47(1).

[162] EqA 2006 (n 10) s 30.

[163] Allen, 'Strategic Enforcement of Antidiscrimination Law' (n 33) 116–23.

[164] Women and Equalities Committee, *Enforcing the Equality Act* (n 22) 14.

[165] Equality Commission for Northern Ireland, 'Policy for the Provision of Legal Advice And Assistance' (2018) 8 <http://www.equalityni.org/ECNI/media/ECNI/Publications/Individuals/DAO/Policy-Provision_of_Legal-Advice_and_Assistance.pdf> accessed 5 June 2020.

[166] Women and Equalities Committee, *Enforcing the Equality Act* (n 22) 15.

[167] ibid 55.

[168] UK94; A118.

[169] Equality and Human Rights Commission, 'Legal Case Search' <https://legal.equalityhumanrights.com/en/search> accessed 15 October 2020.

[170] *Holloway v Ministry of Defence* [2015] UKEAT/0396/14/BA.

[171] Equality Commission for Northern Ireland, 'Legal Services Report: Review of Legal Services 2018–19' (2019) 3.

[172] Dickens, 'The Road is Long' (n 61) 479.

[173] Employment Equality (Age) Regulations (Northern Ireland) 2006 (NI) s 47(1).

Table 8.1 Applications and assistance granted, LFC, 2011–12 to 2019–20

Year	Total LFC applications	Granted assistance	% granted
2011–12	274	85	31.02
2012–13	264	83	31.44
2013–14	315	110	34.92
2014–15	286	59	20.63
2015–16	291	71	24.4
2016–17	255	59	23.14
2017–18	310	52	16.77
2018–19	317	67	21.14
2019–20	337	72	21.36

Source: ECNI Legal Services Reports

high visibility respondents to 'send a general deterrence message'.[174] Each agency has their own strategic priorities, which can change over time,[175] and cases are assessed against those priorities and in-house criteria.[176] The EHRC sets its priorities based on the triennial *Is Britain Fairer?* Report and evidence from stakeholders.[177] While this is a consistent and predictable way of setting priorities, it is also relatively inflexible. In response to the WEC's recommendation that it develop a plan for addressing age discrimination in employment,[178] the EHRC made it clear that it would not shift its priorities to focus on age discrimination in employment, due to the need to take 'a coordinated and strategic approach to determining our priorities'.[179] As one respondent noted, though, 'there is a tendency to talk about [the EHRC's] strategic role as an explanation of what they can't do rather than as a description of what they are doing'.[180]

174 A110. Though Hardy and Howe illustrate the gaps in this logic: Tess Hardy and John Howe, 'Creating Ripples, Making Waves? Assessing the General Deterrence Effects of Enforcement Activities of the Fair Work Ombudsman' (2017) 39 Sydney Law Review 471.

175 Hepple, 'Agency Enforcement of Workplace Equality' (n 4) 62–63.

176 UK94. See Employment Equality (Age) Regulations (Northern Ireland) 2006 (NI) s 47(1); Equality Commission for Northern Ireland (n 165) 4–5.

177 Women and Equalities Committee, *Older People and Employment: Government and Equality and Human Rights Commission Responses to the Committee's Fourth Report of Session 2017-19* (2017–19, HC 1585) 13.

178 Women and Equalities Committee, *Older People and Employment* (2017–19, HC 359) 13.

179 Women and Equalities Committee, *Older People and Employment: Government and EHRC Responses* (n 177) 13.

180 UK81.

The most significant cases are not always the most strategic. One agency is supporting 'ordinary' claims in specific areas, rather than major cases: 'it's been really effective in raising the profile of that type of discrimination . . . and getting access to justice for a lot of people who . . . are struggling to get cases off the ground.'[181] This is not 'about clarifying the law. This is about seeing it applied in practice.'[182] Even when choosing which ordinary claims to pursue, though, attention could be directed to complaints that are recurring frequently, indicating that there is some systemic or widespread problem; or to complaints that are raised rarely, and therefore under-represented in statistics and cases.[183] Age falls in the latter category: 'there would be a good chance of an age discrimination case getting assisted, simply because the profile is not so good, and we might be able to lift that up a little bit.'[184]

In addition to choosing *which* claims to pursue, agencies must also determine *when* to assist claimants. The EHRC tends to intervene in matters only when they progress to appeal; ECNI, by contrast, offers legal support in the early stages of a claim. The risk with the EHRC's approach is that a claim is framed—and ultimately determined—by the evidence and arguments put forward at the first instance hearing; it is hard to retrofit a claim once it has progressed on appeal. Early support for claimants therefore increases the likelihood of success.[185] However, it can be difficult for equality agencies to identify good complaints early on, especially where complaints and enquiries are handled by different agencies, as in GB.[186]

In Australia, it is exceptional for equality agencies to have the power to assist claimants,[187] though the AHRC, South Australian Equal Opportunity Commission (SAEOC),[188] and Western Australian Equal Opportunity Commission (WAEOC)[189] may support individual parties.[190] At the federal level, this support is limited to filling out court forms.[191] The FWO can assist claimants and has powers to initiate and conduct litigation.[192] Critical to this, though, is adequate resourcing, including to translate enquiries into written complaints.[193] Further, the standing of equality agencies to bring complaints and enforcement proceedings on behalf of individual claimants needs to be clarified in some jurisdictions.[194]

181 UK79.
182 UK81.
183 UK97.
184 ibid.
185 ibid.
186 UK79. cf Allen, 'Strategic Enforcement of Anti-Discrimination Law' (n 33) 115.
187 Allen, 'Strategic Enforcement of Anti-Discrimination Law' (n 33) 104.
188 Equal Opportunity Act 1984 (SA) s 95C.
189 Equal Opportunity Act 1984 (WA) s 93A(1).
190 These powers were originally introduced in Victoria when the Equal Opportunity Act 2010 (Vic) was passed, but were subsequently removed with a change in government before the Act came into force.
191 Australian Human Rights Commission Act 1986 (Cth) s 46PT.
192 FWA (n 36) s 682.
193 A101.
194 A102; A105; UK94.

Reform 44: That Australian equality agencies be given powers and funding to assist individual complainants and standing to bring complaints on behalf of individuals.

Even where these powers are available, they are exercised rarely. In South Australia (SA), in 2018–19, the SAEOC provided initial funding for five complainants (ie, to assess prospects of success) across all protected grounds; only one case was fully funded, though three received partial funding.[195] In 2017–18, ten complainants received initial funding, and one case was fully funded.[196]

Australian equality agencies may appear as amicus curiae[197] or intervene in legal proceedings with the leave of the court,[198] to offer their expertise and guidance.[199] While rarely done in practice, this can have an important impact on the shape of discrimination law: 'we've started doing more interventions in court work here partly because you only need a couple of good cases really to start to build and send messages.'[200]

B. Adequate Resourcing

Adequate resourcing is critical if statutory agencies are to be effective enforcers of equality law:

> it all comes down to resourcing.... you can have all the new laws in the world but ... the real issue is how we enforce what we've currently got.... if you're going to get any progress, you've got to have some teeth somewhere in the system.[201]

The UN Paris principles, which set out requirements for human rights agencies,[202] specifically include the need for adequate funding:

195 South Australian Equal Opportunity Commission, 'South Australian Equal Opportunity Commission Annual Report 2018–19' (2019) 21–22.

196 Equal Opportunity Commission South Australia, 'Annual Report 2017–18' (2018) 27.

197 Anti-Discrimination Act 1991 (Qld) s 186; Anti-Discrimination Act 1977 (NSW) s 99; Equal Opportunity Act 1984 (WA) s 113; Australian Human Rights Commission Act 1986 (Cth) s 46PV; Equal Opportunity Act 2010 (Vic) ss 159, 160.

198 A118; Anti-Discrimination Act 1991 (Qld) s 235(j); Anti-Discrimination Act 1998 (Tas) s 7(b); Anti-Discrimination Act 1992 (NT) s13(q); Equal Opportunity Act 2010 (Vic) ss 159, 160; Australian Human Rights Commission Act 1986 (Cth) s 11(1)(o); Sex Discrimination Act 1984 (Cth) s 48(1)(gb).

199 Ronnit Redman, 'Litigating for Gender Equality: The Amicus Curiae Role of the Sex Discrimination Commissioner' (2004) 27 University of New South Wales Law Journal 849.

200 A105.

201 UK87.

202 *Principles Relating to the Status of National Institutions*. United Nation General Assembly Resolution 48/134, December 1993.

> The national institution shall have an infrastructure which is suited to the smooth conduct of its activities, in particular adequate funding. The purpose of this funding should be to enable it to have its own staff and premises, in order to be independent of the Government and not be subject to financial control which might affect its independence.

At 27 November 2019, the AHRC, Canadian Human Rights Commission, ECNI, and EHRC all had 'A' status, being fully compliant with the Paris Principles.[203]

Despite this, statutory equality agencies are still under-resourced given the scale and diversity of their responsibilities:[204] 'They are not funded for the size of their task.'[205] Resources are continually shrinking, meaning the activities of equality agencies are becoming progressively more limited[206] across the enforcement pyramid as staff numbers decline:[207] 'social justice agencies are just being diminished.'[208] Limited resourcing makes it especially difficult for statutory agencies to work proactively.[209]

Increasing agency roles and responsibilities, or expanding the scope of equality law, can stretch statutory agencies beyond their capacity: 'every time you add an attribute, that's another area we have to develop expertise in. And another area that we have to go out and educate [on].'[210] Law reform needs to be accompanied by appropriate resourcing; at the moment, 'we will resource it with passion.'[211] Equality agency staff are stretched thinly, nearly to breaking point: 'every time I feel like I'm drowning, I remind myself not drowning, waving';[212] 'if one of us is taken offline, for a short period even, we struggle to meet our core function let alone [do more].'[213]

This reflects the dramatic reduction in agency staff over time: in one Australian agency, from eight policy and legal officers to just one;[214] another from thirty to nineteen staff in three years.[215] EHRC staff have declined from

[203] Global Alliance of National Human Rights Institutions, 'Chart of the Status of National Institutions' (2019) <https://www.ohchr.org/Documents/Countries/Cooperation/StatusAccreditationChart.pdf> accessed 16 October 2020.
[204] A3; A10; A71; A100; A101; A105; A113; A153; A155; A157; UK78; UK80; UK87; UK97.
[205] A157.
[206] A101; A113.
[207] A10; A101; A113; A155.
[208] A102.
[209] A157.
[210] A99.
[211] ibid.
[212] ibid.
[213] A113.
[214] A10.
[215] A155.

530 to 206 from 2010 to 2019;[216] and the ECNI from 138 to 71 FTE from 2009–10 to 2019–20.[217] Issues of resourcing are acute in both the UK and Australia (Table 8.2 and Table 8.3), though some jurisdictions are far better resourced than others.

As staff numbers decline, certain activities and functions get lost.[218] While it may be politically or legally impossible to abolish an equality agency, cuts to funding and resources are less visible to the electorate.[219] The resulting limits on an agency's operations are seen—in the public eye—as a failing of the agency itself, not the government.[220] The Covid-19 pandemic has made clear, too, that decisions around funding are normative, and reflect the devaluing of equality, rather than financial necessity:

> All the things that couldn't be done before can suddenly be done.... it's actually not about resources. It's about what we think is important.... what government thinks is important. And discrimination is obviously not something that the government—this government, or the last government—thought was important.[221]

Agencies are responding to these funding challenges in creative ways: one has set up a business arm, pitching or bidding for funded work to support its other operations;[222] another uses revenue from its education functions to fund other activities.[223] Some agencies undertake 'blitzes', focusing on enforcement against particular employers or particular industries for a short period of time.[224] This is unlikely to have a broader systemic impact: 'your average discriminating employer is probably not going to get caught, so they needn't bother with that.'[225] To achieve systemic change, agencies need greater funding.

Reform 45: That statutory equality agencies be given increased funding, reflecting their broad and complex range of responsibilities.

[216] Women and Equalities Committee, *Enforcing the Equality Act* (n 22) 25, [76]. Though £10.2 million of this reduction is attributable to the EHRC's functions—like the helpline—being outsourced.
[217] ECNI, 'Annual Report and Accounts 2019–2020' (n 34) 15, 16.
[218] A113.
[219] Margaret Thornton, 'Equivocations of Conciliation: The Resolution of Discrimination Complaints in Australia' (1989) 52 Modern Law Review 733, 750.
[220] ibid.
[221] A113. See also A10.
[222] A113.
[223] A10.
[224] A157.
[225] ibid.

Table 8.2 Statutory agency funding and staffing, Australia, 2019–20

Jurisdiction		Total budget / expenses ($ million)	Government funding ($ million)	Staff		Population ('000)	Population ('000) per staff
				n	FTE		
Fed	FWO	207.5		741		25,687.0	34.7
Fed	AHRC	29.0	16.5	145		25,687.0	177.2
NSW	ADNSW	3.8		33	30	8,164.1	272.1
Vic	VEOHRC		9.6	51	48.9	6,694.9	136.9
Qld	QHRC	7.8	7.4		40.2	5,174.4	128.7
WA	WAEOC	4.0	3.8		20.8	2,661.9	128.0
SA	SAEOC		0.96		5.6	1,769.3	315.9
Tas	EOT	1.7	1.7	9	8.4	540.6	64.4
ACT	ACTHRC*			67	62.5	431.1	6.9
NT	NTADC					246.0	

Source: Annual Reports, Australian Bureau of Statistics (ABS) population data, and author's own calculations
Table notes:

Blank = do not report

Fed = Federal

Vic = Victoria

Qld = Queensland

Tas = Tasmania

ADNSW = Anti-Discrimination NSW

QHRC = Queensland Human Rights Commission

EOT = Equal Opportunity Tasmania

ACTHRC = ACT Human Rights Commission

* ACTHRC includes divisions relating to victims of crime, health services and the public advocate, as well as equality and human rights functions. Its staffing and funding cannot be compared directly to other jurisdictions.

NTADC = NT Anti-Discrimination Commission

Table 8.3 Statutory agency funding, UK, 2019–20

	Staff	Total budget (£ million)	Population ('000)	Funding (£) per head of population
EHRC	199	17.4	64,903	0.27
ECNI	71	5.2	1,894	2.75

Source: Annual Reports, Office for National Statistics (ONS) population data, and author's own calculations

IV. Enhancing Agency Enforcement

Equality agencies must use their powers strategically to maximize their impact and effectiveness in the face of finite resources.[226] Even with repeated budget cuts, there is much that equality agencies can achieve: as the WEC argues,

> [the EHRC] continues to have extensive enforcement powers, a staff of more than 200 people and expenditure of £18.4 million per year. As an organisation it must overcome its timidity and be bolder in using the existing powers that only it has; increasing its own enforcement activity; and doing so in a strategic way that acts as a multiplier across entire sectors in the longer term.[227]

Equality agencies must integrate their various functions, powers, and divisions, to adopt holistic, proactive, and strategic approaches to addressing inequality;[228] this requires strong and targeted leadership.[229] Regulatory choices must be made, at every point of the enforcement pyramid, and within the confines of statutory powers and responsibilities. Improving agency enforcement of age discrimination law therefore primarily depends on enhancing choices within this field.

A. Prioritizing Age

With limited budgets and multiple competing priorities, statutory equality agencies rarely prioritize the enforcement of age discrimination law:[230] age tends to be 'the poor relation'.[231] Equality agencies report limited engagement with age-based non-governmental organization (NGOs) and representative groups.[232]

The comparative neglect of age equality might be attributed to three factors. First, having a single unified equality agency, responsible for addressing discrimination across all protected characteristics, creates a risk that a protected ground will not be prioritized in an agency's activities;[233] indeed, all groups may feel like they are getting insufficient attention.[234] That said, a unified equality body can promote efficiencies in enforcement, and more appropriately reflects the complex, intersectional nature of discrimination. The issue, then, is how unified bodies set their priorities.

[226] The WEC has therefore called on the EHRC 'to refocus its work': Women and Equalities Committee, *Enforcing the Equality Act* (n 22) 3.
[227] ibid.
[228] UK81.
[229] ibid; Dickens, 'The Road is Long' (n 61).
[230] A3; UK79; UK80.
[231] UK117; UK152.
[232] UK97.
[233] UK87.
[234] ibid.

Second, age equality may be deprioritized due to the way age discrimination law is perceived, and the demographics of claimants who file age discrimination claims (who tend to be older, men, and relatively privileged).[235] If those who benefit from age discrimination law are seen as being comparatively privileged, and not requiring support or assistance, it is unsurprising that agencies focus their attention elsewhere.[236]

Third, a limited focus on age equality may reflect the small number of age discrimination complaints filed each year. The exercise of agency powers often depends on individuals complaining or approaching the statutory agency with a problem.[237] Equality agencies use complaint statistics to guide their enforcement activities;[238] agency activities are increasingly data driven.[239] It is difficult for statutory agencies to respond to issues that they are not aware of, or to address issues of avoidance.[240] Resource intensive investigations or enforcement activities are therefore unlikely in areas with few complaints; a 'wave' of complaints provides an 'evidence base' for action.[241] This fails to move agency enforcement beyond the individual enforcement model: 'the [EHRC] continues to rely on affected individuals seeking it out and convincing it to act, instead of leading work to tackle endemic and structural inequalities.'[242]

This reflects a fundamental limitation of responsive or reflexive regulation: it does not speak to the detection or identification of non-compliant behaviour.[243] If agencies and regulators rely on individual complaints—with all their flaws and limitations—to identify issues and direct their actions, then agency enforcement adds little to the enforcement landscape. Individual enforcement is particularly problematic for addressing age discrimination (Chapters 3–6); few complaints do not reflect an absence of age discrimination.[244] The EHRC is therefore 'right to be concerned by the low numbers of age discrimination claims being brought to it'[245] but little has been done to address it.[246]

Further, complaints data and statistics are not neutral: agencies need to be critical of complaint data as a strategy-setting tool. Complaint numbers can be 'gamed' by NGOs and lobby groups: filing complaints is a powerful tool to get certain issues

235 UK79.
236 UK80.
237 A10; A110.
238 A101; A102; A105; UK166; UK167.
239 A99.
240 A110.
241 A101.
242 Women and Equalities Committee, *Enforcing the Equality Act* (n 22) 29.
243 Hardy, Howe, and Cooney (n 111) 570.
244 A101; A159.
245 Women and Equalities Committee, *Older People and Employment* (n 178) 13.
246 ibid.

on an agency's agenda.[247] In areas with limited collective action and few lobby groups—such as age equality (Chapter 9)—data are rarely used instrumentally as a lobbying tactic. Indeed, some practitioners and advocates are not aware that complaint statistics are informing agencies' enforcement functions;[248] if they were, they might encourage their clients to pursue a complaint.

Equality agencies therefore need to prioritize areas that are 'hidden', such as age discrimination and race discrimination:[249] 'I think older people and Aboriginal people experience discrimination on a regular basis and it never gets reported to us.'[250] In NI, the absence of age discrimination claims operates in *favour* of supporting individual claimants;[251] the ECNI has particularly tried to support younger workers and older women to pursue their complaints.[252] Statutory agencies must proactively investigate issues, rather than relying on complaints and enquiry data to structure their response. Few agencies have the powers or resources to do proactive audits,[253] though some have proactively reviewed job advertisements[254] and met with impacted groups to identify barriers and issues.[255]

Recognizing that age compounds and amplifies other forms of inequality (Chapter 2), failing to address age discrimination will have consequences for all other protected grounds. Age must become a renewed priority for equality agencies; with limited case law in this area, equality agencies must 'step up' their work around age discrimination[256] in a proactive way.

Reform 46: That equality agencies prioritize the enforcement of age discrimination law.

In some jurisdictions, a dedicated Commissioner has re-focused attention on age equality, including the Australian federal Age Discrimination Commissioner, the Commissioner for Older People for Northern Ireland, and the Older People's Commissioner for Wales. In Australia, the Age Discrimination Commissioner is part of the AHRC; in the UK, the Commissioners head up separate statutory agencies. Their roles, then, are quite different: Commissioners in the UK might field queries and help individuals to navigate EHRC processes; the Australian Commissioner is part of the equality agency, and must be independent.

247 A99.
248 A100.
249 A113; A159.
250 A113.
251 UK97.
252 ibid.
253 A3.
254 A6.
255 ibid.
256 UK79.

There are significant advantages in having an independent voice for older people:[257] older people feel valued and appreciate that someone is standing up for them.[258] Commissioners can empower older people to understand and assert their rights, challenge other government agencies, and use soft power to influence the private sector.[259] A dedicated Commissioner position itself can raise awareness of age inequality:[260] 'it is important to have the focus that a dedicated Commissioner can bring'.[261]

That said, Commissioners rarely focus on the interests of older people in employment or, at least, have not done so in recent years. Issues of elder care and elder abuse currently dominate the agenda; while this is obviously important, it leaves little space for Commissioners to pursue other issues. Each Commissioner brings their own interests and concerns to their appointment; while each new Commissioner might conduct an inquiry during their tenure, implementation is often left to their successor. As with the Australian *Willing to Work* report, this may mean implementation is minimal. The responsibility, then, rests with the Commissioner's staff to ensure continuity and implementation.[262]

It is notable, too, that UK Commissioners are solely responsible for protecting the interests of older people. There are equivalent Commissioners for children, and young people are sometimes (but not always) included in their remit. Splitting advocacy for older people and young people risks missing the synergies and similarities between how we treat those of non-prime age. While the Australian Age Discrimination Commissioner could represent people of all ages, the remit has been interpreted narrowly to focus only on older people.[263]

Reform 47: That dedicated Commissioners for age equality be appointed, with responsibility for advancing equality across all ages.

B. Communicating and Engaging

Equality agencies need to better promote their work, and to promote themselves as an avenue for making enquiries and complaints,[264] especially to young people. Agencies are not well-known to the public, and there is limited familiarity with the

257 UK86.
258 ibid.
259 ibid.
260 A4.
261 ibid.
262 UK86.
263 A156.
264 A10; A101; A102; A159; A160; UK97.

work they do.[265] This may inhibit claiming: other bodies *are* receiving complaints from young people about discrimination.[266]

These gaps could be addressed through a strategic approach to publicity and public engagement, including re-branding,[267] outreach in schools and tertiary education settings,[268] and targeted website and media publicity that speaks to young people.[269] The question, though, is how to use limited resources in a targeted and strategic way to best enable outreach and education:[270] at present, outreach and promotion is limited by a lack of resourcing and staff.[271] The answer to this question will itself come from outreach and consultation: 'young people can tell us the specifics that they know will actually make a difference.... one of the loudest messages ... is just to talk with young people.'[272] Similarly, equality agencies engaging personally with legal practitioners and community legal centre (CLCs) will have the most impact on how practitioners engage with statutory agencies, and how they advise their clients.[273]

Reform 48: That statutory equality agencies re-focus their efforts on engagement and consultation, including with young people and older women.

V. Conclusion

Statutory equality agencies are critical for moving beyond individual enforcement; they are key players in building capacity, educating, promoting dialogue and understanding, and escalating in cases of non-compliance. However, this impact is constrained in practice by limited statutory enforcement powers and a critical lack of resourcing. Equality agency staff are stretched thin and under stress; agencies are not doing enough to advance age equality, but cannot practically do any more.

Governments must reprioritize equality, and financially and politically support the work of statutory equality agencies. The advancement of age equality depends on strategic, holistic, and integrated enforcement by a strong statutory agency that does not rely on individual complaints for agenda setting. Agencies themselves should adopt a renewed focus on communicating and engaging with the public,

265 A10; A101; A102; A159; A160; A164; UK97.
266 A164.
267 A101.
268 A160.
269 A159; UK97.
270 A101.
271 A10; A101.
272 A159.
273 A107.

including around their existing work and enforcement activity. This would support enforcement and compliance, and could facilitate agenda setting through consultation and engagement with impacted groups. The problem, though, is that there is limited collective presence around age equality and age discrimination, complicating consultation in practice. It is to these issues of collective action that I turn in Chapter 9.

9

Collective Enforcement

I. Introduction

Meaningful engagement and consultation is key for achieving organizational change in a reflexive law framework.[1] However, equality law does not yet harness the social partners or collective bargaining to advance equality,[2] perhaps because, at the point where equality legislation was developed, unions and collective bargaining were more likely to promote *inequality* than equality: they were 'part of the problem'.[3] As unions have become more diverse and representative, and adopted a stronger focus on equality issues, there is a strong argument that they can play a positive role in achieving social change.[4]

Collective enforcement offers significant advantages over the individual enforcement model. It more authentically reflects the lived experience of work, which is collective and communal,[5] and redistributes the costs and risks of enforcement across a group of people, reducing the burden on any one person.[6] Collective approaches help to reframe individual experiences as systemic issues, and enforcement as an exercise of rights. Conversely, framing discrimination as an individual rights issue often fails to identify and address systemic drivers of workplace issues;[7] some systemic problems can only be resolved through collective action,[8] and systemic issues that may never be raised by an individual might be identified by an organization.[9] Collective approaches are therefore important complements to individual enforcement.[10]

[1] Bob Hepple, 'Enforcing Equality Law: Two Steps Forward and Two Steps Backwards for Reflexive Regulation' (2011) 40 Industrial Law Journal 315, 323.

[2] Linda Dickens, 'The Road is Long: Thirty Years of Equality Legislation in Britain' (2007) 45 British Journal of Industrial Relations 463, 484. Though this differs across the UK nations: Deborah Foster, 'Devolution and Disabled Workers: The Experiences of Union Equality Representatives in Wales: Devolution, Disabled Workers and Equality Representatives' (2015) 46 Industrial Relations Journal 153.

[3] Dickens, 'The Road is Long' (n 2) 484.

[4] ibid.

[5] Lizzie Barmes, *Bullying and Behavioural Conflict at Work: The Duality of Individual Rights* (OUP 2016) 259.

[6] A99; A101; A150.

[7] A160.

[8] ibid.

[9] A99; Bob Hepple, 'Agency Enforcement of Workplace Equality' in Linda Dickens (ed), *Making Employment Rights Effective: Issues of Enforcement and Compliance* (Hart Publishing 2012) 58.

[10] A160.

Reforming Age Discrimination Law. Alysia Blackham, Oxford University Press. © Alysia Blackham 2022.
DOI: 10.1093/oso/9780198859284.003.0009

A trend towards collectivized enforcement can already be seen among some vulnerable workers. The Unrepresented Worker Survey, for example, found that the second most frequent action taken to resolve a problem—after approaching managers—was joining with co-workers 'who shared the same concerns to get together as a group to pursue their claims' (24.2 per cent of all respondents, and 28.2 per cent of those who took action).[11] This figure rose to 55.8 per cent when respondents were later asked if their problems were shared by others and, if so, whether they acted to resolve them.[12] Thus, individuals appear inclined to attempt to resolve workplace problems collectively, particularly where those problems are shared or systemic. It is vital that discrimination laws allow, facilitate, and support these attempts.

However, there are potential tensions between collective and individual interests: can collective mechanisms enable effective enforcement, in a system fundamentally concerned with individual rights? Or do individual employment rights displace collective action? This chapter critically examines contradictions and tensions in the collective enforcement of individual rights. It considers the extent to which collective enforcement is viable for age discrimination law, drawing on developments in the United Kingdom (UK), Canada, and Australia.

II. Potential and Contradictions of Collective Enforcement: Facilitating Individual Rights?

There is potentially a deep-seated contradiction between the individualized framing of rights to be protected from age discrimination, and collective enforcement. The growth of individual discrimination rights may undercut the role and powers of collective negotiation.[13] Industrial reforms have moved trade unions from a central position, in which they directly determine and enforce employment standards through collective rights, to a subsidiary position, where they mediate individual rights established by statute.[14] This has led to an emphasis on trade unions' service functions, rather than their regulatory functions.[15]

[11] Anna Pollert and Andy Charlwood, 'The Unorganised Worker: Problems at Work, Routes to Support and Views on Representation' (2008) Working Paper 11, 42 <https://uwe-repository.worktribe.com/output/1021196/the-unorganised-worker-problems-at-work-routes-to-support-and-views-on-representation-the-unrepresented-worker-survey-2004-working-paper-11-who-experiences-problems-at-work-what-problems-do-they-experience-what-do-they-do-about-them-and-what-happen> accessed 28 March 2022.

[12] ibid 47.

[13] Margaret Thornton, 'Equivocations of Conciliation: The Resolution of Discrimination Complaints in Australia' (1989) 52 Modern Law Review 733, 745.

[14] Trevor Colling, 'Trade Union Roles in Making Employment Rights Effective' in Linda Dickens (ed), *Making Employment Rights Effective: Issues of Enforcement and Compliance* (Hart Publishing 2012) 191.

[15] KD Ewing, 'The Function of Trade Unions' (2005) 34 Industrial Law Journal 1, 7.

Individual rights have entrenched this shift from collectivism to individualism at work, embedding an individualized lens for viewing work and workplace benefits.[16] Individual enforcement models then steer parties 'to become combative and confrontational . . . within a distinctly individualist frame',[17] often at the expense of collective structures and solutions.[18] Individual claims are particularly disruptive to collectivist workplaces,[19] but have done little to rebalance power at work, and deliver few material gains for workers.[20] Individual rights have therefore become a 'Trojan horse' for addressing power disparities at work.[21]

However, individual rights and collective bargaining are not discrete and separate forms of regulation; 'individualism' and 'collectivism' can be understood in multiple, conflicting ways, challenging any dichotomous characterization.[22] The 'individual' and the 'collective' can be blended and combined, and rights can have individual elements without being individualistic,[23] as where trade unions enforce rights on behalf of individual members.[24] Though '"individualism" and "collectivism" can seem to be locked in a kind of zero-sum game for supremacy',[25] the reality is more nuanced.

Industrial reform has therefore not undermined collective action in a simplistic or mechanistic way.[26] Heery's 'recombination thesis' posits that unions use and incorporate individual legal rights 'as a precedent, sanction and standard' to support and strengthen collective action and bargaining.[27] Legal claims (especially group claims) support collective bargaining, prompting issues to become part of the bargaining process:[28] 'you create a problem so that you can find a solution for it' through bargaining.[29] Claims can also support legal mobilization.[30]

16 Barmes (n 5) 252.
17 ibid 217.
18 ibid 242.
19 ibid 216.
20 ibid 252.
21 ibid 255.
22 Alan Bogg, '"Individualism" and "Collectivism" in Collective Labour Law' (2017) 46 Industrial Law Journal 72.
23 ibid 77.
24 ibid.
25 ibid 73.
26 Colling (n 14) 184.
27 Edmund James Heery, 'Debating Employment Law: Responses to Juridification' in Paul Robert Blyton, Edmund James Heery, and Peter John Turnbull (eds), *Reassessing the Employment Relationship* (Palgrave Macmillan 2010) 89–90. That said, this complementarity can be undermined by the legal framework: Dickens, 'The Road is Long' (n 2) 483.
28 A111.
29 ibid. In Ireland, see Michelle O'Sullivan and others, 'Is Individual Employment Law Displacing the Role of Trade Unions?' (2015) 44 Industrial Law Journal 222.
30 O'Sullivan and others (n 29) 230–32; Colling (n 14). Though unions may not use claims in this way in practice: O'Sullivan and others (n 29) 239–40, 242. The potential for outcomes to be inspirational or radiating might be limited by both the legal process itself and unions' declining institutional power: Colling (n 14) 198.

The individual and the collective are therefore fundamentally intertwined, and need to be balanced in our quest for decent work.[31] In some cases, individual rights—such as discrimination rights—should prevail over collective rights; neither the individual nor the collective is morally superior all the time.[32] Ultimately, though, the worth of an association—like a union—should be judged by how it contributes to the well-being of its members as individuals.[33]

Strong legal regimes therefore have *complementary* individual and collective legal protections;[34] this extends to age discrimination law.[35] In a New Zealand study of age discrimination in recruitment, for example, Harcourt and others found that unions were 'active defenders and enforcers of individual rights'; weakening collective rights would also undermine the enforcement of individual rights,[36] and high unionization rates reduced the odds of employers asking unlawful questions about age in recruitment.[37] This is consistent with O'Sullivan and others' survey of union officials in Ireland: as they conclude, 'while unions view the law as an inadequate substitute for collective bargaining and recognise its individualising effect, they believe, in general, that the law is "complementary to trade union organization as distinct from being a threat".'[38]

While individual and collective legal protections may be complementary, contradictions or tensions between individual rights and collective enforcement can still emerge. Collectively negotiated responses to discrimination are not always appropriate or desirable for individuals.[39] Similarly, where unions help individuals to enforce their rights, tensions might arise between the union's interests—in pursuing structural change and setting an example—and an individual's interests in resolving a matter as expeditiously and confidentially as possible;[40] it takes a strong individual to resist a settlement offer and continue to run a claim,[41] and it is difficult for a union to tell a member that they cannot take a settlement offer.[42] Unions also encounter tensions in selecting which cases and claimants to support,[43] balancing claims that are strategic and impactful with claims that meet the 'immediate demands' of union members who 'are shouting at us to do something'.[44]

31 Bogg, '"Individualism" and "Collectivism" in Collective Labour Law' (n 22) 77.
32 ibid.
33 ibid 74.
34 ibid 100–01.
35 Mark Harcourt, Geoffrey Wood, and Sondra Harcourt, 'Do Unions Affect Employer Compliance with the Law? New Zealand Evidence for Age Discrimination' (2004) 42 British Journal of Industrial Relations 527.
36 ibid 528.
37 ibid 536.
38 O'Sullivan and others (n 29) 241.
39 A154.
40 A111. This is similar to the tensions that arise where equality agencies support individual claimants (Chapter 8).
41 A111.
42 ibid.
43 UK168.
44 A111.

These tensions between individual rights and collective negotiation are especially evident in age discrimination law: it is an area where unions are 'a bit equivocal'.[45] The demographic make-up of unions leaves them 'internally conflicted' when it comes to age equality, limiting collective negotiation around age equality issues.[46] False assumptions around intergenerational fairness and 'bed blocking' are widely held,[47] and collectively bargained solutions often limit solidarity between generations.[48] In the UK, this is further complicated by the ability to justify direct age discrimination: this can entrench social attitudes, rather than challenging them, and allows unions to adopt a stance that is biased in favour of particular age groups.[49]

While there can be clear tensions between the interests of the collective union and the interests of individual members, 'it's inevitable, [and] something that unions have always faced'.[50] The challenge, then, is to respect and balance these competing interests, in a way that best addresses age discrimination at work.

III. Structures of Collective Enforcement

Collective enforcement of age discrimination law could be facilitated through formal and informal collective structures, including trade unions, community organizations with an interest in age equality, and informal groupings of workers. In relation to claiming, collective enforcement could occur through joint, group, or representative claims.

A. Joint, Group, and Representative Claims

Individuals can work together to collectively enforce their rights through joint or group discrimination claims; or representative actions, where organizations or individuals bring a claim on behalf of a class or group. In practice, though, collective claiming is exceedingly rare.[51] Discrimination claims tend to be fact specific

[45] UK86. In the UK, see Colin Duncan and Wendy Loretto, 'Ageism, Early Exit, and British Trade Unions' (2000) 31 Industrial Relations Journal 220, 231.

[46] UK82.

[47] UK86.

[48] Pnina Alon-Shenker and Lilach Lurie, 'Do Trade Unions Promote Age Diversity and Intergenerational Solidarity in the Workplace? A View from Canada and Israel' (2019) 70 Labor Law Journal 103, 108.

[49] UK82. See, eg, *Barlow v Gallagher Ltd* [2017] NIIT 00924/15IT, where the Northern Ireland (NI) Industrial Tribunal noted that 'the position of the over 65s [age group] was, overall, not a matter pursued with any notable vigour by the unions. The claimant could be forgiven for thinking that his union had effectively abandoned him' in negotiations: at [22].

[50] A111. See also A154.

[51] A101; A106; A115. See Neil Rees, Simon Rice, and Dominique Allen, *Australian Anti-Discrimination and Equal Opportunity Law* (3rd edn, The Federation Press 2018) 808.

and 'personal', with minimal commonality across claims; discrimination claims are therefore less amenable to representative complaints than other areas of law.[52] Further, issues of standing may inhibit claiming, particularly where bringing representative and joint claims engages complex procedural rules.[53] Thus, even in jurisdictions where joint, group, or representative complaints are possible, such complaints are virtually unknown.[54]

1. Australia

This potential complexity is well illustrated by federal Australian procedural rules. Under the Fair Work Act 2009 (Cth) (FWA), general protections provisions can be enforced by the person affected,[55] an industrial association (if they are entitled to represent the industrial interests of those affected),[56] and/or an inspector.[57] In federal discrimination law, a complaint may be lodged with the Australian Human Rights Commission (AHRC) by:

- The person aggrieved (on their own behalf, or on behalf of themselves and others also aggrieved);
- Two or more people aggrieved (on their own behalf, or on behalf of themselves and others also aggrieved); and/or
- A person or trade union on behalf of one or more aggrieved persons.[58]

Representative complaints can only be lodged with the AHRC and Federal Court if they:

- Are against the same respondent;
- Arise from the same, similar, or related circumstances; and
- Involve a substantial common issue of law or fact.[59]

While representative complaints filed with the AHRC need to describe or identify class members, it is not necessary to name class members specifically, or to have their consent before lodgment.[60] In the Federal Court, representative actions require at least seven claimants;[61] this is not a requirement at the AHRC. Provision for representative

[52] A118.
[53] A99; UK94.
[54] A101; A106; A115.
[55] Fair Work Act 2009 (Cth) s 540(1) (hereafter FWA).
[56] ibid s 540(2).
[57] ibid s 539.
[58] Australian Human Rights Commission Act 1986 (Cth) s 46P.
[59] ibid s 46PB(1); Federal Court of Australia Act 1976 (Cth) s 33C(1).
[60] Australian Human Rights Commission Act 1986 (Cth) s 46PB(2)–(4). A class member may later withdraw from the complaint (s 46PC(1)), and the President of the AHRC may direct that notice of the complaint be given to class members (s 46PC(3)).
[61] Federal Court of Australia Act 1976 (Cth) s 33C(1).

actions has not been made for the Federal Circuit Court. In the 2016 *Willing to Work* report, the AHRC therefore recommended a review of standing provisions in federal discrimination law, to ensure consistency between the standing rules to bring a complaint to the AHRC and the standing rules to commence court proceedings.[62]

In the Australian case law sample, there were only five joint or group complaints;[63] most complaints were brought by sole individuals. However, flexible standing provisions significantly assisted younger discrimination claimants: in *Gabryelczyk v Hundt*,[64] the claim was brought by a minor worker's mother on his behalf; in *Shop, Distributive and Allied Employees' Association, Broken Hill Branch v Gateway Investments Pty Ltd*[65] the Shop, Distributive and Allied Employees Association filed an unfair dismissal claim on Hoskins's behalf (age 18).[66]

Reform 49: That Australian federal procedural rules be revised, to provide that those who have standing to bring a complaint to the AHRC can commence court proceedings.

2. UK

Article 9(2) of Council Directive 2000/78/EC of 27 November 2000 establishing a general framework for equal treatment in employment and occupation[67] says:

> Member States shall ensure that associations, organisations or other legal entities which have, in accordance with the criteria laid down by their national law, a legitimate interest in ensuring that the provisions of this Directive are complied with, may engage, either on behalf or in support of the complainant, with his or her approval, in any judicial and/or administrative procedure provided for the enforcement of obligations under this Directive.

In Great Britain (GB), two or more claimants may make their claims on the same form if they 'give rise to common or related issues of fact or law, or if it is otherwise reasonable for their claims to be made on the same claim form'.[68]

[62] AHRC, 'Willing to Work: National Inquiry into Employment Discrimination Against Older Australians and Australians with Disability' (2016) 21.

[63] *Lightning Bolt Co Pty Ltd v Skinner* [2002] QSC 62; *Virgin Blue Airlines Pty Ltd v Stewart* [2007] QSC 75; *Perera v Warehouse Solutions Pty Ltd* [2017] VCAT 1267; *Martin v Powerlink Qld* [2004] QADT 36 (3 November 2004); *McKeown v Carcione Nominees* (1999) EOC 92-990.

[64] [2005] NSWADT 94.

[65] [2005] NSWIRComm 209.

[66] In that case, under pt 6 ch 2 of the Industrial Relations Act 1996 (Cth).

[67] [2000] OJ L303/16 (hereafter the Framework Directive).

[68] Employment Tribunals (Constitution and Rules of Procedure) Regulations 2013, SI 2013/1237, Sch 1, reg 9. This more lenient provision was adopted after the conclusion of this study: The Employment Tribunals (Constitution and Rules of Procedure) (Early Conciliation: Exemptions and

Table 9.1 Early conciliation notifications and group cases, age discrimination, 2014–15 to 2018–19

	Early conciliation notifications	Group cases	Child cases	% Group cases
2014–15	1,415	13	50	0.92
2015–16	1,856	16	175	0.86
2016–17	1,821	14	79	0.77
2017–18	2,000	6	23	0.30
2018–19	2,303	42	250	1.82

Source: Acas and author's own calculations

However, there is no capacity to bring representative or class actions in the context of equality law:[69] while advocated for, this was not included in the Equality Act 2010 (EqA).[70] Each claimant must therefore be individually identified when a claim is commenced.[71]

Group claims are relatively uncommon in age discrimination matters.[72] Acas (the Advisory, Conciliation and Arbitration Service) records the number of group notifications received ('group cases') and how many claimants are involved in group cases ('child cases'). Only a handful of group age discrimination cases are received each year (Table 9.1).

In the UK case law sample, multiple claimants were involved in only twenty-seven cases; of these, thirteen claims were withdrawn. The only successful age discrimination claims with multiple claimants were *Sargeant v London Fire and Emergency Planning Authority*[73] and *McCloud v Lord Chancellor*.[74]

Rules of Procedure) (Amendment) Regulations 2020, SI 1003/2020, reg 6. At the time of this study, claims needed to be based on the same set of facts; this is still the requirement in NI: The Industrial Tribunals and Fair Employment Tribunal (Constitution and Rules of Procedure) Regulations (Northern Ireland) 2020, SI 2020/3, Sch 1, reg 10.

[69] Dickens, 'The Road is Long' (n 2) 481.
[70] Hepple, 'Agency Enforcement of Workplace Equality' (n 9) 58.
[71] ibid.
[72] See similarly LD Irving, 'Challenging Ageism in Employment: An Analysis of the Implementation of Age Discrimination Legislation in England and Wales' (Coventry University 2012) 92–93 <https://curve.coventry.ac.uk/open/file/ffc88163-6994-4400-bead-121298f52bd1/1/Irving%202012.pdf> accessed 2 April 2015.
[73] [2017] UKET 2202235/2015.
[74] [2017] UKET 2201483/2015.

B. Non-Governmental Organizations

Representative actions depend on a strong community sector capable of bringing collective claims;[75] age-based organizations typically lack the resources to use legal mechanisms.[76] While non-governmental organizations (NGOs) could be 'significant "new actors"' in labour law enforcement,[77] there is limited community activism around age equality issues.[78] Community organizing around age is impeded by limited social recognition of age discrimination[79] (Chapter 3). People rarely rally around age, as the consequences of ageing are highly variable.[80] It is therefore rare for people to attribute their problems to (age) group membership, rather than an individual difficulty or failing.[81] Further, community groups typically focus on either older workers *or* younger workers; given these age groups have many things in common as non-prime age workers,[82] it makes sense to work together and combine efforts.

Thus, there is a need to support and enhance the community sector in this area; this will also support the use of representative actions.[83] While NGOs are attempting to create a social movement to advance age equality, and groups are active in this area—such as Council on The Ageing (COTA) and the EveryAGE Counts coalition in Australia, and Age UK and the Centre for Ageing Better in the UK—there is considerable work to do in this space.[84] There is a need to build a stronger social and collective presence in relation to age equality,[85] including by supporting NGO activity.

C. Trade Unions

Trade unions amplify the effects of labour standards in the workplace, linking national and international developments to the shop floor.[86] While this can be

75 A99.
76 A1.
77 Edmund Heery, Brian Abbott, and Stephen Williams, 'The Involvement of Civil Society Organizations in British Industrial Relations: Extent, Origins and Significance' (2012) 50 British Journal of Industrial Relations 47. See also Edmund Heery, Steve Williams and Brian Abbott, 'Civil Society Organizations and Trade Unions: Cooperation, Conflict, Indifference' (2012) 26 Work, Employment and Society 145.
78 UK81; A99.
79 UK81.
80 UK165.
81 UK81.
82 Alysia Blackham, 'Young Workers and Age Discrimination: Tensions and Conflicts' (2019) 48 Industrial Law Journal 1.
83 A99.
84 A1.
85 ibid; UK81.
86 Colling (n 14) 194.

achieved through formal litigation, and by facilitating and supporting individual complaints,[87] it also occurs through organic enforcement, as unions interpret and communicate rights and standards,[88] raising rights awareness. Unions can negotiate and bargain around equality, using 'voice' to enhance equality measures,[89] and putting pressure on employers to '[conform] to normative pressures from the wider society'[90] and address age inequality[91] by increasing organizational visibility, increasing external scrutiny,[92] and limiting the arbitrary power of employers.[93] Trade unions can therefore act as 'champions of sound equal opportunities practice'[94] and support a preventative approach to discrimination.[95] A union presence is associated with both substantive and procedural improvements in how workplaces respond to equality rights.[96]

The extent to which unions can advance collective enforcement is obviously limited by union membership[97] and declining union coverage.[98] Trade union density has declined across Australia, the UK, and Canada, and the proportion of employees with the right to bargain has declined in Canada and the UK (Table 9.2 and Table 9.3).

Collective action is therefore limited by industrial trends: declining unionization both reflects and exacerbates growing individualism in the workplace.[99] The decline of unionization is particularly evident in specific sectors and industries, and with the rise in non-standard work as 'standard' work:[100] 'there are some industries or . . . sectors that are effectively de-unionised.'[101] Unions are rarely involved in the

[87] Nicolas Bacon and Kim Hoque, 'The Role and Impact of Trade Union Equality Representatives in Britain' (2012) 50 British Journal of Industrial Relations 239, 241.

[88] Colling (n 14) 194–95.

[89] Bacon and Hoque (n 87) 241.

[90] Alan Felstead and others, 'Opportunities to Work at Home in the Context of Work-Life Balance' (2002) 12 Human Resource Management Journal 54, 57; Stephen J Wood, Lilian M de Menezes, and Ana Lasaosa, 'Family-Friendly Management in Great Britain: Testing Various Perspectives' (2003) 42 Industrial Relations 221, 223.

[91] Felstead and others (n 90) 57; Wood, de Menezes, and Lasaosa (n 90) 223.

[92] Felstead and others (n 90) 57.

[93] A157.

[94] Mike Noon and Kim Hoque, 'Ethnic Minorities and Equal Treatment: The Impact of Gender, Equal Opportunities Policies and Trade Unions' (2001) 176 National Institute Economic Review 105, 106–07.

[95] A157.

[96] Colling (n 14) 195. See also Kim Hoque and Mike Noon, 'Equal Opportunities Policy and Practice in Britain: Evaluating the "Empty Shell" Hypothesis' (2004) 18 Work, Employment & Society 481, 488; Barbara Kersley and others, *Inside the Workplace: Findings from the 2004 Workplace Employment Relations Survey* (Routledge 2006) 239, 248; Helen Barnes, Deborah Smeaton, and Rebecca Taylor, 'An Ageing Workforce: The Employer's Perspective' (2009) 468 35, 80 <http://www.employment-studies.co.uk/pdflibrary/468.pdf> accessed 28 August 2012; Alysia Blackham, *Extending Working Life for Older Workers: Age Discrimination Law, Policy and Practice* (Hart Publishing 2016) ch 5.

[97] A111; A109; A154; A160; A164; A157.

[98] A164; A157; UK84; UK86.

[99] A164.

[100] Rebecca Zahn, 'Trade Unions, the Gig Economy, and the Feminisation of Work: Lessons from the Past?' in Alysia Blackham, Miriam Kullmann, and Ania Zbyszewska (eds), *Theorising Labour Law in a Changing World: Towards Inclusive Labour Law* (Hart Publishing 2019) 113–18.

[101] A154.

Table 9.2 Employees with the right to bargain (per cent), Australia, Canada, and the UK, 2006–18

	2006	2007	2008	2009	2010	2011	2012	2013	2014	2015	2016	2017	2018
Australia	63.3	..	59.3	..	61.1	..	60.0	..	62.0	..	61.3	..	61.2
Canada	31.7	31.6	31.2	31.5	31.4	31.0	31.3	31.1	30.4	30.6	30.3	30.4	30.1
UK	33.4	34.7	33.7	32.8	30.9	31.2	29.3	29.5	27.5	27.9	26.3	26.0	26.0

Source: OECD (2021), Collective bargaining coverage, OECD/AIAS database on Institutional Characteristics of Trade Unions, Wage Setting, State Intervention and Social Pacts (ICTWSS) <https://stats.oecd.org/index.aspx?DataSetCode=CBC> accessed 25 October 2021

Table 9.3 Trade union density (per cent), Australia, Canada and the UK, 2006–18

	2006	2007	2008	2009	2010	2011	2012	2013	2014	2015	2016	2017	2018
Australia	20.4	18.8	18.8	19.6	18.4	18.4	18.2	17.0	15.1	..	14.6	..	13.7
Canada	27.4	27.3	27.0	27.3	27.2	26.9	27.2	27.1	26.4	26.5	26.3	26.3	25.9
UK	28.3	28.0	27.5	27.4	26.6	26.0	26.1	25.6	25.0	24.7	23.6	23.3	23.4

Source: OECD (2021), Trade Union Dataset, OECD/AIAS database on Institutional Characteristics of Trade Unions, Wage Setting, State Intervention and Social Pacts (ICTWSS) <https://stats.oecd.org/Index.aspx?DataSetCode=TUD> accessed 25 October 2021

shadow economy, where wage theft and discrimination 'thrives',[102] and collective action is harder where workplaces are dispersed, sectors are dominated by small employers, or in remote or regional areas.[103] Industrial law also curtails employees' capacity to organize collectively[104] and a union's ability to enter and inspect workplace records for compliance;[105] this limits unions' ability to represent the interests of groups who are likely to be discriminated against.[106]

The demographics of union members may also limit unions' capacity to support the enforcement of age discrimination law. Union members are the 'luckiest

[102] A157.
[103] A160.
[104] A157.
[105] A160. In Australia, see Tess Hardy and John Howe, 'Partners in Enforcement? The New Balance between Government and Trade Union Enforcement of Employment Standards in Australia' (2009) 22 Australian Journal of Labour Law 306. In the UK, see Tonia Novitz, 'Freedom of Association and "Fairness at Work": An Assessment of the Impact and Relevance of ILO Convention No. 87 on its Fiftieth Anniversary' (1998) 27 Industrial Law Journal 169; Alan Bogg, 'Beyond Neo-Liberalism: The Trade Union Act 2016 and the Authoritarian State' (2016) 45 Industrial Law Journal 299.
[106] A157.

Table 9.4 Trade union membership in connection with main job, by demographic characteristics, Australia, August 2018

	Trade union member ('000)	Not a trade union member ('000)	Total employees ('000)	% in union
Sex				
Male	735.2	4,225.7	5,327.0	13.80
Female	800.6	4,148.8	5,185.1	15.44
Age group				
15–19	26.3	589.1	660.3	3.98
20–24	89.2	974.4	1,174.1	7.60
25–34	293.4	2,181.6	2,667.6	11.00
35–44	317.2	1,823.4	2,254.3	14.07
45–54	410.2	1,552.3	2,039.0	20.12
55–59	214.5	616.0	863.0	24.85
60–64	132.7	393.5	549.1	24.17
65 and over	52.3	244.3	304.7	17.15
Total	**1,535.7**	**8,374.5**	**10,512.0**	14.61

Source: ABS, 6333.0 Characteristics of employment, Australia, August 2018

workers';[107] those in a short-term role or on a short-term visa are unlikely to join a union.[108] Union membership traditionally favours men[109] and older workers,[110] who are less likely to be employed precariously;[111] this has major consequences for rights enforcement and accessing union support.[112] That said, Australian Bureau of Statistics (ABS) data on Australian union membership shows that women are more likely to be a member of a union (Table 9.4), perhaps due to their over-representation in industries with high union density. However, union membership remains exceptional for younger workers, with less than 4 per cent of those aged 15 to 19 being a member of a union in connection with their main job; for those aged 55 to 59, this figure is nearly 25 per cent.

107 A154.
108 A157.
109 A113.
110 A111; A157.
111 A113.
112 ibid. See Zahn (n 100) 121–22.

The UK Trades Union Congress (TUC) *Equality Audit 2018* (sent to TUC-affiliated unions, with responses covering 97 per cent of all TUC-affiliated union members),[113] also found that women were more likely to be union members than men,[114] and disabled workers were more likely to be union members than non-disabled workers.[115] That said, black and minority ethnic (BME) workers[116] and young workers[117] were under-represented among union members: 40 per cent of union members were aged 50 and over, compared with 29 per cent of all employees; and 4 per cent of union members were aged under 25, compared with 13 per cent of all employees.[118] Women, BME workers, and young workers were also all under-represented in union positions.[119]

1. Supporting complaints

Trade unions can support their members to bring individual, joint, or group claims; they are key enablers of enforcement. Individuals may be more willing to challenge their employer if they have the backing of a trade union;[120] adding 'a union's "collective voice" to the worker's "individual voice" can improve the cost–benefit trade-offs in initiating a grievance or complaint.'[121] Legal advice has become one of the key services unions provide to their members.[122] The 2018 Survey of Employment Tribunal Applications (SETA) found that 26 per cent of claimants (across all areas) sought advice from a trade union or worker representative before filing an ET1 claim; for union members, this rose to 79 per cent of claimants (compared to 5 per cent of non-members).[123] Once a claim was filed, 16 per cent of ET claimants had a trade union representative as a day-to-day representative; for 13 per cent of claimants, a trade union representative was their main source of day-to-day help.[124] Union members were over-represented in the SETA sample: 28 per cent of claimants were members of a trade union or staff association (compared to the 23 per cent of all employees who are union members);[125] in discrimination cases, 40 per cent of claimants were members of a trade union or staff association.[126] Thus,

[113] TUC, 'TUC Equality Audit 2018' (2018) 5.
[114] ibid 6.
[115] ibid 7.
[116] ibid 6.
[117] ibid 8.
[118] ibid.
[119] ibid 12–14.
[120] See Colling (n 14) 195–96.
[121] Harcourt, Wood, and Harcourt (n 35) 529.
[122] Colling (n 14) 196.
[123] 'Survey of Employment Tribunal Applications: Findings from the 2018 Survey' (2020) BEIS Research Paper Number 2020/007, 29–30. In the 2004 Unrepresented Worker Survey, few respondents (5.2 per cent) approached trade unions for advice: Pollert and Charlwood (n 11) 36–37.
[124] 'Survey of Employment Tribunal Applications: Findings from the 2018 Survey' (n 123) 44.
[125] ibid 81.
[126] ibid.

unions can be active supporters of individual claims, and trade union members appear more likely than non-members to bring a claim of discrimination.

However, union support of equality complaints appears variable.[127] Unions often struggle to resolve discrimination disputes on the shop floor;[128] many delegates lack expertise in age discrimination law.[129] There is a need, then, for unions to use legal mechanisms, especially where an issue is systemic, complex, or sector-wide.[130] Despite this, a lack of union support often underscores individual powerlessness in a discrimination claim.[131] Unions may not support a claim or claimant for a variety of reasons:

> the union's obtuseness, the complainant is challenging union policies regarding the existence of discrimination, there is a conflict of interests between union members or because the victim does not even belong to a union at all.[132]

Unions are only involved in age discrimination matters 'by exception':[133] 'we've not run a single age discrimination claim and I don't know of any other union that has.'[134] Like equality agencies (Chapter 8), unions direct their efforts to areas with a high number of complaints;[135] if individuals are not raising issues with the union, the union dedicates its efforts elsewhere.[136] Again, this replicates the limits of the individual enforcement model. Further, union members may not approach the union as their first point of support;[137] unions therefore need to promote understanding of the support they offer to their members,[138] especially younger workers.[139] Where complaints are made, some unions apply a merit test to potential claims;[140] more marginal or risky cases are unlikely to be supported, potentially limiting support for age discrimination claims (Chapter 6). There can also be clear tensions between collectively negotiated solutions or policies and the interests of specific individuals.[141] In the UK case law sample, for example, some

[127] A112.
[128] A111.
[129] ibid. In the UK, the appointment of trade union Equality Representatives may address this to some extent (discussed in Part III.C.2): Tessa Wright, Hazel Conley, and Sian Moore, 'Addressing Discrimination in the Workplace on Multiple Grounds: The Experience of Trade Union Equality Representatives' (2011) 40 Industrial Law Journal 460.
[130] A111.
[131] Thornton (n 13) 745.
[132] ibid.
[133] UK168.
[134] A111.
[135] ibid.
[136] ibid.
[137] A109.
[138] ibid.
[139] A160.
[140] UK78; Colling (n 14) 199.
[141] Kenneth WM Thornicroft, 'The Uncertain State of Mandatory Retirement in Canada' (2016) 67 Labor Law Journal 397, 405.

age discrimination cases related to processes negotiated with unions;[142] in these scenarios, unions may seek to uphold the status quo and protect their position,[143] rather than support an individual complaint.

Australian equality agencies therefore rarely see complaints lodged by unions.[144] Some unions lack experience and expertise in this area,[145] meaning they 'miss' equality issues when they arise.[146] Alternatively, unions may prefer to use the industrial jurisdiction to bring a complaint,[147] as discrimination law is seen as 'complex and unsatisfactory':[148] 'I've had clients tell me before "the union said if you want to bring a discrimination claim you have to call Legal Aid. We won't help you." '[149] Bringing a discrimination claim is expensive and requires dedicated expertise;[150] that cost will rarely be recouped through the remedies available in discrimination law.[151]

In the UK case law sample, unions were identified as supporting claimants in five cases, and as providing initial advice in nine cases. In the Australian case sample, unions lodged two cases on behalf of members, both in the industrial jurisdiction.[152] Other claims might have been lodged with union support, without that being noted in the decision;[153] most unions will have a relationship with a law firm, and will refer members to that firm to assist with complaints.[154] Overall, though, unions need to be more assertive and bring more claims in this area.[155]

Reform 50: That trade unions prioritize support for age discrimination complaints.

2. Bargaining and consultation

Addressing age discrimination requires the adoption of age-conscious policies and practices, such as those that can be achieved through union-led bargaining and consultation.[156] Effective bargaining and consultation requires employers to

142 *Yang v Amec Foster Wheeler Group Ltd* [2017] UKET 2404452/2016; *Sharp v Plympton Academy* [2018] UKET 1400688/2017; *Barlow v Gallagher Ltd* [2017] NIIT 00924/15IT.
143 UK168.
144 A153.
145 A112.
146 A101; A111.
147 A101; A112; A157.
148 A157.
149 A112.
150 A111.
151 A112.
152 *Shop, Distributive and Allied Employees' Association, Broken Hill Branch v Gateway Investments Pty Ltd* [2005] NSWIRComm 209; *Yaxley v Trust Bank of Tasmania* [1996] IRCA 95.
153 A154.
154 ibid.
155 A111.
156 Alon-Shenker and Lurie (n 48) 104. See also Trevor Colling and Linda Dickens, 'Selling the Case for Gender Equality: Deregulation and Equality Bargaining' (1998) 36 British Journal of Industrial Relations 389, 394, 405; Helen Bewley and Sue Fernie, 'What Do Unions Do for Women?' in Howard

engage with and support the process.[157] Bargaining must also encompass equality issues. Unions often attempt to build equality considerations into bargaining, but this occurs more often in relation to disability than age discrimination.[158]

In the UK, trade unions have appointed thousands of equality representatives to give advice and support on equality issues in the workplace.[159] In the TUC *Equality Audit 2018*, 84 per cent of members of respondent unions were in unions with a rule or practice on workplace or branch equality representatives;[160] 65 per cent of those members were in unions with young members' representatives.[161] These equality representatives do not have statutory backing, or any rights to time off to perform their role;[162] this limits the number of local equality officers[163] and constrains participation in the day-to-day implementation of individual rights.[164]

Where equality representatives are in place, they can have a positive impact: in a 2009 survey of equality representatives (n = 209), over half (56 per cent) of respondents reported having impacted positively on employer age practices, though only 6 per cent felt they had had 'a lot' of impact.[165] Positive impact was more likely to be reported where respondents had contact with any level of management at least once a month, where respondents attended equality committees or forums,[166] and in workplaces with negotiation over equality policies and practices (but not necessarily in workplaces with consultation).[167] Equality representatives also reported having a positive impact where they had supported and represented employees suffering discrimination and harassment on the basis of age;[168] thus, unions' various roles are mutually reinforcing and supportive in this area.

However, less than half (46.9 per cent) of equality representatives in that survey were located in workplaces with equality forums, and only 28.2 per cent of equality representatives regularly attended such a forum; 25.8 per cent of equality representatives reported that negotiation over equality occurred in their workplace; and 37.3 per cent of respondents had contact with any level of management in their role as equality representative at least once a month.[169] This likely constrains the impact of equality representatives in most workplaces. Thus, where there is no legal duty

F Gospel and Stephen Wood (eds), *Representing Workers: Trade Union Recognition and Membership in Britain* (Routledge 2003) 116–17.

157 Bacon and Hoque (n 87) 243.
158 A111; A154. In Canada, see Alon-Shenker and Lurie (n 48).
159 Hepple, 'Agency Enforcement of Workplace Equality' (n 9) 60.
160 TUC (n 113) 15.
161 ibid 16.
162 Bacon and Hoque (n 87) 245.
163 TUC (n 113) 16.
164 Barmes (n 5) 242–43, 259.
165 Bacon and Hoque (n 87) 248.
166 ibid 248–53.
167 ibid 253–54.
168 ibid 253.
169 ibid 261.

to consult or involve unions in equality issues, employer willingness and support is key; despite this, only 29.7 per cent of respondents agreed that managers valued their equality representative activities.[170]

There is a need, then, for increased participation and the inclusion of employee perspectives in the day-to-day implementation of individual rights,[171] 'simultaneously challeng[ing] employer dominance of extreme kinds and help[ing] more receptive organizations to arrive at just solutions to multifaceted conflicts'.[172] This could be assisted, for example, by a Public Sector Equality Duty (PSED)-style obligation on organizations to help resolve conflicts, 'to encourage participation in implementation and dispute resolution'.[173]

Reform 51: That there be a legal duty to consult and engage on equality issues.

IV. Conclusion: Enhancing Collective Enforcement

Collective enforcement of age discrimination law is currently limited: joint, group, and representative claims mechanisms are under-utilized; trade unions rarely prioritize age equality; and there is limited social and NGO activity in this space. However, this chapter has illustrated that collective action and individual rights can be complementary and mutually supportive; while there are tensions between individual and collective mechanisms, these can be navigated and worked through.

Individual age discrimination rights can therefore be effectively advanced through collective structures. Engaging unions with issues of age equality can develop collective presence and voice in this area.[174] As Alon-Shenker and Lurie argue 'The key is to avoid framing the interests and special needs of older and young workers as competing or conflicting. They are often quite similar ... and when different, can be mutually and integratively promoted' through intergenerational policies.[175] Thus, this chapter has flagged broader questions about social and cultural change, and illustrated the ways in which broader attitudes to age and age equality might imbue collective workplace mechanisms. These issues and questions are taken up in Chapter 10, which concludes this volume.

170 ibid.
171 Barmes (n 5) 242–43, 259.
172 ibid 259.
173 ibid 261.
174 UK86.
175 Alon-Shenker and Lurie (n 48) 105.

10

Conclusion

Reforming Age Discrimination Law

I. Introduction

There are major gaps in the enforcement of age discrimination law. This reflects the nature of age discrimination, which is subtle, often internalized, and socially accepted. Ambivalence towards age equality, extensive exceptions to age discrimination law, enduring age norms, and—in the United Kingdom (UK)—the ability to justify direct age discrimination, have left age discrimination law in a derelict state. However, this also reveals broader problems with relying on the individual enforcement model to address discrimination and remedy inequality. Individual enforcement has major theoretical and practical flaws as a tool for achieving societal change. As the law is currently framed, the costs and risks of complaining far outweigh any perceived benefits.

To move beyond individual enforcement, I put forward a fourfold model of reform, embracing improvements to the individual enforcement model (Chapters 4 to 6); strengthening positive duties (Chapter 7); bolstering the roles of statutory agencies (Chapter 8); and enhancing collective enforcement, whether by trade unions, groups of individuals, or the third sector (Chapter 9). These reforms best work as mutually reinforcing and mutually supportive strategies operating in tandem. As Dickens argues:

> A diversity and variety of administrative, judicial, individual and collective approaches, enforcement and remedies could deliver such a multiplicity of risks to help tackle discrimination and drive equality action.[1]

The common challenge, though, in pursuing these fourfold reforms, is to keep age on the agenda as a matter of concern, equal to other protected grounds.[2] Age equality is rarely a priority for statutory equality agencies,[3] legal practitioners,[4]

[1] Linda Dickens, 'The Road is Long: Thirty Years of Equality Legislation in Britain' (2007) 45 British Journal of Industrial Relations 463, 481.
[2] UK86.
[3] UK162; UK165.
[4] UK78.

Reforming Age Discrimination Law. Alysia Blackham, Oxford University Press. © Alysia Blackham 2022.
DOI: 10.1093/oso/9780198859284.003.0010

governments[5] or unions. Rather, age discrimination is seen as a lesser, less serious or more socially acceptable form of discrimination[6] (Chapter 2). We can *choose* to make age a priority: age can, should and must be prioritized. Key to prioritizing age is overcoming social ambivalence towards age equality: we need to better address and counter the perceived tensions inherent in both age discrimination law itself and in its enforcement; and recognize the normative case for advancing age equality (Chapter 2).

II. Overcoming the Tensions of Age Discrimination Law

A. Towards Intergenerational Solidarity

Intergenerational 'tensions' are grounded in generalizations, assumptions, and stereotypes,[7] which are damaging to both younger and older people.[8] Rather than focusing on intergenerational conflict, we should embrace a *solidarity approach*, valuing interaction, solidarity, and enrichment across generations, and seeing the interests of different age groups as being mutually enhancing.[9] A solidarity approach emphasizes the ways different generations can work together to achieve positive outcomes; we can simultaneously advance the interests of those who are young *and* old.[10]

To embrace a solidarity approach, we must tackle assumptions, stereotypes, and misconceptions about age. We can then start to address policy failures which disadvantage both older and younger people.[11] First, intersectionality helps us recognize the diversity of 'young people' and 'older people' (Chapter 2). Embracing the diversity of age cohorts helps to break down ageist stereotypes, build intergenerational bridges, and overcome real or imagined conflicts between different age groups.

Second, we can build solidarity by emphasizing the similarities and commonalities between and across generations. Current generations have a point of similarity, as they are all alive *now*, and can all make a difference now.[12] Focusing on

[5] UK80. That said, the Scottish government was seen as very active in this space, and had made ageing issues a priority: UK88.
[6] UK165.
[7] UK167; UK80; Josephine M Wildman and others, 'Intergenerational Equity, Equality and Reciprocity in Economically and Politically Turbulent Times: Narratives from across Generations' (2021) Ageing & Society 1, 3.
[8] UK80.
[9] Pnina Alon-Shenker and Lilach Lurie, 'Do Trade Unions Promote Age Diversity and Intergenerational Solidarity in the Workplace? A View from Canada and Israel' (2019) 70 Labor Law Journal 103, 106.
[10] UK85.
[11] See, eg, Wildman and others (n 7) 12.
[12] UK85.

the things that unite us, rather than what divides us, can bridge perceived tensions between generations. Ironically, too, older and younger generations are united by our shared experience of age discrimination: 'we all have a vested interest in age discrimination. . . . it's something that we have in common.'[13]

Third, then, measures that address points of vulnerability experienced by both older and younger workers could help build intergenerational solidarity. For example, a universal basic income would help address issues of insecure and low-paid work, un- and under-employment, and inadequate retirement pensions,[14] supporting both older and younger cohorts.[15] The Australian government's response to Covid-19 job losses—which included new JobKeeper and more accessible JobSeeker payments—offers an example of how a universal basic income might be implemented, even in neo-liberal economies.[16]

Fourth, intergenerational solidarity can be promoted through intergenerational interaction and exposure, to break down age-based stereotypes.[17] This could take the form of multi-generational workplaces; housing, social, and cultural events;[18] and intergenerational care and education models.[19] A National Intergenerational Week has been held in the UK since 2020, celebrating the many ways in which generations might work together. These programmes aim to challenge bias through new experiences and exposure:

> It's all about experience. If you have no experience in that space, you will, as a human being, create bias and that bias will leak out of every pore of your body unless you have a different experience that challenges it.[20]

Embracing a solidarity approach has dramatic implications for age discrimination law; it represents a shift to a human rights model of age discrimination law, bolstering protections for people of all ages, and across all contexts. With an emphasis

[13] A99.

[14] See, eg, Guy Standing, *Basic Income: And How We Can Make It Happen* (Pelican 2017).

[15] Don Arthur, 'Basic Income: A Radical Idea Enters the Mainstream' (Parliament of Australia, 18 November 2016) <https://www.aph.gov.au/About_Parliament/Parliamentary_Departments/Parliamentary_Library/pubs/rp/rp1617/BasicIncome#_Toc467232178> accessed 1 March 2019.

[16] Anthony Forsyth, 'COVID-19 and Labour Law: Australia' (2020) 13 Italian Labour Law e-Journal <https://illej.unibo.it/article/view/10812> accessed 16 February 2021. Acknowledging, though, that many groups were excluded from these payments, such as migrant workers.

[17] A1; UK89; UK90; David Burnes and others, 'Interventions to Reduce Ageism Against Older Adults: A Systematic Review and Meta-Analysis' (2019) 109 American Journal of Public Health e1; Jonathan Cadieux, Alison L Chasteen, and Dominic J Packer, 'Intergenerational Contact Predicts Attitudes Toward Older Adults Through Inclusion of the Outgroup in the Self' (2019) 74 The Journals of Gerontology. Series B, Psychological Sciences and Social Sciences 575.

[18] Peta S Cook, Anthea Vreugdenhil, and Brienna Macnish, 'Confronting Ageism: The Potential of Intergenerational Contemporary Art Events to Increase Understandings of Older Adults and Ageing' (2018) 37 Australasian Journal on Ageing E110.

[19] Elia E Femia and others, 'Intergenerational Preschool Experiences and the Young Child: Potential Benefits to Development' (2008) 23 Early Childhood Research Quarterly 272.

[20] UK88.

on intergenerational solidarity, using 'intergenerational fairness' arguments to justify direct age discrimination is unlikely to be appropriate in most cases. Instead, we should be more critically examining why direct age discrimination is required, and why measures that support all generations cannot be deployed, including through collective bargaining. A solidarity approach therefore challenges the many exceptions to age discrimination law, undermining the arbitrary limits that have been put on protection. This creates a better balance between individual needs and the needs of the 'collective' (Chapter 2).

B. Transparency and Secrecy

Like discrimination law generally, the enforcement of age discrimination law places excessive weight on secrecy, at the expense of transparency and accountability.[21] Limiting the use of non-disclosure agreements (NDAs),[22] moving to a presumption of openness for conciliated outcomes, and publicizing the outcomes of complaints[23] all serve to make the enforcement of discrimination law more transparent and open.

A lack of transparency means data on age discrimination law and its enforcement are piecemeal, incomplete, unreliable, haphazard, and inconsistent. It is difficult to make meaningful comparisons across jurisdictions, or even to undertake detailed analysis within a particular jurisdiction. In Australia, this is further complicated by the federal structure, and agencies tasked with pursuing age equality at state, territory, and federal level, and under both discrimination law and industrial relations law. Even in the UK, though, quality data is rarely collected on the enforcement of age discrimination law.

This lack of transparency and lack of data is a major barrier to reform. If something is not measured, it is difficult to identify problems, or to mount an argument for change. We need better, more consistent data—across all jurisdictions—to better inform the work of governments, equality agencies, and unions:

> If we know things, if we have information, then we'll know where the bigger problems are. We'll know where to put resources in. If we've got information that a particular industry is particularly problematic, maybe the equality bodies can

[21] Dominique Allen and Alysia Blackham, 'Under Wraps: Secrecy, Confidentiality and the Enforcement of Equality Law in Australia and the UK' (2019) 43 Melbourne University Law Review 384.

[22] Equality and Human Rights Commission, 'Turning the Tables: Ending Sexual Harassment at Work' (2018) 16–17 <https://www.equalityhumanrights.com/sites/default/files/ending-sexual-harassment-at-work.pdf> accessed 3 May 2018.

[23] Equality Commission for Northern Ireland, 'Policy for the Provision of Legal Advice and Assistance' (2018) 8 <http://www.equalityni.org/ECNI/media/ECNI/Publications/Individuals/DAO/Policy-Provision_of_Legal-Advice_and_Assistance.pdf> accessed 5 June 2020.

> be there or the bodies and the unions can be working together to resolve [the] issue.[24]

Statutory agencies and courts therefore need to collect more comprehensive, intersectional data on (1) those who make enquiries and complaints and file proceedings; (2) those who fail to pursue enquiries, complaints, and proceedings; (3) conciliations and mediations that are conducted; and (4) the outcomes achieved in conciliation and mediation. This data should be made publicly accessible in de-identified form, consistent with statutory secrecy obligations.[25]

Data from statutory agencies and courts could be complemented by better organizational data. Just as employers are required to report on their progress in achieving gender equality and the gender pay gap, they could be required to report on the age make-up of the organization. As noted by the House of Commons Women and Equalities Committee (WEC):

> Transparency can drive progress, and facilitate accountability for change. The Government has instigated voluntary publication by companies of data on women on boards, and has introduced regulations requiring large employers to publish data on their gender pay gap.... if employers were required to disclose data concerning the age make-up of their employees it would show where the issues lie, as an important starting point in achieving that cultural change.[26]

A focus on data collection and transparency would both complement and be facilitated by positive duties on employers (Chapter 7).[27] These structured forms of transparency challenge the embedded confidentiality and secrecy in age discrimination law, achieving a better balance between (individual) confidentiality and (institutional) transparency. Transparency can shift cultural norms away from a social acceptance of age discrimination and inequality, better addressing systemic problems.[28] A renewed focus on transparency is therefore key to ensuring the effectiveness of age discrimination law.

[24] A160.

[25] Allen and Blackham, 'Under Wraps' (n 21).

[26] Women and Equalities Committee, *Older People and Employment* (2017–19, HC 359) 16.

[27] Alysia Blackham, 'Positive Equality Duties: The Future of Equality and Transparency?' (2021) 37(2) Law in Context 98.

[28] Equality and Human Rights Commission, 'Turning the Tables: Ending Sexual Harassment at Work' (n 22) 17.

C. Consistency and Diversity

Federalism and devolution create significant scope for diversity and positive experimentation across the Australian states and territories and the UK nations (Chapter 3). This might enable innovative developments in regulation and enforcement, as in the adoption of human rights statutes in the Australian states and territories, and the development of specific duties under the Public Sector Equality Duty (PSED). However, this diversity might also lead to regulatory gaps, and increase the complexity of individual enforcement. This is especially evident in Australia, where claimants must quickly navigate complex choices about where to bring a claim. 'Duplication' of this nature might signify a healthy democracy, offering individuals multiple possible routes to redress.[29] Quality, accessible legal advice is essential to ensure individuals can make a meaningful and informed choice (Chapter 4).

Age equality is a complex field: while this study has focused on work, 'age touches everything'.[30] Age is not confined to one particular social sphere[31] and issues cannot be seen in isolation.[32] Despite this, many statutory agencies have a limited and confined remit,[33] and multiple agencies can have overlapping or closely related remits.[34] Again, this makes the system difficult for individuals to navigate: in Great Britain (GB), for example, functions relating to equality at work are split across the Equality Advisory and Support Service (EASS), the Equality and Human Rights Commission (EHRC), Acas (the Advisory, Conciliation and Arbitration Service), and the Government Equalities Office. In Australia, there is overlap across state, territory, and federal equality bodies; state and territory industrial bodies; the Australian Taxation Office; and the Australian Competition and Consumer Commission.[35] Agencies attempt to coordinate their efforts,[36] including through joint working groups[37] and regular meetings,[38] the sharing of data,[39] cross-referral of matters,[40] and monitoring of proceedings and enforcement action in other jurisdictions.[41] This is made more complex, though, by the need for some organizations—like the Fair Work Commission (FWC) and Fair Work Ombudsman (FWO)—to be separate to preserve their institutional integrity.[42]

29 A6.
30 UK90.
31 ibid.
32 A6.
33 UK94.
34 ibid; A6.
35 A6.
36 ibid; UK94; UK117.
37 UK117.
38 ibid; A6.
39 A6.
40 ibid.
41 ibid.
42 ibid.

There is still significant scope for a more coordinated, joined up approach: across regions, jurisdictions, and the various remits of statutory agencies. We must adopt a holistic approach to pursuing age equality, maximizing the impact of the many agencies working in this area.

III. Reforming Age Discrimination Law: A Call to Action

I end this study, then, with a call to action. Reform of age discrimination law needs to be both coordinated and holistic; it demands the coordinated efforts of all actors in the field. **Organizations and employers** have a clear role to play in monitoring and proactively acting on age inequality in their workplace. Workplace culture change and employer initiatives to value diversity are key for addressing age discrimination at work:[43] 'culture is ... where it is really at.'[44]

That said, employers do not bear all responsibility for change: some areas are best led by government; this includes addressing age bias and age discrimination.[45] Law must underpin and encourage cultural change.[46] This study therefore has implications for **government action and law reform**, identifying essential changes to the individual enforcement model, the need for increased funding for statutory agencies, and the case for positive duties to advance age equality. With this funding, **statutory agencies** must collect more consistent, comprehensive, and transparent data on enquiries, complaints, and conciliations; promote accessibility and openness in their operations; implement measures to better translate enquiries to complaints; and prioritize age in enforcement activity.

These findings also have implications for **unions**, requiring them to better prioritize age equality, support their members to address issues of age discrimination and inequality, overcome age-based stereotypes, and up-skill to identify age issues as they emerge. We must enhance collective action in the field of age equality, through the work of unions, but also non-governmental organizations (NGOs) and groups of workers. We must also seek greater voice for and consultation of both older and younger workers,[47] in the workplace and through participatory research.

While it has been beyond the scope of this study to undertake participatory research with workers of different ages, this is an obvious and necessary next step in advancing scholarship in the area; this represents a call to action for **academics and researchers**. This study also reveals important gaps in **legal education and**

[43] A3; A4; A103; A104; UK152; UK82.

[44] House of Commons, 'Oral Evidence: Older People and Employment' (2018) HC 359 Q96 <http://data.parliament.uk/writtenevidence/committeeevidence.svc/evidencedocument/women-and-equalities-committee/older-people-and-employment/oral/76656.html> accessed 28 March 2022.

[45] Women and Equalities Committee, *Older People and Employment* (n 26) 35.

[46] House of Commons (n 44) Q96.

[47] A156; A159; UK87.

practice, emphasizing the need for comprehensive legal education in discrimination law, and continuing legal education for practitioners and judges. This should be taken up by law schools, law societies, bar councils and judicial bodies.

More generally, too, this study flags the need for a fundamental shift in **community values**,[48] and a cultural change to respect and value age equality.[49] We must fundamentally recast 'how much [age] equality is acceptable'[50] to address the 'fundamental', 'endemic', and 'deep-seated' ageism in society.[51] We need to celebrate and support workers of all ages,[52] recognizing the rights and legitimacy of people as individuals.[53] This has implications for how we educate young people, to embed a democratic approach in education;[54] and for how we educate the general population, including through campaigns, advertising, and training.[55] We need to address the ageist messages 'we're all subtly sending out',[56] including messages in the media and on social media,[57] to turn the narrative of ageing on its head.[58] Short term action is not enough—work to address ageism 'needs to be sustained ... reinforced and reinforced and reinforced'.[59]

Taking action is a responsibility for us all. While age discrimination is endemic, it can shift. Using the tools and reforms put forward in this book, it is possible for all of us to achieve real and meaningful change, and to reform age discrimination law.

48 A101; A110; UK82; UK152; A154.
49 A113.
50 UK80.
51 A103; A109; A4.
52 A164.
53 UK80.
54 A164.
55 A1; A3; A4; A98; A102; A103; A104; A106; A112; A113; A150; A151; UK152.
56 UK84.
57 UK89; UK92.
58 UK90; A98; A103; A4.
59 UK84.

APPENDIX 1

Reforming age discrimination law

Reform 1: That age discrimination complaints be reframed as a positive assertion of rights with broader significance.

Reform 2: That equality agencies develop training and outreach programmes to promote empathy and understanding for those who are impacted by discrimination.

Reform 3: That equality agencies better promote successful age discrimination claims and cases.

Reform 4: That equality agencies continue to build their evidence-based outreach and training activities in relation to age equality.

Reform 5: That there be better support and funding of community organizations to advance age equality.

Reform 6: That all jurisdictions establish a specialist equality law programme to assist claimants.

Reform 7: That equality law be part of legal education and ongoing professional training for law students, practitioners, judges, and tribunal members.

Reform 8: That equality agencies, courts, and tribunals continue to review the ways in which they promote access to justice, including through the use of accessible language, and by physically opening up premises to the public.

Reform 9: That equality legislation be amended to adopt a more flexible approach to time limits.

Reform 10: That governments increase funding for Acas, to facilitate intensive conciliation in appropriate discrimination matters.

Reform 11: That governments more closely regulate the use of non-disclosure agreements in discrimination cases, including through legislative change.

Reform 12: That jurisdictions develop and publicize a register of conciliated outcomes to inform and educate potential claimants.

Reform 13: That jurisdictions publicly state how matters are selected for inclusion on the register of conciliated outcomes.

Reform 14: That equality agencies monitor complaint outcomes by gender.

Reform 15: That equality agencies consider how complainants can be encouraged to progress their claims to conciliation.

Reform 16: That statutory secrecy provisions in equality law be clarified or repealed.

Reform 17: That governments provide statutory agencies with targeted funding to improve data collection and reporting.

Reform 18: That statutory agencies adopt comprehensive data management systems that facilitate data extraction and reporting.

Reform 19: That practitioners seek to limit the scope of non-disclosure agreements.

Reform 20: That conciliators encourage parties to settle without a non-disclosure agreement.

Reform 21: That governments extend or adopt transparency requirements that include age as a protected characteristic.

Reform 22: That the questionnaire procedure be reinstated in the UK, and adopted in Australia.

Reform 23: That governments consider introducing qualified, one-way costs shifting, allowing costs to be recovered by claimants only.
Reform 24: That a shifting burden of proof be adopted in Australian discrimination law.
Reform 25: That there be explicit recognition of intersectional discrimination in UK and Australian discrimination law.
Reform 26: That the ability to objectively justify direct age discrimination in the UK be removed and replaced by more specific exceptions if required.
Reform 27: That reasonable accommodations be required for all grounds, including age.
Reform 28: That Australian jurisdictions adopt a human rights framework, including equality rights.
Reform 29: That governments and non-governmental organizations actively support the adoption of a United Nations Convention on the rights of older persons, and consider how United Nations conventions could better advance the rights of young people.
Reform 30: That Australian jurisdictions provide judges and tribunal members with training on how to deal with discrimination matters.
Reform 31: That positive duties be strengthened to require both proper consideration and proportionate action to eliminate discrimination and advance equality of opportunity.
Reform 32: That statutory agencies re-emphasize their role in organizational capacity building, to better support the implementation of positive duties.
Reform 33: That English and Australian positive duties be amended to require consultation and engagement.
Reform 34: That positive duties include general principles for how engagement processes should be conducted.
Reform 35: That positive duties be enforceable by a direct cause of action to the relevant tribunal, with the possibility of damages, in a similar jurisdiction to that established under discrimination laws.
Reform 36: That equality agencies be given statutory powers to receive and conciliate complaints relating to positive duties.
Reform 37: That positive duties be adopted in the Australian states and territories, and federally.
Reform 38: That positive duties apply to both the public and private sectors in their role as employers.
Reform 39: That the equality helpline be insourced and returned to the Equality and Human Rights Commission.
Reform 40: That equality agencies enable anonymous reporting of issues via their website to facilitate intelligence gathering, allowing people to indicate on the form if they want to be contacted.
Reform 41: That statutory equality agencies review and re-prioritize strategic public messaging and the gathering and communication of data.
Reform 42: That statutory equality agencies be given more extensive powers to escalate enforcement in the event of non-compliance.
Reform 43: That statutory equality agencies be given adequate funding to enable the strategic exercise of their enforcement powers.
Reform 44: That Australian equality agencies be given powers and funding to assist individual complainants and standing to bring complaints on behalf of individuals.
Reform 45: That statutory equality agencies be given increased funding, reflecting their broad and complex range of responsibilities.
Reform 46: That equality agencies prioritize the enforcement of age discrimination law.

Reform 47: That dedicated Commissioners for age equality be appointed, with responsibility for advancing equality across all ages.
Reform 48: That statutory equality agencies re-focus their efforts on engagement and consultation, including with young people and older women.
Reform 49: That Australian federal procedural rules be revised, to provide that those who have standing to bring a complaint to the Australian Human Rights Commission can commence court proceedings.
Reform 50: That trade unions prioritize support for age discrimination complaints.
Reform 51: That there be a legal duty to consult and engage on equality issues.

Index

For the benefit of digital users, indexed terms that span two pages (e.g., 52–53) may, on occasion, appear on only one of those pages.